Table of Conten

MW00983390

Introduction . . . .

Operations and Algebraic Thinking

▶ **Represent and solve problems involving multiplication and division.**

Lesson 1 CC.3.OA.1 Count Equal Groups **1**
Lesson 2 CC.3.OA.1 **Algebra** • Relate Addition and Multiplication **3**
Lesson 3 CC.3.OA.2 Size of Equal Groups **5**
Lesson 4 CC.3.OA.2 Number of Equal Groups **7**
Lesson 5 CC.3.OA.2 Model with Bar Models **9**
Lesson 6 CC.3.OA.3 Skip Count on a Number Line **11**
Lesson 7 CC.3.OA.3 Model with Arrays **13**
Lesson 8 CC.3.OA.3 Multiply with 2 and 4 . . . . **15**
Lesson 9 CC.3.OA.3 Multiply with 5 and 10 . . . . **17**
Lesson 10 CC.3.OA.3 Multiply with 3 and 6 . . . . **19**
Lesson 11 CC.3.OA.3 **Problem Solving** • Model Division **21**
Lesson 12 CC.3.OA.3 **Algebra** • Relate Subtraction and Division **23**
Lesson 13 CC.3.OA.3 **Investigate** • Model with Arrays **25**
Lesson 14 CC.3.OA.3 Divide by 2 . . . . **27**
Lesson 15 CC.3.OA.3 Divide by 5 . . . . **29**
Lesson 16 CC.3.OA.4 **Algebra** • Find Unknown Factors **31**
Lesson 17 CC.3.OA.4 Divide by 8 . . . . **33**

▶ **Understand properties of multiplication and the relationship between multiplication and division.**

Lesson 18 CC.3.OA.5 **Algebra** • Commutative Property of Multiplication . . . **35**
Lesson 19 CC.3.OA.5 **Algebra** • Multiply with 1 and 0 . . . . **37**
Lesson 20 CC.3.OA.5 **Algebra** • Distributive Property **39**
Lesson 21 CC.3.OA.5 **Algebra** • Associative Property of Multiplication **41**
Lesson 22 CC.3.OA.5 **Algebra** • Division Rules for 1 and 0 . . . . **43**
Lesson 23 CC.3.OA.6 **Algebra** • Relate Multiplication and Division **45**

▶ **Multiply and divide within 100.**

Lesson 24 CC.3.OA.7 Multiply with 7 . . . . **47**
Lesson 25 CC.3.OA.7 Multiply with 8 . . . . **49**
Lesson 26 CC.3.OA.7 Multiply with 9 . . . . **51**
Lesson 27 CC.3.OA.7 **Algebra** • Write Related Facts **53**
Lesson 28 CC.3.OA.7 Divide by 10 . . . . **55**
Lesson 29 CC.3.OA.7 Divide by 3 . . . . **57**
Lesson 30 CC.3.OA.7 Divide by 4 . . . . **59**
Lesson 31 CC.3.OA.7 Divide by 6 . . . . **61**
Lesson 32 CC.3.OA.7 Divide by 7 . . . . **63**
Lesson 33 CC.3.OA.7 Divide by 9 . . . . **65**

▶ **Solve problems involving the four operations, and identify and explain patterns in arithmetic.**

Lesson 34 CC.3.OA.8 **Problem Solving** • Model Addition and Subtraction . . **67**
Lesson 35 CC.3.OA.8 **Problem Solving** • Model Multiplication **69**
Lesson 36 CC.3.OA.8 **Problem Solving** • Multiplication **71**

© Houghton Mifflin Harcourt Publishing Company

Lesson 37	CC.3.OA.8	**Problem Solving** • Two-Step Problems	**73**
Lesson 38	CC.3.OA.8	**Investigate** • Order of Operations	**75**
Lesson 39	CC.3.OA.9	**Algebra** • Number Patterns	**77**
Lesson 40	CC.3.OA.9	**Algebra** • Patterns on the Multiplication Table	**79**
Lesson 41	CC.3.OA.9	**Algebra** • Describe Patterns	**81**

Number and Operations in Base Ten

▶ **Use place value understanding and properties of operations to perform multi-digit arithmetic.**

Lesson 42	CC.3.NBT.1	Round to the Nearest Ten or Hundred	**83**
Lesson 43	CC.3.NBT.1	Estimate Sums	**85**
Lesson 44	CC.3.NBT.1	Estimate Differences	**87**
Lesson 45	CC.3.NBT.2	Mental Math Strategies for Addition	**89**
Lesson 46	CC.3.NBT.2	**Algebra** • Use Properties to Add	**91**
Lesson 47	CC.3.NBT.2	Use the Break Apart Strategy to Add	**93**
Lesson 48	CC.3.NBT.2	Use Place Value to Add	**95**
Lesson 49	CC.3.NBT.2	Mental Math Strategies for Subtraction	**97**
Lesson 50	CC.3.NBT.2	Use Place Value to Subtract	**99**
Lesson 51	CC.3.NBT.2	Combine Place Values to Subtract	**101**
Lesson 52	CC.3.NBT.3	**Problem Solving** • Use the Distributive Property	**103**
Lesson 53	CC.3.NBT.3	Multiplication Strategies with Multiples of 10	**105**
Lesson 54	CC.3.NBT.3	Multiply Multiples of 10 by 1-Digit Numbers	**107**

Number and Operations – Fractions

▶ **Develop understanding of fractions as numbers.**

Lesson 55	CC.3.NF.1	Equal Parts of a Whole	**109**
Lesson 56	CC.3.NF.1	Equal Shares	**111**
Lesson 57	CC.3.NF.1	Unit Fractions of a Whole	**113**
Lesson 58	CC.3.NF.1	Fractions of a Whole	**115**
Lesson 59	CC.3.NF.1	Fractions of a Group	**117**
Lesson 60	CC.3.NF.1	Find Part of a Group Using Unit Fractions	**119**
Lesson 61	CC.3.NF.1	**Problem Solving** • Find the Whole Group Using Unit Fractions	**121**
Lesson 62	CC.3.NF.2a CC.3.NF.2b	Fractions on a Number Line	**123**
Lesson 63	CC.3.NF.3a	**Investigate** • Model Equivalent Fractions	**125**
Lesson 64	CC.3.NF.3b	Equivalent Fractions	**127**
Lesson 65	CC.3.NF.3c	Relate Fractions and Whole Numbers	**129**
Lesson 66	CC.3.NF.3d	**Problem Solving** • Compare Fractions	**131**
Lesson 67	CC.3.NF.3d	Compare Fractions with the Same Denominator	**133**
Lesson 68	CC.3.NF.3d	Compare Fractions with the Same Numerator	**135**
Lesson 69	CC.3.NF.3d	Compare Fractions	**137**
Lesson 70	CC.3.NF.3d	Compare and Order Fractions	**139**

Measurement and Data

▶ **Solve problems involving measurement and estimation of intervals of time, liquid volumes, and masses of objects.**

Lesson 71	CC.3.MD.1	Time to the Minute	**141**
Lesson 72	CC.3.MD.1	A.M. and P.M.	**143**

© Houghton Mifflin Harcourt Publishing Company

Lesson 73	CC.3.MD.1	Measure Time Intervals	**145**
Lesson 74	CC.3.MD.1	Use Time Intervals	**147**
Lesson 75	CC.3.MD.1	**Problem Solving** • Time Intervals	**149**
Lesson 76	CC.3.MD.2	Estimate and Measure Liquid Volume	**151**
Lesson 77	CC.3.MD.2	Estimate and Measure Mass	**153**
Lesson 78	CC.3.MD.2	Solve Problems About Liquid Volume and Mass	**155**

▶ **Represent and interpret data.**

Lesson 79	CC.3.MD.3	**Problem Solving** • Organize Data	**157**
Lesson 80	CC.3.MD.3	Use Picture Graphs	**159**
Lesson 81	CC.3.MD.3	Make Picture Graphs	**161**
Lesson 82	CC.3.MD.3	Use Bar Graphs	**163**
Lesson 83	CC.3.MD.3	Make Bar Graphs	**165**
Lesson 84	CC.3.MD.3	Solve Problems Using Data	**167**
Lesson 85	CC.3.MD.4	Use and Make Line Plots	**169**
Lesson 86	CC.3.MD.4	Measure Length	**171**

▶ **Geometric measurement: understand concepts of area and relate area to multiplication and to addition.**

Lesson 87	CC.3.MD.5 CC.3.MD.5a	Understand Area	**173**
Lesson 88	CC.3.MD.5b CC.3.MD.6	Measure Area	**175**
Lesson 89	CC.3.MD.7a	Use Area Models	**177**
Lesson 90	CC.3.MD.7b	**Problem Solving** • Area of Rectangles	**179**
Lesson 91	CC.3.MD.7c CC.3.MD.7d	Area of Combined Rectangles	**181**

▶ **Geometric measurement: recognize perimeter as an attribute of plane figures and distinguish between linear and area measures.**

Lesson 92	CC.3.MD.8	**Investigate** • Model Perimeter	**183**
Lesson 93	CC.3.MD.8	Find Perimeter	**185**
Lesson 94	CC.3.MD.8	**Algebra** • Find Unknown Side Lengths	**187**
Lesson 95	CC.3.MD.8	Same Perimeter, Different Areas	**189**
Lesson 96	CC.3.MD.8	Same Area, Different Perimeters	**191**

Geometry

▶ **Reason with shapes and their attributes.**

Lesson 97	CC.3.G.1	Describe Plane Shapes	**193**
Lesson 98	CC.3.G.1	Describe Angles in Plane Shapes	**195**
Lesson 99	CC.3.G.1	Identify Polygons	**197**
Lesson 100	CC.3.G.1	Describe Sides of Polygons	**199**
Lesson 101	CC.3.G.1	Classify Quadrilaterals	**201**
Lesson 102	CC.3.G.1	Draw Quadrilaterals	**203**
Lesson 103	CC.3.G.1	Describe Triangles	**205**
Lesson 104	CC.3.G.1	**Problem Solving** • Classify Plane Shapes	**207**
Lesson 105	CC.3.G.2	**Investigate** • Relate Shapes, Fractions, and Area	**209**

Answer Key **211**

Common Core Standards **264**

© Houghton Mifflin Harcourt Publishing Company

Introduction

Core Standards for Math offers two-page lessons for every content standard in the *Common Core State Standards for Mathematics.* The first page of each lesson introduces the concept or skill being taught by providing step-by-step instruction and modeling and checks students' understanding through open-ended practice items. The second page includes multiple-choice practice items as well as problem-solving items.

Common Core State Standards for Mathematics: Content Standards

Content Standards define what students should understand and be able to do. These standards are organized into clusters of related standards to emphasize mathematical connections. Finally, domains represent larger groups of related standards. At the elementary (K–6) level, there are ten content domains. Each grade addresses four or five domains. The table below shows how the domains are placed across Grades K–6.

	Grade Levels						
Domains	**K**	**1**	**2**	**3**	**4**	**5**	**6**
Counting and Cardinality (CC)	•						
Operations and Algebraic Thinking (OA)	•	•	•	•	•	•	
Numbers and Operations in Base Ten (NBT)	•	•	•	•	•	•	
Measurement and Data (MD)	•	•	•	•	•	•	
Geometry (G)	•	•	•	•	•	•	•
Numbers and Operations—Fractions (NF)				•	•	•	
Ratios and Proportional Relationships (RP)							•
The Number System (NS)							•
Expressions and Equations (EE)							•
Statistics and Probability (SP)							•

The lessons in ***Core Standards for Math*** are organized by content standard. The content standard is listed at the top right-hand corner of each page. The entire text of the standards is provided on pages 264–268. The lesson objective listed below the content standard number indicates what part of the standard is emphasized in the lesson. You may choose to have students complete all the lessons for a particular standard or select lessons based on the more focused objectives.

© Houghton Mifflin Harcourt Publishing Company

Name ______________________________

Lesson 1

COMMON CORE STANDARD CC.3.OA.1

Lesson Objective: Model and skip count objects in equal groups to find how many there are.

Count Equal Groups

Equal groups have the same number in each group.

There are 3 tulips in each of 4 vases. How many tulips are there in all?

Step 1 Think: there are 4 vases, so draw **4** circles to show **4** equal groups.

Step 2 Think: there are 3 tulips in each vase, so draw **3** dots in each group.

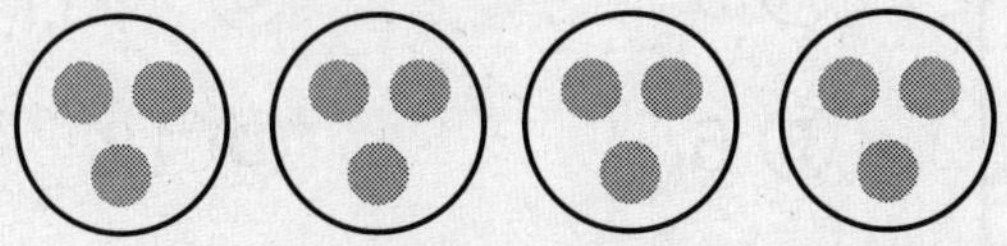

Step 3 Skip count by 3s to find how many in all: 3, **6**, **9**, **12**

There are **4** equal groups with **3** tulips in each group.

So, there are **12** tulips in all.

1. Draw 3 groups of 5. Skip count to find how many.

_____ in all

Count equal groups to find how many.

2.

____ groups of ____

____ in all

3.

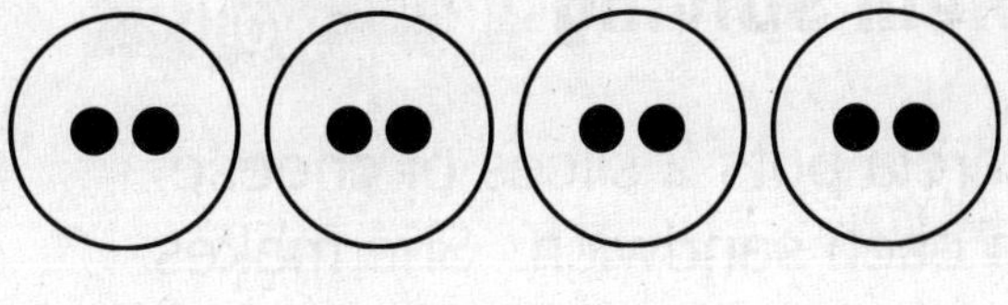

____ groups of ____

____ in all

© Houghton Mifflin Harcourt Publishing Company

1. There are 5 tables in the library. Four students are sitting at each table.

How many students are sitting in the library?

Ⓐ 9
Ⓑ 16
Ⓒ 20
Ⓓ 24

2. Alondra made 3 bracelets. There are 7 beads on each bracelet.

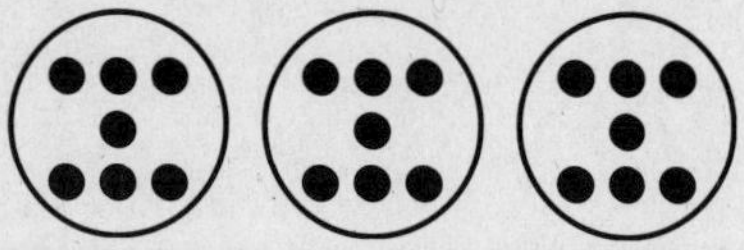

How many beads did Alondra use to make the bracelets?

Ⓐ 10
Ⓑ 14
Ⓒ 21
Ⓓ 24

3. Stella decorated using 4 groups of balloons. She drew this model to show the number of balloons.

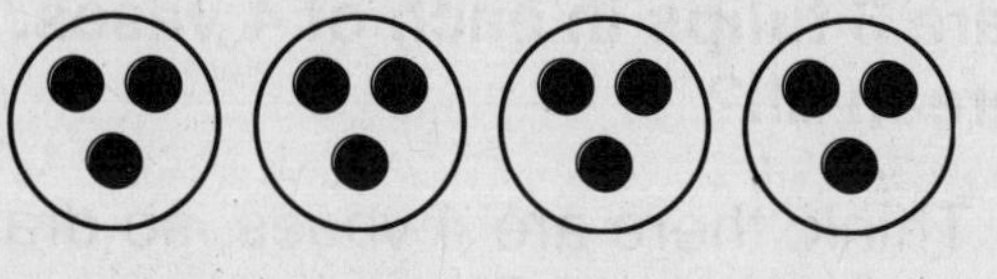

How many balloons did Stella use to decorate?

Ⓐ 3
Ⓑ 6
Ⓒ 9
Ⓓ 12

4. Mrs. Bennett sorted spools of thread into 3 containers. Each container held 3 spools.

How many spools of thread does Mrs. Bennett have in all?

Ⓐ 6
Ⓑ 9
Ⓒ 10
Ⓓ 12

Problem Solving REAL WORLD

5. Marcia puts 2 slices of cheese on each sandwich. She makes 4 cheese sandwiches. How many slices of cheese does Marcia use in all?

____

6. Tomas works in a cafeteria kitchen. He puts 3 cherry tomatoes on each of 5 salads. How many tomatoes does he use?

____

© Houghton Mifflin Harcourt Publishing Company

Name ______________________________

Lesson 2

COMMON CORE STANDARD CC.3.OA.1

Lesson Objective: Write an addition sentence and a multiplication sentence for a model.

Algebra • Relate Addition and Multiplication

You can add to find how many in all.

You can also multiply to find how many in all when you have equal groups.

2 + 2 + 2

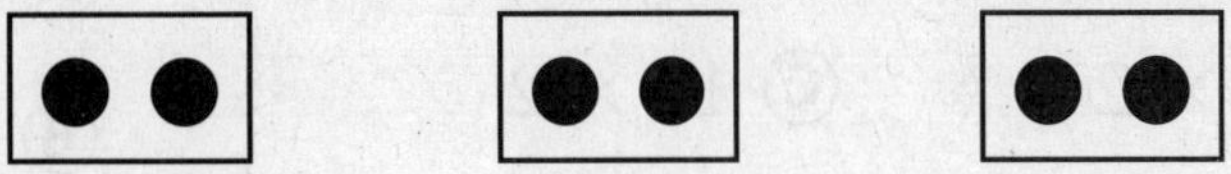

3 × 2 = 6

The **factors** are 3 and 2.
The **product** is 6.

So, 2 + 2 + 2 = **6** and 3 × 2 = **6**.

Write related addition and multiplication sentences for the model.

1.

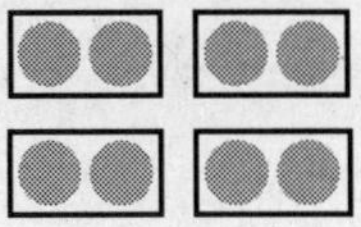

___ + ___ + ___ + ___ = ___

___ × ___ = ___

2.

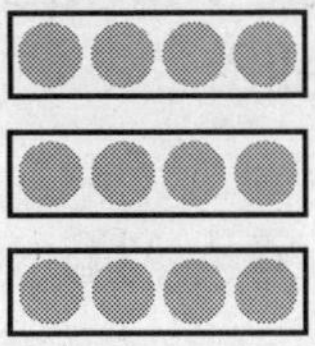

___ + ___ + ___ = ___

___ × ___ = ___

Draw a quick picture to show the equal groups. Then write related addition and multiplication sentences.

3. 4 groups of 3

___ + ___ + ___ + ___ = ___

___ × ___ = ___

4. 2 groups of 3

___ + ___ = ___

___ × ___ = ___

© Houghton Mifflin Harcourt Publishing Company

Name ______________________________

Lesson 2
CC.3.OA.1

1. Eric was doing his math homework. Eric wrote:

$$2 + 2 + 2 + 2 + 2$$

Which is another way to show what Eric wrote?

Ⓐ 2×2 Ⓒ 10×2

Ⓑ 5×2 Ⓓ $5 + 2$

2. Dallas and Mark each sharpened 4 pencils before school.

Which sentence shows the number of pencils sharpened in all?

Ⓐ $2 + 2 = 4$ Ⓒ $4 \times 4 = 16$

Ⓑ $4 + 2 = 6$ Ⓓ $2 \times 4 = 8$

3. A pet store has some fish bowls on display. There are 3 fish in each of 5 bowls. Which number sentence shows how many fish there are in all?

Ⓐ $5 \times 3 = 15$ Ⓒ $5 + 3 = 8$

Ⓑ $5 \times 5 = 25$ Ⓓ $3 \times 3 = 9$

4. Carlos spent 5 minutes working on each of 8 math problems. He can use 8×5 to find the total number of minutes he spent on the problems. Which is equal to 8×5?

Ⓐ $8 + 5$

Ⓑ $8 + 8 + 8$

Ⓒ $5 + 5 + 5 + 5 + 5$

Ⓓ $5 + 5 + 5 + 5 + 5 + 5 + 5 + 5$

Problem Solving REAL WORLD

5. There are 6 jars of pickles in a box. Ed has 3 boxes of pickles. How many jars of pickles does he have in all? Write a multiplication sentence to find the answer.

___ × ___ = ___ jars

6. Each day, Jani rides her bike 5 miles. How many miles does Jani ride in all in 4 days? Write a multiplication sentence to find the answer.

___ × ___ = ___ miles

© Houghton Mifflin Harcourt Publishing Company

Name ______________________________

Lesson 3

COMMON CORE STANDARD CC.3.OA.2

Lesson Objective: Use models to explore the meaning of partitive (sharing) division.

Size of Equal Groups

When you **divide**, you separate into equal groups.

Use counters or draw a quick picture. Make equal groups. Complete the table.

Counters	Number of Equal Groups	Number in Each Group
24	6	■

The number in each group is unknown, so divide.

Place 1 counter at a time in each group until all 24 counters are used.

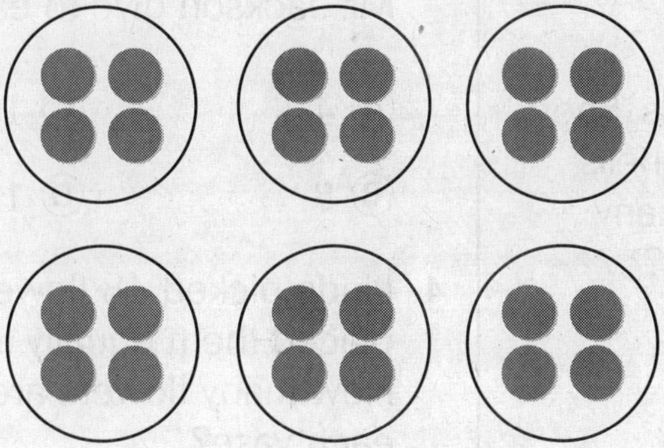

There are 4 counters in each of 6 groups.

Use counters or draw a quick picture. Make equal groups. Complete the table.

	Counters	Number of Equal Groups	Number in Each Group
1.	12	2	
2.	10	5	
3.	16	4	
4.	24	3	
5.	15	5	

© Houghton Mifflin Harcourt Publishing Company

Name ______________________

Lesson 3
CC.3.OA.2

1. Derek has 12 sweaters. He places an equal number of sweaters into 2 drawers.

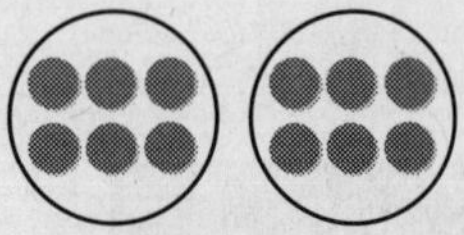

How many sweaters are in each drawer?

Ⓐ 2 Ⓒ 6
Ⓑ 4 Ⓓ 8

2. Megan found 36 seashells. She put an equal number of shells in each of 4 piles. How many seashells are in each pile?

Ⓐ 32
Ⓑ 9
Ⓒ 6
Ⓓ 4

3. Mr. Jackson has 16 flashcards. He gives an equal number of flashcards to 4 groups.

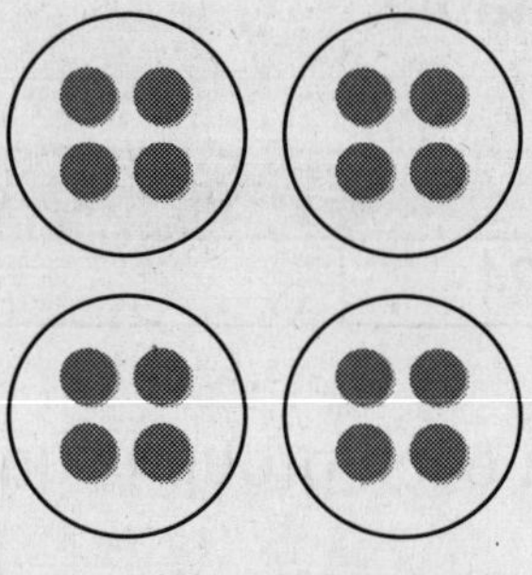

How many flashcards does Mr. Jackson give to each group?

Ⓐ 4 Ⓒ 12
Ⓑ 8 Ⓓ 16

4. Linda picked 48 flowers. She placed them equally into 8 vases. How many flowers are in each vase?

Ⓐ 4 Ⓒ 6
Ⓑ 5 Ⓓ 7

Problem Solving REAL WORLD

5. Alicia has 12 eggs that she will use to make 4 different cookie recipes. If each recipe calls for the same number of eggs, how many eggs will she use in each recipe?

____

6. Brett picked 27 flowers from the garden. He plans to give an equal number of flowers to each of 3 people. How many flowers will each person get?

____

© Houghton Mifflin Harcourt Publishing Company

Name ___________________________

COMMON CORE STANDARD CC.3.OA.2

Lesson Objective: Use models to explore the meaning of quotative (measurement) division.

Number of Equal Groups

Complete the table. Use counters to help find the number of equal groups.

Counters	Number of Equal Groups	Number in Each Group
18	■	3

The number of equal groups is unknown, so divide.
Circle groups of 3 counters until all 18 counters are in a group.

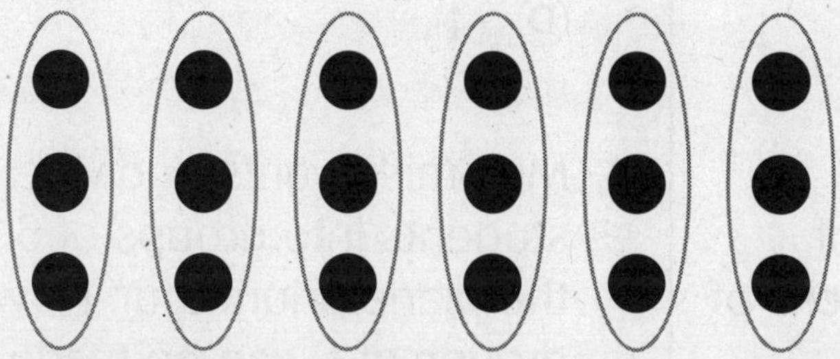

There are **6** groups of **3** counters each.

Draw counters. Then circle equal groups.
Complete the table.

	Counters	Number of Equal Groups	Number in Each Group
1.	24		4
2.	20		5
3.	21		7
4.	36		4

© Houghton Mifflin Harcourt Publishing Company

Name ______________________

1. Elle puts 24 charms into groups of 4. How many groups of charms are there?

Ⓐ 4

Ⓑ 6

Ⓒ 20

Ⓓ 28

2. A sporting goods store has 72 baseball caps in stacks of 8 caps each. How many stacks of baseball caps are there?

Ⓐ 7

Ⓑ 8

Ⓒ 9

Ⓓ 11

3. Heather places 32 stamps into groups of 8. How many groups of stamps are there?

Ⓐ 12

Ⓑ 8

Ⓒ 6

Ⓓ 4

4. Mr. Smith wants to divide his students into groups of 6 for the planetarium tour. How many groups of 6 can be made with 18 students?

Ⓐ 2

Ⓑ 3

Ⓒ 6

Ⓓ 9

Problem Solving REAL WORLD

5. In his bookstore, Toby places 21 books on shelves, with 7 books on each shelf. How many shelves does Toby need?

____

6. Mr. Holden has 32 quarters in stacks of 4 on his desk. How many stacks of quarters are on his desk?

____

© Houghton Mifflin Harcourt Publishing Company

Name ______________________

Lesson 5

COMMON CORE STANDARD CC.3.OA.2

Lesson Objective: Model division by using equal groups and bar models.

Model with Bar Models

Use counters to find 15 ÷ 5.

Step 1 Use 15 counters. Draw 5 circles to show the number of equal groups.

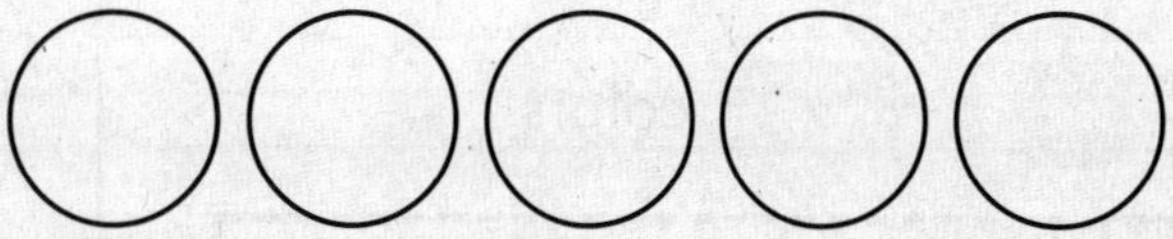

Step 2 Place 1 counter at a time in each circle.

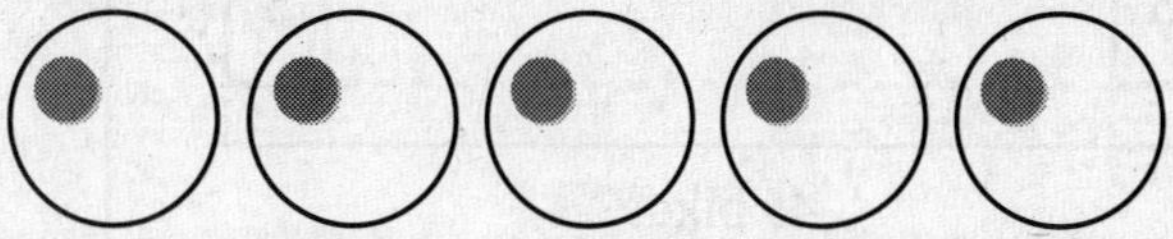

Step 3 Continue until you have placed all 15 counters.

Step 4 Count the number of counters in each circle.

There are 3 counters in each of the 5 groups.

You can use a bar model to show how the parts of a problem are related.

- There are 15 counters.
- There are 5 equal groups.
- There are 3 counters in each group.

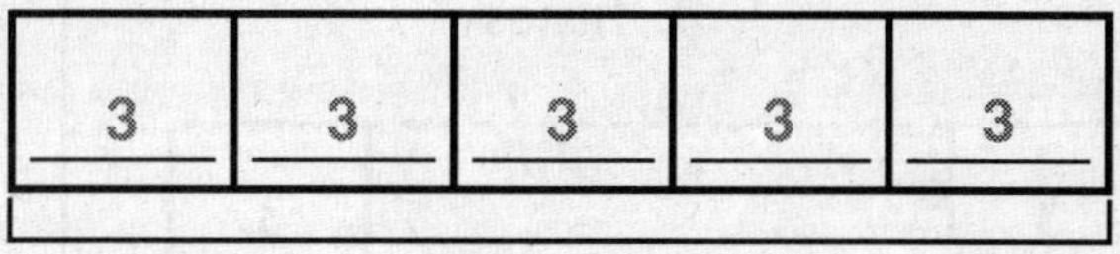

Write a division equation for the model.

15 ÷ 5 = 3

Write a division equation for the picture.

1.

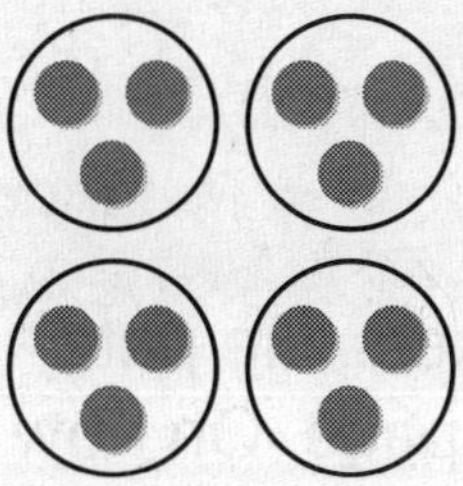

____

____

2.

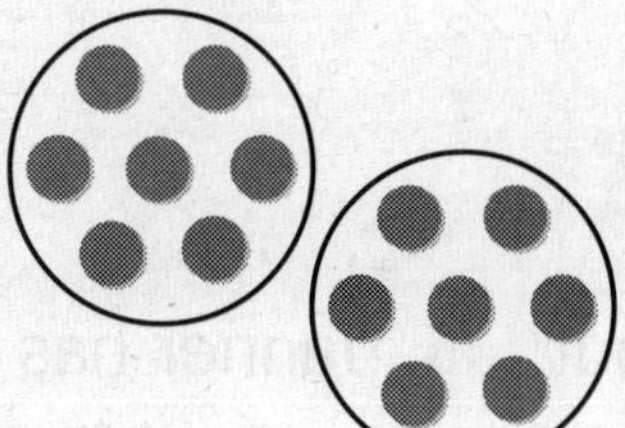

____

____

3.

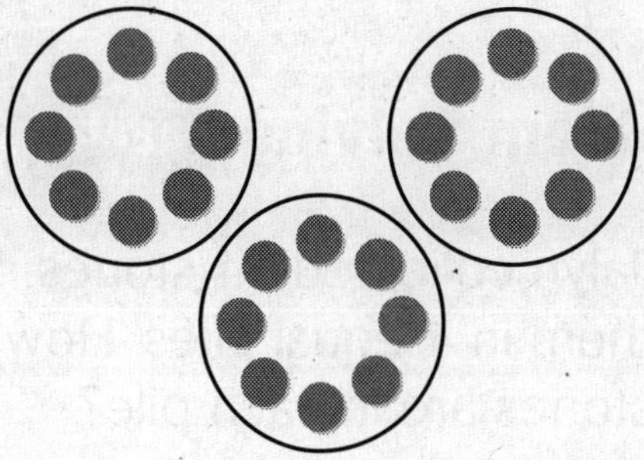

____

____

© Houghton Mifflin Harcourt Publishing Company

1. The Bike Shack displays 45 bikes grouped by color. There are 5 bikes in each group. How many colors of bikes are on display?

▭ colors

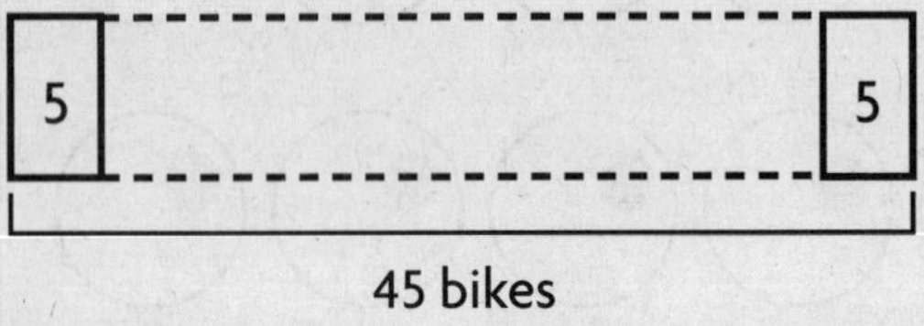

Ⓐ 5 Ⓒ 8

Ⓑ 7 Ⓓ 9

2. Rico went for a 12 mile bike ride. He stopped every 3 miles to take pictures. How many times did Rico stop during his bike ride?

▭ times

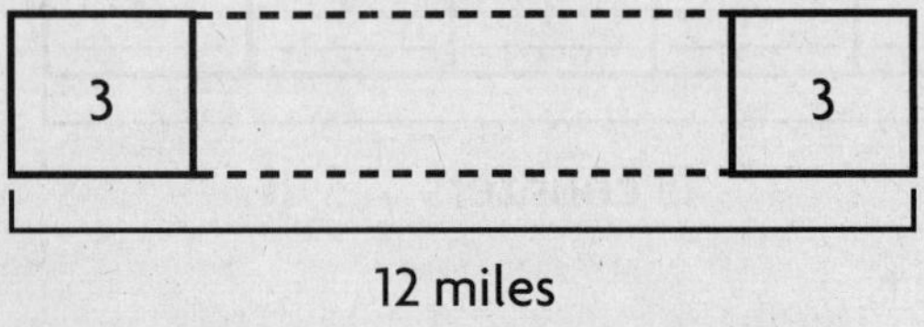

Ⓐ 3 Ⓒ 9

Ⓑ 4 Ⓓ 15

3. Amber divided her marbles evenly among 3 friends.

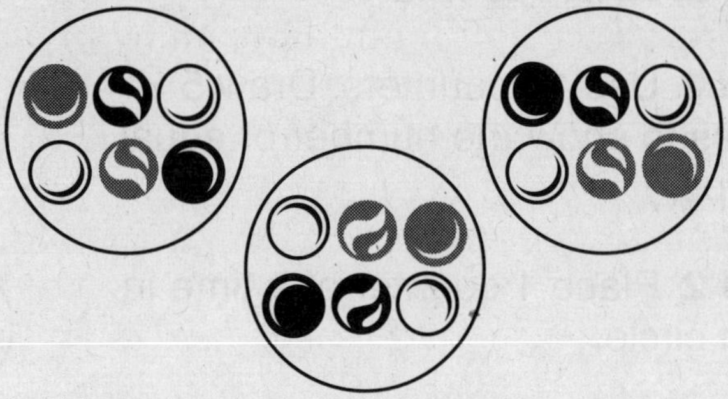

Which division equation is represented by the picture?

Ⓐ $3 \div 3 = 1$

Ⓑ $18 \div 3 = 6$

Ⓒ $18 \div 2 = 9$

Ⓓ $21 \div 3 = 7$

Problem Solving REAL WORLD

4. Jalyn collected 24 stones. She put them in 4 equal piles. How many stones are in each pile?

____

5. Tanner has 30 stickers. He puts 6 stickers on each page. On how many pages does he put stickers?

____

© Houghton Mifflin Harcourt Publishing Company

Name ________________________________

Lesson 6

COMMON CORE STANDARD CC.3.OA.3

Lesson Objective: Model and skip count on a number line to find how many there are.

Skip Count on a Number Line

When you have **equal groups**, you can skip count on a number line to find how many in all.

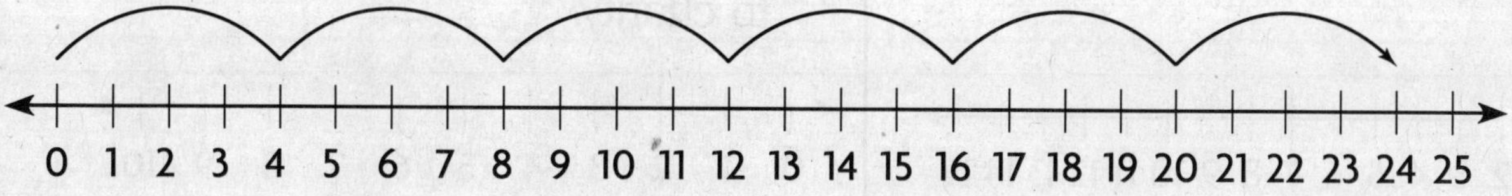

How many jumps are there? **6**

How long is each jump? **4 spaces**

Think: 6 jumps of 4 shows 6 groups of 4.

Multiply. **6 × 4**

6 × 4 = **24**

1. Skip count by drawing jumps on the number line. Find how many in 4 jumps of 4. Then write the product.

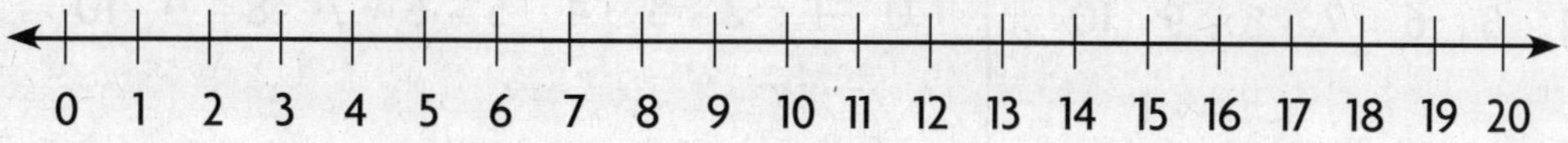

4 × 4 = _____

2. Draw jumps on the number line to show 6 groups of 3. Then find the product.

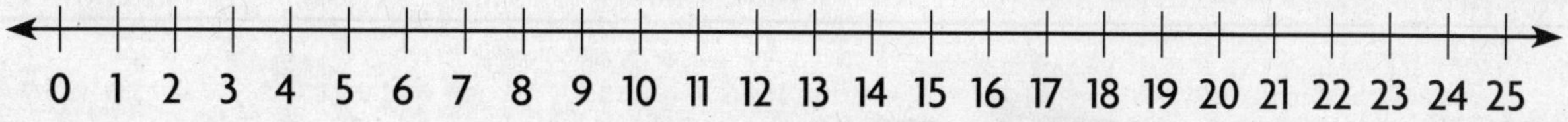

6 × 3 = _____

3. Write the multiplication sentence the number line shows.

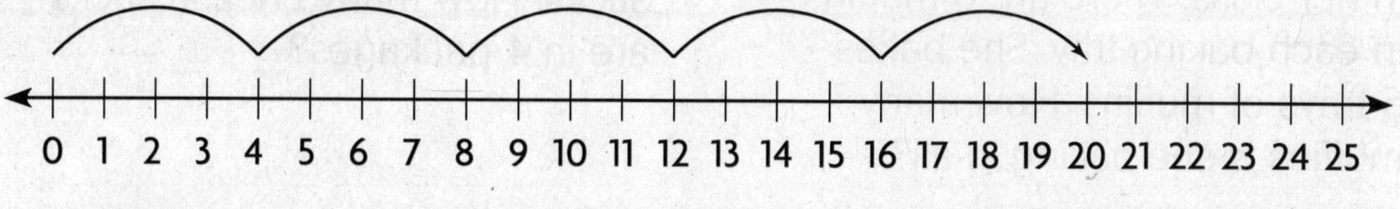

_____ × _____ = _____

© Houghton Mifflin Harcourt Publishing Company

Name ______________________________

1. Julio has a collection of coins. He puts the coins in 2 equal groups. There are 7 coins in each group.

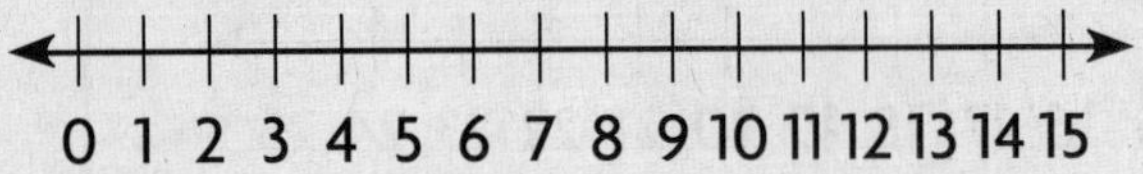

How many coins does Julio have in all?

Ⓐ 7 Ⓑ 9 Ⓒ 14 Ⓓ 15

2. Mrs. Riley buys 3 packages of mangos to make a large fruit salad. Each package contains 2 mangos.

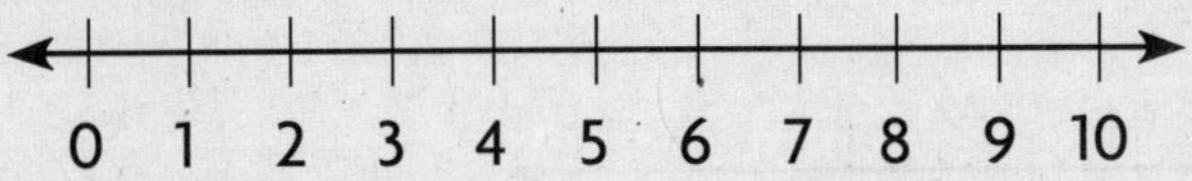

How many mangos does Mrs. Riley have in all?

Ⓐ 4 Ⓑ 5 Ⓒ 6 Ⓓ 8

3. Mr. Walters was cleaning his closet. He packed 2 shoes in each of 5 shoeboxes to donate to charity.

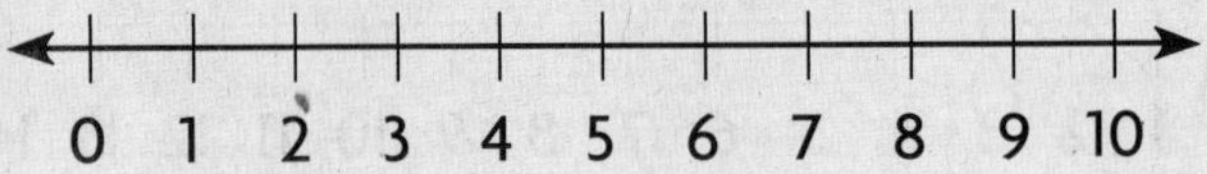

How many shoes did he pack in all?

Ⓐ 3 Ⓑ 7 Ⓒ 9 Ⓓ 10

4. Luis has 3 boxes of cars. There are 3 cars in each box.

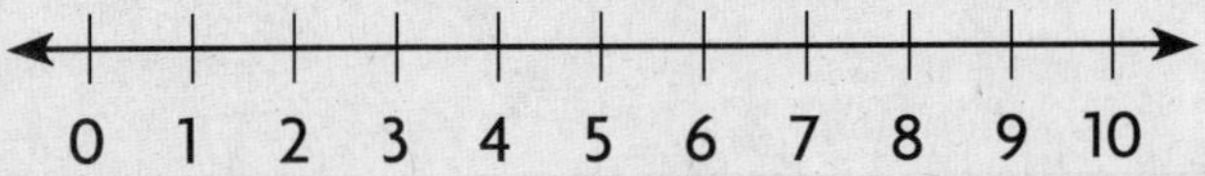

How many cars does Luis have in all?

Ⓐ 10 Ⓑ 9 Ⓒ 8 Ⓓ 6

Problem Solving REAL WORLD

5. Allie is baking muffins for students in her class. There are 6 muffins in each baking tray. She bakes 5 trays of muffins. How many muffins is she baking in all?

____

6. A snack package has 4 cheese sticks. How many cheese sticks are in 4 packages?

____

© Houghton Mifflin Harcourt Publishing Company

Name ________________________________

Lesson 7

COMMON CORE STANDARD CC.3.OA.3

Lesson Objective: Use arrays to model products and factors.

Model with Arrays

An **array** is a set of objects arranged in rows and columns.

Write a multiplication sentence for each array.

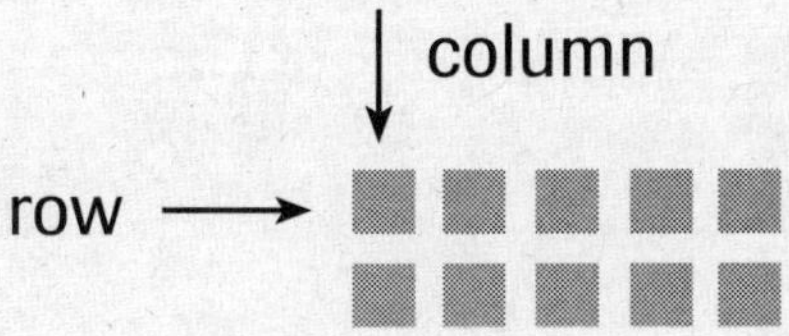

This array has **2** rows and **5** columns.	This array has **5** rows and **2** columns.
Count by fives.	Count by twos.
2 rows of 5 are 10.	5 rows of 2 are 10.
The multiplication sentence is $2 \times 5 = \mathbf{10}$.	The multiplication sentence is $5 \times 2 = \mathbf{10}$.

Write a multiplication sentence for the array.

1.

___ × ___ = ___

2.

___ × ___ = ___

3.

___ × ___ = ___

4.

___ × ___ = ___

© Houghton Mifflin Harcourt Publishing Company

1. Carson drew this array to show the number of pictures on one page of her photo album.

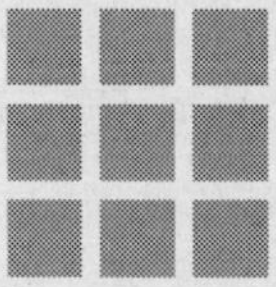

Which multiplication sentence does this array show?

Ⓐ $2 \times 3 = 6$ Ⓒ $3 \times 3 = 9$

Ⓑ $4 \times 4 = 16$ Ⓓ $3 \times 2 = 6$

2. Paco drew an array with 3 rows. Each row has 7 squares. Which multiplication sentence describes the array?

Ⓐ $2 \times 8 = 16$ Ⓒ $3 \times 7 = 21$

Ⓑ $2 \times 9 = 18$ Ⓓ $3 \times 8 = 24$

3. Rita arranged counters in 5 rows with 7 counters in each row. Which array shows how many counters she arranged in all?

Ⓐ 

Ⓑ 

Ⓒ 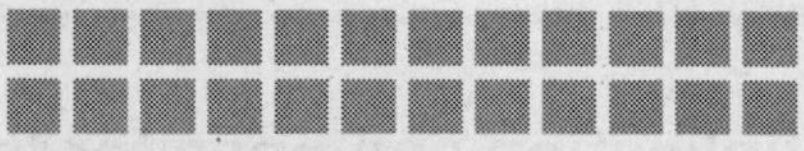

Ⓓ 

Problem Solving REAL WORLD

4. Lenny is moving tables in the school cafeteria. He places all the tables in a 7×4 array. How many tables are in the cafeteria?

____

5. Ms. DiMeo directs the school choir. She has the singers stand in 3 rows. There are 8 singers in each row. How many singers are there in all?

____

© Houghton Mifflin Harcourt Publishing Company

Name ____________________

Lesson 8

COMMON CORE STANDARD CC.3.OA.3

Lesson Objective: Draw a picture, count by 2s, or use doubles to multiply with the factors 2 and 4.

Multiply with 2 and 4

You can skip count to help you find a product.

Find the product. 4×3

Step 1 Use cubes to model 4 groups of 3.

Step 2 Skip count by 3s four times to find how many in all.

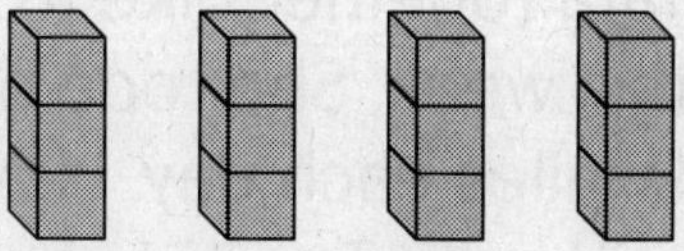

3, 6, 9, 12

4 groups of 3 is equal to **12**.

So, $4 \times 3 = 12$.

Write a multiplication sentence for the model.

1.

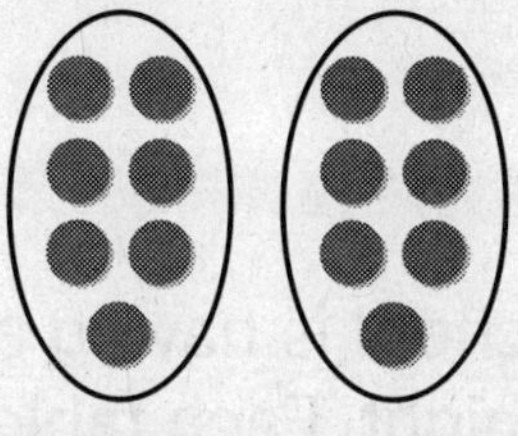

____ × ____ = ____

2.

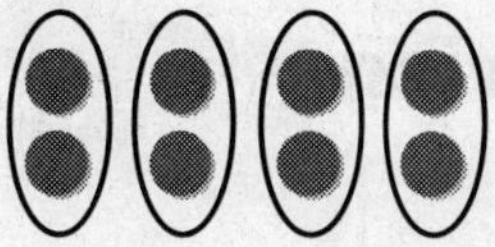

____ × ____ = ____

Find the product.

3. $\begin{array}{r} 2 \\ \times\ 3 \\ \hline \end{array}$ **4.** $\begin{array}{r} 4 \\ \times\ 8 \\ \hline \end{array}$ **5.** $\begin{array}{r} 2 \\ \times\ 6 \\ \hline \end{array}$ **6.** $\begin{array}{r} 4 \\ \times\ 1 \\ \hline \end{array}$ **7.** $\begin{array}{r} 2 \\ \times\ 9 \\ \hline \end{array}$

8. $\begin{array}{r} 2 \\ \times\ 2 \\ \hline \end{array}$ **9.** $\begin{array}{r} 4 \\ \times\ 9 \\ \hline \end{array}$ **10.** $\begin{array}{r} 2 \\ \times\ 5 \\ \hline \end{array}$ **11.** $\begin{array}{r} 4 \\ \times\ 5 \\ \hline \end{array}$ **12.** $\begin{array}{r} 4 \\ \times\ 7 \\ \hline \end{array}$

© Houghton Mifflin Harcourt Publishing Company

Name ______________________________

Lesson 8
CC.3.OA.3

1. There are 4 tables in the school library. Four students are sitting at each table. Brett made this model with counters to show the total number of students sitting in the library. How many students are sitting in the library?

Ⓐ 8
Ⓑ 10
Ⓒ 12
Ⓓ 16

2. Lily goes on 6 rides at the carnival. The cost of each ride is $2. How much do the rides cost in all?

Ⓐ $14
Ⓑ $12
Ⓒ $10
Ⓓ $8

3. Tara rode her bike to work 4 days this week. She rode a total of 9 miles each day. How many total miles did Tara ride her bike?

Ⓐ 13 miles
Ⓑ 18 miles
Ⓒ 36 miles
Ⓓ 45 miles

Problem Solving REAL WORLD

4. On Monday, Steven read 9 pages of his new book. To finish the first chapter on Tuesday, he needs to read double the number of pages he read on Monday. How many pages does he need to read on Tuesday?

____

5. Courtney's school is having a family game night. Each table has 4 players. There are 7 tables in all. How many players are at the game night?

____

© Houghton Mifflin Harcourt Publishing Company

Name ______________________________

Lesson 9

COMMON CORE STANDARD CC.3.OA.3

Lesson Objective: Use skip counting, a number line, or a bar model to multiply with the factors 5 and 10.

Multiply with 5 and 10

You can use an array to multiply with 5.

Find the product. 5×4

Step 1 Make an array to show 5×4. Show 5 rows of 4 tiles.

Step 2 Count the tiles.
5 rows of 4 tiles = 20 tiles

So, $5 \times 4 =$ **20**.

You can use doubles to multiply with 10.

Find the product. 6×10

Think: $5 + 5 = 10$

Multiply with 5. $6 \times 5 =$ **30**

Then double the product. **30** $+$ **30** $=$ **60**

So, $6 \times 10 =$ **60**.

Find the product.

1. $2 \times 5 =$ ____ **2.** $10 \times 2 =$ ____ **3.** $5 \times 5 =$ ____ **4.** $5 \times 1 =$ ____

5. $10 \times 1 =$ ____ **6.** $10 \times 5 =$ ____ **7.** $3 \times 5 =$ ____ **8.** $10 \times 7 =$ ____

9. 10×4 **10.** 6×5 **11.** 9×5 **12.** 10×3

13. 5×2 **14.** 10×6 **15.** 8×5 **16.** 10×8

© Houghton Mifflin Harcourt Publishing Company

Name ______________________________

1. Kyle bought 4 erasers at the school store. Each eraser cost 10¢.

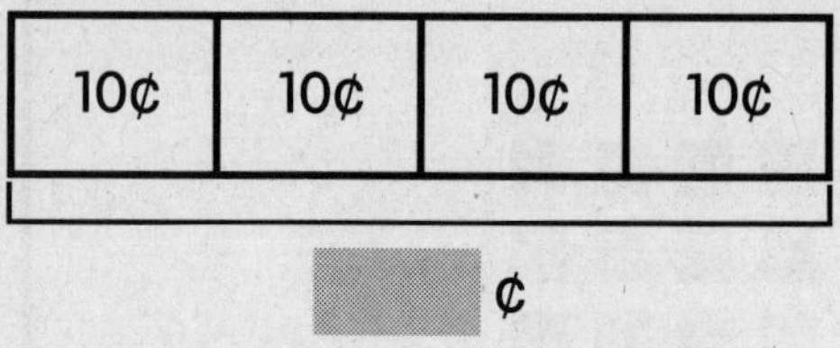

How much did the erasers cost in all?

Ⓐ 14¢ Ⓒ 40¢

Ⓑ 20¢ Ⓓ 44¢

2. Mrs. Howard's students stack their chairs at the end of the day. Each stack contains 5 chairs. If there are 6 stacks of chairs, how many chairs are stacked?

Ⓐ 15 Ⓒ 25

Ⓑ 20 Ⓓ 30

3. Aleesha has 10 packages of beads. There are 6 beads in each package. How many beads does Aleesha have altogether?

Ⓐ 16 Ⓒ 60

Ⓑ 30 Ⓓ 66

4. Tran buys an apple. He gives the store clerk 9 nickels. Each nickel has a value of 5 cents. How many cents does Tran give the store clerk?

Ⓐ 45 cents

Ⓑ 35 cents

Ⓒ 14 cents

Ⓓ 10 cents

Problem Solving REAL WORLD

5. Ginger takes 10 nickels to buy some pencils at the school store. How many cents does Ginger have to spend?

____

6. The gym at Evergreen School has three basketball courts. There are 5 players on each of the courts. How many players are there in all?

____

© Houghton Mifflin Harcourt Publishing Company

Name ______________________________

Lesson 10

COMMON CORE STANDARD CC.3.OA.3

Lesson Objective: Draw a picture, use 5s facts and addition, doubles, or a multiplication table to multiply with the factors 3 and 6.

Multiply with 3 and 6

You can use a number line to multiply with 3 or 6.

Find the product. 6×3

The factor 6 tells you to make **6 jumps**.

The factor 3 tells you each jump should be **3 spaces**.

Step 1 Start at 0.
Make 6 jumps of 3 spaces.

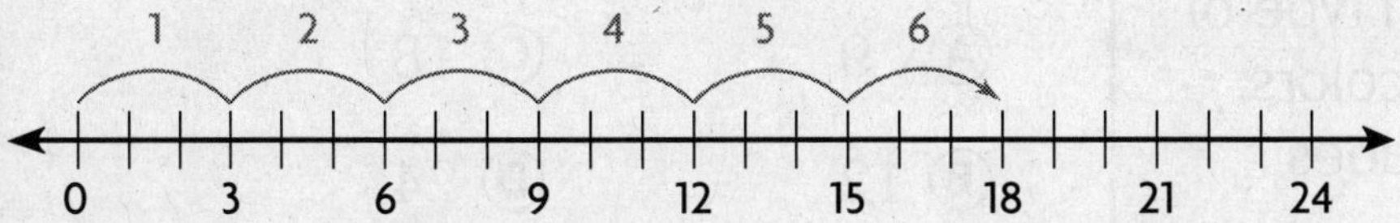

Step 2 The number you land on is the product.

So, $6 \times 3 = $ **18**.

Find the product.

1. $3 \times 1 =$ _____
2. _____ $= 2 \times 6$
3. $8 \times 3 =$ _____
4. $6 \times 6 =$ _____
5. $3 \times 0 =$ _____
6. $5 \times 6 =$ _____
7. _____ $= 3 \times 5$
8. $9 \times 6 =$ _____
9. $\begin{array}{r} 3 \\ \times\ 9 \\ \hline \end{array}$
10. $\begin{array}{r} 6 \\ \times\ 4 \\ \hline \end{array}$
11. $\begin{array}{r} 7 \\ \times\ 3 \\ \hline \end{array}$
12. $\begin{array}{r} 1 \\ \times\ 6 \\ \hline \end{array}$
13. $\begin{array}{r} 10 \\ \times\ 6 \\ \hline \end{array}$
14. $\begin{array}{r} 3 \\ \times\ 6 \\ \hline \end{array}$
15. $\begin{array}{r} 6 \\ \times\ 7 \\ \hline \end{array}$
16. $\begin{array}{r} 4 \\ \times\ 3 \\ \hline \end{array}$

© Houghton Mifflin Harcourt Publishing Company

Name ______________________________ **Lesson 10**

CC.3.OA.3

1. Jason has 6 bookshelves in his room. There are 6 books on each shelf. How many books are there in all?

(A) 12 (C) 36

(B) 24 (D) 42

2. Madison makes 4 types of hair ribbons. She makes each type of ribbon using 3 different colors. How many hair ribbons does Madison make?

(A) 12

(B) 10

(C) 9

(D) 7

3. Dora is making hexagons with straws. She uses 6 straws for each hexagon. If she makes 3 hexagons, how many straws does Dora use?

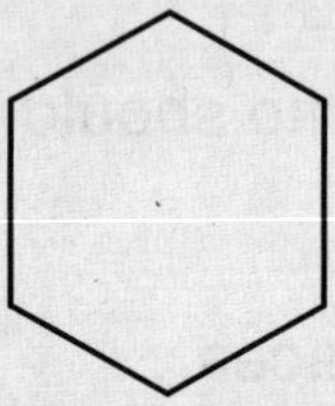

(A) 9 (C) 18

(B) 12 (D) 24

4. Elvira bought 4 packages of stickers. There are 6 stickers in each package. How many stickers did Elvira buy?

(A) 12 (C) 30

(B) 24 (D) 36

Problem Solving REAL WORLD

5. James got 3 hits in each of his baseball games. He has played 4 baseball games. How many hits has he had in all?

____

6. Mrs. Burns is buying muffins. There are 6 muffins in each box. If she buys 5 boxes, how many muffins will she buy?

____

© Houghton Mifflin Harcourt Publishing Company

Name ______________________________

Lesson 11

COMMON CORE STANDARD CC.3.OA.3

Lesson Objective: Solve division problems by using the strategy *act it out.*

Problem Solving • Model Division

There are 35 people going to the amusement park. They will all travel in 5 vans with the same number of people in each van. How many people will travel in each van?

Read the Problem

What do I need to find?

I need to find the number of people who will travel in each van.

What information do I need to use?

There are 35 people. 5 vans are taking all the people to the amusement park.

How will I use the information?

I can act out the problem by making equal groups with counters.

Solve the Problem

Describe how to act out the problem to solve.

Step 1 Start with 35 counters.

Step 2 Make 5 equal groups. Place 1 counter at a time in each group until all 35 counters are used.

Step 3 Count the number of counters in each group. 7

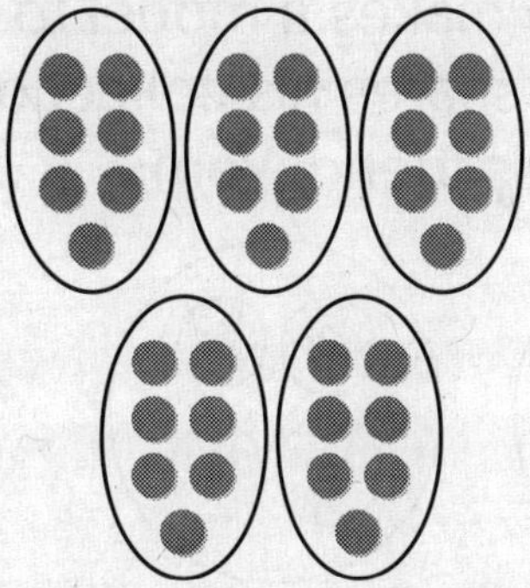

So, 7 people will travel in each van.

1. José packs 54 CDs into small boxes. Each box holds 9 CDs. How many boxes does José pack to hold all 54 CDs?

____

2. Mary volunteers at the library. She has 36 books to put on 4 empty shelves. If Mary puts an equal number of books on each shelf, how many books will be on each shelf?

____

© Houghton Mifflin Harcourt Publishing Company

Name ____________________

1. During a field trip, 30 students in Mrs. Beckman's class were placed into groups of 6 students each for a tour of the museum. How many groups were there?

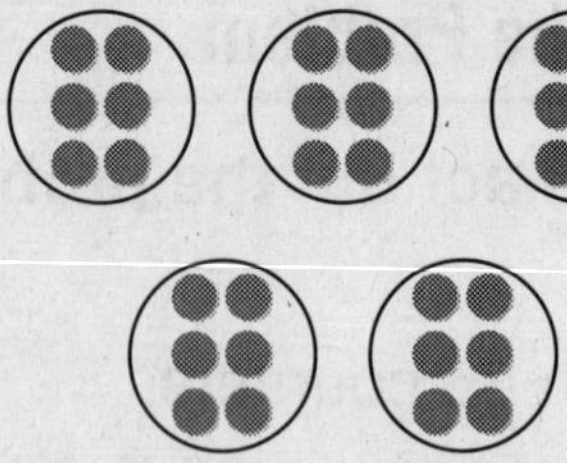

Ⓐ 5 Ⓒ 7

Ⓑ 6 Ⓓ 8

2. Tao has 8 sand dollars in his collection. He makes a model to show how he shares his collection equally with his friend, Yom.

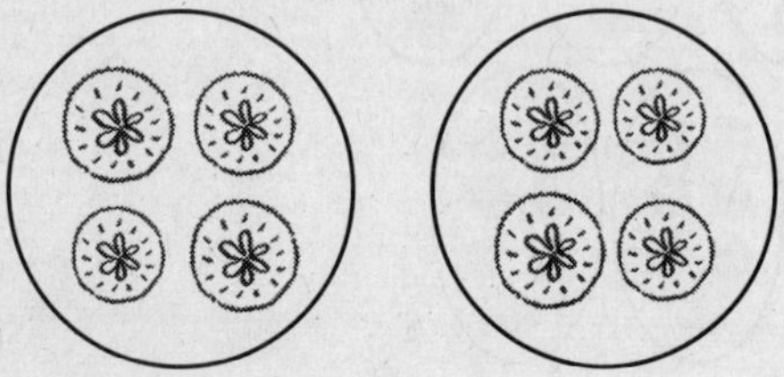

How many sand dollars does each boy get?

Ⓐ 2 Ⓒ 6

Ⓑ 4 Ⓓ 8

3. Barry has 15 comic books. He wants to place his books in 3 equal piles. Which model shows how many comic books Barry should put in each pile?

Ⓐ 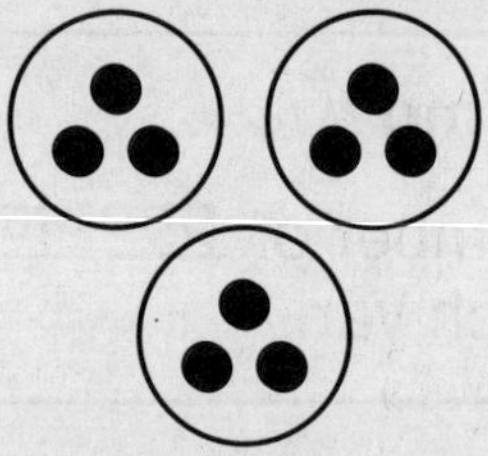

Ⓑ 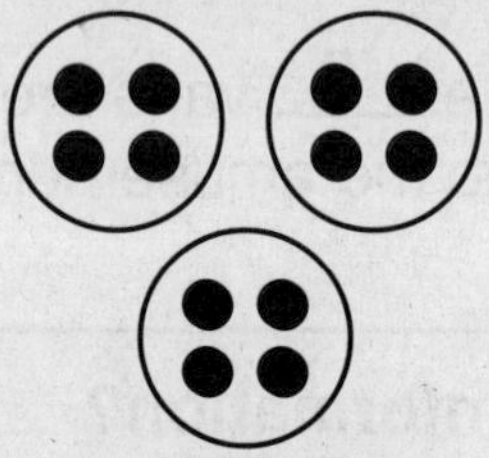

Ⓒ 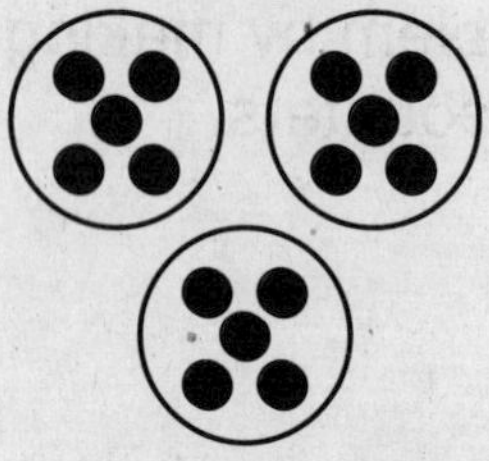

Ⓓ 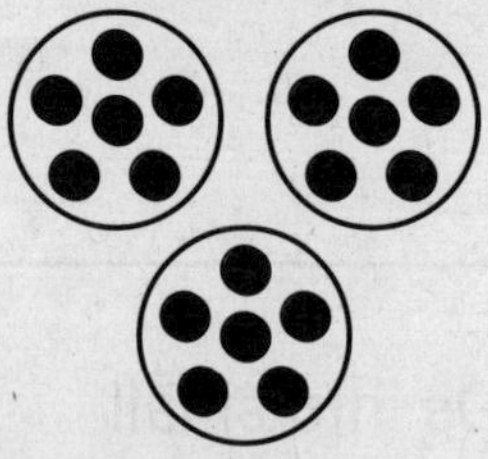

4. There are 54 party favors. Each of 6 tables will have the same number of party favors. How many party favors will go on each table? Explain how you can act out the problem with counters.

____

____

© Houghton Mifflin Harcourt Publishing Company

Name ______________________________

Lesson 12

COMMON CORE STANDARD CC.3.OA.3

Lesson Objective: Use repeated subtraction and a number line to relate subtraction to division.

Algebra • Relate Subtraction and Division

Find 18 ÷ 6.

	Use base-ten blocks.	**Use repeated subtraction.**
Step 1 Start with the number you are dividing, 18.	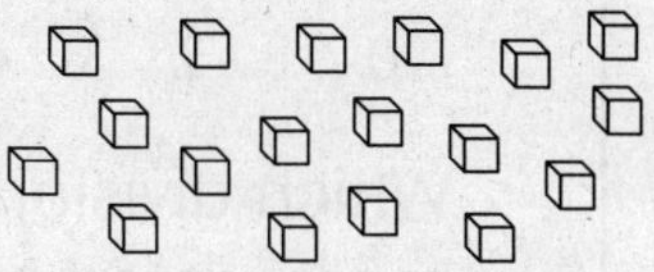	
Step 2 Subtract the number you are dividing by, 6.	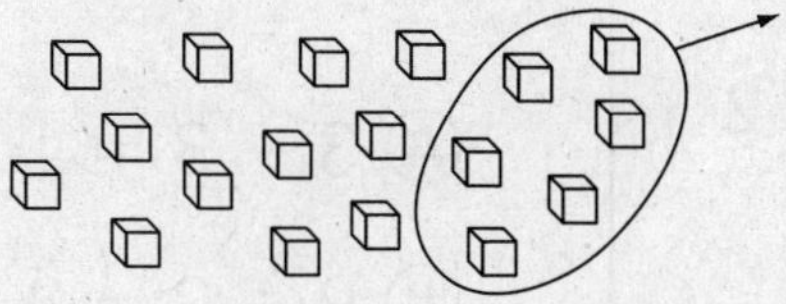	$18 - 6 = 12$
Step 3 There are more than 6 left. Subtract 6 again.	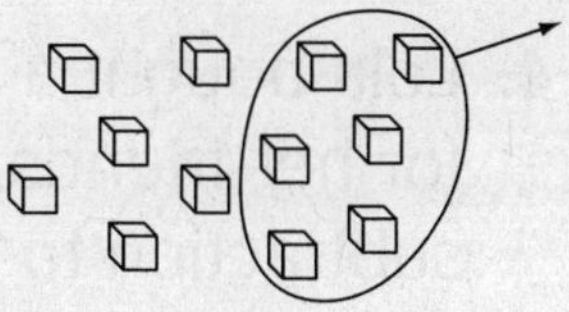	$18 - 6 = 12$ → $12 - 6 = 6$
Step 4 There are 6 left. Subtract 6 again.	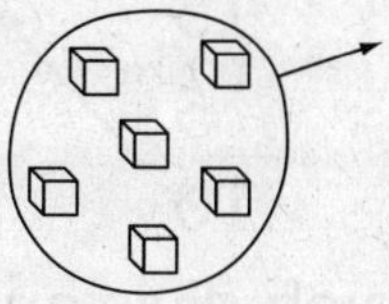	$18 - 6 = 12$ → $12 - 6 = 6$ → $6 - 6 = 0$

Step 5 Count the number of times you subtract 6.

You subtract 6 three times, so there are **3** groups of 6 in 18.

Write: 18 ÷ 6 = **3**

Write a division equation.

1. $27 - 9 = 18$ → $18 - 9 = 9$ → $9 - 9 = 0$

____

2. $16 - 4 = 12$ → $12 - 4 = 8$ → $8 - 4 = 4$ → $4 - 4 = 0$

____

© Houghton Mifflin Harcourt Publishing Company

Name ______________________________

Lesson 12
CC.3.OA.3

1. Mr. Burt shared 12 olives equally with each person in his family.

Which division equation is represented by the number line?

Ⓐ $12 \div 3 = 4$ Ⓒ $12 \div 2 = 6$

Ⓑ $3 \div 3 = 1$ Ⓓ $12 \div 6 = 2$

2. Lionel bought a bag of favors for his party guests. He used repeated subtraction to help him divide the favors equally among his guests.

$$\begin{array}{r}16\\-\ 4\\\hline 12\end{array}\nearrow\begin{array}{r}12\\-\ 4\\\hline 8\end{array}\nearrow\begin{array}{r}8\\-\ 4\\\hline 4\end{array}\nearrow\begin{array}{r}4\\-\ 4\\\hline 0\end{array}$$

Which division equation matches the repeated subtraction?

Ⓐ $16 \div 2 = 8$ Ⓒ $12 \div 3 = 4$

Ⓑ $4 \div 4 = 1$ Ⓓ $16 \div 4 = 4$

3. Marco's mother bought 9 toy cars. She asked Marco to share the cars equally among his friends. Marco used a number line to help.

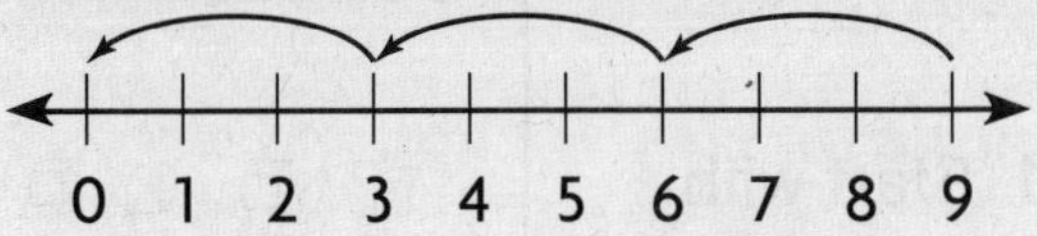

Which division equation is represented by the number line?

Ⓐ $3 \div 3 = 1$ Ⓒ $9 \div 9 = 1$

Ⓑ $9 \div 3 = 3$ Ⓓ $6 \div 3 = 2$

4. Lola bought a bag of 15 apples for her friends. She used repeated subtraction to help her divide the apples equally among her friends.

$$\begin{array}{r}15\\-\ 5\\\hline 10\end{array}\nearrow\begin{array}{r}10\\-\ 5\\\hline 5\end{array}\nearrow\begin{array}{r}5\\-\ 5\\\hline 0\end{array}$$

Which division equation matches the repeated subtraction?

Ⓐ $15 \div 15 = 1$ Ⓒ $15 \div 5 = 3$

Ⓑ $10 \div 5 = 2$ Ⓓ $15 \div 1 = 15$

---

5. How is repeated subtraction like counting back on a number line? Explain how both methods help you divide.

____

____

____

____

© Houghton Mifflin Harcourt Publishing Company

Name ______________________________

Lesson 13

COMMON CORE STANDARD CC.3.OA.3

Lesson Objective: Model division by using arrays.

Model with Arrays

You can use arrays to model division.

How many rows of 6 tiles each can you make with 24 tiles?

Use square tiles to make an array. Solve.

Step 1 Use 24 tiles.

Step 2 Make as many rows of 6 as you can.

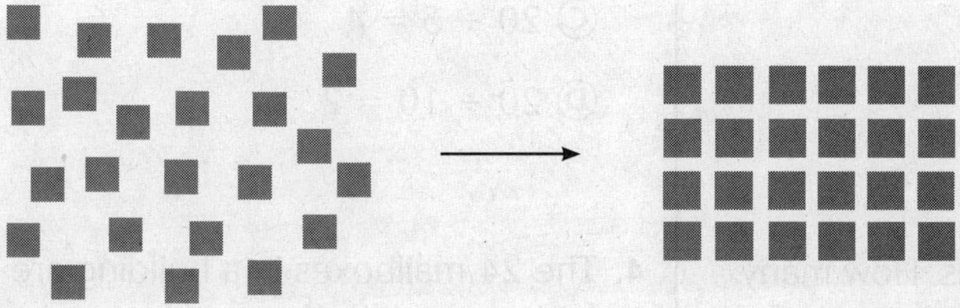

You can make **4** rows of 6.

So, there are **4** rows of 6 tiles in 24.

Use square tiles to make an array. Solve.

1. How many rows of 7 are in 28? ______

2. How many rows of 5 are in 15? ______

Make an array. Then write a division equation.

3. 18 tiles in 3 rows ______

4. 20 tiles in 4 rows ______

5. 14 tiles in 2 rows ______

6. 36 tiles in 4 rows ______

© Houghton Mifflin Harcourt Publishing Company

1. Which division sentence best fits the array?

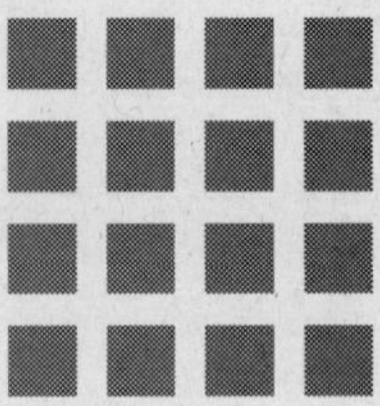

Ⓐ 16 ÷ 16 = 1

Ⓑ 16 ÷ 8 = 2

Ⓒ 16 ÷ 4 = 4

Ⓓ 16 ÷ 1 = 16

2. Damian has 30 tiles. How many rows of 10 tiles can he make?

Ⓐ 27

Ⓑ 15

Ⓒ 10

Ⓓ 3

3. Which division sentence best fits the array?

Ⓐ 21 ÷ 1 = 21

Ⓑ 21 ÷ 3 = 7

Ⓒ 20 ÷ 5 = 4

Ⓓ 20 ÷ 10 = 2

4. The 24 mailboxes in a building are in an array with 6 rows. How many mailboxes are in each row?

Ⓐ 4 Ⓒ 8

Ⓑ 6 Ⓓ 12

Problem Solving REAL WORLD

5. A dressmaker has 24 buttons. He needs 3 buttons to make one dress. How many dresses can he make with 24 buttons?

____

6. Liana buys 36 party favors for her 9 guests. She gives an equal number of favors to each guest. How many party favors does each guest get?

____

© Houghton Mifflin Harcourt Publishing Company

Name ________________________________

Lesson 14

COMMON CORE STANDARD CC.3.OA.3

Lesson Objective: Use models to represent division by 2.

Divide by 2

You can draw a picture to show how to divide.

Find the quotient. $16 \div 2$

Step 1 Draw 16 counters.

Step 2 Circle groups of 2. Continue circling groups of 2 until all 16 counters are in groups.

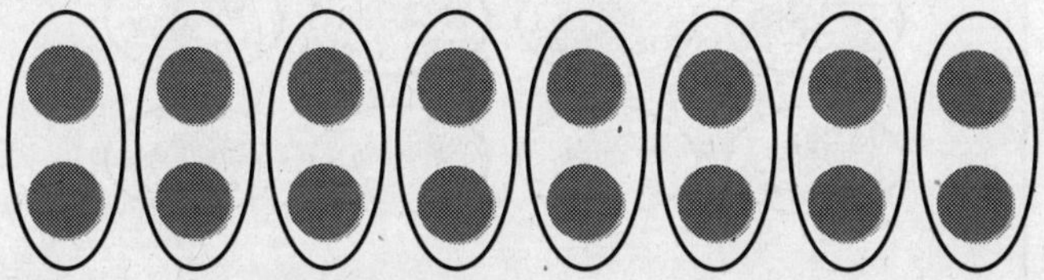

There are **8** groups of **2**.

So, $16 \div 2 = \mathbf{8}$.

Write a division equation for the picture.

1.

2.

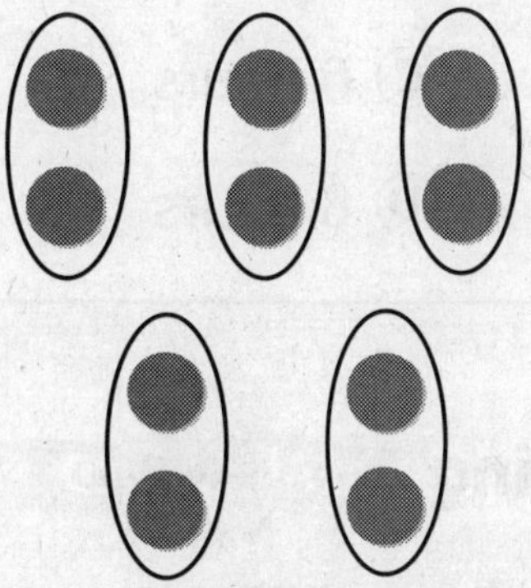

______________________ ______________________

© Houghton Mifflin Harcourt Publishing Company

1. Lionel has 14 mittens.

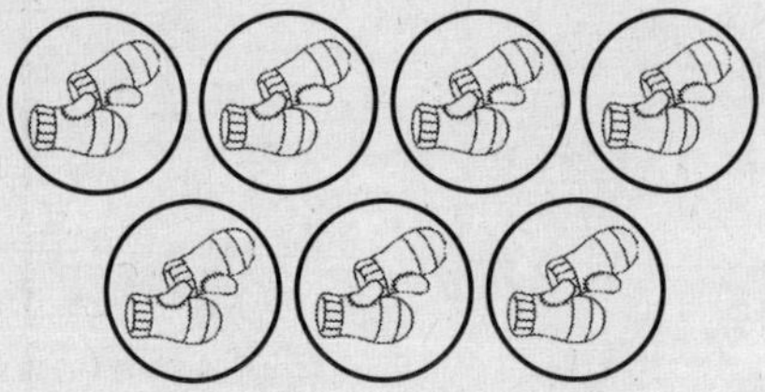

Which division equation is represented by the picture?

Ⓐ $7 \div 7 = 1$

Ⓑ $2 \div 2 = 1$

Ⓒ $14 \div 14 = 1$

Ⓓ $14 \div 2 = 7$

2. Garret practiced on the piano for the same amount of time each day for 2 days. He practiced a total of 4 hours. How many hours did Garret practice each day?

Ⓐ 1 hour Ⓒ 6 hours

Ⓑ 2 hours Ⓓ 8 hours

3. Ben needs 2 oranges to make a glass of orange juice. If oranges come in bags of 10, how many glasses of orange juice can he make using one bag of oranges?

Ⓐ 4 Ⓒ 6

Ⓑ 5 Ⓓ 8

4. Mrs. Conner has 16 shoes.

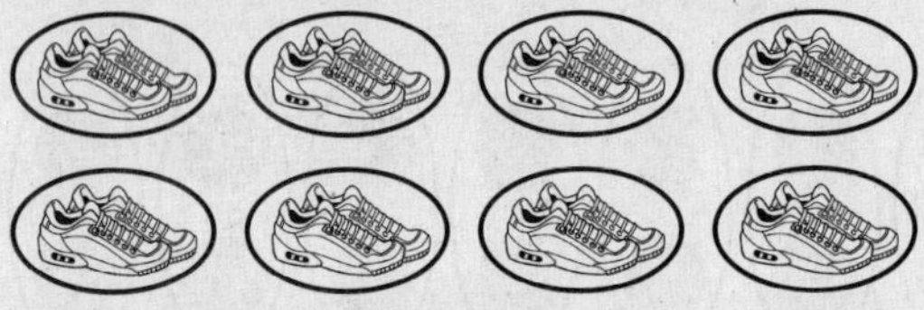

What division sentence is represented by the picture?

Ⓐ $80 \div 8 = 1$

Ⓑ $16 \div 16 = 1$

Ⓒ $16 \div 2 = 8$

Ⓓ $2 \div 2 = 1$

Problem Solving REAL WORLD

5. Mr. Reynolds, the gym teacher, divided a class of 16 students into 2 equal teams. How many students were on each team?

____

6. Sandra has 10 books. She divides them into groups of 2 each. How many groups can she make?

____

© Houghton Mifflin Harcourt Publishing Company

Name ______________________

Lesson 15

COMMON CORE STANDARD CC.3.OA.3

Lesson Objective: Count up by 5s, count back on a number line, or use 10s facts and doubles to divide by 5.

Divide by 5

You can use a hundred chart and count up to help you divide.

Find the quotient. 30 ÷ 5

Step 1 Count up by 5s until you reach 30. Circle the numbers you say in the count.

1	2	3	4	(5)	6	7	8	9	(10)
11	12	13	14	15	16	17	18	19	20
21	22	23	24	25	26	27	28	29	30
31	32	33	34	35	36	37	38	39	40
41	42	43	44	45	46	47	48	49	50
51	52	53	54	55	56	57	58	59	60
61	62	63	64	65	66	67	68	69	70
71	72	73	74	75	76	77	78	79	80
81	82	83	84	85	86	87	88	89	90
91	92	93	94	95	96	97	98	99	100

Step 2 Count the number of times you count up.

5, 10, 15, ____, ____, ____

1 2, ____, ____, ____, ____

Step 3 Use the number of times you count up to complete the equation.

You counted up by 5 ______ times.

So, 30 ÷ 5 = _____.

Use the hundred chart and count up to solve.

1. 20 ÷ 5 = _____

2. 35 ÷ 5 = _____

3. 40 ÷ 5 = _____

Find the quotient.

4. 25 ÷ 5 = _____

5. _____ = 45 ÷ 5

6. 10 ÷ 5 = _____

7. _____ = 15 ÷ 5

8. 50 ÷ 5 = _____

9. _____ = 5 ÷ 5

© Houghton Mifflin Harcourt Publishing Company

1. The Bike Shack displays 45 bikes grouped by color. There are 5 bikes in each group. How many colors of bikes does the store have?

Ⓐ 7

Ⓑ 9

Ⓒ 20

Ⓓ 40

2. Mrs. Alvarez printed 35 pictures. She will group them into sets of 5. How many sets of pictures can she make?

Ⓐ 40 Ⓒ 7

Ⓑ 30 Ⓓ 6

3. Hannah made $40 selling hats. Each hat costs $5. She wants to know how many hats she sold. Hannah used a number line to help her.

Which division equation is represented by the number line?

Ⓐ $6 \div 6 = 1$

Ⓑ $40 \div 10 = 4$

Ⓒ $40 \div 4 = 10$

Ⓓ $40 \div 5 = 8$

Problem Solving REAL WORLD

4. A model car maker puts 5 wheels in each kit. A machine makes 30 wheels at a time. How many packages of 5 wheels can be made from the 30 wheels?

____

5. A doll maker puts a small bag with 5 hair ribbons inside each box with a doll. How many bags of 5 hair ribbons can be made from 45 hair ribbons?

____

© Houghton Mifflin Harcourt Publishing Company

Name ______________________

COMMON CORE STANDARD CC.3.OA.4

Lesson Objective: Use an array or a multiplication table to find an unknown factor.

Algebra • Find Unknown Factors

Lily has 20 stuffed animals. She wants to put the same number of stuffed animals on each of 5 shelves. How many stuffed animals will Lily put on each shelf?

Find the unknown factor. $5 \times c = 20$

You can use counters to find the unknown factor.

Step 1 Use 20 counters.

Step 2 Make **5** equal groups. Place 1 counter in each of the groups until you have placed all 20 counters.

Step 3 Count the number of counters in each group.
4 counters

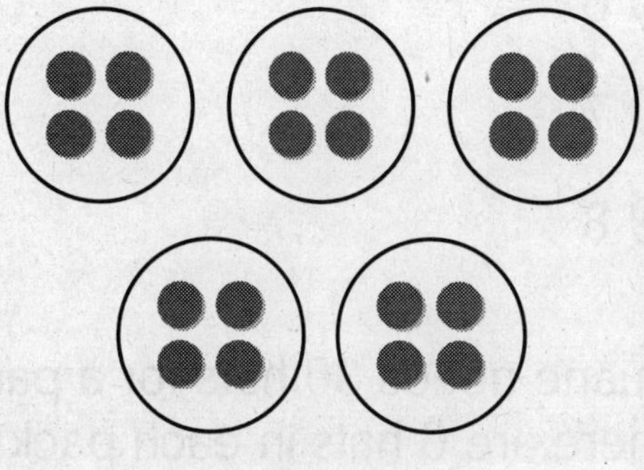

$c = 4$

So, Lily will put **4** stuffed animals on each of the 5 shelves.

$5 \times 4 = 20$

Find the unknown factor.

1. $3 \times b = 24$ $b =$ ______
2. $n \times 7 = 21$ $n =$ ______
3. $36 = 4 \times z$ $z =$ ______
4. $s \times 8 = 56$ $s =$ ______
5. $r \times 5 = 45$ $r =$ ______
6. ■ $\times 4 = 40$ ■ $=$ ______
7. $12 = 3 \times p$ $p =$ ______
8. $m \times 6 = 42$ $m =$ ______
9. $6 \times h = 36$ $h =$ ______
10. $63 = 7 \times d$ $d =$ ______
11. $3 \times y = 6$ $y =$ ______
12. $32 = 4 \times$ ▲   ▲ $=$ ______

© Houghton Mifflin Harcourt Publishing Company

1. The volleyball club plans to have 7 teams. There were 42 students who signed up to play. How many students will be on each team?

$7 \times \blacksquare = 42$

Ⓐ 5

Ⓑ 6

Ⓒ 7

Ⓓ 8

2. Duane needs 36 hats for a party. There are 6 hats in each package. How many packages of hats does Duane need to buy?

$p \times 6 = 36$

Ⓐ 2 Ⓒ 18

Ⓑ 6 Ⓓ 30

3. Pilar spent $48 on 6 books. The cost of each book was the same. Which equation can be used to find the cost of one book?

Ⓐ $\$48 \times \blacksquare = 6$

Ⓑ $3 \times \blacksquare = 6$

Ⓒ $\$48 \times \blacksquare = 8$

Ⓓ $6 \times \blacksquare = \$48$

4. Mr. Perkins plans to teach 4 reading groups. If he has 28 students, how many students will be in each reading group?

$4 \times \blacksquare = 28$

Ⓐ 24 Ⓒ 7

Ⓑ 8 Ⓓ 6

Problem Solving REAL WORLD

5. Carmen spent $42 for 6 hats. How much did each hat cost?

____

6. Mark has a baking tray with 24 cupcakes. The cupcakes are arranged in 4 equal rows. How many cupcakes are in each row?

____

© Houghton Mifflin Harcourt Publishing Company

Name ________________________________

Lesson 17

COMMON CORE STANDARD CC.3.OA.4

Lesson Objective: Use repeated subtraction, a related multiplication fact, or a multiplication table to divide by 8.

Divide by 8

You can use a number line to divide by 8.

Find the quotient. 24 ÷ 8

Step 1 Start at 24. Count back by 8s as many times as you can until you reach 0. Draw the jumps on the number line.

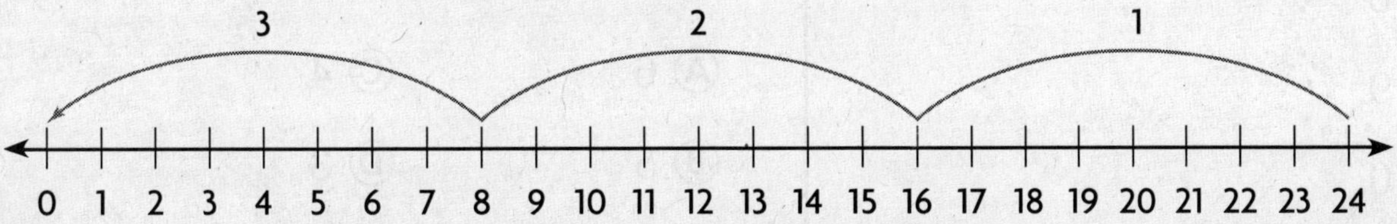

Step 2 Count the number of times you jumped back 8.

You jumped back by 8 **three** times.

So, 24 ÷ 8 = **3**.

Find the unknown factor and quotient.

1. ____ × 8 = 72   72 ÷ 8 = ____

2. 8 × ____ = 48   48 ÷ 8 = ____

3. 8 × ____ = 40   40 ÷ 8 = ____

4. ____ × 8 = 16   16 ÷ 8 = ____

Find the quotient.

5. 32 ÷ 8 = ____

6. ____ = 8 ÷ 8

7. 64 ÷ 8 = ____

8. 56 ÷ 8 = ____

9. ____ = 16 ÷ 8

10. 40 ÷ 8 = ____

11. 24 ÷ 8 = ____

12. ____ = 72 ÷ 8

13. 48 ÷ 8 = ____

© Houghton Mifflin Harcourt Publishing Company

Name ______________________________

1. Brian is dividing 64 baseball cards equally among 8 friends. How many baseball cards will each friend get?

Ⓐ 7

Ⓑ 8

Ⓒ 9

Ⓓ 10

2. Adam and his friends raked enough leaves to fill 48 bags. Each person filled 8 bags. How many people raked leaves?

Ⓐ 6

Ⓑ 5

Ⓒ 4

Ⓓ 3

3. Students celebrated Earth Day by planting 24 seedlings at 8 different locations in town. They planted the same number of seedlings at each location. How many seedlings did they plant at each location?

Ⓐ 6 Ⓒ 4

Ⓑ 5 Ⓓ 3

4. Keith arranged 40 toy cars in 8 equal rows. How many toy cars are in each row?

Ⓐ 4

Ⓑ 5

Ⓒ 6

Ⓓ 32

Problem Solving REAL WORLD

5. Sixty-four students are going on a field trip. There is 1 adult for every 8 students. How many adults are there?

____

6. Mr. Chen spends $32 for tickets to a play. If the tickets cost $8 each, how many tickets does Mr. Chen buy?

____

© Houghton Mifflin Harcourt Publishing Company

Name ______________________________

Lesson 18

COMMON CORE STANDARD CC.3.OA.5

Lesson Objective: Model the Commutative Property of Multiplication and use it to find products.

Algebra • Commutative Property of Multiplication

The **Commutative Property of Multiplication** states that you can change the order of the factors and the product stays the same.

There are **4** rows of **5** tiles.

Think: 4 equal groups of 5

$5 + 5 + 5 + 5 = 20$

Multiply. $4 \times 5 =$ **20**

There are **5** rows of **4** tiles.

Think: 5 equal groups of 4

$4 + 4 + 4 + 4 + 4 = 20$

Multiply. $5 \times 4 =$ **20**

The factors are 4 and 5. The product is 20.

Write a multiplication sentence for the array.

1.

____

2.

____

3.

____

Write a multiplication sentence for the model. Then use the Commutative Property of Multiplication to write a related multiplication sentence.

4.

___ × ___ = ___

___ × ___ = ___

5.

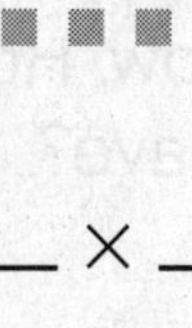

___ × ___ = ___

___ × ___ = ___

6.

___ × ___ = ___

___ × ___ = ___

© Houghton Mifflin Harcourt Publishing Company

1. Donna wrote $5 \times 9 = 45$. Which is a related number sentence?

Ⓐ $5 + 4 = 9$
Ⓑ $9 \times 5 = 45$
Ⓒ $5 \times 5 = 25$
Ⓓ $4 \times 5 = 20$

2. Matthew made arrays with counters to show the Commutative Property of Multiplication.

Which multiplication sentences are shown by his arrays?

Ⓐ $3 \times 4 = 12$ and $4 \times 3 = 12$
Ⓑ $6 \times 4 = 24$ and $4 \times 6 = 24$
Ⓒ $6 \times 2 = 12$ and $2 \times 6 = 12$
Ⓓ $2 \times 7 = 14$ and $7 \times 2 = 14$

3. Greta put 6 coins into each of 3 stacks. She wrote $3 \times 6 = 18$. Which is a related number sentence?

Ⓐ $6 \times 3 = 18$
Ⓑ $6 + 3 = 9$
Ⓒ $3 + 3 + 3 = 9$
Ⓓ $6 \times 6 = 36$

4. Ben put 10 color pencils into each of 6 bags. He wrote $6 \times 10 = 60$ to represent the total. Which is a related multiplication sentence?

Ⓐ $10 \times 10 = 100$
Ⓑ $5 \times 12 = 60$
Ⓒ $6 \times 6 = 36$
Ⓓ $10 \times 6 = 60$

Problem Solving REAL WORLD

5. A garden store sells trays of plants. Each tray holds 2 rows of 8 plants. How many plants are in one tray?

____

6. Jeff collects toy cars. They are displayed in a case that has 4 rows. There are 6 cars in each row. How many cars does Jeff have?

____

© Houghton Mifflin Harcourt Publishing Company

Name ___________________________

Lesson 19

COMMON CORE STANDARD CC.3.OA.5

Lesson Objective: Model multiplication with the factors 1 and 0.

Algebra • Multiply with 1 and 0

Find the product.

4 × 0 = ■

Model 4 × 0.
Each circle contains 0 counters.

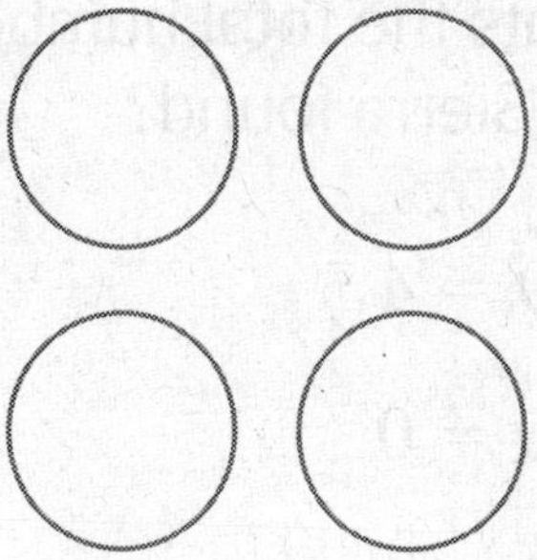

4 circles × 0 counters = 0 counters

Zero Property of Multiplication
The product of zero and any number is zero.

So, 4 × 0 = **0** and 0 × 4 = **0**.

Find the product.

6 × 1 = ■

Model 6 × 1.
Each circle contains 1 star.

6 circles × 1 star = 6 stars

Identity Property of Multiplication
The product of any number and 1 is that number.

So, 6 × 1 = **6** and 1 × 6 = **6**.

Find the product.

1. 9 × 0 = ______ **2.** 1 × 5 = ______ **3.** 0 × 10 = ______ **4.** 8 × 1 = ______

5. 0 × 3 = ______ **6.** 7 × 1 = ______ **7.** 5 × 0 = ______ **8.** 1 × 2 = ______

© Houghton Mifflin Harcourt Publishing Company

Name ___________________________

1. Sierra looked in 4 jars for marbles. In each jar she found 0 marbles. Which number sentence represents the total number of marbles Sierra found?

Ⓐ $4 + 0 = 4$

Ⓑ $4 \times 0 = 0$

Ⓒ $4 \times 1 = 4$

Ⓓ $4 - 4 = 0$

2. Robin found 1 pinecone under each of 3 trees. Which number sentence shows how many pinecones Robin found?

Ⓐ $3 - 3 = 0$

Ⓑ $3 + 0 = 3$

Ⓒ $3 \times 0 = 0$

Ⓓ $3 \times 1 = 3$

3. Juan bought a golf ball display case with 10 shelves. There are 0 golf balls on each shelf. Which number sentence shows how many golf balls Juan has in the display case now?

Ⓐ $10 - 0 = 10$

Ⓑ $1 \times 10 = 10$

Ⓒ $10 \times 0 = 0$

Ⓓ $10 + 0 = 10$

4. Aiden saw 4 lifeguard towers at the beach. Each tower had 1 lifeguard. Which number sentence represents the total number of lifeguards Aiden saw?

Ⓐ $4 \times 4 = 16$

Ⓑ $4 \times 1 = 4$

Ⓒ $1 \times 1 = 1$

Ⓓ $4 + 1 = 5$

Problem Solving REAL WORLD

5. Peter is in the school play. His teacher gave 1 copy of the play to each of 6 students. How many copies of the play did the teacher hand out?

____

6. There are 4 egg cartons on the table. There are 0 eggs in each carton. How many eggs are there in all?

____

© Houghton Mifflin Harcourt Publishing Company

Name ______________________________

Lesson 20

COMMON CORE STANDARD CC.3.OA.5

Lesson Objective: Use the Distributive Property to find products by breaking apart arrays.

Algebra • Distributive Property

A garden has 4 rows of 7 corn stalks. How many corn stalks in all are in the garden?

You can use the **Distributive Property** to break an array into smaller arrays to help you find the answer.

Find 4 × 7.

Step 1 Make an array to show 4 rows of 7.

4 rows of 7, or 4 × 7

Step 2 Break apart the array to make two smaller arrays for facts you know.

4 × 4 + 4 × 3

16 + 12 = 28

Step 3 Write the multiplication for the new arrays. Multiply and then add the products to find the answer.

4 × 7 = (4 × 4) + (4 × 3)
4 × 7 = 16 + 12
4 × 7 = 28

So, there are 28 corn stalks in all in the garden.

Write one way to break apart the array. Then find the product.

1.

____

____

2.

____

____

© Houghton Mifflin Harcourt Publishing Company

Name ______________________________

1. Henry and 5 friends are going to the movies. Tickets cost \$8 each. Henry used this model to help him find the total cost of tickets.

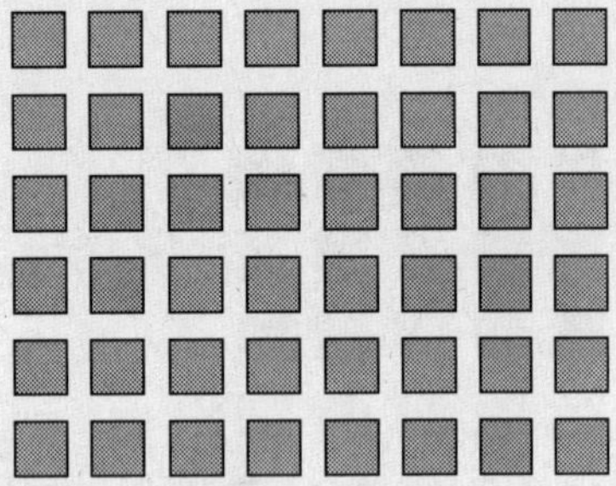

Which shows one way to break apart the array to find the product?

Ⓐ $(6 \times 5) + (6 \times 3)$

Ⓑ $(3 \times 8) + (6 \times 8)$

Ⓒ $(6 \times 6) + (6 \times 4)$

Ⓓ $6 + (4 \times 4)$

2. Which number sentence is an example of the Distributive Property of Multiplication?

Ⓐ $7 \times 8 = 50 + 6$

Ⓑ $7 \times 8 = 7 \times (2 \times 4)$

Ⓒ $7 \times 8 = 8 \times 7$

Ⓓ $7 \times 8 = (7 \times 4) + (7 \times 4)$

3. Which is equal to 7×9?

Ⓐ $(7 \times 3) + (7 \times 3)$

Ⓑ $(7 \times 3) \times (7 \times 3)$

Ⓒ $(7 \times 3) + (7 \times 6)$

Ⓓ $(7 \times 3) \times (7 \times 6)$

Problem Solving REAL WORLD

4. There are 2 rows of 8 chairs set up in the library for a puppet show. How many chairs are there in all? Use the Distributive Property to solve.

____

5. A marching band has 4 rows of trumpeters with 10 trumpeters in each row. How many trumpeters are in the marching band? Use the Distributive Property to solve.

____

© Houghton Mifflin Harcourt Publishing Company

Name ______________________________

Lesson 21

COMMON CORE STANDARD CC.3.OA.5

Lesson Objective: Use the Associative Property of Multiplication to multiply with three factors.

Algebra • Associative Property of Multiplication

You can use the **Associative Property of Multiplication** to multiply 3 factors. If you change the grouping of factors, the product remains the same.

Find 4 × (3 × 1).

Step 1 Start inside the parentheses. Make 3 groups of 1 counter.

(3 × 1)

Step 2 Multiply by 4, the number outside the parentheses. Make 4 groups of the counters in Step 1.

4 × (3 × 1)

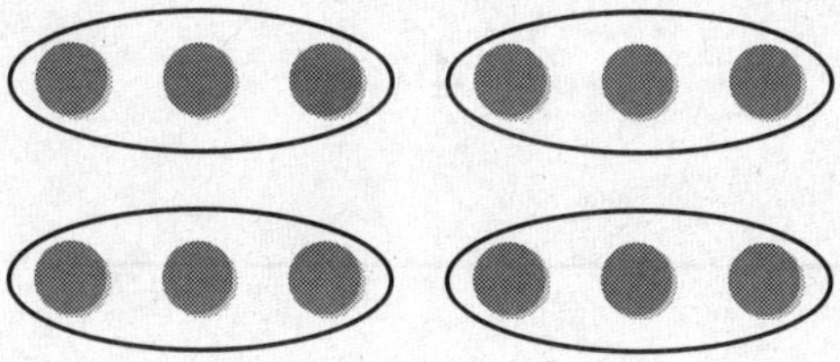

Step 3 Count the total number of counters. 12 counters

Find (4 × 3) × 1.

Step 1 Start inside the parentheses. Make 4 groups of 3 counters.

(4 × 3)

Step 2 Multiply by 1, the number outside the parentheses. Make 1 group of the counters in Step 1.

(4 × 3) × 1

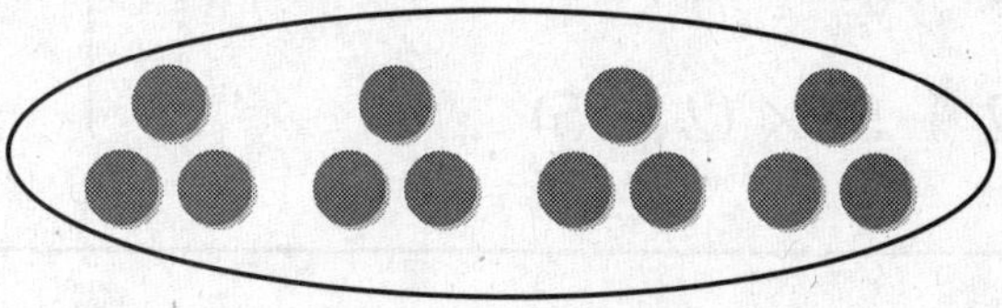

Step 3 Count the total number of counters. 12 counters

So, 4 × (3 × 1) = **12** and (4 × 3) × 1 = **12**.

Write another way to group the factors. Then find the product.

1. (2 × 3) × 2 ______________

2. 2 × (4 × 2) ______________

3. 2 × (3 × 1) ______________

4. 5 × (7 × 1) ______________

5. 8 × (4 × 1) ______________

6. 2 × (2 × 6) ______________

© Houghton Mifflin Harcourt Publishing Company

Name ________________________________

1. Which number sentence is an example of the Associative Property of Multiplication?

Ⓐ $4 \times 2 = 2 \times 4$

Ⓑ $(4 \times 2) \times 2 = 4 \times (2 \times 2)$

Ⓒ $4 \times 2 = (4 \times 1) + (4 \times 1)$

Ⓓ $4 \times (2 + 2) = (4 \times 2) + (4 \times 2)$

2. Which is equal to $(2 \times 2) \times 5$?

Ⓐ $2 \times (2 + 5)$

Ⓑ $2 \times (2 \times 5)$

Ⓒ $(2 \times 2) \times (2 \times 5)$

Ⓓ $(2 + 5) \times (2 + 5)$

3. Corey has 3 stacks of boxes. In each stack are 3 boxes with 2 trains in each box. How many trains does he have in all?

Ⓐ 6

Ⓑ 9

Ⓒ 18

Ⓓ 27

4. There are 2 walls in Yolanda's classroom that each have 2 rows of pictures. Each row has 3 pictures. How many pictures are on these walls in Yolanda's classroom?

Ⓐ 12

Ⓑ 7

Ⓒ 6

Ⓓ 4

Problem Solving REAL WORLD

5. Beth and Maria are going to the county fair. Admission costs $4 per person for each day. They plan to go for 3 days. How much will the girls pay in all?

____

6. Randy's garden has 3 rows of carrots with 3 plants in each row. Next year he plans to plant 4 times the number of rows of 3 plants. How many plants will he have next year?

____

© Houghton Mifflin Harcourt Publishing Company

Name ____________________

Lesson 23

COMMON CORE STANDARD CC.3.OA.6

Lesson Objective: Use bar models and arrays to relate multiplication and division as inverse operations.

Algebra • Relate Multiplication and Division

You can use an array to complete 21 ÷ 3 = ____.

Use 21 counters.
Make 3 equal rows.

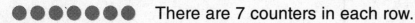

There are 7 counters in each row.

3 rows of 7 = 21

So, 21 ÷ 3 = 7

The 21 tells the total number of counters in the array.
The 3 stands for the number of equal rows.
The 7 stands for the number of counters in each row.

You can use a related multiplication fact to check your answer.

21 ÷ 3 = 7   **3 × 7 = 21**

So, 3 rows of 7 represents **21** ÷ 3 = 7 or 3 × 7 = **21**.

Complete.

1. 

6 rows of ____ = 24

6 × ____ = 24

24 ÷ 6 = ____

2. 

3 rows of ____ = 27

3 × ____ = 27

27 ÷ 3 = ____

3. 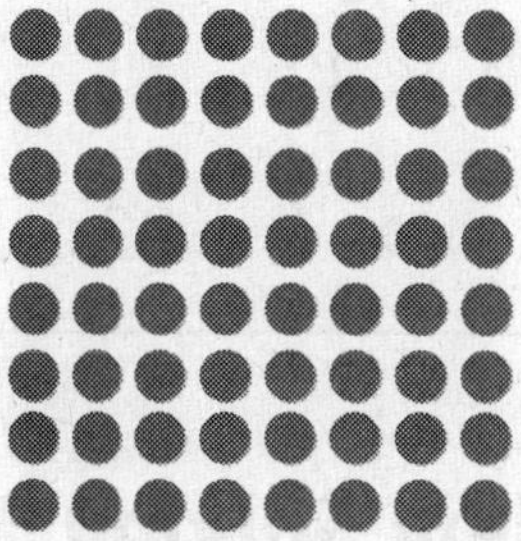

8 rows of ____ = 64

8 × ____ = 64

64 ÷ 8 = ____

Complete the equations.

4. 6 × ____ = 42   42 ÷ ____ = 6

5. 9 × ____ = 54   54 ÷ ____ = 9

© Houghton Mifflin Harcourt Publishing Company

Name ______________________________

1. Cindy made 24 bracelets using 8 different colors. She made the same number of bracelets of each color. How many bracelets of each color did she make?

$8 \times \blacksquare = 24 \quad 24 \div 8 = \blacksquare$

Ⓐ 2
Ⓑ 3
Ⓒ 4
Ⓓ 8

2. There are 32 chairs in Mr. Owen's art room. There are 4 chairs at each table. Which equation can be used to find the number of tables in the art room?

Ⓐ $4 + \blacksquare = 32$
Ⓑ $32 + 4 = \blacksquare$
Ⓒ $4 \times 32 = \blacksquare$
Ⓓ $\blacksquare \times 4 = 32$

3. Yolanda knitted 15 scarves in 3 different colors. She knitted the same number of scarves of each color. How many scarves of each color did she make?

$3 \times \blacksquare = 15 \quad 15 \div 3 = \blacksquare$

Ⓐ 5
Ⓑ 8
Ⓒ 9
Ⓓ 12

4. Mike wrote these related equations. Which number completes both equations?

$6 \times \blacksquare = 48 \quad 48 \div 6 = \blacksquare$

Ⓐ 9
Ⓑ 8
Ⓒ 7
Ⓓ 6

Problem Solving REAL WORLD

5. Mr. Martin buys 36 muffins for a class breakfast. He places them on plates for his students. If he places 9 muffins on each plate, how many plates does Mr. Martin use?

____

6. Ralph read 18 books during his summer vacation. He read the same number of books each month for 3 months. How many books did he read each month?

____

© Houghton Mifflin Harcourt Publishing Company

Name ______________________

Lesson 24

COMMON CORE STANDARD CC.3.OA.7

Lesson Objective: Use the Commutative or Distributive Property or known facts to multiply with the factor 7.

Multiply with 7

Pablo is making gift bags for his party. He puts 7 pencils in each bag. How many pencils will he need for 3 gift bags?

Find 3 × 7.

You can use a number line to find the product.

Step 1 Draw a number line.

Step 2 Start at 0. Draw 3 jumps of 7.

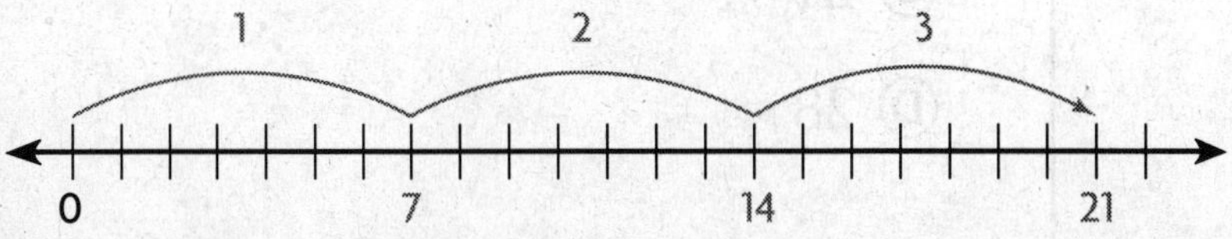

$3 \times 7 =$ **21**

So, Pablo will need <u>21</u> pencils for 3 gift bags.

Find the product.

1. _____ $= 0 \times 7$ **2.** $5 \times 7 =$ _____ **3.** $4 \times 7 =$ _____ **4.** _____ $= 6 \times 7$

5. $7 \times 7 =$ _____ **6.** _____ $= 7 \times 9$ **7.** $1 \times 7 =$ _____ **8.** _____ $= 7 \times 2$

9. 10×7 **10.** 7×8 **11.** 7×0 **12.** 7×3 **13.** 9×7

14. 6×7 **15.** 7×5 **16.** 1×7 **17.** 7×7 **18.** 4×7

© Houghton Mifflin Harcourt Publishing Company

Name ______________________________

1. There are 7 apartments on every floor of Sean's apartment building. The building has 5 floors. How many apartments are in Sean's apartment building?

Ⓐ 12

Ⓑ 21

Ⓒ 35

Ⓓ 42

2. Sandy made greeting cards for a craft show. She put 7 greeting cards in each of 7 boxes. How many greeting cards did Sandy make altogether?

Ⓐ 56

Ⓑ 49

Ⓒ 28

Ⓓ 14

3. Mike sent 7 postcards to each of 4 friends when he was on vacation. How many postcards did Mike send altogether?

Ⓐ 11

Ⓑ 14

Ⓒ 21

Ⓓ 28

4. There are 9 vans taking students to the museum. Each van is carrying 7 students. How many students are in the vans?

Ⓐ 16

Ⓑ 63

Ⓒ 70

Ⓓ 77

Problem Solving REAL WORLD

5. Julie buys a pair of earrings for $7. Now she would like to buy the same earrings for 2 of her friends. How much will she spend for all 3 pairs of earrings?

____

6. Owen and his family will go camping in 8 weeks. There are 7 days in 1 week. How many days are in 8 weeks?

____

© Houghton Mifflin Harcourt Publishing Company

Name ______________________

Lesson 25

COMMON CORE STANDARD CC.3.OA.7

Lesson Objective: Use doubles, a number line, or the Associative Property of Multiplication to multiply with the factor 8.

Multiply with 8

You can break apart arrays to multiply with 8.

Candace works at a candle shop.
She places candles in a box for display.
The box has 7 rows of 8 candles.
How many candles are in the box in all?

You can break apart an array to find 7 × 8.

Step 1 Draw 7 rows of 8 squares.

Step 2 Draw a dashed line to break apart the array into two smaller arrays to show facts you know.

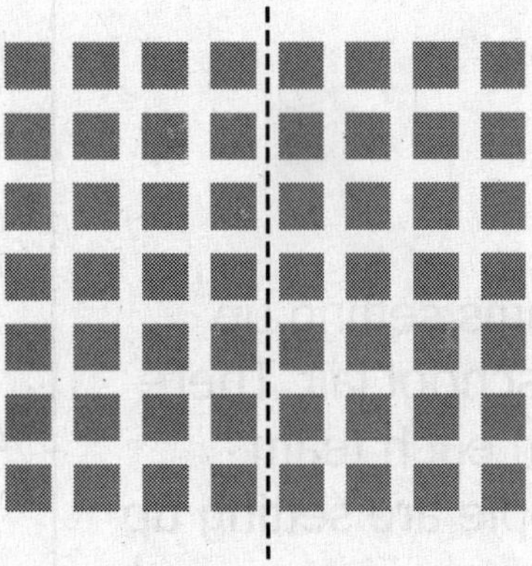

7 × 4   7 × 4

7 × 8 = (7 × 4) + (7 × 4)

7 × 8 = **28** + **28**

7 × 8 = **56**

So, there are **56** candles in the box.

Find the product.

1. 3 × 8 = _____ **2.** _____ = 0 × 8 **3.** 2 × 8 = _____ **4.** 4 × 8 = _____

5. _____ = 9 × 8 **6.** 5 × 8 = _____ **7.** 8 × 10 = _____ **8.** _____ = 8 × 8

9. 7 × 8 **10.** 10 × 8 **11.** 8 × 4 **12.** 8 × 3 **13.** 1 × 8

© Houghton Mifflin Harcourt Publishing Company

Name ____________________

1. Ashley buys 8 fishbowls. There are 2 goldfish in each bowl. How many goldfish did Ashley buy?

Ⓐ 4

Ⓑ 8

Ⓒ 16

Ⓓ 24

2. There are 8 teams setting up booths for the school fair. There are 7 people on each team. How many people are setting up booths?

Ⓐ 28
Ⓑ 48
Ⓒ 56
Ⓓ 64

3. Students' exhibits at a science fair are judged in 5 categories. Akio's exhibit received 8 points in each category. How many total points did Akio's exhibit receive?

Ⓐ 20

Ⓑ 40

Ⓒ 48

Ⓓ 56

4. Liz buys 6 flowerpots. There are 8 flowers in each pot. How many flowers did Liz buy?

Ⓐ 4
Ⓑ 14
Ⓒ 40
Ⓓ 48

Problem Solving REAL WORLD

5. There are 6 teams in the basketball league. Each team has 8 players. How many players are there in all?

____

6. Lynn has 4 stacks of quarters. There are 8 quarters in each stack. How many quarters does Lynn have in all?

____

7. Tomas is packing 7 baskets for a fair. He is placing 8 apples in each basket. How many apples are there in all?

____

8. There are 10 pencils in each box. If Jenna buys 8 boxes, how many pencils will she buy?

____

© Houghton Mifflin Harcourt Publishing Company

Name ______________________________

COMMON CORE STANDARD CC.3.OA.7

Lesson Objective: Use the Distributive Property with addition or subtraction or patterns to multiply with the factor 9.

Multiply with 9

Ana goes to the pet store to buy a fish. The store has 3 fish tanks. Each tank has 9 fish. How many fish in all are in the tanks?

You can use counters to find the product.

Find 3 × 9.

Step 1 Make 3 groups of 9 counters.

Step 2 Skip count by 9s to find the total number of counters.

9, 18, 27 counters

$3 \times 9 = 27$

So, there are 27 fish in all in the tanks.

Find the product.

1. $4 \times 9 =$ ____ **2.** $6 \times 9 =$ ____ **3.** $3 \times 9 =$ ____ **4.** $7 \times 9 =$ ____

5. $1 \times 9 =$ ____ **6.** ____ $= 8 \times 9$ **7.** $9 \times 5 =$ ____ **8.** ____ $= 0 \times 9$

9. $\begin{array}{r} 2 \\ \times\ 9 \\ \hline \end{array}$ **10.** $\begin{array}{r} 9 \\ \times\ 9 \\ \hline \end{array}$ **11.** $\begin{array}{r} 9 \\ \times\ 3 \\ \hline \end{array}$ **12.** $\begin{array}{r} 9 \\ \times\ 4 \\ \hline \end{array}$ **13.** $\begin{array}{r} 10 \\ \times\ 9 \\ \hline \end{array}$

© Houghton Mifflin Harcourt Publishing Company

1. Mika bought 3 boxes of bouncy balls. Each box contains 9 bouncy balls. How many bouncy balls did Mika buy in all?

Ⓐ 12

Ⓑ 18

Ⓒ 24

Ⓓ 27

2. There are 8 students in the camera club. Each student took 9 pictures. How many pictures did the students take altogether?

Ⓐ 81

Ⓑ 72

Ⓒ 64

Ⓓ 17

3. Shana bought 5 bags of hard pretzels. Each bag contains 9 pretzels. How many hard pretzels did Shana buy in all?

Ⓐ 14

Ⓑ 40

Ⓒ 45

Ⓓ 50

4. Raul has 6 shoeboxes on his bookshelf. If he has 9 toy robots in each shoebox, how many toy robots does Raul have?

Ⓐ 63

Ⓑ 54

Ⓒ 36

Ⓓ 15

Problem Solving REAL WORLD

5. There are 9 positions on the softball team. Three people are trying out for each position. How many people in all are trying out?

____

6. Carlos bought a book for $9. Now he would like to buy 4 other books for the same price. How much will he have to pay in all for the other 4 books?

____

© Houghton Mifflin Harcourt Publishing Company

Name ______________________________

Lesson 27

COMMON CORE STANDARD CC.3.OA.7

Lesson Objective: Write related multiplication and division facts.

Algebra • Write Related Facts

Related facts are a set of related multiplication and division equations.

Write the related facts for the array.

There are 4 equal rows of tiles.
There are 6 tiles in each row.
There are 24 tiles.
Write 2 multiplication equations and 2 division equations for the array.

factor × factor = product   dividend ÷ divisor = quotient

$\boxed{4} \times \boxed{6} = 24$ $24 \div \boxed{4} = \boxed{6}$

$\boxed{6} \times \boxed{4} = 24$ $24 \div \boxed{6} = \boxed{4}$

The equations show how the numbers 4, 6, and 24 are related.

So, the related facts are $4 \times 6 = 24$, $6 \times 4 = 24$, $24 \div 4 = 6$, and $24 \div 6 = 4$.

Write the related facts for the array.

1.

________________ ________________

________________ ________________

2.

________________ ________________

________________ ________________

3.

________________ ________________

________________ ________________

4.

________________ ________________

________________ ________________

© Houghton Mifflin Harcourt Publishing Company

1. Han wrote a set of related facts for the array below. Which equation is **not** related to this array?

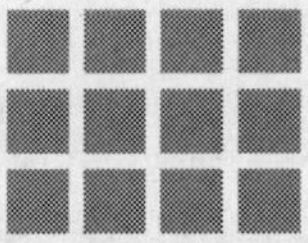

Ⓐ $3 \times 4 = 12$

Ⓑ $6 \times 2 = 12$

Ⓒ $12 \div 4 = 3$

Ⓓ $12 \div 3 = 4$

2. Lucy writes a set of related facts. One of the facts she writes is $24 \div 6 = 4$. Which equation is related to this fact?

Ⓐ $8 \times 3 = 24$

Ⓑ $24 \div 8 = 3$

Ⓒ $6 \times 4 = 24$

Ⓓ $24 \div 3 = 8$

3. Fritz wrote a set of related facts for the array below. Which equation is **not** related to this array?

Ⓐ $6 \times 3 = 18$

Ⓑ $6 \div 2 = 3$

Ⓒ $3 \times 2 = 6$

Ⓓ $2 \times 3 = 6$

4. Alex uses the numbers 3, 4, and 12 to write multiplication and division related facts. Which equation is one of the related facts that Alex writes?

Ⓐ $3 + 4 = 7$

Ⓑ $12 - 8 = 4$

Ⓒ $12 \div 6 = 2$

Ⓓ $4 \times 3 = 12$

Problem Solving REAL WORLD

5. CDs are on sale for $5 each. Jennifer has $45 and wants to buy as many as she can. How many CDs can Jennifer buy?

____

6. Mr. Moore has 21 feet of wallpaper. He cuts it into sections that are each 3 feet long. How many sections does Mr. Moore have?

____

© Houghton Mifflin Harcourt Publishing Company

Name ____________________________

Lesson 28

COMMON CORE STANDARD CC.3.OA.7

Lesson Objective: Use repeated subtraction, a number line, or a multiplication table to divide by 10.

Divide by 10

You can use a multiplication table to divide by 10.

Find the quotient. 30 ÷ 10

Think of a related multiplication fact.

10 × ■ = 30

Step 1 Find the row for the factor, 10. This number is the divisor.

Step 2 Look across the row to find the product, 30. This number is the dividend.

×	0	1	2	3	4	5	6	7	8	9	10
0	0	0	0	0	0	0	0	0	0	0	0
1	0	1	2	3	4	5	6	7	8	9	10
2	0	2	4	6	8	10	12	14	16	18	20
3	0	3	6	9	12	15	18	21	24	27	30
4	0	4	8	12	16	20	24	28	32	36	40
5	0	5	10	15	20	25	30	35	40	45	50
6	0	6	12	18	24	30	36	42	48	54	60
7	0	7	14	21	28	35	42	49	56	63	70
8	0	8	16	24	32	40	48	56	64	72	80
9	0	9	18	27	36	45	54	63	72	81	90
10	0	10	20	30	40	50	60	70	80	90	100

Step 3 Look up to the top row to find the unknown factor, **3**. This is the quotient.

Since 10 × **3** = 30, then 30 ÷ 10 = **3**.

So, 30 ÷ 10 = **3**.

Find the unknown factor and quotient.

1. 10 × _____ = 70 _____ = 70 ÷ 10

2. 10 × _____ = 20 20 ÷ 10 = _____

Find the quotient.

3. 60 ÷ 10 = _____

4. 80 ÷ 10 = _____

5. 100 ÷ 10 = _____

6. 10)$\overline{50}$

7. 10)$\overline{90}$

8. 10)$\overline{30}$

© Houghton Mifflin Harcourt Publishing Company

1. Larah found 50 pinecones. She put 10 pinecones in each bag. How many bags did Larah use?

Ⓐ 5

Ⓑ 6

Ⓒ 9

Ⓓ 10

2. Michael wants to display his model car collection on shelves. He has 60 model cars. He puts 10 cars on each shelf. How many shelves does Michael use?

Ⓐ 6

Ⓑ 8

Ⓒ 10

Ⓓ 70

3. There are 20 students in science class. There are 10 students sitting at each table. Which division sentence shows how many tables have students at them?

Ⓐ $20 \div 4 = 5$

Ⓑ $20 \div 10 = 2$

Ⓒ $10 \div 5 = 2$

Ⓓ $10 \div 10 = 1$

4. Stickers cost 10¢ each. How many stickers can Todd buy with 80¢?

Ⓐ 10

Ⓑ 9

Ⓒ 8

Ⓓ 7

Problem Solving REAL WORLD

5. Pencils cost 10¢ each. How many pencils can Brent buy with 90¢?

____

6. Mrs. Marks wants to buy 80 pens. If the pens come in packs of 10, how many packs does she need to buy?

____

© Houghton Mifflin Harcourt Publishing Company

Name ____________________

Lesson 29

COMMON CORE STANDARD CC.3.OA.7

Lesson Objective: Use equal groups, a number line, or a related multiplication fact to divide by 3.

Divide by 3

You can draw a picture to show how to divide.

Find the quotient.

21 ÷ 3

Step 1 Draw 21 counters to show the dividend.

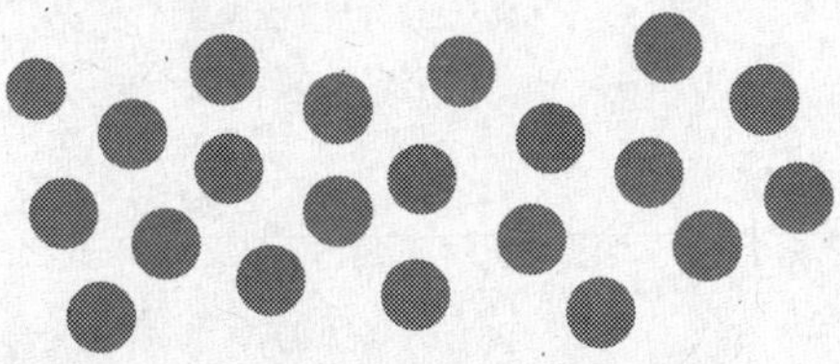

Step 2 Circle groups of 3 to show the divisor.

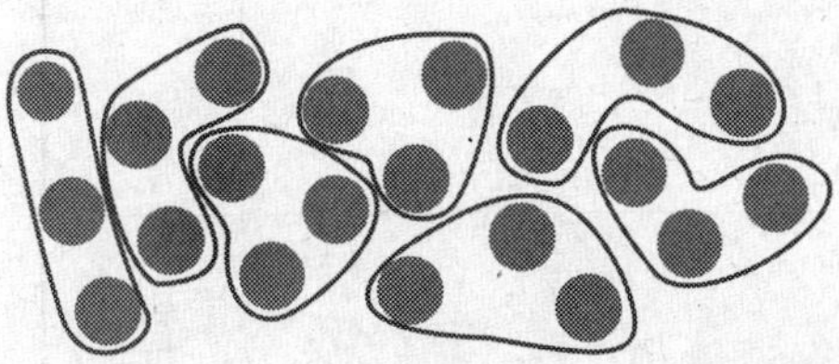

Step 3 Count the groups.

There are 7 groups of 3. So, the quotient is 7.

You can use a related multiplication fact to check your answer.

Think: 7 × 3 = 21

So, 21 ÷ 3 = **7**.

Circle groups of 3 to find the quotient.

1. 9 ÷ 3 = ____

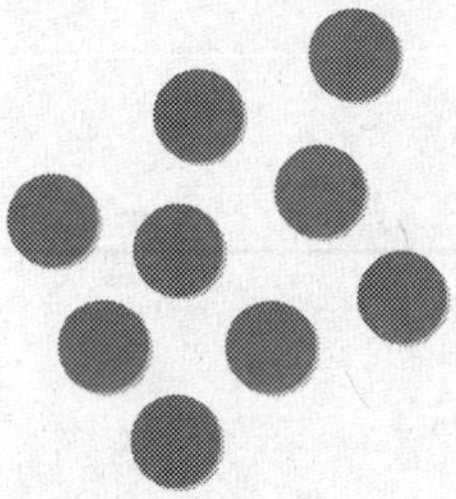

2. 15 ÷ 3 = ____

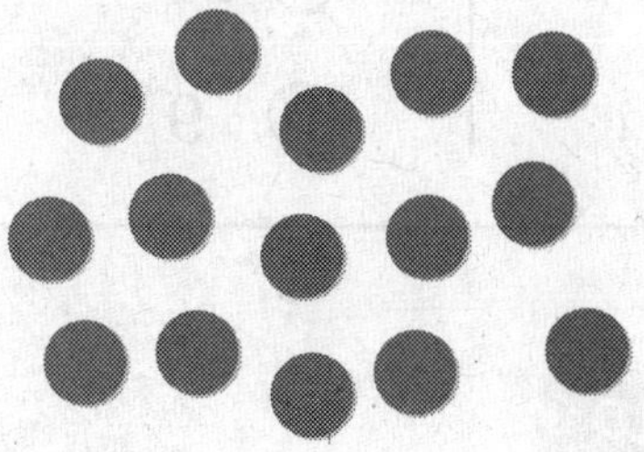

3. ____ = 6 ÷ 3

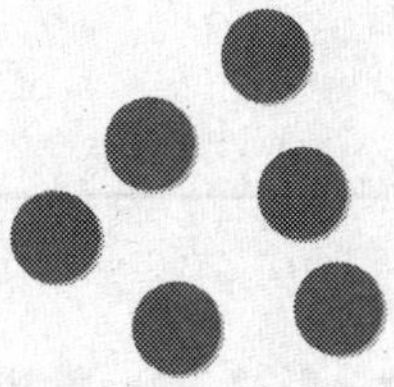

Find the quotient.

4. 12 ÷ 3 = ____ **5.** 18 ÷ 3 = ____ **6.** 24 ÷ 3 = ____ **7.** 27 ÷ 3 = ____

© Houghton Mifflin Harcourt Publishing Company

Name ______________________________

Lesson 29
CC.3.OA.7

1. Steve and his family traveled 12 miles on a sunset cruise. Every 3 miles, the boat stopped for people to take pictures. How many times did the boat stop for pictures?

Ⓐ 4

Ⓑ 6

Ⓒ 9

Ⓓ 15

2. Martina plays tennis. She gets 21 new tennis balls. They come in cans of 3. How many cans of tennis balls did Martina get?

Ⓐ 18

Ⓑ 8

Ⓒ 7

Ⓓ 6

3. Jake walked 15 miles in a walk-a-thon. Every 3 miles, he stopped for a rest. How many times did Jake stop for a rest?

Ⓐ 4

Ⓑ 5

Ⓒ 6

Ⓓ 12

4. There are 27 students in Mr. Garcia's class. The class is going on a field trip to a water park. Mr. Garcia separates the students into groups of 3. How many groups will Mr. Garcia make?

Ⓐ 30

Ⓑ 24

Ⓒ 14

Ⓓ 9

Problem Solving REAL WORLD

5. The principal at Miller Street School has 12 packs of new pencils. She will give 3 packs to each third-grade class. How many third-grade classes are there?

____

6. Mike has $21 to spend at the mall. He spends all of his money on bracelets for his sisters. Bracelets cost $3 each. How many bracelets does he buy?

____

© Houghton Mifflin Harcourt Publishing Company

Name ____________________

Lesson 30

COMMON CORE STANDARD CC.3.OA.7

Lesson Objective: Use an array, equal groups, factors, or a related multiplication fact to divide by 4.

Divide by 4

One way to divide is to count back on a number line.

Find the quotient.
12 ÷ 4

Start at 12.

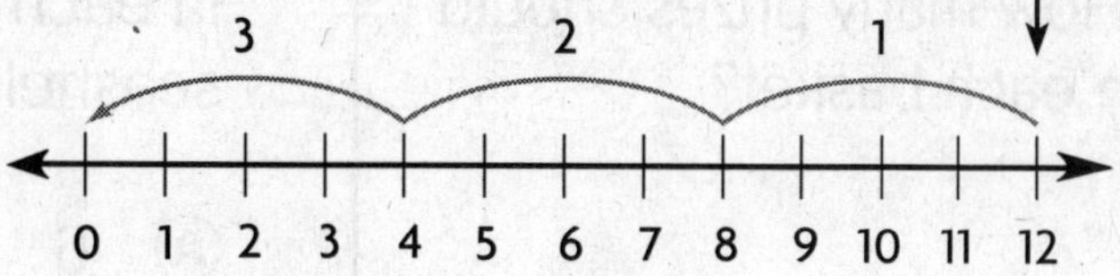

Count back by 4s as many times as you can until you reach 0.

Count the number of times you jumped back 4. **3 times**

So, 12 ÷ 4 = 3.

Find the quotient.
32 ÷ 4

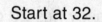

Start at 32.

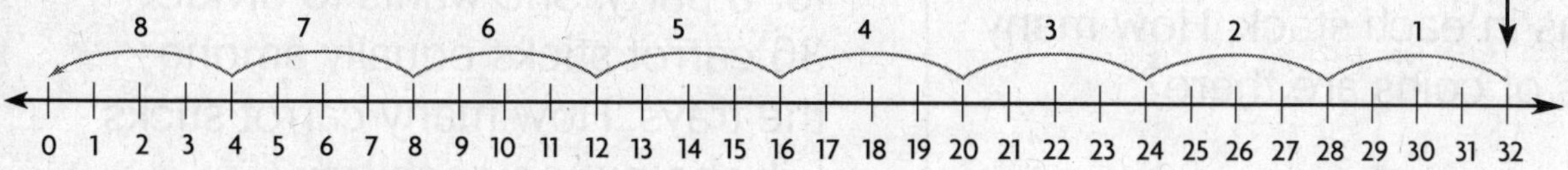

Count back by 4s as many times as you can until you reach 0.

Count the number of times you jumped back 4. **8 times**

So, 32 ÷ 4 = 8.

Find the quotient.

1. 24 ÷ 4 = ____ **2.** ____ = 12 ÷ 3 **3.** 16 ÷ 4 = ____ **4.** ____ = 8 ÷ 4

5. 4 ÷ 2 = ____ **6.** ____ = 28 ÷ 4 **7.** 36 ÷ 4 = ____ **8.** 20 ÷ 4 = ____

Find the unknown number.

9. 4 ÷ 4 = ▲ **10.** 40 ÷ 10 = t **11.** 8 ÷ 2 = g **12.** 21 ÷ 7 = m

▲ = ____ t = ____ g = ____ m = ____

© Houghton Mifflin Harcourt Publishing Company

Name ______________________

1. Ellen is making 4 gift baskets for her friends. She has 16 prizes she wants to divide equally among the baskets. How many prizes should she put in each basket?

Ⓐ 4
Ⓑ 8
Ⓒ 12
Ⓓ 20

2. Casey has 20 coins. She places them in equal stacks. There are 4 coins in each stack. How many stacks of coins are there?

Ⓐ 5
Ⓑ 6
Ⓒ 7
Ⓓ 8

3. Jim collected 28 seashells at the beach. He arranged them in equal rows. There are 4 seashells in each row. How many rows of seashells are there?

Ⓐ 6
Ⓑ 7
Ⓒ 24
Ⓓ 30

4. Holly is making 4 veggie trays for a party. She wants to divide 36 carrot sticks equally among the trays. How many carrot sticks will she put on each tray?

Ⓐ 7
Ⓑ 8
Ⓒ 9
Ⓓ 32

Problem Solving REAL WORLD

5. Ms. Higgins has 28 students in her gym class. She puts them in 4 equal groups. How many students are in each group?

____

6. Andy has 36 CDs. He buys a case that holds 4 CDs in each section. How many sections can he fill?

____

© Houghton Mifflin Harcourt Publishing Company

Name ______________________________

Lesson 31

COMMON CORE STANDARD CC.3.OA.7

Lesson Objective: Use equal groups, a related multiplication fact, or factors to divide by 6.

Divide by 6

You can use a multiplication table to divide by 6.

Find the quotient. 42 ÷ 6

Think of a related multiplication fact.
6 × ■ = 42

Find the row for the factor, 6.

Look right to find the product, **42**.

Look up to find the unknown factor, 7.

7 is the factor you multiply by 6 to get the product, 42.

So, 6 × **7** = 42.

Use this related multiplication fact to find the quotient.

Since 6 × **7** = 42, then 42 ÷ 6 = **7**.

So, 42 ÷ 6 = **7**.

×	0	1	2	3	4	5	6	7	8	9	10
0	0	0	0	0	0	0	0	0	0	0	0
1	0	1	2	3	4	5	6	7	8	9	10
2	0	2	4	6	8	10	12	14	16	18	20
3	0	3	6	9	12	15	18	21	24	27	30
4	0	4	8	12	16	20	24	28	32	36	40
5	0	5	10	15	20	25	30	35	40	45	50
6	0	6	12	18	24	30	36	42	48	54	60
7	0	7	14	21	28	35	42	49	56	63	70
8	0	8	16	24	32	40	48	56	64	72	80
9	0	9	18	27	36	45	54	63	72	81	90
10	0	10	20	30	40	50	60	70	80	90	100

Find the unknown factor and quotient.

1. 6 × ____ = 30 30 ÷ 6 = ____

2. 6 × ____ = 48 48 ÷ 6 = ____

3. 6 × ____ = 18 18 ÷ 6 = ____

4. 6 × ____ = 24 24 ÷ 6 = ____

Find the quotient.

5. 6 ÷ 6 = ____

6. 48 ÷ 6 = ____

7. 54 ÷ 6 = ____

8. 12 ÷ 6 = ____

9. 0 ÷ 6 = ____

10. 36 ÷ 6 = ____

11. 6 ÷ 1 = ____

12. 18 ÷ 6 = ____

© Houghton Mifflin Harcourt Publishing Company

1. Pedro uses 30 game pieces to play a game. He gives 6 players the same number of game pieces. How many game pieces does each player get?

Ⓐ 4 Ⓒ 10
Ⓑ 5 Ⓓ 15

2. Each team at a hockey tournament has 6 players. How many teams are there if 42 players are at the tournament?

Ⓐ 5
Ⓑ 6
Ⓒ 7
Ⓓ 8

3. There are picnic tables at the park. Each picnic table seats 6 people. How many picnic tables are needed to seat 24 people?

Ⓐ 3
Ⓑ 4
Ⓒ 5
Ⓓ 6

4. Luis uses 36 marbles to play a game. There are 6 players in the game. If each player gets the same number of marbles, how many marbles does each player get?

Ⓐ 30 Ⓒ 12
Ⓑ 18 Ⓓ 6

Problem Solving REAL WORLD

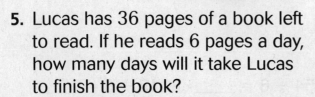

5. Lucas has 36 pages of a book left to read. If he reads 6 pages a day, how many days will it take Lucas to finish the book?

____

6. Juan has $24 to spend at the bookstore. If books cost $6 each, how many books can he buy?

____

© Houghton Mifflin Harcourt Publishing Company

Name ____________________

Lesson 32

COMMON CORE STANDARD CC.3.OA.7

Lesson Objective: Use an array, a related multiplication fact, or equal groups to divide by 7.

Divide by 7

You can use counters to divide by 7.

Find the quotient. 35 ÷ 7

Step 1 Draw 7 circles to show 7 groups. Place 1 counter in each group.

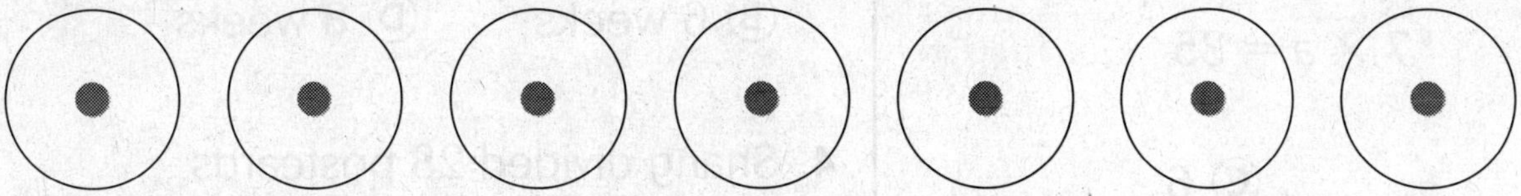

Step 2 Continue placing 1 counter at a time in each group until all 35 counters are placed.

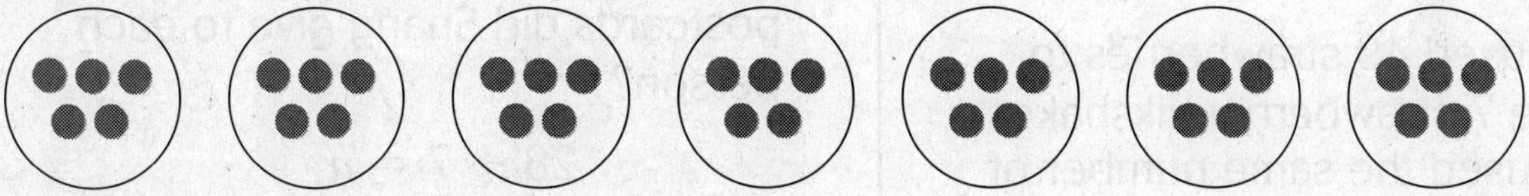

There are **5** counters in each group.

So, 35 ÷ 7 = **5**.

Find the unknown factor and quotient.

1. 7 × ____ = 63 63 ÷ 7 = ____ **2.** 7 × ____ = 7 7 ÷ 7 = ____

3. 7 × ____ = 14 14 ÷ 7 = ____ **4.** 7 × ____ = 28 28 ÷ 7 = ____

Find the quotient.

5. ____ = 56 ÷ 7 **6.** 21 ÷ 7 = ____ **7.** 42 ÷ 7 = ____ **8.** 28 ÷ 7 = ____

9. ____ = 35 ÷ 7 **10.** 63 ÷ 7 = ____ **11.** 49 ÷ 7 = ____ **12.** 70 ÷ 7 = ____

© Houghton Mifflin Harcourt Publishing Company

Name ______________________________

1. Ming divided 35 marbles among 7 different friends. Each friend received the same number of marbles. How many marbles did Ming give to each friend?

$35 \div 7 = a$

$7 \times a = 35$

Ⓐ 4 Ⓒ 6

Ⓑ 5 Ⓓ 7

2. Ana used 49 strawberries to make 7 strawberry milkshakes. She used the same number of strawberries in each milkshake. How many strawberries did Ana use in each milkshake?

Ⓐ 4 Ⓒ 6

Ⓑ 5 Ⓓ 7

3. Joni texted her dad every day for 42 days. How many weeks did Joni text her dad? [Hint: 1 week has 7 days.]

Ⓐ 5 weeks Ⓒ 7 weeks

Ⓑ 6 weeks Ⓓ 8 weeks

4. Shang divided 28 postcards among 7 different people. Each person received the same number of postcards. How many postcards did Shang give to each person?

$28 \div 7 = n$

$7 \times n = 28$

Ⓐ 4 Ⓒ 6

Ⓑ 5 Ⓓ 21

Problem Solving REAL WORLD

5. Twenty-eight players sign up for basketball. The coach puts 7 players on each team. How many teams are there?

____

6. Roberto read 42 books over 7 months. He read the same number of books each month. How many books did Roberto read each month?

____

© Houghton Mifflin Harcourt Publishing Company

Name ____________________________

Lesson 33

COMMON CORE STANDARD CC.3.OA.7

Lesson Objective: Use equal groups, factors, or a related multiplication fact to divide by 9.

Divide by 9

You can use repeated subtraction to divide by 9.

Find the quotient.
36 ÷ 9

Step 1 Start with 36. Subtract 9 as many times as you can until you reach 0. Write the answers.

$$\begin{array}{r} 36 \\ -\ 9 \\ \hline 27 \end{array} \rightarrow \begin{array}{r} 27 \\ -\ 9 \\ \hline 18 \end{array} \rightarrow \begin{array}{r} 18 \\ -\ 9 \\ \hline 9 \end{array} \rightarrow \begin{array}{r} 9 \\ -9 \\ \hline 0 \end{array}$$

Step 2 Count the number of times you subtract 9.

You subtracted 9 **four** times.

So, 36 ÷ 9 = **4**.

Find the quotient.

1. 9 ÷ 9 = ____
2. 27 ÷ 9 = ____
3. 18 ÷ 9 = ____
4. 36 ÷ 9 = ____
5. ____ = 72 ÷ 9
6. ____ = 63 ÷ 9
7. 45 ÷ 9 = ____
8. ____ = 18 ÷ 9
9. ____ = 54 ÷ 9
10. $9\overline{)63}$
11. $9\overline{)81}$
12. $9\overline{)36}$
13. $8\overline{)48}$
14. $4\overline{)36}$
15. $7\overline{)28}$

© Houghton Mifflin Harcourt Publishing Company

Name ______________________________

Lesson 33
CC.3.OA.7

1. Mrs. Torres separates 45 students into 9 equal groups for a field trip. How many students are in each group?

Ⓐ 4 Ⓒ 6
Ⓑ 5 Ⓓ 7

2. Carla sells homemade pretzels in bags with 9 pretzels in each bag. She sells 54 pretzels in all. How many bags of pretzels does she sell?

Ⓐ 6 Ⓒ 4
Ⓑ 5 Ⓓ 3

3. A flower shop sells tulips in bunches of 9. It sells 27 tulips. How many bunches of tulips does the shop sell?

Ⓐ 2 Ⓒ 4
Ⓑ 3 Ⓓ 9

4. There are 36 athletes at a baseball workshop. A baseball team has 9 players. How many teams can be formed?

Ⓐ 7 Ⓒ 5
Ⓑ 6 Ⓓ 4

Problem Solving REAL WORLD

5. A crate of oranges has trays inside that hold 9 oranges each. There are 72 oranges in the crate. If all trays are filled, how many trays are there?

____

6. Van has 45 new baseball cards. He puts them in a binder that holds 9 cards on each page. How many pages does he fill?

____

© Houghton Mifflin Harcourt Publishing Company

Name ______________________________

Lesson 34

COMMON CORE STANDARD CC.3.OA.8

Lesson Objective: Solve addition and subtraction problems by using the strategy *draw a diagram.*

Problem Solving • Model Addition and Subtraction

Kim sold 127 tickets to the school play. Jon sold 89 tickets. How many more tickets did Kim sell than Jon?

Read the Problem	Solve the Problem
What do I need to find? I need to find how many more tickets Kim sold than Jon ______.	Complete the bar model. 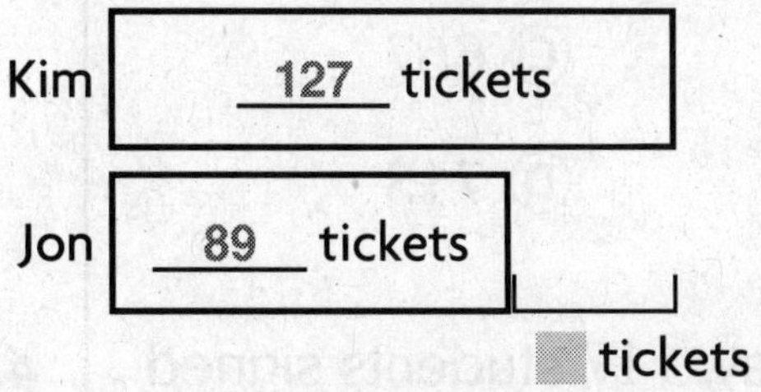
What information do I need to use? I know that Kim sold 127 tickets and Jon sold 89 tickets.	Subtract to find the unknown part. 127 − 89 = 38 ■ = 38 tickets
How will I use the information? I will draw a bar model to help me see what operation to use to solve the problem.	So, Kim sold 38 more tickets than Jon.

1. Kasha collected 76 fall leaves. She collects 58 more leaves. How many leaves does she have now?

____

2. Max has 96 stamps. Pat has 79 stamps. How many more stamps does Max have than Pat?

____

© Houghton Mifflin Harcourt Publishing Company

Name ______________________________

1. During the first week of school, 345 students bought their lunch. During the second week of school, 23 fewer students bought their lunch than the week before. How many students bought their lunch in those two weeks?

Ⓐ 322 Ⓒ 667

Ⓑ 368 Ⓓ 713

2. On Monday, 117 students signed up to plant trees in the park. On Tuesday, 16 fewer students signed up than on Monday. How many students signed up to plant trees on Monday and Tuesday?

Ⓐ 218 Ⓒ 118

Ⓑ 158 Ⓓ 101

3. In one week, 103 students were absent. The next week, 17 fewer students were absent than the week before. How many students were absent in those two weeks?

Ⓐ 86 Ⓒ 189

Ⓑ 120 Ⓓ 223

4. For two days, Imani counted taxis that passed her house from 4:30 to 4:45 P.M. She counted 33 taxis on Monday. That was 19 fewer than the number of taxis she counted on Tuesday. How many taxis did Imani count on both days?

Ⓐ 14 Ⓒ 52

Ⓑ 33 Ⓓ 85

5. Draw bar models to solve 45 + 92 = ■ and 92 − ■ = 45. Explain how the models are alike and how they are different.

____

____

____

____

© Houghton Mifflin Harcourt Publishing Company

Name ______________________

Lesson 35

COMMON CORE STANDARD CC.3.OA.8

Lesson Objective: Solve one- and two-step problems by using the strategy *draw a diagram.*

Problem Solving • Model Multiplication

There are 2 rows of flute players in a marching band. Each row has 7 students. How many flute players are there in all?

Read the Problem	Solve the Problem
What do I need to find? I need to find how many flute players are in the marching band.	Complete the bar model to show the flute players. Write 7 in each box to show the 7 students in each of the 2 groups.
What information do I need to use? I know there are 2 rows. There are 7 students in each row.	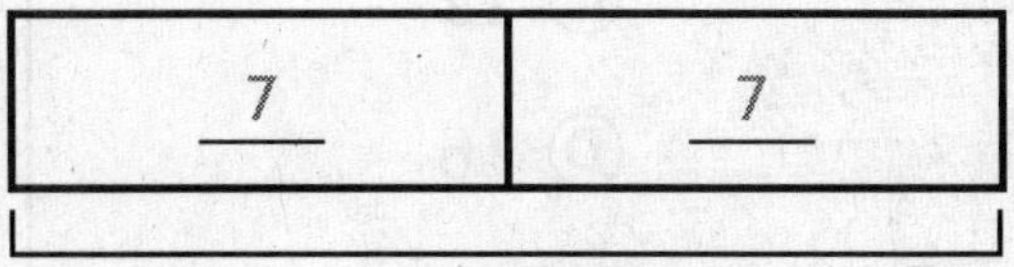 14 students
How will I use the information? I will draw a bar model to help me see what operation I need to use to solve the problem.	Since there are equal groups, I can multiply to find the number of flute players in the band. 2 × 7 = 14 So, there are 14 flute players in all.

1. The Coopers put a new floor in the bathroom. There are 5 rows of 6 red tiles. How many tiles did they use?

____

2. Tommy has a jar of coins. He makes 8 piles of 4 quarters. How many quarters does Tommy have in all?

____

© Houghton Mifflin Harcourt Publishing Company

Name ______________________________

1. Edith sorts buttons into 4 groups. Each group contains 3 buttons. How many buttons does Edith sort?

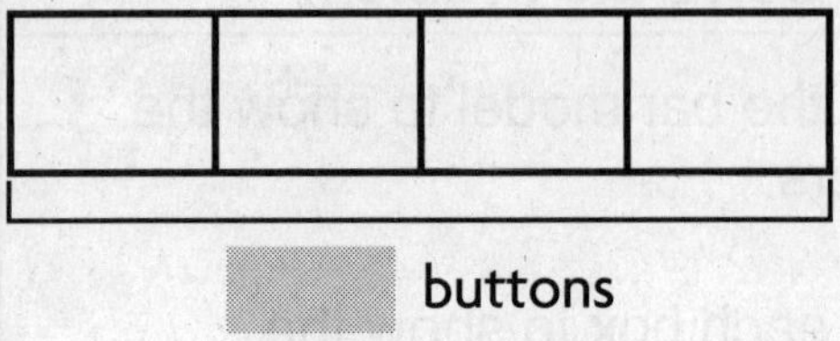

Ⓐ 4 Ⓒ 12

Ⓑ 11 Ⓓ 16

2. Hector has 4 groups of blocks with 2 blocks in each group. He uses 3 of the blocks for a project. How many blocks does Hector have left?

Ⓐ 3 Ⓒ 9

Ⓑ 5 Ⓓ 11

3. John sold 3 baskets of peaches at the market. Each basket contained 6 peaches. How many peaches did John sell?

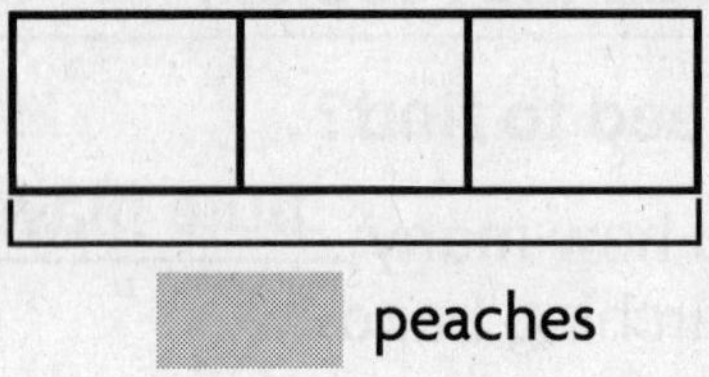

Ⓐ 36 Ⓒ 18

Ⓑ 30 Ⓓ 9

4. Sophia buys 3 baskets of apples to make applesauce. Each basket has 9 apples in it. How many apples does Sophia buy in all?

Ⓐ 27 Ⓒ 18

Ⓑ 24 Ⓓ 9

5. Landon sorted his trading cards into 3 groups. Each group had 7 cards. How many trading cards does he have in all? Use the bar model to solve. Explain your answer.

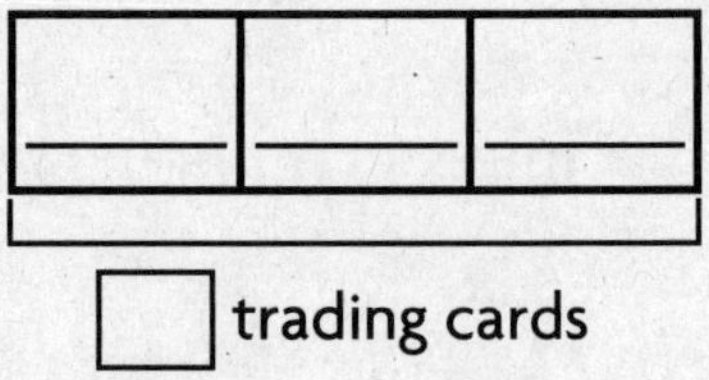

____

____

____

© Houghton Mifflin Harcourt Publishing Company

Name ______________________

Lesson 36

COMMON CORE STANDARD CC.3.OA.8

Lesson Objective: Solve multiplication problems by using the strategy *make a table*.

Problem Solving • Multiplication

Lucy's mother is making punch for the students. For each pitcher, she uses 1 can of fruit juice, 1 bottle of ginger ale, and 6 scoops of sherbet. How much of each ingredient will she need to make 5 pitchers of punch?

Read the Problem

What do I need to find?

I need to find how much of each ingredient Lucy's mother needs to make 5 pitchers of punch.

What information do I need to use?

Lucy's mother uses __1__ can of fruit juice, __1__ bottle of ginger ale, and __6__ scoops of sherbet for each pitcher.

How will I use the information?

I will make a __table__ to show the total amounts of each ingredient Lucy's mother needs.

Solve the Problem

First, make a table with the information.

Number of Pitchers	1	2	3	4	5
Cans of Fruit Juice	1	2	3	4	5
Bottles of Ginger Ale	1	2	3	4	5
Scoops of Sherbet	6	12	18	24	30

Next, look for information in the table that will help you solve the problem.

Look for a pattern. The cans of fruit juice and the bottles of ginger ale increase by 1. The scoops of sherbet increase by 6. Complete the table.

So, Lucy's mother will need 5 cans of fruit juice, 5 bottles of ginger ale, and 30 scoops of sherbet.

1. Suppose Lucy's mother decides to make 2 more pitchers of punch. How many scoops of sherbet would she need for 7 pitchers of punch? **Explain** your answer.

____

____

2. Jake gives his dog 4 chew bones and 1 dog toy each month. How many chew bones and how many toys will Jake give his dog in 5 months?

____

© Houghton Mifflin Harcourt Publishing Company

1. Bella is planning to write in her journal. Some pages will have two journal entries on them, and other pages will have three journal entries on them. If Bella wants to make 18 entries, how many different ways can she write them in her journal?

Ⓐ 2 Ⓒ 5

Ⓑ 4 Ⓓ 10

2. Jayme wants to make $1.50 using dollars, half dollars, and quarters. How many different ways can she make $1.50?

Ⓐ 4 Ⓒ 6

Ⓑ 5 Ⓓ 7

3. Toddrick has a photo album. Some pages have one photo on them, and other pages have two photos on them. If Toddrick has 9 photos, how many different ways can he put them in the album?

Ⓐ 2 Ⓒ 4

Ⓑ 3 Ⓓ 5

4. Myra has 30 cousins. Each month for the past 5 months, she has seen 2 different cousins. How many more cousins does she have to see before she has seen all 30 cousins?

Ⓐ 18 Ⓒ 25

Ⓑ 20 Ⓓ 28

5. Erin wants to arrange flower bouquets in rows for a reception. Each row can have 4 or 6 bouquets. She has a total of 22 bouquets and wants to know how many different ways she can arrange them. Explain how Erin could make a table to find how many different ways she can arrange the bouquets.

____

____

____

____

____

____

© Houghton Mifflin Harcourt Publishing Company

Name ____________________

Lesson 37

COMMON CORE STANDARD CC.3.OA.8

Lesson Objective: Solve two-step problems by using the strategy *act it out.*

Problem Solving • Two-Step Problems

Chloe bought 5 sets of books. Each set had the same number of books. She donated 9 books to her school. Now she has 26 books left. How many books were in each set that Chloe bought?

Read the Problem

What do I need to find?

I need to find how many **books** were in each **set**.

What information do I need to use?

I need to use the information given:

Chloe bought **5** sets of books.

She donated **9** books.

She has **26** books left.

How will I use the information?

I will use the information to **act out** the problem.

Solve the Problem

First, begin with the number of books left. Add the number of books donated.

books left		books donated		*t*, total number of books
↓		↓		↓
26	+	9	=	*t*
		35	=	*t*

Then divide to find the number of books in each set.

t, total number of books		sets of books		*s*, books in each set
↓		↓		↓
35	÷	5	=	*s*
		7	=	*s*

So, **7** books were in each set.

Solve the problem.

1. Jackie had 6 equal packs of pencils. Her friend gave her 4 more pencils. Now she has 52 pencils. How many pencils were in each pack?

____

2. Tony had 4 equal sets of sports cards. He gave his friends 5 cards. Now he has 31 cards. How many cards were in each set?

____

© Houghton Mifflin Harcourt Publishing Company

1. Gary bought 4 packs of cards. Each pack had the same number of cards. A friend gave him 3 more cards. Now he has 35 cards in all. How many cards were in each pack?

Ⓐ 42 Ⓒ 8

Ⓑ 28 Ⓓ 7

2. Mrs. Jackson bought 5 packages of juice boxes. Each package had the same number of juice boxes. She opened one package and gave 3 juice boxes away. Now she has 27 juice boxes. How many juice boxes were in each package?

Ⓐ 6 Ⓒ 24

Ⓑ 8 Ⓓ 35

3. Ms. King bought 7 packages of raisin boxes. Each package had the same number of raisin boxes. She opened one package and gave 5 raisin boxes away. Now she has 51 raisin boxes. How many raisin boxes were in each package?

Ⓐ 56 Ⓒ 8

Ⓑ 12 Ⓓ 7

4. George had 6 sheets of animal stickers. Each sheet had the same number of stickers. A friend gave him 4 more animal stickers. Now he has 40 animal stickers. How many animal stickers were on each sheet?

Ⓐ 50 Ⓒ 10

Ⓑ 24 Ⓓ 6

5. Ruby saved $12 to buy cat toys. Her uncle gives her $3 more. Each cat toy costs $5. Explain the steps needed to find how many cat toys Ruby can buy.

____

____

____

____

____

© Houghton Mifflin Harcourt Publishing Company

Name ______________________________

Lesson 38

COMMON CORE STANDARD CC.3.OA.8

Lesson Objective: Perform operations in order when there are no parentheses.

Order of Operations

Danny buys a marker for $4. He also buys 5 pens for $2 each. How much money does he spend?

You can write $4 + 5 \times 2 = c$ to describe and solve the problem.

Find $4 + 5 \times 2 = c$.

When there is more than one type of operation in an equation, use the **order of operations**, or the set of rules for the order in which to do operations.

Order of Operations

First: Multiply and divide from left to right.

Then: Add and subtract from left to right.

Step 1 Multiply from left to right.

$\$4 + 5 \times \$2 = c$

multiply

$\$4 + \$10 = c$

Step 2 Next, add from left to right.

$\$4 + \$10 = c$

add

$\$14 = c$

So, Danny spends $14 .

Write *correct* if the operations are listed in the correct order. If not correct, write the correct order of operations.

1. $5 + 6 \times 3$ add, multiply

____

2. $20 \div 4 - 3$ divide, subtract

____

Follow the order of operations to find the unknown number.

3. $9 - 7 + 2 = k$

$k =$ _____

4. $8 + 2 \times 5 = m$

$m =$ _____

5. $7 \times 8 - 6 = g$

$g =$ _____

6. $16 + 4 \div 2 = s$

$s =$ _____

7. $12 - 6 \div 2 = y$

$y =$ _____

8. $36 \div 6 + 13 = f$

$f =$ _____

© Houghton Mifflin Harcourt Publishing Company

Name ______________________

Lesson 38
CC.3.OA.8

1. Amber uses the order of operations to solve the equation below.

$$63 - 49 \div 7 = b$$

What is the unknown number?

Ⓐ $b = 2$
Ⓑ $b = 14$
Ⓒ $b = 55$
Ⓓ $b = 56$

2. Aki uses the order of operations to solve the equation below.

$$3 + 12 \div 3 = c$$

What is the unknown number?

Ⓐ $c = 7$
Ⓑ $c = 6$
Ⓒ $c = 5$
Ⓓ $c = 4$

3. Kayla uses the order of operations to solve the equation below.

$$78 - 54 \div 6 = h$$

What is the unknown number?

Ⓐ $h = 4$
Ⓑ $h = 24$
Ⓒ $h = 69$
Ⓓ $h = 70$

4. Deon uses the order of operations to solve the equation below.

$$3 + 7 \times 3 = x$$

What is the unknown number?

Ⓐ $x = 13$
Ⓑ $x = 21$
Ⓒ $x = 24$
Ⓓ $x = 30$

Problem Solving REAL WORLD

5. Shelley bought 3 kites for \$6 each. She gave the clerk \$20. How much change should Shelley get?

____

6. Tim has 5 apples and 3 bags with 8 apples in each bag. How many apples does Tim have in all?

____

© Houghton Mifflin Harcourt Publishing Company

Name ______________________________

Lesson 39

COMMON CORE STANDARD CC.3.OA.9

Lesson Objective: Identify and describe whole-number patterns and solve problems.

Algebra • Number Patterns

A **pattern** is an ordered set of numbers or objects. The order helps you predict what will come next.

Use the addition table to find patterns.

+	0	1	2	3	4
0	0	1	2	3	4
1	1	2	3	4	5
2	2	3	4	5	6
3	3	4	5	6	7
4	4	5	6	7	8

- Color the row that starts with 1. What pattern do you see?

  The numbers increase by 1.

- Color the column that starts with 1. What pattern do you see?

  The numbers increase by 1. The numbers are the same as in the row starting with 1.

- Circle the sum of 4 in the column you colored. Circle the addends for that sum. What two addition sentences can you write for that sum of 4?

  3 + 1 = 4 and 1 + 3 = 4

  The addends are the same. The sum is the same.

The **Commutative Property of Addition** states that you can add two or more numbers in any order and get the same sum.

Use the addition table to find the sum.

1. 2 + 3 = ___ 3 + 2 = ___

2. 2 + 0 = ___ 0 + 2 = ___

Find the sum. Then use the Commutative Property of Addition to write the related addition sentence.

3. 3 + 0 = ___

   ___ + ___ = ___

4. 4 + 1 = ___

   ___ + ___ = ___

5. 2 + 3 = ___

   ___ + ___ = ___

© Houghton Mifflin Harcourt Publishing Company

Name ___________________________

1. Kara wrote this number sentence to show how many yellow stickers and green stickers she earned. Which describes Kara's number sentence?

$$7 + 0 = 7$$

Ⓐ Commutative Property of Addition

Ⓑ Identity Property of Addition

Ⓒ odd + odd = odd

Ⓓ even + even = even

2. Pablo finds the sum of two addends. The sum is odd. Which statement is **true** about the addends?

Ⓐ Both addends are odd.

Ⓑ Both addends are even.

Ⓒ The addends are both odd or both even.

Ⓓ One addend is odd and one addend is even.

3. Maria wrote the number sentence $4 + 7 = 11$. Which number sentence shows the Commutative Property of Addition?

Ⓐ $11 - 4 = 7$

Ⓑ $3 + 4 = 7$

Ⓒ $4 + 7 = 11$

Ⓓ $7 + 4 = 11$

4. Gregory finds the sum of two addends. The sum is even. Which could **not** be Gregory's addends?

Ⓐ $3 + 10$

Ⓑ $7 + 1$

Ⓒ $7 + 7$

Ⓓ $10 + 12$

5. Ruby says she has read an even number of books. She has read 9 fiction books and 8 nonfiction books. Is Ruby correct? Explain your answer.

____

____

____

© Houghton Mifflin Harcourt Publishing Company

Name ____________________

Lesson 40

COMMON CORE STANDARD CC.3.OA.9

Lesson Objective: Identify and explain patterns on the multiplication table.

Algebra • Patterns on the Multiplication Table

You can use a multiplication table to explore number patterns.

Step 1 Shade the columns for 5 and 10 on the multiplication table.

Step 2 Look for patterns in the shaded numbers.

- The products in the 5s column end in 0 or 5.
- The products in the 5s column repeat—even, odd.
- All the products in the 10s column are even.

×	0	1	2	3	4	5	6	7	8	9	10
0	0	0	0	0	0	0	0	0	0	0	0
1	0	1	2	3	4	5	6	7	8	9	10
2	0	2	4	6	8	10	12	14	16	18	20
3	0	3	6	9	12	15	18	21	24	27	30
4	0	4	8	12	16	20	24	28	32	36	40
5	0	5	10	15	20	25	30	35	40	45	50
6	0	6	12	18	24	30	36	42	48	54	60
7	0	7	14	21	28	35	42	49	56	63	70
8	0	8	16	24	32	40	48	56	64	72	80
9	0	9	18	27	36	45	54	63	72	81	90
10	0	10	20	30	40	50	60	70	80	90	100

Is the product even or odd? Write *even* or *odd*.

1. 5 × 5 ________ **2.** 6 × 4 ________ **3.** 7 × 1 ________ **4.** 8 × 6 ________

Use the multiplication table. Describe a pattern you see.

5. in the row for 2

____
____
____
____

6. in the column for 3

____
____
____
____

© Houghton Mifflin Harcourt Publishing Company

Name ______________________

Use the multiplication table for 1–3.

×	0	1	2	3	4	5	6	7	8	9	10
0	0	0	0	0	0	0	0	0	0	0	0
1	0	1	2	3	4	5	6	7	8	9	10
2	0	2	4	6	8	10	12	14	16	18	20
3	0	3	6	9	12	15	18	21	24	27	30
4	0	4	8	12	16	20	24	28	32	36	40
5	0	5	10	15	20	25	30	35	40	45	50
6	0	6	12	18	24	30	36	42	48	54	60
7	0	7	14	21	28	35	42	49	56	63	70
8	0	8	16	24	32	80	48	56	64	72	80
9	0	9	18	27	36	45	54	63	72	81	90
10	0	10	20	30	40	50	60	70	80	90	100

1. Which row of the table has only even numbers?

Ⓐ the row for 3

Ⓑ the row for 4

Ⓒ the row for 7

Ⓓ the row for 9

2. Which describes a pattern in the column for 5?

Ⓐ All the products are even.

Ⓑ All the products are odd.

Ⓒ Each product is twice the product above it.

Ⓓ Each product is 5 more than the product above it.

3. Which product is even?

Ⓐ 3×7

Ⓑ 4×5

Ⓒ 5×3

Ⓓ 9×1

Problem Solving REAL WORLD

4. Carl shades a row in the multiplication table. The products in the row are all even. The ones digits in the products repeat 0, 4, 8, 2, 6. What row does Carl shade?

____

5. Jenna says that no row or column contains products with only odd numbers. Do you agree? **Explain.**

____

____

____

____

© Houghton Mifflin Harcourt Publishing Company

Name ______________________________

Lesson 41

COMMON CORE STANDARD CC.3.OA.9

Lesson Objective: Identify and describe a number pattern shown in a function table.

Algebra • Describe Patterns

The table shows the number of candles in different numbers of packs. How many candles will be in 4 packs?

Packs	1	2	3	4
Candles	2	4	6	■

Describe a pattern in the columns.

Step 1 Look for a pattern by comparing the columns in the table. You can multiply the number of packs by 2 to find the number of candles in all.

$1 \times 2 = 2$

$2 \times 2 = 4$

$3 \times 2 = 6$

Multiply by **2** candles for each pack.

Step 2 Use the pattern to find the number of candles in 4 packs.

$4 \times 2 = 8$

So, there are **8** candles in 4 packs.

Describe a pattern for the table. Then complete the table.

1.

Tricycles	1	2	3	4	5
Wheels	3	6	9		

____

____

2.

Boxes	1	2	3	4	5
Baseballs	6	12	18		

____

____

© Houghton Mifflin Harcourt Publishing Company

1. Lori is making bracelets. The table shows how many beads she will need. Which two numbers come next?

Bracelets	2	3	4	5	6
Beads	10	15	20	■	■

Ⓐ 25 and 30 Ⓒ 30 and 35

Ⓑ 25 and 35 Ⓓ 30 and 40

2. Sofia is making omelets. The table shows how many eggs she will need. Which of the following describes a pattern in this table?

Omelets	2	3	4	5	6
Eggs	6	9	12	15	18

Ⓐ Add 4. Ⓒ Multiply by 3.

Ⓑ Subtract 3. Ⓓ Multiply by 4.

3. Stephanie and John made a table about spiders. Which of the following describes a pattern in this table?

Spiders	2	3	4	5	6
Legs	16	24	32	40	48

Ⓐ Add 14. Ⓒ Multiply by 6.

Ⓑ Subtract 35. Ⓓ Multiply by 8.

4. Bobby made a table about ants. Which number completes the pattern in this table?

Ants	3	4	5	6	7
Legs	18	24	30	■	42

Ⓐ 6 Ⓒ 36

Ⓑ 35 Ⓓ 40

Problem Solving REAL WORLD

5. Caleb buys 5 cartons of yogurt. Each carton has 8 yogurt cups. How many yogurt cups does Caleb buy?

____

6. Libby bought 4 packages of pencils. Each package has 6 pencils. How many pencils did Libby buy?

____

© Houghton Mifflin Harcourt Publishing Company

Name ______________________________

Lesson 42

COMMON CORE STANDARD CC.3.NBT.1

Lesson Objective: Round 2- and 3-digit numbers to the nearest ten or hundred.

Round to the Nearest Ten or Hundred

When you **round** a number, you find a number that tells you *about* how much or *about* how many.

Use place value to round 76 to the nearest ten.

Step 1 Look at the digit to the right of the tens place.

- If the ones digit is 5 or more, the tens digit increases by one.
- If the ones digit is less than 5, the tens digit stays the same.

Step 2 Write zero for the ones digit.

76
↑
ones place

The digit in the ones place is 6.

$6 > 5$

So, the digit 7 in the tens place increases to 8.

So, 76 rounded to the nearest ten is **80**.

Think: To round to the nearest hundred, look at the tens digit. So, 128 rounded to the nearest hundred is **100**.

128
↑
tens place

Round to the nearest ten.

1. 24 ____________ **2.** 15 ____________ **3.** 47 ____________

4. 42 ____________ **5.** 81 ____________ **6.** 65 ____________

Round to the nearest hundred.

7. 176 ____________ **8.** 395 ____________ **9.** 431 ____________

10. 421 ____________ **11.** 692 ____________ **12.** 470 ____________

© Houghton Mifflin Harcourt Publishing Company

Name ______________________________

Lesson 42
CC.3.NBT.1

1. On Friday, 209 people attended a show. What is 209 rounded to the nearest ten?

   Ⓐ 100
   Ⓑ 200
   Ⓒ 210
   Ⓓ 220

2. There are 852 mystery books in the school library. What is 852 rounded to the nearest ten?

   Ⓐ 800
   Ⓑ 850
   Ⓒ 860
   Ⓓ 900

3. There are 487 books in the classroom library. What is 487 rounded to the nearest ten?

   Ⓐ 480
   Ⓑ 490
   Ⓒ 500
   Ⓓ 510

4. Pizza Place sold 581 pizzas on Friday night. What is 581 rounded to the nearest hundred?

   Ⓐ 600
   Ⓑ 590
   Ⓒ 580
   Ⓓ 500

Problem Solving REAL WORLD

5. The baby elephant weighs 435 pounds. What is its weight rounded to the nearest hundred pounds?

   ____

6. Jayce sold 218 cups of lemonade at his lemonade stand. What is 218 rounded to the nearest ten?

   ____

© Houghton Mifflin Harcourt Publishing Company

Name ____________________

Lesson 43

COMMON CORE STANDARD CC.3.NBT.1

Lesson Objective: Use compatible numbers and rounding to estimate sums.

Estimate Sums

An **estimate** is a number close to an exact amount.

You can use **compatible numbers** to estimate. Compatible numbers are easy to compute mentally and are close to the real numbers.

Estimate. Use compatible numbers.

73 + 21 = ■

So, 73 + 21 is about **100**.

73	⟶	75
+ 21	⟶	+ 25
		100

Another way to estimate is to round numbers to the same place value.

Estimate. Round each number to the nearest hundred. 214 + 678 = ■

Step 1 Look at the digit to the right of the hundreds place.

- 1 < 5, so the digit 2 stays the same.
- 7 > 5, so the digit 6 increases by 1 to become 7.

214	⟶	200
+ 678	⟶	+ 700
		900

Step 2 Write zeros for the tens and ones places.

So, 214 + 678 is about **900**.

Use rounding or compatible numbers to estimate the sum.

1. 42 + 36 → ____ + ____

2. 523 + 117 → ____ + ____

3. 235 + 374 → ____ + ____

4. 23 + 99 → ____ + ____

5. 254 + 167 → ____ + ____

6. 299 + 199 → ____ + ____

© Houghton Mifflin Harcourt Publishing Company

1. Amber and her friends collected shells. The table shows how many shells each person collected.

Shells Collected

Name	Number of Shells
Amber	372
Melba	455
Pablo	421
Tom	515

Which is the **best** estimate of the total number of shells Amber and Pablo collected?

Ⓐ 600 Ⓒ 800

Ⓑ 700 Ⓓ 900

2. The parking lot at the grocery store had 574 parking spaces. Another 128 parking spaces were added to the parking lot. Which is the **best** estimate of the total number of parking spaces in the parking lot now?

Ⓐ 800 Ⓒ 600

Ⓑ 700 Ⓓ 500

3. Mavis and her friends collected bottle caps. The table shows how many bottle caps each person collected.

Bottle Caps Collected

Name	Number of Bottle Caps
Karen	372
Mavis	255
Pedro	121
John	315

Which is the **best** estimate of the total number of bottle caps Mavis and Pedro collected?

Ⓐ 100 Ⓒ 300

Ⓑ 200 Ⓓ 400

4. Umiko made 47 origami birds last week and 62 origami birds this week. About how many origami birds did she make in the two weeks?

Ⓐ 10 Ⓒ 110

Ⓑ 60 Ⓓ 200

5. Bruce wants to use compatible numbers to estimate 173 + 327. Suggest two compatible numbers he could use to estimate the sum. Explain your choices.

____

____

© Houghton Mifflin Harcourt Publishing Company

Name ______________________________

Lesson 44

COMMON CORE STANDARD CC.3.NBT.1

Lesson Objective: Use compatible numbers and rounding to estimate differences.

Estimate Differences

You can use what you know about estimating sums to estimate differences.

Estimate. Use compatible numbers.
78 − 47 = ■

Think: Compatible numbers are easy to subtract.

78	⟶	75
− 47	⟶	− 50
		25

So, 78 − 47 is about **25**.

Another way to estimate is to round to the same place value.

Estimate. Round each number to the earest hundred. 687 − 516 = ■

Step 1 Look at the digit to the right of the hundreds place.

- 8 > 5, so the digit in the hundreds place increases by 1.
- 1 < 5, so the digit in the hundreds place stays the same.

Step 2 Write zeros for the tens and ones places.

687	⟶	200
− 516	⟶	− 700
		900

So, 687 − 516 is about **200**.

Use rounding or compatible numbers to estimate the difference.

1. 92 − 43 → ____ − ____ = ____

2. 271 − 152 → ____ − ____ = ____

3. 517 − 249 → ____ − ____ = ____

4. 445 − 112 → ____ − ____ = ____

5. 92 − 65 → ____ − ____ = ____

6. 776 − 384 → ____ − ____ = ____

© Houghton Mifflin Harcourt Publishing Company

1. Three classes had a reading contest. The table shows how many books the students in each class read.

Reading Contest

Class	Number of Books
Mr. Lopez	273
Ms. Martin	403
Mrs. Wang	147

Which is the **best** estimate of how many more books Ms. Martin's class read than Mr. Lopez's class?

Ⓐ 100 Ⓒ 300

Ⓑ 200 Ⓓ 400

2. Abby and Cruz are playing a game. Abby's score is 168 points less than Cruz's score. Cruz's score is 754. Which is the **best** estimate of Abby's score?

Ⓐ 300 Ⓒ 500

Ⓑ 400 Ⓓ 600

3. Three classes had a spelling contest. The table shows how many words the students in each class spelled correctly.

Spelling Contest

Class	Number of Words
Mr. Silva	719
Ms. Parker	660
Mrs. Cheng	847

Which is the **best** estimate of how many more words Mrs. Cheng's class spelled correctly than Mr. Silva's class?

Ⓐ 100 Ⓒ 300

Ⓑ 200 Ⓓ 400

4. Andre and Salma collect stamps. Andre has 287 stamps. Salma has 95 stamps. About how many more stamps does Andre have than Salma has?

Ⓐ 400 Ⓒ 200

Ⓑ 300 Ⓓ 100

5. To estimate 512 − 87, Kim rounded the numbers to 510 − 90 and subtracted. What is another way that Kim could have estimated to subtract? Explain why it might be easier.

____

____

____

© Houghton Mifflin Harcourt Publishing Company

Name ____________________

Lesson 45

COMMON CORE STANDARD CC.3.NBT.2

Lesson Objective: Count by tens and ones, use a number line, make compatible numbers, or use friendly numbers to find sums mentally.

Mental Math Strategies for Addition

You can count by tens and ones to find a sum.

Find 58 + 15.

Step 1 Count on to the nearest ten. Start at 58. Count to 60.

Step 2 Count by tens. Start at 60. Count to 70.

Step 3 Then count by ones. Start at 70. Count to 73.

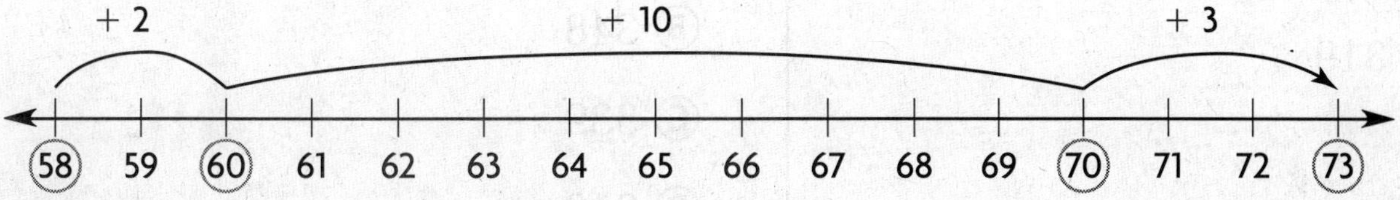

Think: 58 + 2 + 10 + 3 = 73

So, 58 + 15 = 73.

You can also count on by tens first and then by ones.

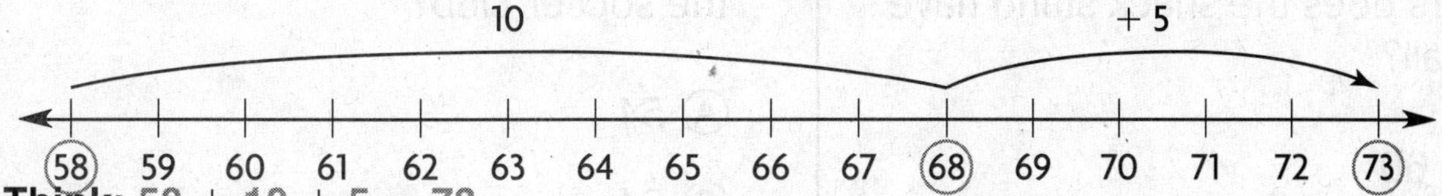

Think: 58 + 10 + 5 = 73

So, 58 + 15 = 73.

1. Count by tens and ones to find 54 + 26. Draw jumps and label the number line to show your thinking.

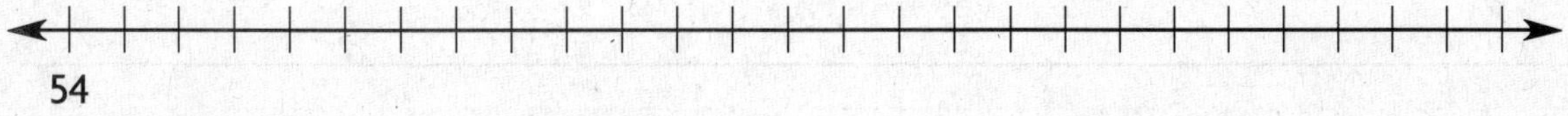

54 + 26 = _____

© Houghton Mifflin Harcourt Publishing Company

Name ______________________

1. On Monday, 114 girls and 205 boys wore jeans to school. How many students wore jeans to school on Monday?

Ⓐ 219

Ⓑ 299

Ⓒ 309

Ⓓ 319

2. The snack stand has 28 honey granola bars and 42 maple granola bars. How many granola bars does the snack stand have in all?

Ⓐ 60

Ⓑ 68

Ⓒ 70

Ⓓ 78

3. The Smoothie Stop sold 216 banana smoothies and 132 peach smoothies for breakfast. How many banana smoothies and peach smoothies did the Smoothie Stop sell combined?

Ⓐ 358

Ⓑ 348

Ⓒ 339

Ⓓ 248

4. There are 37 second graders and 27 third graders in the soccer club. How many students are in the soccer club?

Ⓐ 54

Ⓑ 64

Ⓒ 67

Ⓓ 74

5. Aya has to find the sum of 67 + 34. Explain a mental math strategy she can use to find the sum.

____

____

____

© Houghton Mifflin Harcourt Publishing Company

Name ______________________________

Lesson 46

COMMON CORE STANDARD CC.3.NBT.2

Lesson Objective: Use the Commutative and Associative Properties of Addition to add more than two addends.

Algebra • Use Properties to Add

You can use addition properties and strategies to help you add.

<table>
<tr>
<td>

Find 3 + 14 + 21.

The **Commutative Property of Addition** states that you can add numbers in any order and still get the same sum.

Step 1 Look for numbers that are easy to add.
Think: Make doubles.
3 + 1 = 4 and 4 + 4 = 8.

Step 2 Use the Commutative Property to change the order.
3 + 14 + 21 = 3 + 21 + 14

Step 3 Add.

3 + 21 + 14 = **24** + 14

24 + 14 = **30** + **8**

So, 3 + 14 + 21 = **38**.

</td>
<td>

Find 7 + (3 + 22).

The **Associative Property of Addition** states that you can group addends in different ways and still get the same sum.

Step 1 Look for numbers that are easy to add.
Think: Make a ten. 7 + 3 = 10

Step 2 Use the Associative Property to change the grouping.
7 + (3 + 22) = (7 + 3) + 22

Step 3 Add.

(7 + 3) + 22 = **10** + 22

10 + 22 = **32**

So, 7 + (3 + 22) = **32**.

</td>
</tr>
</table>

Use addition properties and strategies to find the sum.

1. 2 + 15 + 8 = _____

2. 19 + 36 + 1 = _____

3. 25 + 44 + 5 = _____

4. 12 + 36 + 18 + 14 = _____

5. 23 + 14 + 23 = _____

6. 11 + 15 + 19 + 14 = _____

© Houghton Mifflin Harcourt Publishing Company

Name ____________________________

1. Amy writes a number sentence that shows the Commutative Property of Addition. Which could be Amy's number sentence?

Ⓐ $(53 + 9) + 41 = 53 + (9 + 41)$

Ⓑ $53 + 0 = 53$

Ⓒ $41 = 40 + 1$

Ⓓ $53 + 9 = 9 + 53$

2. Mr. Rios bought 24 apples, 16 bananas, and 14 pears at the store. How many pieces of fruit did he buy?

Ⓐ 64

Ⓑ 54

Ⓒ 40

Ⓓ 38

3. Mario writes a number sentence that shows the Commutative Property of Addition. Which could be Mario's number sentence?

Ⓐ $37 = 36 + 1$

Ⓑ $0 + 23 = 23$

Ⓒ $37 + 13 = 13 + 37$

Ⓓ $(37 + 13) + 23 = 37 + (13 + 23)$

4. John writes the following number sentences. Which shows the Associative Property of Addition?

Ⓐ $7 + (13 + 8) = (7 + 13) + 8$

Ⓑ $44 + (56 + 13) = 44 + (13 + 56)$

Ⓒ $44 + 56 = 40 + 60$

Ⓓ $44 + 56 = 100$

Problem Solving REAL WORLD

5. A pet shelter has 26 dogs, 37 cats, and 14 gerbils. How many of these animals are in the pet shelter in all?

____

6. The pet shelter bought 85 pounds of dog food, 50 pounds of cat food, and 15 pounds of gerbil food. How many pounds of animal food did the pet shelter buy?

____

© Houghton Mifflin Harcourt Publishing Company

Name ____________________

Lesson 47

COMMON CORE STANDARD CC.3.NBT.2

Lesson Objective: Use the break apart strategy to add 3-digit numbers.

Use the Break Apart Strategy to Add

You can use the break apart strategy to add.

Add. 263 + 215

Think and Record

Step 1 Estimate. Round to the nearest hundred.

300 + 200 = **500**

Step 2 Start with the hundreds. Break apart the addends. Then add each place value.

263 = 200 + 60 + 3
215 = 200 + 10 + 5
400 + 70 + 8

Step 3 Add the sums.

400 + 70 + 8 = **478**

So, 263 + 215 = **478**.

Model

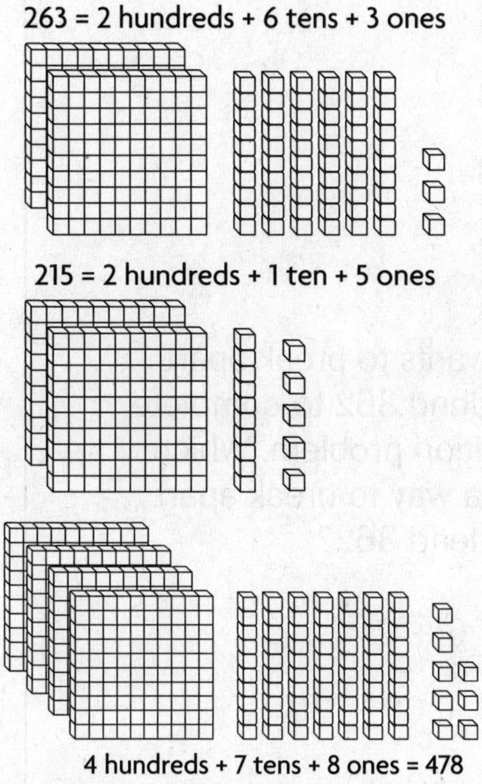

Estimate. Then use the break apart strategy to find the sum.

1. Estimate: ______

242 =
+ 536 = ____________

2. Estimate: ______

469 =
+ 413 = ____________

3. Estimate: ______

385 =
+ 519 = ____________

4. Estimate: ______

527 =
+ 266 = ____________

© Houghton Mifflin Harcourt Publishing Company

Name ______________________________

1. A Rent-A-Raft store rented 213 rafts in June and 455 rafts in July. How many rafts did the Rent-A-Raft store rent in June and July altogether?

Ⓐ 658

Ⓑ 668

Ⓒ 678

Ⓓ 778

2. Omar wants to break apart the addend 362 to complete an addition problem. Which shows a way to break apart the addend 362?

Ⓐ 3 + 6 + 2

Ⓑ 300 + 60 + 20

Ⓒ 30 + 62

Ⓓ 300 + 60 + 2

3. Marcus took 242 pictures with his new camera and 155 pictures with his camera phone. How many pictures did Marcus take in all?

Ⓐ 397

Ⓑ 387

Ⓒ 297

Ⓓ 292

4. The number of campers at Arrowhead Camp was 412 in July and 443 in August. How many campers were at Arrowhead Camp in July and August combined?

Ⓐ 865

Ⓑ 855

Ⓒ 843

Ⓓ 455

---

5. Explain how you can tell that the sum of 575 and 338 is greater than 900 without finding the exact sum.

____

____

____

____

© Houghton Mifflin Harcourt Publishing Company

Name ______________________________

Lesson 48

COMMON CORE STANDARD CC.3.NBT.2

Lesson Objective: Use place value to add 3-digit numbers.

Use Place Value to Add

You can use place value to add 3-digit numbers.

Add. 268 + 195 **Estimate.** 300 + 200 = **500**

Step 1 Add the ones. If there are 10 or more ones, regroup as tens and ones.

$$\begin{array}{r} {}^{1} \\ 268 \\ +\ 195 \\ \hline 3 \end{array}$$

8 ones + **5** ones = **13** ones

13 ones = **1** ten **3** ones

Step 2 Add the tens. Regroup the tens as hundreds and tens.

$$\begin{array}{r} {}^{1\,1} \\ 268 \\ +\ 195 \\ \hline 63 \end{array}$$

1 ten + **6** tens + **9** tens = **16** tens

16 tens = **1** hundred **6** tens

Step 3 Add the hundreds.

$$\begin{array}{r} {}^{1\,1} \\ 268 \\ +\ 195 \\ \hline 463 \end{array}$$

1 hundred + **2** hundreds + **1** hundred = **4** hundreds

So, 268 + 195 = **463**.

Estimate. Then find the sum.

1. Estimate: ____

$$\begin{array}{r} 156 \\ +\ 323 \\ \hline \end{array}$$

2. Estimate: ____

$$\begin{array}{r} 347 \\ +\ 390 \\ \hline \end{array}$$

3. Estimate: ____

$$\begin{array}{r} 472 \\ +\ 108 \\ \hline \end{array}$$

4. Estimate: ____

$$\begin{array}{r} 239 \\ +\ 570 \\ \hline \end{array}$$

5. Estimate: ____

$$\begin{array}{r} 110 \\ +\ 576 \\ \hline \end{array}$$

6. Estimate: ____

$$\begin{array}{r} 258 \\ +\ 324 \\ \hline \end{array}$$

7. Estimate: ____

$$\begin{array}{r} 471 \\ +\ 269 \\ \hline \end{array}$$

8. Estimate: ____

$$\begin{array}{r} 585 \\ +\ 309 \\ \hline \end{array}$$

© Houghton Mifflin Harcourt Publishing Company

Name ______________________________

1. The table shows the number of students visiting the zoo each day.

Field Trips This Week

Day	Number of Students
Monday	346
Tuesday	518
Wednesday	449
Thursday	608

How many students will visit the zoo on Monday and Tuesday combined?

Ⓐ 814 Ⓒ 864

Ⓑ 854 Ⓓ 964

2. Mr. Rodriguez drove 136 miles to Main City. Then he drove another 146 miles to Rock Town. How many miles did Mr. Rodriguez drive?

Ⓐ 212 miles Ⓒ 272 miles

Ⓑ 270 miles Ⓓ 282 miles

3. The table shows the number of students who bought lunch in the school cafeteria one week.

Bought Lunch in Cafeteria

Day	Number of Students
Monday	236
Tuesday	319
Wednesday	225
Thursday	284
Friday	306

How many students bought lunch in the cafeteria on Wednesday and Friday combined?

Ⓐ 261 Ⓒ 531

Ⓑ 521 Ⓓ 631

4. Mrs. Carlson drove 283 miles to Plant City. She then drove 128 miles to Bond Town. How far did Mrs. Carlson drive?

Ⓐ 411 miles Ⓒ 365 miles

Ⓑ 401 miles Ⓓ 311 miles

5. Bryce has 317 baseball cards. Elin has 168 baseball cards and Jeff has 425 baseball cards. Which two people together have fewer than 500 cards? Explain your answer.

____

____

____

© Houghton Mifflin Harcourt Publishing Company

Name ______________________________

Lesson 49

COMMON CORE STANDARD CC.3.NBT.2

Lesson Objective: Use a number line, friendly numbers, or the break apart strategy to find differences mentally.

Mental Math Strategies for Subtraction

You can count up on a number line to find a difference.

Find 53 – 27.

Step 1 Count up by tens. Start at 27. Count up to 47.

Step 2 Count up by ones. Start at 47. Count up to 53.

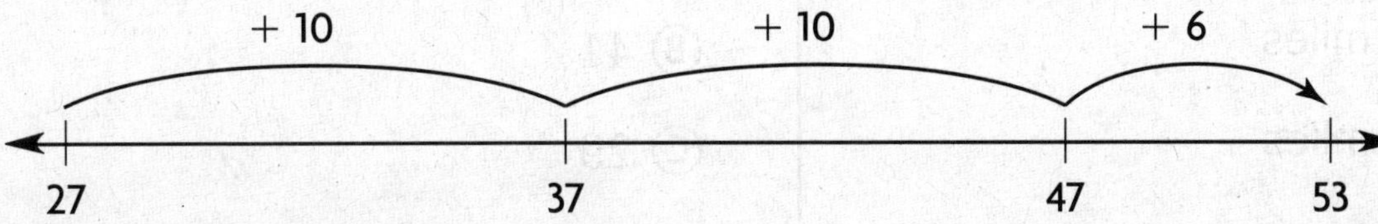

Think: 10 + 10 + 6 = 26.

So, 53 − 27 = 26.

You can take away tens and ones to find a difference.

Step 1 Take away tens. Start at 53.

Step 2 Take away ones. Start at 33.

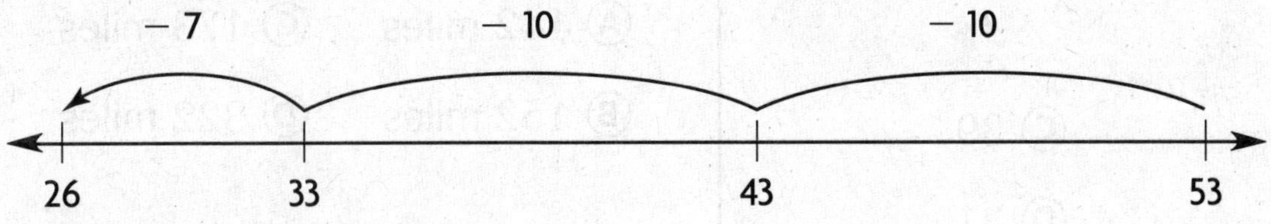

Think: 53 − 10 − 10 − 7 = 26.

So, 53 − 27 = 26.

1. Find 92 − 65. Draw jumps and label the number line to show your thinking.

92 − 65 = ______.

© Houghton Mifflin Harcourt Publishing Company

Name ______________________

1. Mikio drove a total of 267 miles in 2 days. He drove 125 miles the first day. How many miles did he drive the second day?

Ⓐ 142 miles

Ⓑ 162 miles

Ⓒ 242 miles

Ⓓ 392 miles

2. The Fruity Yogurt Company sold 86 banana yogurt bars and 47 strawberry yogurt bars. How many more banana yogurt bars were sold than strawberry yogurt bars?

Ⓐ 49 Ⓒ 39

Ⓑ 41 Ⓓ 31

3. The Party Popcorn Company sold 58 bags of cheese popcorn and 39 bags of nutty popcorn. How many more bags of cheese popcorn were sold than nutty popcorn?

Ⓐ 97

Ⓑ 41

Ⓒ 29

Ⓓ 19

4. Lin drove a total of 346 miles in 2 days. She drove 204 miles the first day. How many miles did she drive the second day?

Ⓐ 142 miles Ⓒ 173 miles

Ⓑ 152 miles Ⓓ 322 miles

Problem Solving REAL WORLD

5. Ruby has 78 books. Thirty-one of the books are on shelves. The rest are still packed in boxes. How many of Ruby's books are still in boxes?

____

6. Kyle has 130 pins in his collection. He has 76 of the pins displayed on his wall. The rest are in a drawer. How many of Kyle's pins are in a drawer?

____

© Houghton Mifflin Harcourt Publishing Company

Name ______________________________

Lesson 50

COMMON CORE STANDARD CC.3.NBT.2

Lesson Objective: Use place value to subtract 3-digit numbers.

Use Place Value to Subtract

You can use place value to subtract 3-digit numbers.

Subtract. 352 − 167 **Estimate.** 400 − 200 = **200**

Step 1 Subtract the ones.

```
  4 12
 3 5 2
-1 6 7
     5
```

Are there enough ones to subtract 7?
There are not enough ones.
Regroup **5** tens **2** ones as **4** tens **12** ones.
12 ones − 7 ones = **5** ones

Step 2 Subtract the tens.

```
   14
 2  4 12
 3  5  2
-1  6  7
    8  5
```

Are there enough tens to subtract 6?
There are not enough tens.
Regroup **3** hundreds **4** tens as **2** hundreds **14** tens.
14 tens − 6 tens = **8** tens

Step 3 Subtract the hundreds.

```
   14
 2  4 12
 3  5  2
-1  6  7
 1  8  5
```

2 hundreds − **1** hundred = **1** hundred

So, 352 − 167 = **185**.

Estimate. Then find the difference.

1. Estimate: ______

537
− 123

2. Estimate: ______

268
− 157

3. Estimate: ______

426
− 218

4. Estimate: ______

785
− 549

5. Estimate: ______

354
− 206

6. Estimate: ______

679
− 482

7. Estimate: ______

787
− 378

8. Estimate: ______

843
− 675

© Houghton Mifflin Harcourt Publishing Company

Name ______________________________

Lesson 50
CC.3.NBT.2

1. The school store had 136 notepads. It sold 109 notepads. How many notepads are left?

Ⓐ 27

Ⓑ 33

Ⓒ 37

Ⓓ 43

2. Mr. Ruiz's art students used 159 green beads and 370 orange beads to make necklaces. How many more orange beads than green beads did they use?

Ⓐ 201

Ⓑ 211

Ⓒ 221

Ⓓ 229

3. The craft store had 151 bags of beads. It sold 128 bags. How many bags of beads are left?

Ⓐ 37

Ⓑ 33

Ⓒ 27

Ⓓ 23

4. A movie theater has 245 seats in the main section, and 78 seats up in the balcony. How many more seats are in the main section?

Ⓐ 137

Ⓑ 167

Ⓒ 187

Ⓓ 233

Problem Solving REAL WORLD

5. Mrs. Cohen has 427 buttons. She uses 195 buttons to make puppets. How many buttons does Mrs. Cohen have left?

____

6. There were 625 ears of corn and 247 tomatoes sold at a farm stand. How many more ears of corn were sold than tomatoes?

____

© Houghton Mifflin Harcourt Publishing Company

Name ______________________

Lesson 51

COMMON CORE STANDARD CC.3.NBT.2

Lesson Objective: Use the combine place values strategy to subtract 3-digit numbers.

Combine Place Values to Subtract

You can combine place values to subtract. Think of two digits next to each other as one number.

Subtract. 354 − 248

Estimate. 350 − 250 = **100**

Step 1 Look at the digits in the ones place.	Step 2 Combine the tens and ones places.	Step 3 Subtract the hundreds.
Think: 8 > 4, so combine place values.	**Think:** There are 54 ones and 48 ones. Subtract the ones. Write 0 for the tens.	
$\begin{array}{r} 354 \\ -\,248 \\ \hline \end{array}$	$\begin{array}{r} 354 \\ -\,248 \\ \hline 06 \end{array}$	$\begin{array}{r} 354 \\ -\,248 \\ \hline 106 \end{array}$

So, 354 − 248 = **106**.

Remember: You can also combine hundreds and tens to subtract.

Estimate. Then find the difference.

1. Estimate: ______
$\begin{array}{r} 485 \\ -\,376 \\ \hline \end{array}$

2. Estimate: ______
$\begin{array}{r} 657 \\ -\,424 \\ \hline \end{array}$

3. Estimate: ______
$\begin{array}{r} 347 \\ -\,198 \\ \hline \end{array}$

4. Estimate: ______
$\begin{array}{r} 623 \\ -\,397 \\ \hline \end{array}$

5. Estimate: ______
$\begin{array}{r} 443 \\ -\,207 \\ \hline \end{array}$

6. Estimate: ______
$\begin{array}{r} 500 \\ -\,338 \\ \hline \end{array}$

7. Estimate: ______
$\begin{array}{r} 835 \\ -\,548 \\ \hline \end{array}$

8. Estimate: ______
$\begin{array}{r} 712 \\ -\,289 \\ \hline \end{array}$

© Houghton Mifflin Harcourt Publishing Company

1. Students want to sell 420 tickets to the school fair. They have sold 214 tickets. How many more tickets do they need to sell to reach their goal?

Ⓐ 106

Ⓑ 206

Ⓒ 214

Ⓓ 634

2. A website received 724 visitors last month. This month, there were 953 visitors. How many more visitors did the website have this month than last month?

Ⓐ 1,677 Ⓒ 229

Ⓑ 231 Ⓓ 129

3. The owners of a new discount store expect 350 shoppers the day the store opens. By noon, there are 143 shoppers. How many more shoppers do they need to reach their goal?

Ⓐ 107

Ⓑ 207

Ⓒ 217

Ⓓ 223

4. A popular ride at a theme park has 200 seats. Only 84 people got tickets for the last ride of the day. How many empty seats were there?

Ⓐ 184 Ⓒ 126

Ⓑ 124 Ⓓ 116

Problem Solving REAL WORLD

5. Bev scored 540 points. This was 158 points more than Ike scored. How many points did Ike score?

____

6. A youth group earned $285 washing cars. The group's expenses were $79. How much profit did the group make washing cars?

____

© Houghton Mifflin Harcourt Publishing Company

Name ______________________________

Lesson 52

COMMON CORE STANDARD CC.3.NBT.3

Lesson Objective: Solve multiplication problems by using the strategy *draw a diagram.*

Problem Solving • Use the Distributive Property

There are 6 rows of singers in a performance. There are 20 singers in each row. How many singers are in the performance?

Read the Problem

What do I need to find?

I need to find how many singers are in the performance.

What information do I need to use?

There are __6__ rows of singers.

Each row has __20__ singers.

How will I use the information?

I can draw a diagram and use the Distributive Property to break apart the factor 20 into 10 + 10 to use facts I know.

Solve the Problem

Record the steps you used to solve the problem.

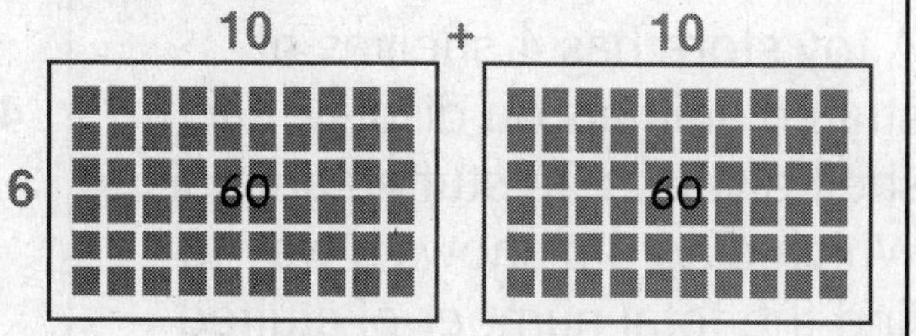

First, I draw and label a diagram to show __6__ rows of __20__ singers.

Next, I break apart 20 into 10 + 10 and find the products of the two smaller rectangles.

$6 \times 10 =$ _____ $6 \times 10 =$ _____

Then, I find the sum of the two products.

_____ + _____ = _____

$6 \times 20 =$ _____

So, there are _____ singers.

1. Eight teams play in a Little League series. Each team has 20 players. How many players are in the series?

   ____

2. The assembly room has 6 rows with 30 chairs in each row. If third graders fill 3 rows, how many third graders are in the room?

   ____

© Houghton Mifflin Harcourt Publishing Company

Name ______________________________

1. Uncle Tito has 4 nephews. He gives each boy a $30 gift card to a hobby shop. What is the total cost of the 4 gift cards?

Ⓐ $34 Ⓒ $120

Ⓑ $80 Ⓓ $150

2. A toy store has 4 shelves of stuffed animals on display. Each shelf displays 20 stuffed animals. Which diagram shows a way to find the total number of stuffed animals on display?

Ⓐ 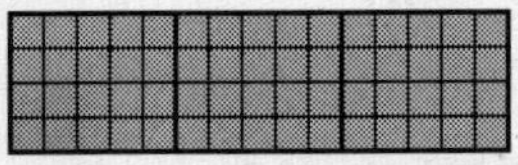

Ⓑ 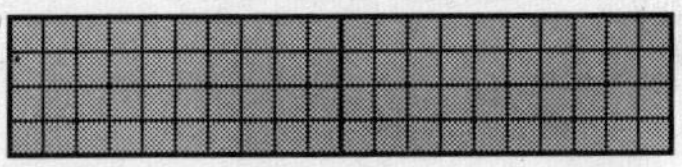

Ⓒ 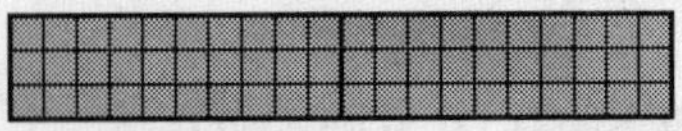

Ⓓ 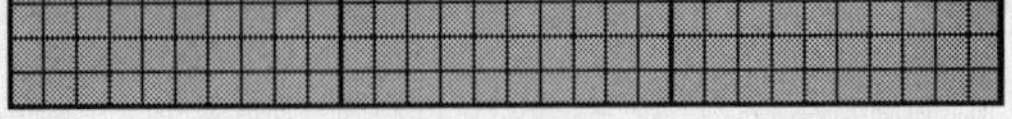

3. Wendy buys 7 boxes of envelopes. There are 80 envelopes in each box. How many envelopes does Wendy buy altogether?

Ⓐ 56 Ⓒ 630

Ⓑ 560 Ⓓ 640

4. Aunt Sonya has 5 nieces. She gives each girl a $40 gift card to the museum shop. What is the total cost of the 5 gift cards?

Ⓐ $45

Ⓑ $50

Ⓒ $160

Ⓓ $200

5. Corey sold 5 kites to each of 20 people. How many kites did Corey sell altogether? Explain your answer.

____

____

____

____

____

© Houghton Mifflin Harcourt Publishing Company

Name ______________________________

Lesson 53

COMMON CORE STANDARD CC.3.NBT.3

Lesson Objective: Use base-ten blocks, a number line, or place value to multiply with multiples of 10.

Multiplication Strategies with Multiples of 10

You can use place value to multiply with multiples of 10.

Find 5 × 20.

Step 1 Use a multiplication fact you know.

Think: 5 × 2 = 10, so
5 × 2 ones = 10 ones

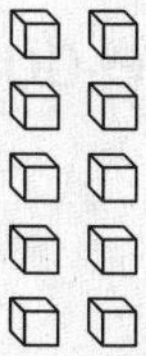

Step 2 Use place value to find the product.

Think: 5 × 2 tens = 10 tens, or 100

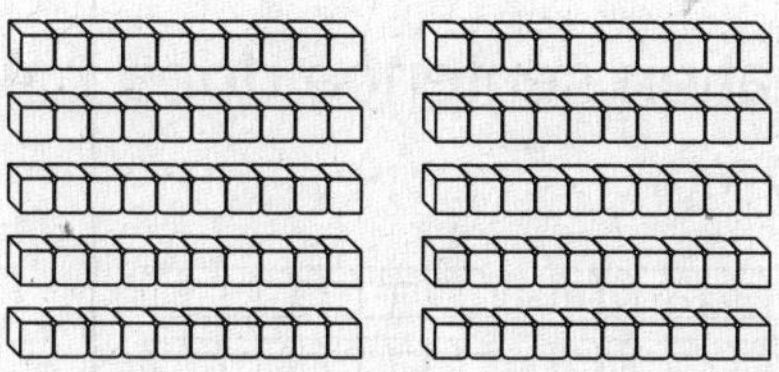

So, 5 × 20 = 100.

You can also use a number line to multiply with multiples of 10.

Find 4 × 30.

Think: There are 4 groups of 30. Draw 4 jumps of 30.

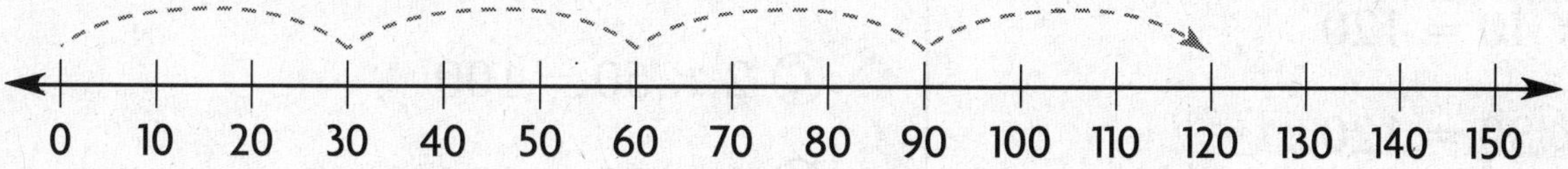

So, 4 × 30 = 120.

Use place value to find the product.

1. 6 × 40 = 6 × _____ tens
= _____ tens = _____

2. 50 × 7 = _____ tens × 7
= _____ tens = _____

3. Use a number line to find the product. 3 × 50 = _____

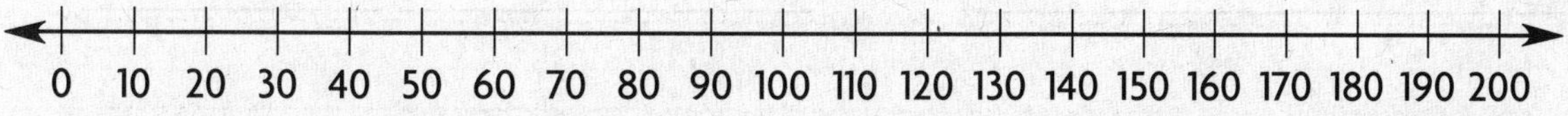

© Houghton Mifflin Harcourt Publishing Company

1. Lucia takes care of farm animals. She works 5 days each week. Last week she took care of 60 farm animals each day she worked. How many farm animals did Lucia take care of last week?

(A) 360
(B) 300
(C) 240
(D) 65

2. What multiplication sentence does the model show?

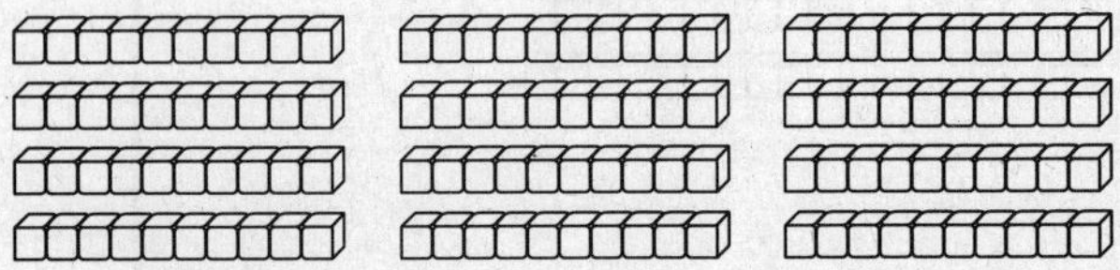

(A) $3 \times 4 = 12$
(B) $2 \times 60 = 120$
(C) $3 \times 40 = 120$
(D) $4 \times 30 = 120$

3. Each school bus has seats for 30 students. On a recent third-grade field trip, 7 buses were filled with students. How many students went on the field trip?

(A) 21
(B) 37
(C) 180
(D) 210

4. What multiplication sentence does the model show?

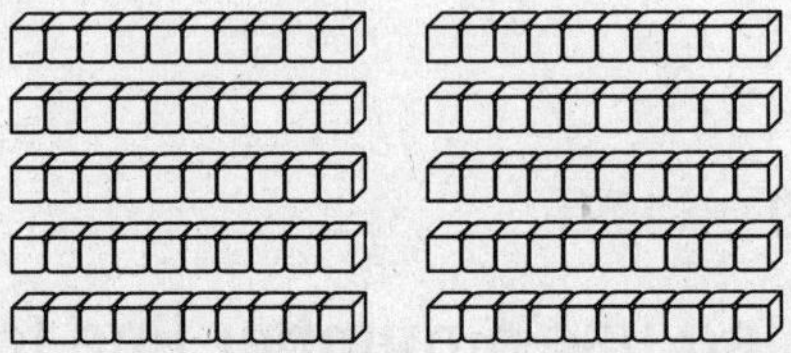

(A) $2 \times 5 = 10$
(B) $3 \times 40 = 120$
(C) $2 \times 50 = 100$
(D) $2 \times 60 = 120$

Problem Solving REAL WORLD

5. One exhibit at the aquarium has 5 fish tanks. Each fish tank holds 50 gallons of water. How much water do the 5 tanks hold in all?

____

6. In another aquarium display, there are 40 fish in each of 7 large tanks. How many fish are in the display in all?

____

© Houghton Mifflin Harcourt Publishing Company

Name ______________________________

Lesson 54

COMMON CORE STANDARD CC.3.NBT.3

Lesson Objective: Model and record multiplication with multiples of 10.

Multiply Multiples of 10 by 1-Digit Numbers

You can use place value and regrouping to multiply multiples of 10.

Find 3 × 40.

Step 1 Use quick pictures to draw 3 groups of 40.

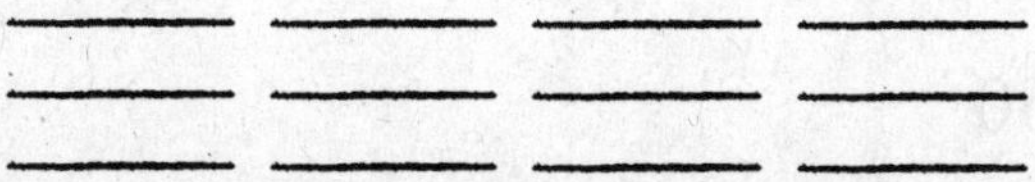

THINK

Multiply the ones.

3 × 0 ones = **0** ones.

RECORD

$$\begin{array}{r} 40 \\ \times\ 3 \\ \hline \mathbf{0} \end{array}$$

Step 2 Regroup the 12 tens.

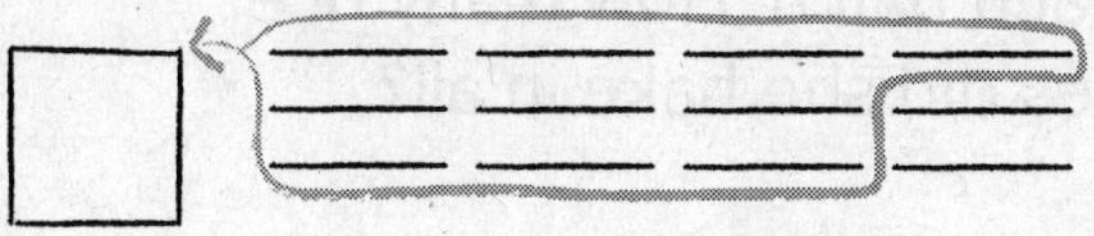

Multiply the tens.

3 × **4** tens = **12** tens

Regroup the **12** tens as **1** hundred **2** tens

$$\begin{array}{r} 40 \\ \times\ 3 \\ \hline \mathbf{120} \end{array}$$

So, 3 × 40 = **120**.

Find the product. Draw a quick picture.

1. 4 × 50 = _____

2. 7 × 30 = _____

3. _____ = 9 × 20

4. 6 × 70 = _____

© Houghton Mifflin Harcourt Publishing Company

Name ______________________________

1. A bank makes rolls of 40 nickels. How many nickels would there be in 8 rolls?

Ⓐ 640

Ⓑ 320

Ⓒ 80

Ⓓ 64

2. Claire bought 6 bags of beads. There are 80 beads in each bag. How many beads did Claire buy?

Ⓐ 480

Ⓑ 460

Ⓒ 400

Ⓓ 380

3. Mr. Chandler planted 5 rows of bean seedlings. He planted 50 seedlings in each row. How many seedlings did Mr. Chandler plant?

Ⓐ 55

Ⓑ 200

Ⓒ 250

Ⓓ 350

4. Mei-Ling baked 6 batches of rice cakes. There were 30 rice cakes in each batch. How many rice cakes did she bake in all?

Ⓐ 36

Ⓑ 120

Ⓒ 150

Ⓓ 180

Problem Solving REAL WORLD

5. Each model car in a set costs $4. There are 30 different model cars in the set. How much would it cost to buy all the model cars in the set?

____

6. Amanda exercises for 50 minutes each day. How many minutes will she exercise in 7 days?

____

© Houghton Mifflin Harcourt Publishing Company

Name ______________________________

Lesson 55

COMMON CORE STANDARD CC.3.NF.1

Lesson Objective: Explore and identify equal parts of a whole.

Equal Parts of a Whole

When you divide a shape into **equal parts**, each part must be exactly the same size.

This rectangle is divided into **2** equal parts, or **halves**.

This rectangle is divided into **3** equal parts, or **thirds**.

This rectangle is divided into **4** equal parts, or **fourths**.

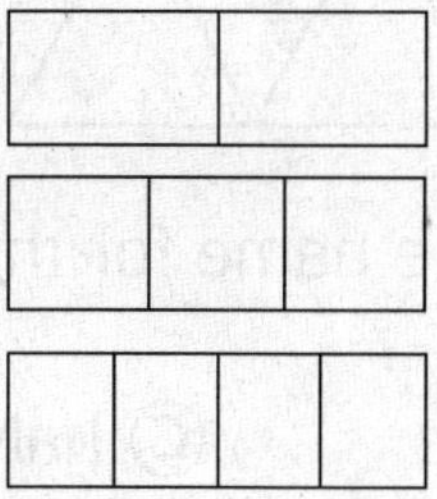

Write the number of equal parts. Then write the name for the parts.

1.

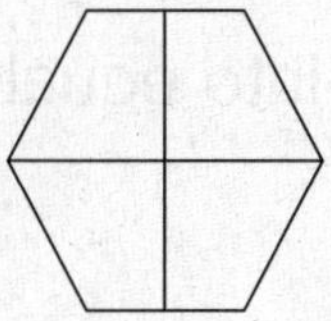

____ equal parts

____

2.

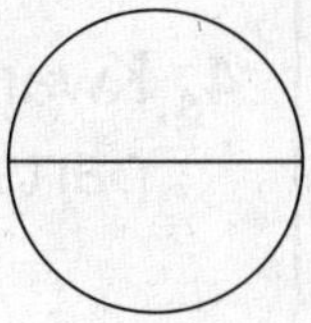

____ equal parts

____

3.

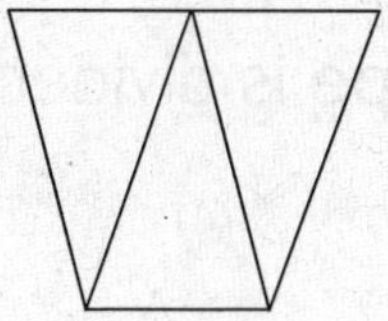

____ equal parts

____

Write whether each shape is divided into *equal* parts or *unequal* parts.

4.

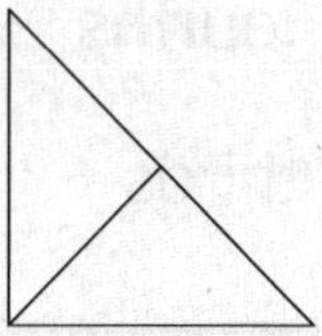

______________ parts

5.

______________ parts

6.

______________ parts

Draw lines to divide the squares into equal parts.

7. 3 thirds

8. 6 sixths

9. 8 eighths

© Houghton Mifflin Harcourt Publishing Company

Name ______________________________

Lesson 55
CC.3.NF.1

1. This shape is divided into equal parts.

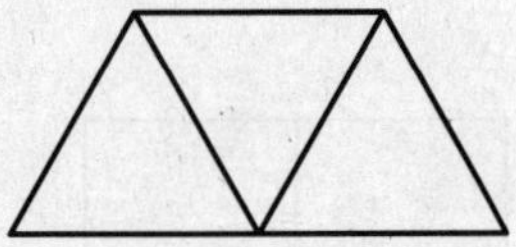

What is the name for the parts?

Ⓐ eighths
Ⓑ fourths
Ⓒ halves
Ⓓ thirds

2. This shape is divided into equal parts.

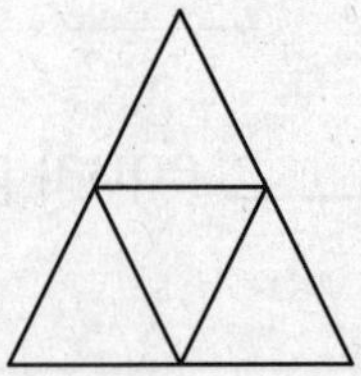

What is the number of equal parts?

Ⓐ 8
Ⓑ 4
Ⓒ 3
Ⓓ 2

3. Jamal folded a piece of cloth into equal parts.

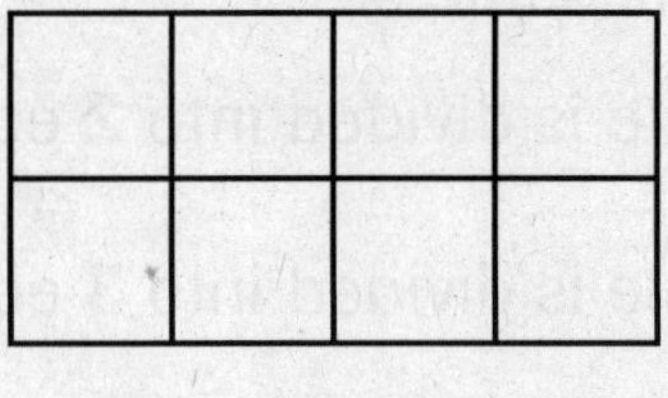

What is the name for the parts?

Ⓐ eighths
Ⓑ fourths
Ⓒ thirds
Ⓓ halves

4. Kwan folded a circle into equal parts.

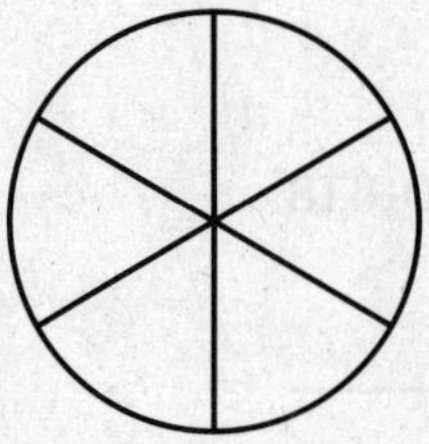

What is the name for the parts?

Ⓐ eighths
Ⓑ sixths
Ⓒ fourths
Ⓓ thirds

Problem Solving REAL WORLD

5. Diego cuts a round pizza into eight equal slices. What is the name for the parts?

____

6. Madison is making a place mat. She divides it into 6 equal parts to color. What is the name for the parts?

____

© Houghton Mifflin Harcourt Publishing Company

Name ______________________________

COMMON CORE STANDARD CC.3.NF.1

Lesson Objective: Divide models to make equal shares.

Equal Shares

Six brothers share 5 sandwiches equally. How much does each brother get? Draw to model the problem.

Step 1 Draw 5 squares for the sandwiches.

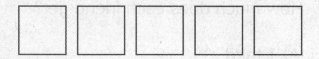

Step 2 There are 6 brothers. Draw lines to divide each sandwich into 6 equal parts.

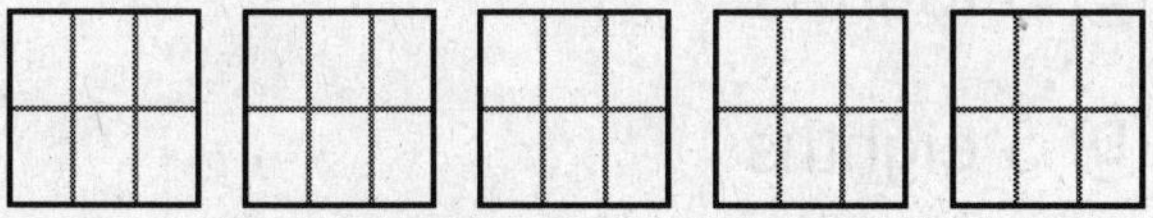

Step 3 Each brother will get 1 equal part from each sandwich.

So, each brother gets **5 sixths** of a sandwich.

Draw lines to show how much each person gets. Write the answer.

1. 4 sisters share 3 pies equally.

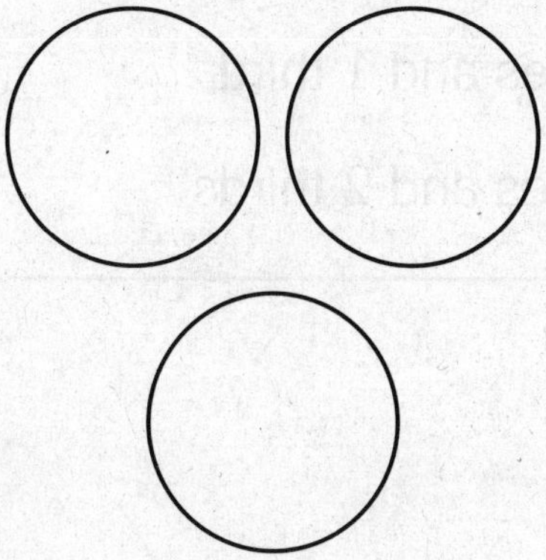

____

2. 6 friends share 3 fruit bars equally.

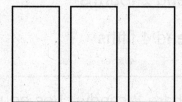

____

© Houghton Mifflin Harcourt Publishing Company

Name ____________________

1. Three friends share 6 graham crackers equally.

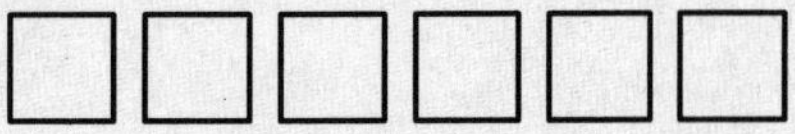

How much does each friend get?

Ⓐ 2 wholes

Ⓑ 2 wholes and 1 half

Ⓒ 3 wholes

Ⓓ 3 wholes and 1 half

2. Four brothers share 5 cookies equally.

How much does each brother get?

Ⓐ 1 whole and 1 fifth

Ⓑ 1 whole and 1 fourth

Ⓒ 1 whole and 2 fourths

Ⓓ 1 whole and 4 fifths

3. Four friends share 3 fruit bars equally.

How much does each friend get?

Ⓐ 1 third

Ⓑ 2 thirds

Ⓒ 3 fourths

Ⓓ 5 eighths

4. Three teachers share 7 brownies equally.

How much does each teacher get?

Ⓐ 1 whole and 1 third

Ⓑ 1 whole and 2 thirds

Ⓒ 2 wholes and 1 third

Ⓓ 2 wholes and 2 thirds

---

5. Two moms share 3 sandwiches equally.

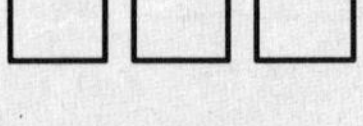

Shade the squares to show how much each mom gets.
Then write the answer.

____

____

© Houghton Mifflin Harcourt Publishing Company

Name ______________________________

Lesson 57

COMMON CORE STANDARD CC.3.NF.1

Lesson Objective: Use a fraction to name one part of a whole that is divided into equal parts.

Unit Fractions of a Whole

A **fraction** is a number. It names part of a whole or part of a group.

The top number tells how many equal parts are being counted.
The bottom number tells how many equal parts are in the whole.
A **unit fraction** names 1 equal part of a whole. It always has 1 as its top number.

How much is 1 part of a fruit bar that is cut into 8 equal parts?

Step 1 Use fraction strips. Make a strip showing 8 equal parts, or eighths.

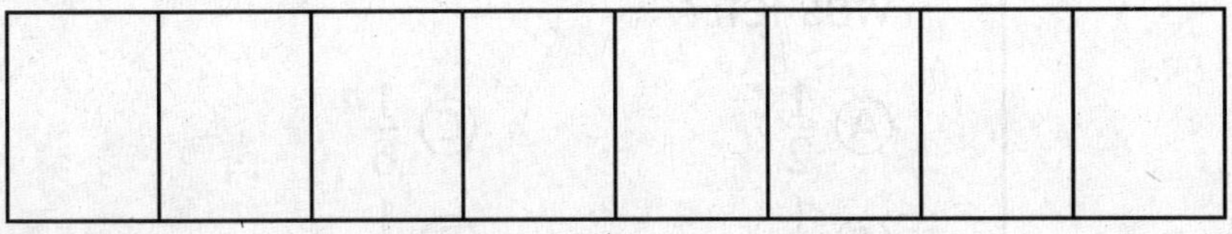

Step 2 Shade 1 of the parts and name it.

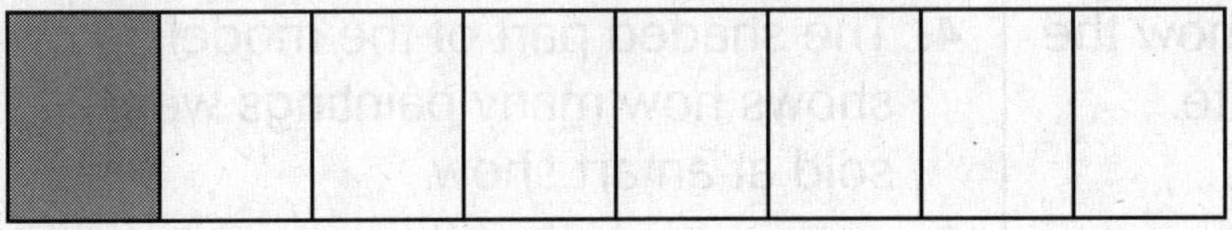

This fraction is called $\frac{1}{8}$.

So, 1 part of a fruit bar that can be divided into 8 equal parts is $\frac{1}{8}$.

**Write the number of equal parts in the whole.
Then write the fraction that names the shaded part.**

1. 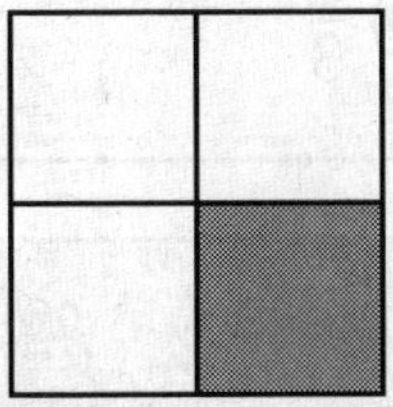

_____ equal parts

_____

2. 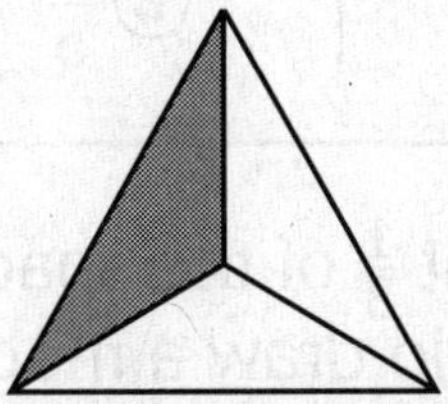

_____ equal parts

_____

3. 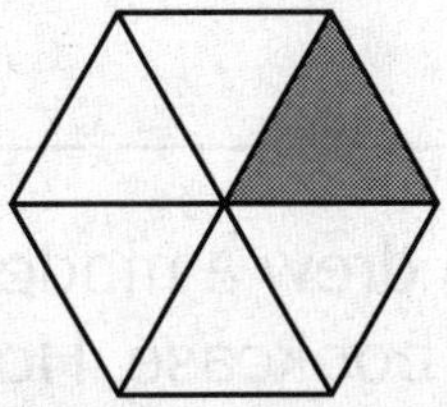

_____ equal parts

_____

© Houghton Mifflin Harcourt Publishing Company

Name ______________________________

Lesson 57
CC.3.NF.1

1. The shaded part of the model shows how much cornbread was left after dinner.

What fraction of the cornbread was left?

Ⓐ $\frac{1}{3}$ Ⓒ $\frac{1}{6}$

Ⓑ $\frac{1}{4}$ Ⓓ $\frac{1}{8}$

2. Riley shaded a model to show the amount of sandwich she ate.

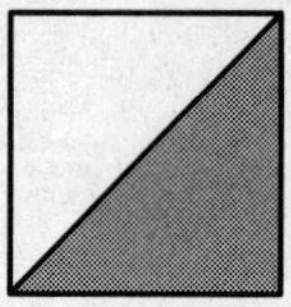

What fraction of the sandwich did Riley eat?

Ⓐ $\frac{1}{4}$ Ⓒ $\frac{1}{2}$

Ⓑ $\frac{1}{3}$ Ⓓ $\frac{1}{1}$

3. Kareena made potato salad. She shaded a model to show how much salad was left.

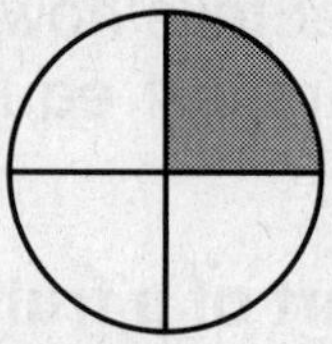

What fraction of the potato salad was left?

Ⓐ $\frac{1}{2}$ Ⓒ $\frac{1}{6}$

Ⓑ $\frac{1}{4}$ Ⓓ $\frac{1}{8}$

4. The shaded part of the model shows how many paintings were sold at an art show.

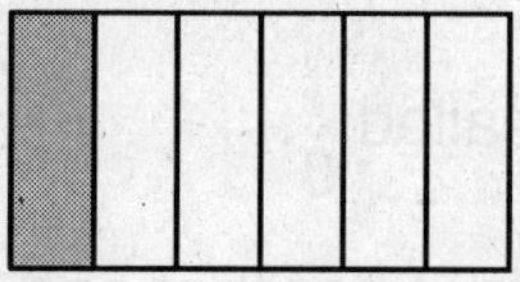

What fraction of the paintings were sold?

Ⓐ $\frac{1}{6}$ Ⓒ $\frac{1}{4}$

Ⓑ $\frac{1}{5}$ Ⓓ $\frac{1}{3}$

5. Mario drew a model to represent $\frac{1}{3}$ of the space in his bookcase. How could Mario draw a model to represent all the space in his bookcase?

____

____

____

© Houghton Mifflin Harcourt Publishing Company

Name ________________________________

Lesson 58

COMMON CORE STANDARD CC.3.NF.1

Lesson Objective: Read, write, and model fractions that represent more than one part of a whole that is divided into equal parts.

Fractions of a Whole

Some shapes can be cut into equal parts.
A fraction can name more than 1 equal part of a whole.

Write a fraction in words and in numbers to name the shaded part.

How many equal parts make up the whole shape? **6 equal parts**

How many parts are shaded? **3 parts**

So, 3 parts out of 6 equal parts are shaded. Read: **three sixths**. Write: $\frac{3}{6}$.

1. Shade three parts out of eight equal parts. Write a fraction in words and in numbers to name the shaded part.

Read: ________ eighths

Write: ________

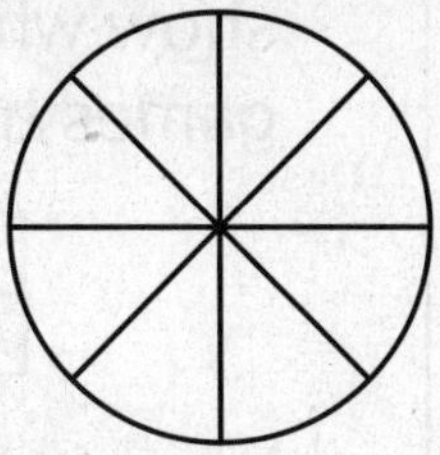

Write the fraction that names each part. Write a fraction in words and in numbers to name the shaded part.

2.

Each part is ________.

________ sixths

____

3.

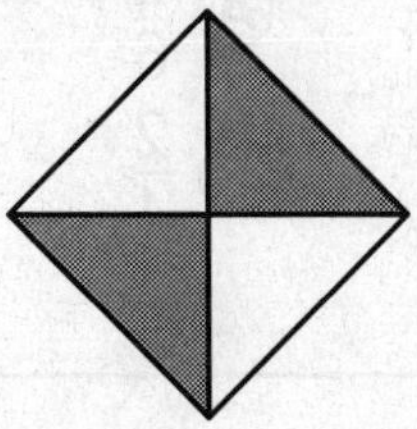

Each part is ________.

________ fourths

____

4.

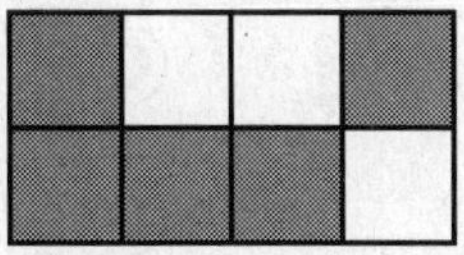

Each part is ________.

________ eighths

____

© Houghton Mifflin Harcourt Publishing Company

Name ______________________________

1. What fraction names the shaded part of the page?

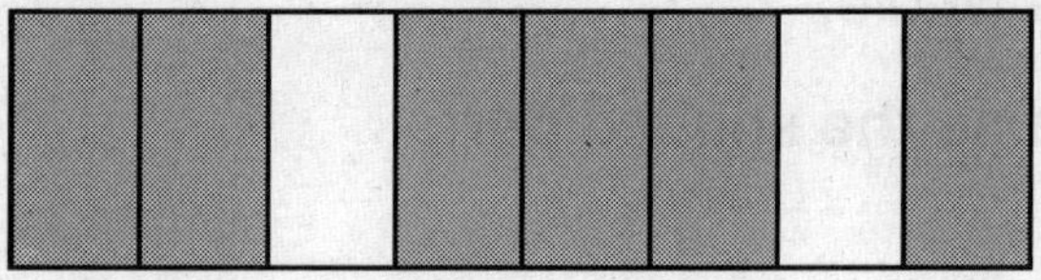

Ⓐ eight sixths

Ⓑ eight eighths

Ⓒ six eighths

Ⓓ two sixths

2. Lilly shaded this model to show what part of all the books she read are fiction.

What fraction of the books Lilly read are fiction?

Ⓐ $\frac{3}{3}$ Ⓒ $\frac{3}{4}$

Ⓑ $\frac{5}{6}$ Ⓓ $\frac{3}{6}$

3. What fraction names the shaded part of the shape?

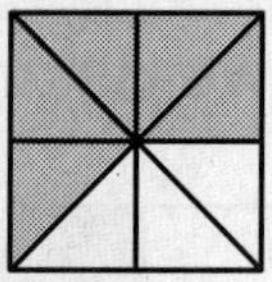

Ⓐ three eighths

Ⓑ five eighths

Ⓒ six eighths

Ⓓ eight eighths

4. Bailey shaded this model to show what part of all the baseball games his team won last season.

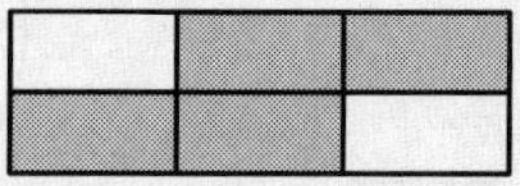

What fraction of the games did Bailey's team win?

Ⓐ $\frac{2}{6}$ Ⓒ $\frac{4}{6}$

Ⓑ $\frac{2}{4}$ Ⓓ $\frac{6}{4}$

5. Ashleigh shaded a model to show what part of the bracelets she made are blue. Explain how the model can be used to describe what part of the bracelets Ashleigh made are not blue.

____

____

____

© Houghton Mifflin Harcourt Publishing Company

Name ______________________________

Lesson 59

COMMON CORE STANDARD CC.3.NF.1

Lesson Objective: Model, read, and write fractional parts of a group.

Fractions of a Group

Adam has a collection of cars.

What fraction names the shaded part of the collection?

Step 1 Count how many cars are shaded. There are **3** shaded cars. This number will be the **numerator**, or the top number of the fraction.

Step 2 Count the total number of cars. **8** This number will be the **denominator**, or the bottom number of the fraction.

Step 3 Read the fraction: three eighths, or three out of eight.

So, $\frac{3}{8}$ of Adam's cars are shaded.

Write a fraction to name the shaded part of each group.

1.

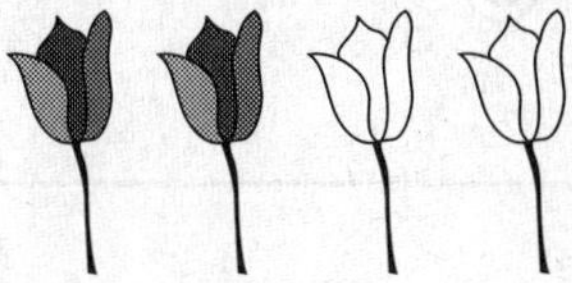

____

2.

____

Write a whole number and a fraction greater than 1 to name the part filled.

3.

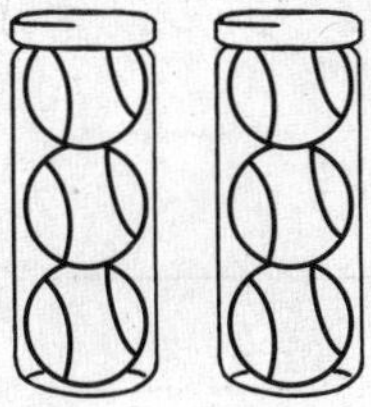

Think: 1 can = 1

__________ __________

4.

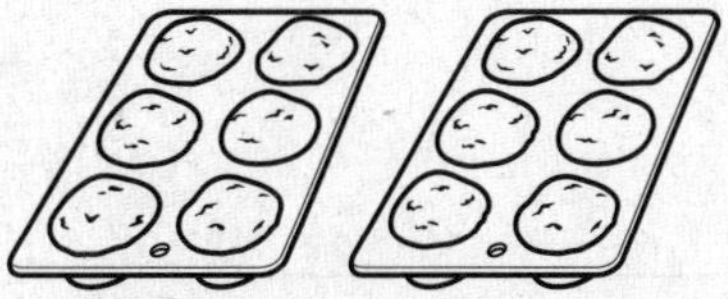

Think: 1 pan = 1

__________ __________

© Houghton Mifflin Harcourt Publishing Company

1. There are 8 rows of chairs in the auditorium. Three of the rows are empty. What fraction of the rows of chairs are empty?

   (A) $\frac{5}{8}$ (C) $\frac{3}{8}$

   (B) $\frac{4}{8}$ (D) $\frac{1}{8}$

2. Greyson has 3 baseballs. He brings 2 baseballs to school. What fraction of his baseballs does Greyson bring to school?

   (A) $\frac{1}{3}$ (C) $\frac{2}{3}$

   (B) $\frac{1}{2}$ (D) $\frac{3}{2}$

3. David sold 6 apple trees. He sold 5 of the apple trees to Max. What fraction of the apple trees did David sell to Max?

   (A) $\frac{1}{6}$ (C) $\frac{5}{6}$

   (B) $\frac{3}{16}$ (D) $\frac{6}{5}$

4. Maria has 8 tulip bulbs. She gives 3 of the tulip bulbs to her neighbor. What fraction of her tulip bulbs does Maria give to her neighbor?

   (A) $\frac{3}{8}$ (C) $\frac{3}{5}$

   (B) $\frac{5}{8}$ (D) $\frac{8}{3}$

Problem Solving REAL WORLD

5. Brian has 3 basketball cards and 5 baseball cards. What fraction of Brian's cards are baseball cards?

   ____

6. Sophia has 3 pink tulips and 3 white tulips. What fraction of Sophia's tulips are pink?

   ____

© Houghton Mifflin Harcourt Publishing Company

Name ______________________________

Lesson 60

COMMON CORE STANDARD CC.3.NF.1

Lesson Objective: Find fractional parts of a group using unit fractions.

Find Part of a Group Using Unit Fractions

Lauren bought 12 stamps for postcards. She gave Brianna $\frac{1}{6}$ of them. How many stamps did Lauren give to Brianna?

Step 1 Find the total number of stamps. **12** stamps

Step 2 Since you want to find $\frac{1}{6}$ of the group, there should be **6** equal groups. Circle one of the groups to show $\frac{1}{6}$.

Step 3 Find $\frac{1}{6}$ of the stamps. How many stamps are in 1 group? **2** stamps

So, Lauren gave Brianna 2 stamps. $\frac{1}{6}$ of 12 = **2**

Circle equal groups to solve. Count the number of shapes in 1 group.

1. $\frac{1}{4}$ of 8 = __________

2. $\frac{1}{3}$ of 9 = __________

3. $\frac{1}{4}$ of 16 = __________

4. $\frac{1}{6}$ of 18 = __________

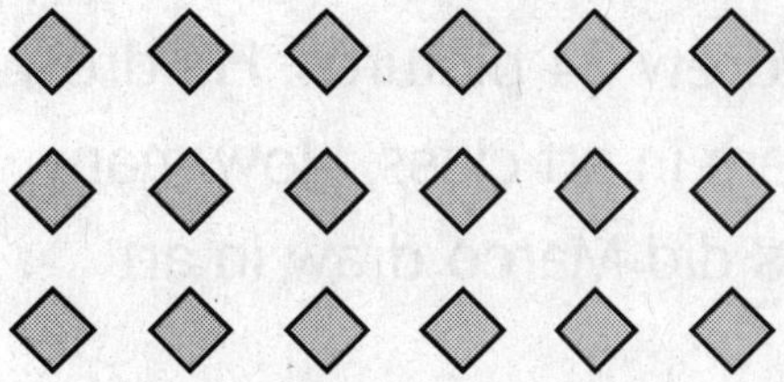

© Houghton Mifflin Harcourt Publishing Company

1. Charlotte bought 16 songs. One fourth of the songs are pop songs.

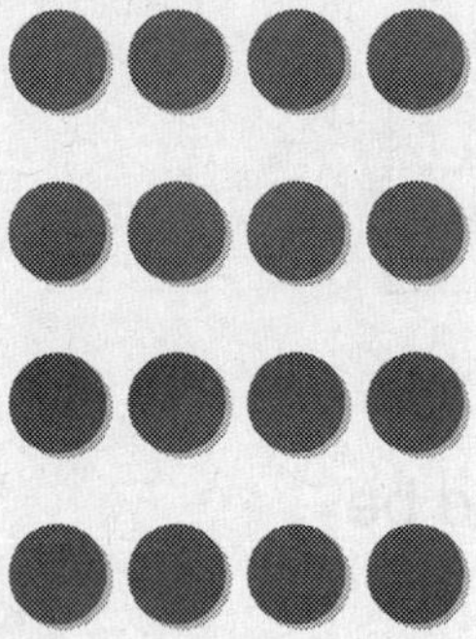

How many of the songs are pop songs?

Ⓐ 16 Ⓒ 4
Ⓑ 12 Ⓓ 1

2. Sophie uses 18 beads to make a necklace. One sixth of the beads are purple. How many of the beads are purple?

Ⓐ 1 Ⓒ 6
Ⓑ 3 Ⓓ 18

3. Mr. Walton ordered 12 pizzas for the art class celebration. One fourth of the pizzas had only mushrooms.

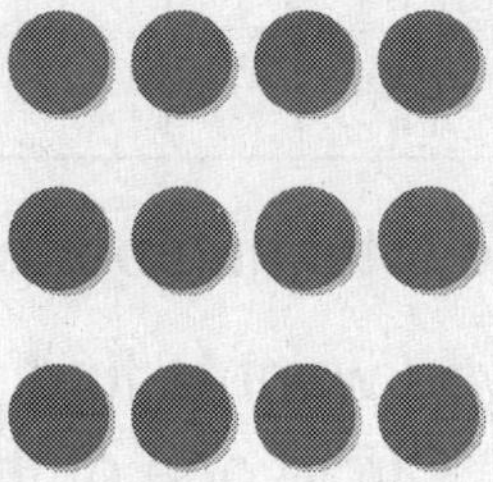

How many of the pizzas had only mushrooms?

Ⓐ 1 Ⓒ 4
Ⓑ 3 Ⓓ 9

4. Caleb took 24 photos at the zoo. One eighth of his photos are of giraffes. How many of Caleb's photos are of giraffes?

Ⓐ 1 Ⓒ 8
Ⓑ 3 Ⓓ 24

Problem Solving REAL WORLD

5. Marco drew 24 pictures. He drew $\frac{1}{6}$ of them in art class. How many pictures did Marco draw in art class?

____

6. Caroline has 16 marbles. One eighth of them are blue. How many of Caroline's marbles are blue?

____

© Houghton Mifflin Harcourt Publishing Company

Name ______________________________

Lesson 61

COMMON CORE STANDARD CC.3.NF.1

Lesson Objective: Solve fraction problems by using the strategy *draw a diagram.*

Problem Solving • Find the Whole Group Using Unit Fractions

There are 3 apple juice boxes in the cooler. One fourth of the juice boxes in the cooler are apple juice. How many juice boxes are in the cooler?

Read the Problem	Solve the Problem
What do I need to find? I need to find <u>how many juice boxes</u> are in the cooler.	**Describe how to draw a diagram to solve.** The denominator in $\frac{1}{4}$ tells you that there are <u>4</u> parts in the whole group. Draw 4 circles to show <u>4</u> parts. Since 3 juice boxes are $\frac{1}{4}$ of the group, draw <u>3</u> counters in the first circle. Since there are <u>3</u> counters in the first circle, draw <u>3</u> counters in each of the remaining circles. Then count all of the counters. 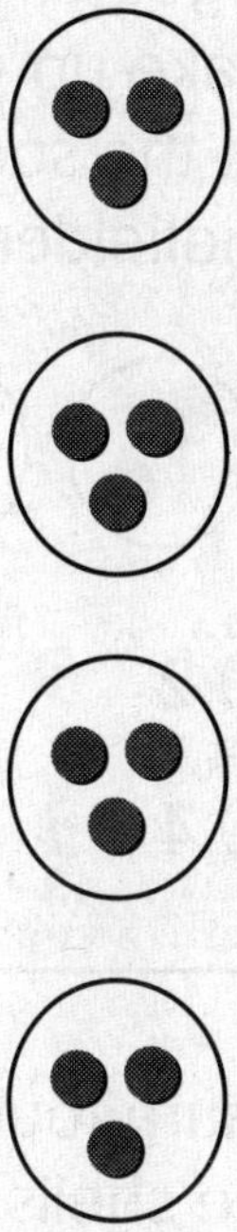 So, there are <u>12</u> juice boxes in the cooler.
What information do I need to use? There are <u>3</u> apple juice boxes. <u>One fourth</u> of the juice boxes are apple juice.	
How will I use the information? I will use the information in the problem to draw a diagram.	

1. Max has 3 beta fish in his fish tank. One half of his fish are beta fish. How many fish does Max have in his tank?

____

2. Two boys are standing in line. One sixth of the students in line are boys. How many students are standing in line?

____

© Houghton Mifflin Harcourt Publishing Company

1. Samuel brought 2 autographed baseballs for show and tell. They are $\frac{1}{6}$ of his whole collection. How many autographed baseballs are in Samuel's whole collection?

Ⓐ 3 Ⓒ 12

Ⓑ 4 Ⓓ 13

2. Together, Dillon and Leon make up $\frac{1}{4}$ of the midfielders on the soccer team. How many midfielders are on the team?

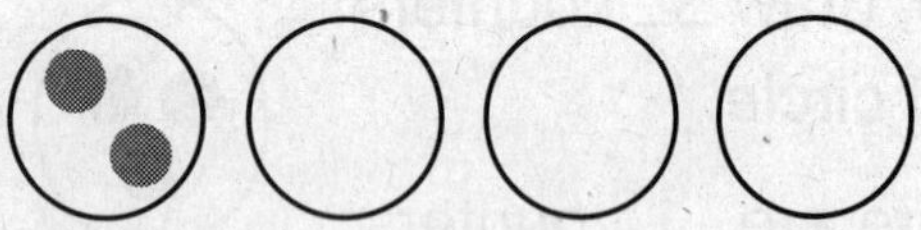

Ⓐ 2 Ⓒ 6

Ⓑ 4 Ⓓ 8

3. Ben has 12 model cars in his room. These cars represent $\frac{1}{2}$ of the model cars in Ben's whole collection. How many model cars does Ben have in his whole collection?

Ⓐ 24 Ⓒ 15

Ⓑ 18 Ⓓ 6

4. A garden has 2 yellow rose plants. These rose plants represent $\frac{1}{8}$ of the plants in the entire garden. How many plants are in the entire garden?

Ⓐ 4 Ⓒ 10

Ⓑ 6 Ⓓ 16

5. Laura found 5 shells on a trip to the beach. These shells represent $\frac{1}{3}$ of the shells in her whole collection. How many shells does Laura have in her whole collection? Draw a diagram to find the answer.

© Houghton Mifflin Harcourt Publishing Company

Name ________________________________

Lesson 62

COMMON CORE STANDARDS
CC.3.NF.2a, CC.3.NF.2b

Lesson Objective: Represent and locate fractions on a number line.

Fractions on a Number Line

Use the fraction strips to help name the points on the number line.

Draw a point to show $\frac{1}{3}$.

Step 1 The denominator is 3, so use fraction strips for **thirds**. Place the fraction strips above the number line. Use the fraction strips to divide the number line into three equal lengths.

Step 2 Label each mark on the number line.
Think: The distance between each mark is $\frac{1}{3}$ of the total distance, so count the number of $\frac{1}{3}$ lengths.

Step 3 Draw a point on the number line to show $\frac{1}{3}$.

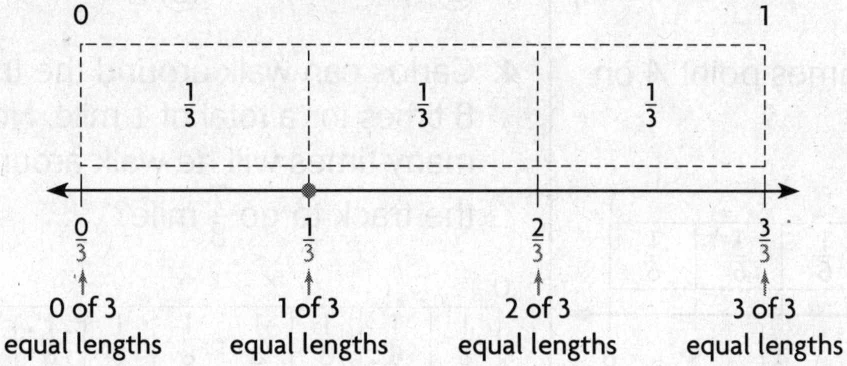

1. Complete the number line. Draw a point to show $\frac{2}{4}$.

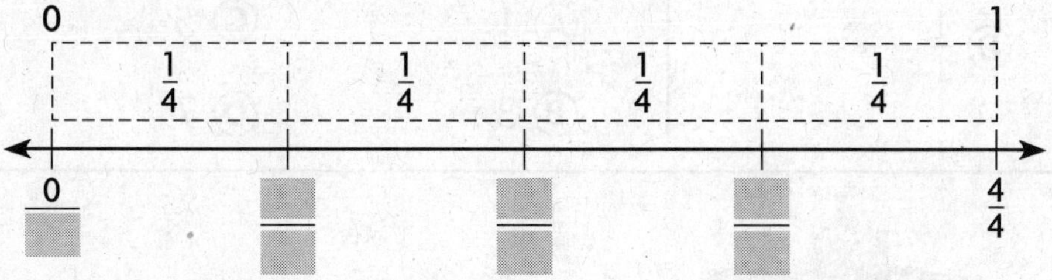

Write the fraction that names the point.

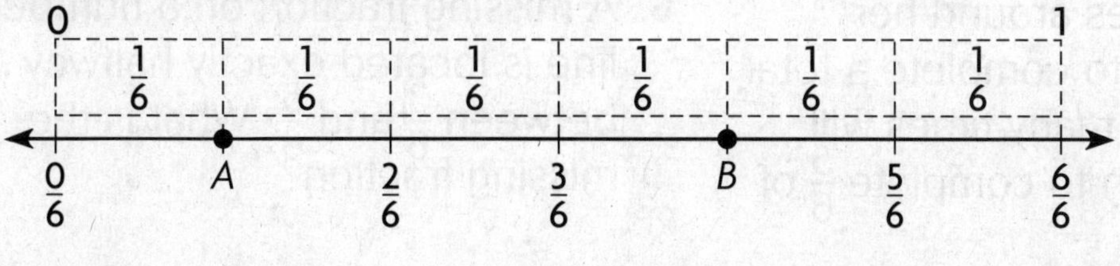

2. point *A* ________

3. point *B* ________

© Houghton Mifflin Harcourt Publishing Company

Name ____________________

Lesson 62
CC.3.NF.2a, CC.3.NF.2b

1. Which fraction names point *A* on the number line?

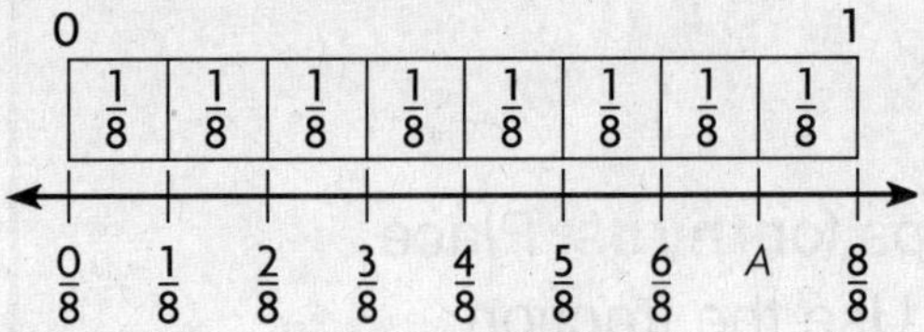

Ⓐ $\frac{1}{8}$ Ⓒ $\frac{7}{8}$

Ⓑ $\frac{6}{8}$ Ⓓ $\frac{8}{8}$

2. Which fraction names point *A* on the number line?

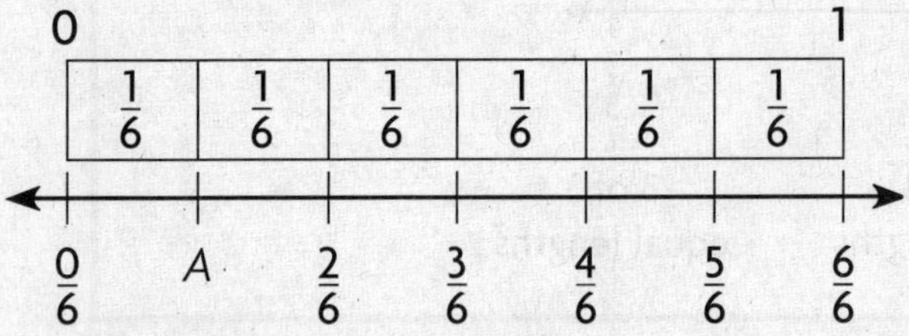

Ⓐ $\frac{1}{6}$ Ⓒ $\frac{3}{6}$

Ⓑ $\frac{2}{6}$ Ⓓ $\frac{1}{1}$

3. Lucy can ride her bike around the block 4 times for a total of 1 mile. How many times will she ride around the block to go $\frac{3}{4}$ mile?

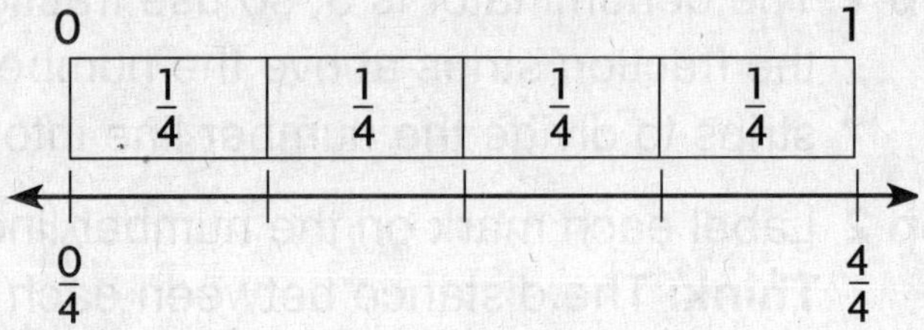

Ⓐ 2 Ⓒ 6

Ⓑ 3 Ⓓ 8

4. Carlos can walk around the track 8 times for a total of 1 mile. How many times will he walk around the track to go $\frac{7}{8}$ mile?

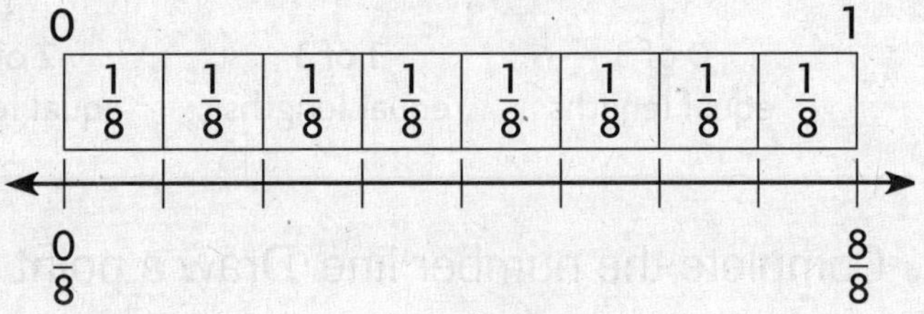

Ⓐ 1 Ⓒ 5

Ⓑ 3 Ⓓ 7

Problem Solving REAL WORLD

5. Jade ran 6 times around her neighborhood to complete a total of 1 mile. How many times will she need to run to complete $\frac{5}{6}$ of a mile?

____

6. A missing fraction on a number line is located exactly halfway between $\frac{3}{6}$ and $\frac{5}{6}$. What is the missing fraction?

____

© Houghton Mifflin Harcourt Publishing Company

Name ______________________________

Lesson 63

COMMON CORE STANDARD CC.3.NF.3a

Lesson Objective: Model equivalent fractions by folding paper, using area models, and using number lines.

Model Equivalent Fractions

Equivalent fractions are two or more fractions that name the same amount.

You can use fraction circles to model equivalent fractions.

Find a fraction that is equivalent to $\frac{1}{2}$. $\frac{1}{2} = \frac{\blacksquare}{4}$

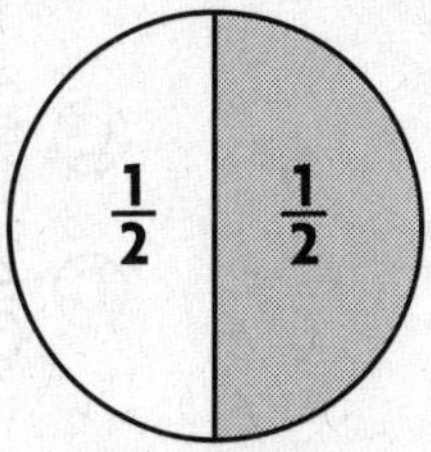

Step 1 Look at the first circle. It is divided into 2 equal parts. Shade one part to show $\frac{1}{2}$.

Step 2 Draw a line to divide the circle into 4 equal parts because 4 is the denominator in the second fraction.

Step 3 Count the number of parts shaded now. There are 2 parts out of 4 parts shaded.

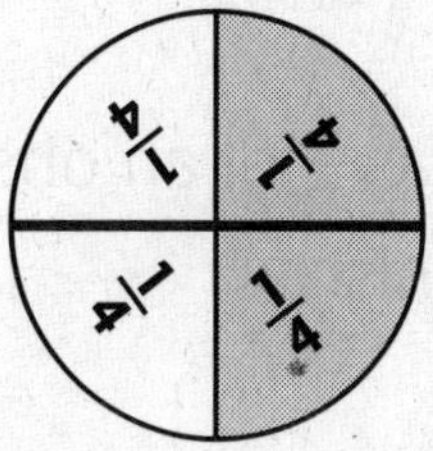

$\frac{1}{2} = \frac{2}{4}$ So, $\frac{1}{2}$ is equivalent to $\frac{2}{4}$.

Shade the model. Then divide the pieces to find the equivalent fraction.

1.

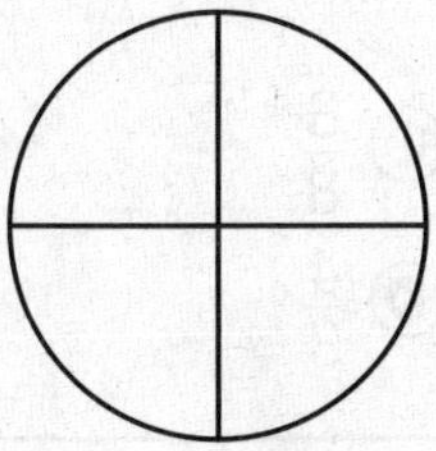

$\frac{1}{4} = \frac{\blacksquare}{8}$

2.

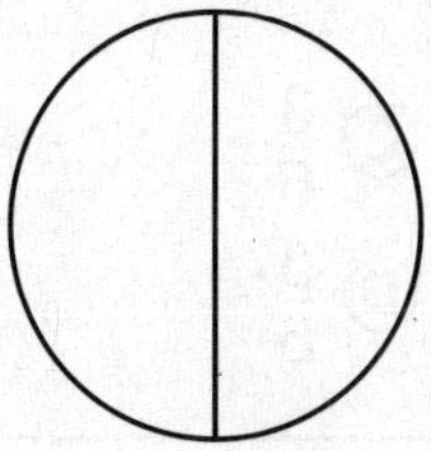

$\frac{1}{2} = \frac{\blacksquare}{8}$

3.

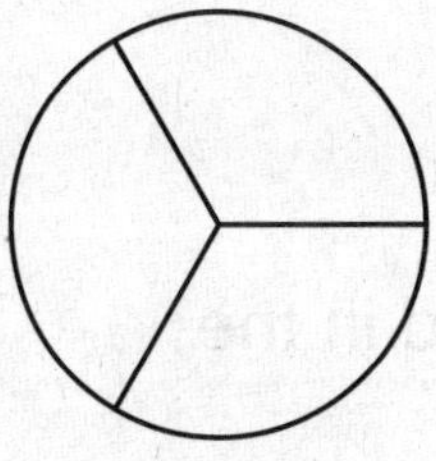

$\frac{2}{3} = \frac{\blacksquare}{6}$

4.

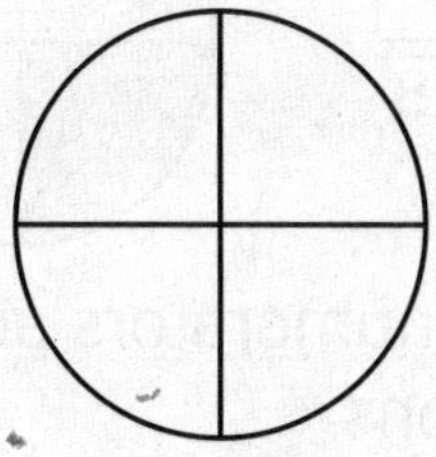

$\frac{3}{4} = \frac{\blacksquare}{8}$

© Houghton Mifflin Harcourt Publishing Company

Name ______________________________

Lesson 63
CC.3.NF.3a

1. Brenda paints $\frac{1}{2}$ of a wall green.

Which fraction is equivalent to $\frac{1}{2}$?

Ⓐ $\frac{4}{8}$ Ⓒ $\frac{2}{1}$

Ⓑ $\frac{1}{6}$ Ⓓ $\frac{2}{6}$

2. Maria has $\frac{1}{2}$ of an obstacle course left to finish.

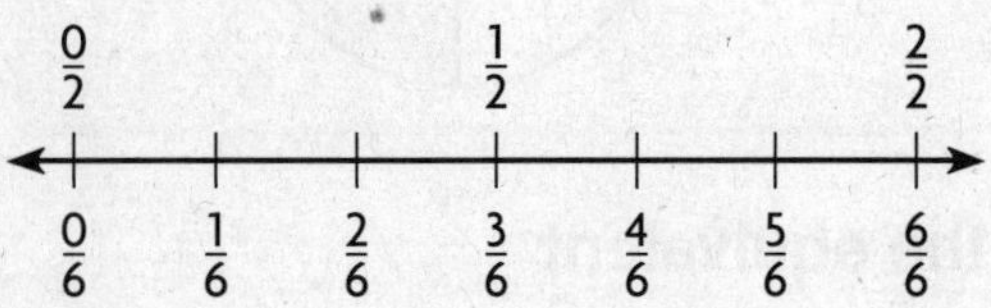

Which fraction is equivalent to $\frac{1}{2}$?

Ⓐ $\frac{2}{1}$ Ⓒ $\frac{3}{6}$

Ⓑ $\frac{2}{6}$ Ⓓ $\frac{5}{6}$

3. Ming-Na has read $\frac{2}{3}$ of a book. Glenn has read the same amount of the book.

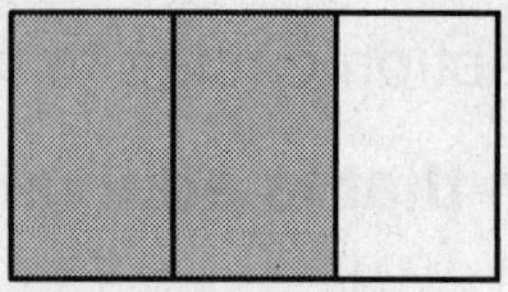

Which fraction is equivalent to $\frac{2}{3}$?

Ⓐ $\frac{1}{2}$ Ⓒ $\frac{3}{4}$

Ⓑ $\frac{5}{8}$ Ⓓ $\frac{4}{6}$

4. Mrs. Reid needs $\frac{3}{4}$ cup of brown sugar for a recipe.

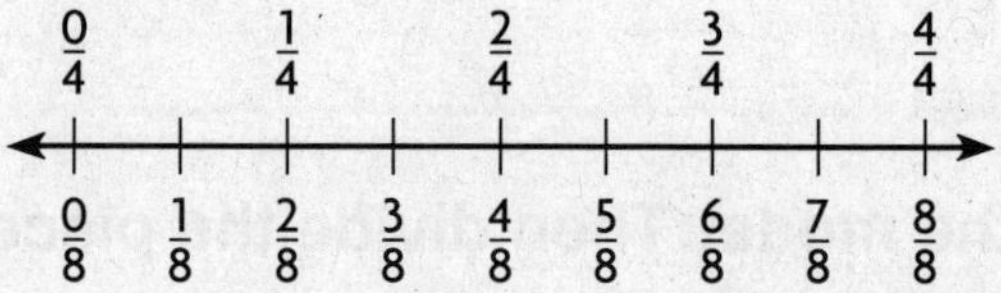

Which fraction is equivalent to $\frac{3}{4}$?

Ⓐ $\frac{7}{8}$ Ⓒ $\frac{3}{8}$

Ⓑ $\frac{6}{8}$ Ⓓ $\frac{4}{3}$

5. Use the fraction circles to complete the statement.

$\frac{1}{4} = \frac{\square}{8}$

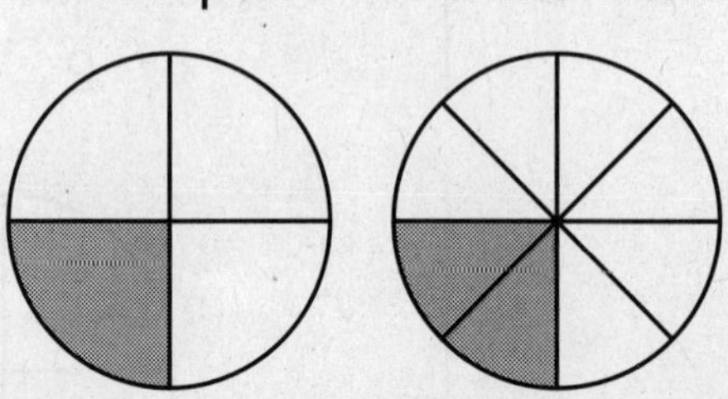

Explain how the numerators and denominators are related in the equivalent fractions.

____

____

© Houghton Mifflin Harcourt Publishing Company

Name ______________________________

Lesson 64

COMMON CORE STANDARD CC.3.NF.3b

Lesson Objective: Generate equivalent fractions by using models.

Equivalent Fractions

Kaitlyn used $\frac{3}{4}$ of a sheet of wrapping paper.

Find a fraction that is equivalent to $\frac{3}{4}$. $\frac{3}{4} = \frac{\square}{8}$

Step 1 The top fraction strip is divided into 4 equal parts. Shade $\frac{3}{4}$ of the strip to show how much paper Kaitlyn used.

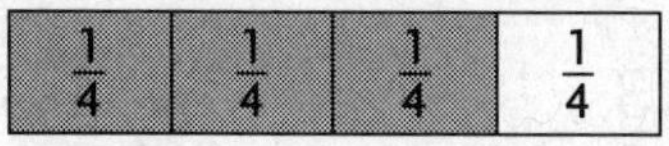

Step 2 The bottom strip is divided into 8 equal parts. Shade parts of the strip until the same amount is shaded as in the top strip.
6 parts of the bottom strip are shaded.

$\frac{3}{4} = \frac{6}{8}$

So, $\frac{6}{8}$ is equivalent to $\frac{3}{4}$.

Each shape is 1 whole. Shade the model to find the equivalent fraction.

1. 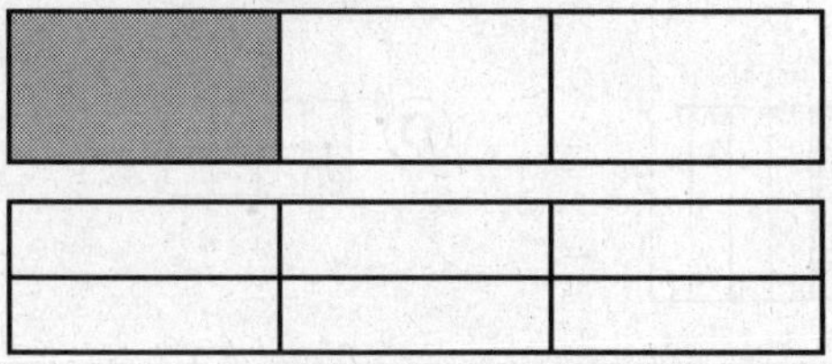

$\frac{1}{3} = \frac{\square}{6}$

2. 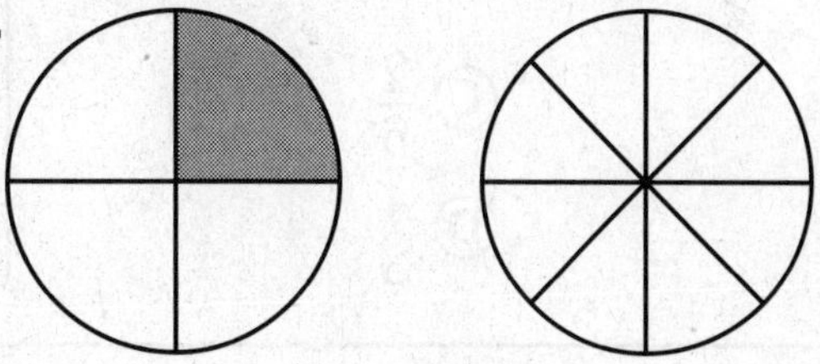

$\frac{1}{4} = \frac{\square}{8}$

3. 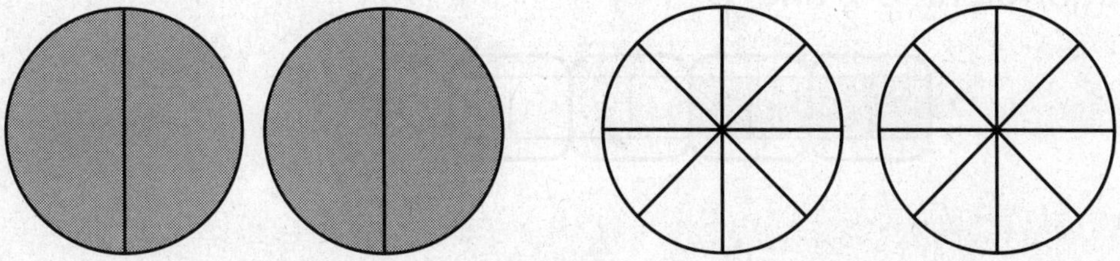

$\frac{4}{2} = \frac{\square}{8}$

© Houghton Mifflin Harcourt Publishing Company

Name ______________________________

Lesson 64
CC.3.NF.3b

1. Sam went for a ride on a sailboat. The ride lasted $\frac{3}{4}$ hour.

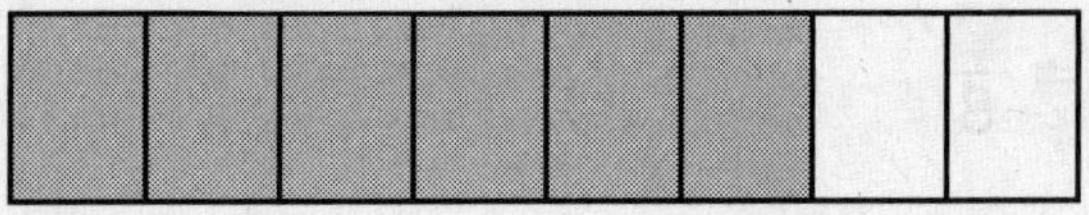

Which fraction is equivalent to $\frac{3}{4}$?

Ⓐ $\frac{3}{6}$
Ⓑ $\frac{4}{8}$
Ⓒ $\frac{3}{8}$
Ⓓ $\frac{6}{8}$

2. Tom rode his horse for $\frac{4}{6}$ mile. Liz rode her horse for an equal distance.

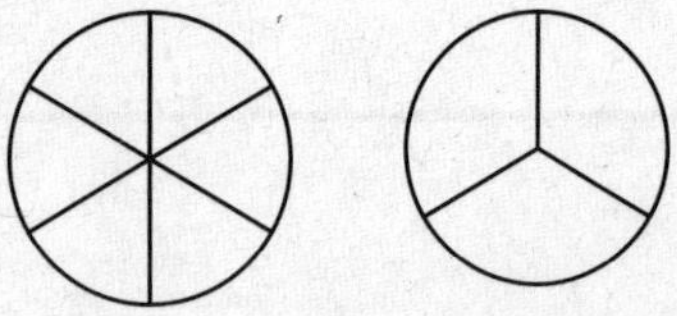

Which fraction is equivalent to $\frac{4}{6}$?

Ⓐ $\frac{1}{3}$
Ⓑ $\frac{2}{3}$
Ⓒ $\frac{2}{6}$
Ⓓ $\frac{4}{3}$

3. Pedro is doing his math homework. He has completed $\frac{8}{8}$ of the problems. Which fraction is equivalent to $\frac{8}{8}$?

Ⓐ $\frac{0}{8}$
Ⓑ $\frac{1}{8}$
Ⓒ $\frac{6}{6}$
Ⓓ $\frac{3}{6}$

4. Aaron is planting a vegetable garden. He made room in $\frac{1}{4}$ of his garden for beans. Which shape has a shaded part equivalent to $\frac{1}{4}$?

Ⓐ 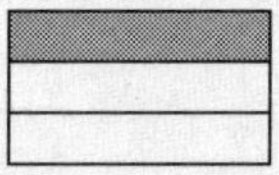
Ⓒ 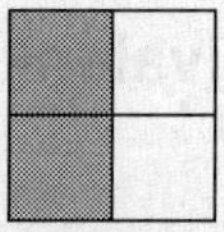
Ⓑ 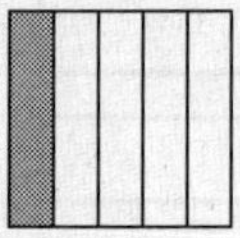
Ⓓ 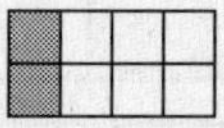

5. Danielle's model shows $\frac{1}{2} = \frac{2}{4}$. Describe a different way you could circle equal groups to show another equivalent fraction. Explain how you know your fraction is equivalent to $\frac{1}{2}$ and $\frac{2}{4}$.

____

____

____

© Houghton Mifflin Harcourt Publishing Company

Name ______________________________

Lesson 65

COMMON CORE STANDARD CC.3.NF.3c

Lesson Objective: Relate fractions and whole numbers by expressing whole numbers as fractions and recognizing fractions that are equivalent to whole numbers.

Relate Fractions and Whole Numbers

A **fraction greater than 1** has a numerator greater than its denominator.

Jason ran 2 miles and Tyra ran $\frac{6}{3}$ miles. Did Jason and Tyra run the same distance?

Step 1 Use fraction strips to show the distances.
Use 2 whole strips to show Jason's distance.
Use six $\frac{1}{3}$-strips to show Tyra's distance.

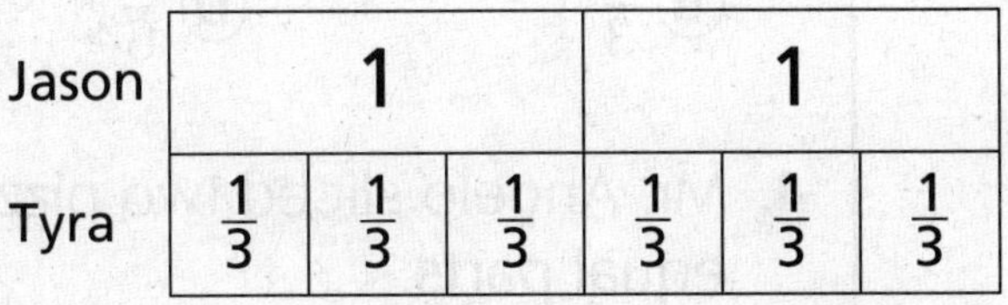

$1 = \frac{3}{3}$ $2 = \frac{6}{3}$

Step 2 Compare the fraction strips.
Since the fraction strips for 2 and $\frac{6}{3}$ are the same length, they are equal.

So, Jason and Tyra ran the same distance.

Use the number line to find whether the two numbers are equal. Write *equal* or *not equal*.

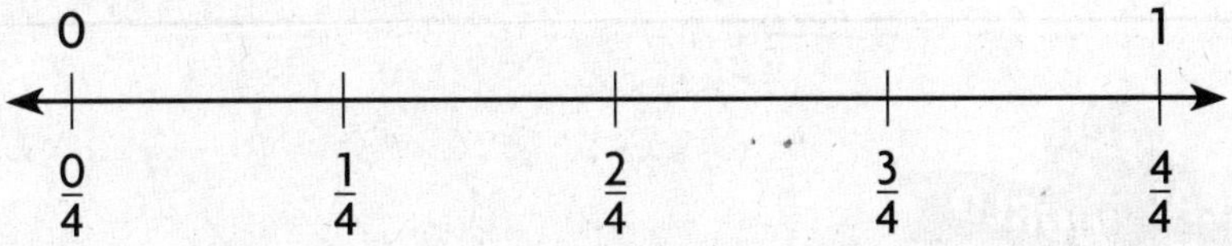

1. $\frac{4}{4}$ and 1 ____________

2. 1 and $\frac{3}{4}$ ____________

3. $\frac{1}{4}$ and $\frac{4}{4}$ ____________

© Houghton Mifflin Harcourt Publishing Company

Name ______________________________

Lesson 65
CC.3.NF.3c

1. Which numbers from the number line are equal?

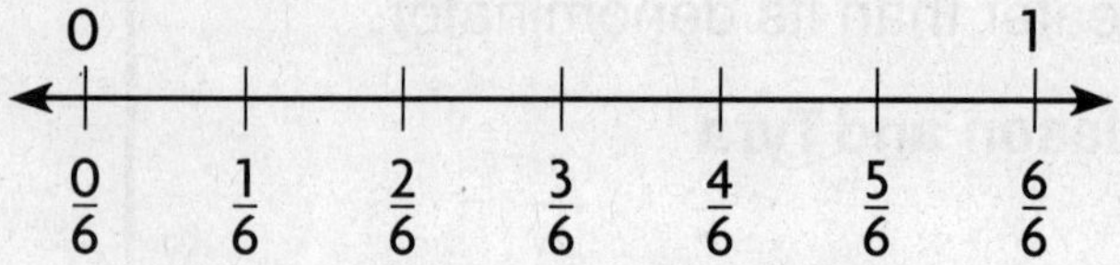

Ⓐ $\frac{6}{6}$ and 1
Ⓑ $\frac{3}{6}$ and $\frac{6}{6}$
Ⓒ $\frac{0}{6}$ and 1
Ⓓ $\frac{0}{6}$ and $\frac{6}{6}$

3. Emma colored some shapes. What fraction greater than 1 names the parts that she shaded?

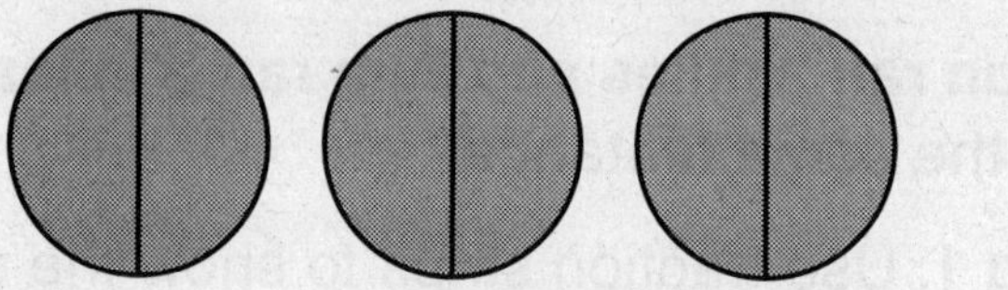

Ⓐ $\frac{6}{2}$
Ⓑ $\frac{6}{3}$
Ⓒ $\frac{2}{3}$
Ⓓ $\frac{2}{6}$

2. Cora cuts the apple pies into equal parts.

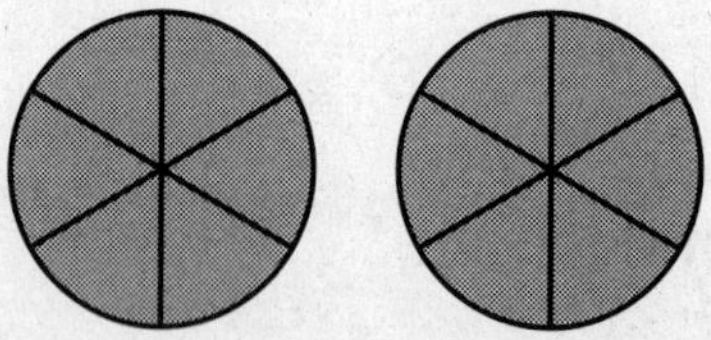

What fraction greater than 1 names both apple pies?

Ⓐ $\frac{2}{6}$
Ⓑ $\frac{6}{12}$
Ⓒ $\frac{6}{6}$
Ⓓ $\frac{12}{6}$

4. Mr. Angelo sliced two pizzas into equal parts.

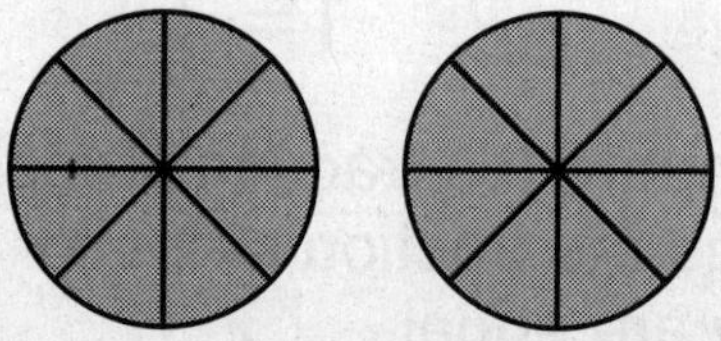

What fraction greater than 1 names both pizzas?

Ⓐ $\frac{2}{16}$
Ⓑ $\frac{8}{16}$
Ⓒ $\frac{16}{8}$
Ⓓ $\frac{16}{4}$

Problem Solving REAL WORLD

5. Rachel jogged along a trail that was $\frac{1}{4}$ of a mile long. She jogged along the trail 8 times. How many miles did Rachel jog in all?

____

6. Jon ran around a track that was $\frac{1}{8}$ of a mile long. He ran around the track 24 times. How many miles did Jon run in all?

____

© Houghton Mifflin Harcourt Publishing Company

Name ______________________________

Lesson 66

COMMON CORE STANDARD CC.3.NF.3d

Lesson Objective: Solve comparison problems by using the strategy *act it out.*

Problem Solving • Compare Fractions

Nick walked $\frac{2}{4}$ mile to the gym. Then he walked $\frac{3}{4}$ mile to the store. Which distance is shorter?

Read the Problem	**Solve the Problem**
What do I need to find? I need to find which distance is shorter. **What information do I need to use?** Nick walked $\frac{2}{4}$ mile to the gym. Then he walked $\frac{3}{4}$ mile to the store. **How will I use the information?** I will use fraction strips and compare the lengths of the models to find which distance is shorter.	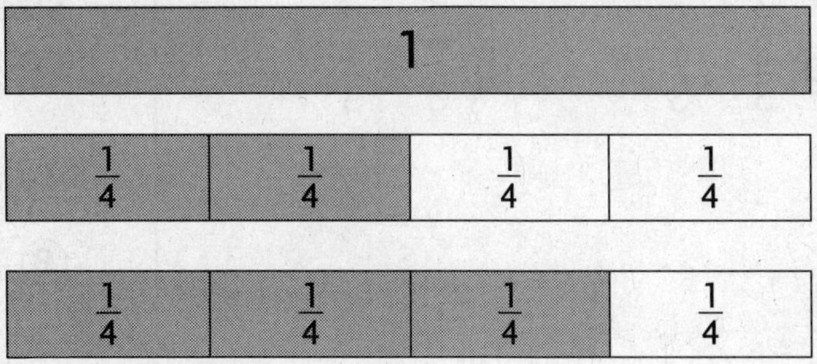 **Compare the lengths.** $\frac{2}{4} < \frac{3}{4}$ The length of the $\frac{2}{4}$ model is less than the length of the $\frac{3}{4}$ model. So, the distance to the gym is shorter.

1. Mariana and Shawn each had 6 pages to read. Mariana read $\frac{2}{3}$ of her pages. Shawn read $\frac{1}{3}$ of his pages. Who read more pages? **Explain.**

____

____

2. Carlos ran $\frac{3}{8}$ of the race course. Lori ran $\frac{3}{6}$ of the same race course. Who ran farther? **Explain.**

____

____

____

© Houghton Mifflin Harcourt Publishing Company

Name ______________________________

Lesson 66

CC.3.NF.3d

1. Bill used $\frac{1}{3}$ cup of raisins and $\frac{2}{3}$ cup of banana chips to make a snack. Which statement correctly compares the fractions?

   Ⓐ $\frac{1}{3} > \frac{2}{3}$
   Ⓑ $\frac{2}{3} < \frac{1}{3}$
   Ⓒ $\frac{2}{3} > \frac{1}{3}$
   Ⓓ $\frac{2}{3} = \frac{1}{3}$

2. Mavis mixed $\frac{1}{4}$ quart of red paint with $\frac{3}{4}$ quart of yellow paint to make orange paint. Which of the following statements is **true**?

   Ⓐ Mavis used less yellow paint than red paint.
   Ⓑ Mavis used more red paint than yellow paint.
   Ⓒ Mavis used equal amounts of red and yellow paint.
   Ⓓ Mavis used more yellow paint than red paint.

3. Carlos found that $\frac{1}{2}$ of the apples in one basket are Granny Smith apples and $\frac{1}{6}$ of the apples in another basket are Granny Smith apples. The baskets are the same size. Which statement correctly compares the fractions?

   Ⓐ $\frac{1}{2} = \frac{1}{6}$
   Ⓑ $\frac{1}{2} < \frac{1}{6}$
   Ⓒ $\frac{1}{2} > \frac{1}{6}$
   Ⓓ $\frac{1}{6} > \frac{1}{2}$

4. Of the stars on the Monroe Elementary School flag, $\frac{2}{4}$ are gold and $\frac{2}{8}$ are black. Which statement correctly compares the fractions?

   Ⓐ $\frac{2}{8} > \frac{2}{4}$
   Ⓑ $\frac{2}{8} < \frac{2}{4}$
   Ⓒ $\frac{2}{4} = \frac{2}{8}$
   Ⓓ $\frac{2}{4} < \frac{2}{8}$

5. Tess ate $\frac{3}{8}$ of her granola bar. Gino ate $\frac{3}{4}$ of his granola bar. Both granola bars were the same size. Who ate more? Describe how you could use fraction strips to solve the problem.

____

____

____

© Houghton Mifflin Harcourt Publishing Company

Name ______________________________ **Lesson 67**

COMMON CORE STANDARD CC.3.NF.3d

Lesson Objective: Compare fractions with the same denominator by using models and reasoning strategies.

Compare Fractions with the Same Denominator

Pete's Prize Pizzas makes a special pizza. Of the toppings, $\frac{1}{4}$ is peppers and $\frac{3}{4}$ is ham. Does the pizza have more peppers or ham?

Compare $\frac{1}{4}$ and $\frac{3}{4}$.

Step 1 The denominators of both fractions are the same, **4**. Use fraction circles divided into fourths to model the fractions.

Step 2 Shade 1 part of the first circle to show $\frac{1}{4}$.

Shade **3** parts of the second circle to show $\frac{3}{4}$.

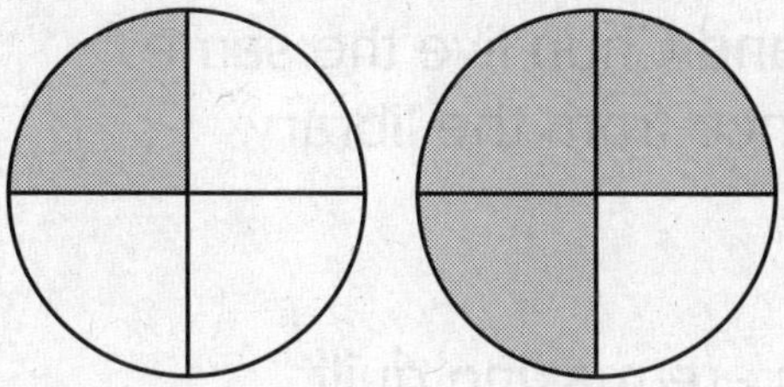

Step 3 Compare. **3** parts is more than **1** part.

$\frac{3}{4} > \frac{1}{4}$

So, the pizza has more **ham**.

Compare. Write <, >, or =.

1.

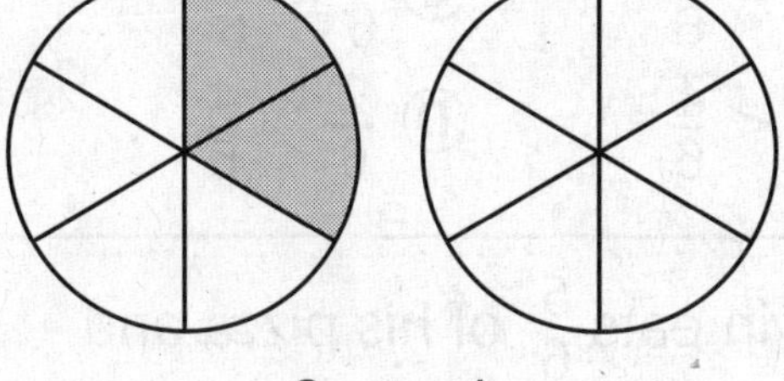

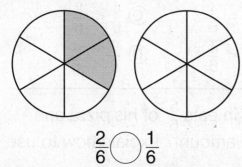

$\frac{2}{6}$ ◯ $\frac{1}{6}$

2.

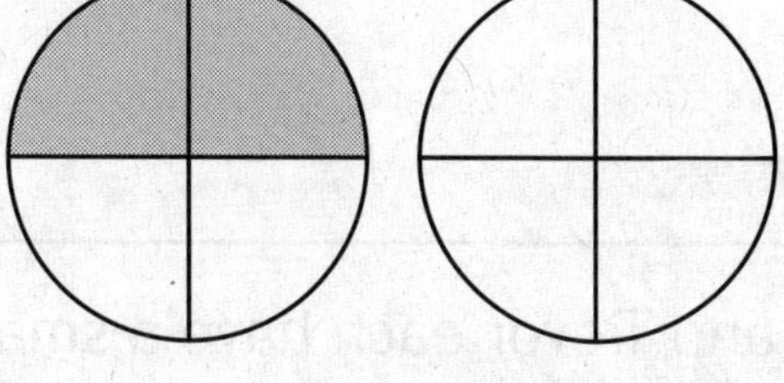

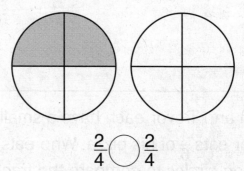

$\frac{2}{4}$ ◯ $\frac{2}{4}$

3. $\frac{1}{3}$ ◯ $\frac{2}{3}$

4. $\frac{5}{8}$ ◯ $\frac{3}{8}$

5. $\frac{1}{4}$ ◯ $\frac{3}{4}$

6. $\frac{4}{8}$ ◯ $\frac{4}{8}$

© Houghton Mifflin Harcourt Publishing Company

1. Dan and David are on the track team. Dan runs $\frac{1}{4}$ mile each day. David runs $\frac{3}{4}$ mile each day. Which statement is correct?

Ⓐ David runs farther than Dan each day.

Ⓑ David runs more than 1 mile each day.

Ⓒ David runs the same distance as Dan each day.

Ⓓ Dan runs farther than David each day.

2. Isabel and Raul are playing a game with fraction circles. Which statement is correct?

Ⓐ $\frac{1}{3} > \frac{2}{3}$

Ⓑ $\frac{2}{3} = \frac{1}{3}$

Ⓒ $\frac{2}{3} < \frac{1}{3}$

Ⓓ $\frac{2}{3} > \frac{1}{3}$

3. Chun lives $\frac{3}{8}$ mile from the library. Gail lives $\frac{5}{8}$ mile from the library. Which statement is correct?

Ⓐ Chun lives more than 1 mile from the library.

Ⓑ Chun lives farther from the library than Gail.

Ⓒ Gail lives farther from the library than Chun.

Ⓓ Gail and Chun live the same distance from the library.

4. Students are making quilt squares. They want $\frac{2}{6}$ of the quilt squares to be red and $\frac{4}{6}$ of the quilt squares to be white. Which statement correctly compares the fractions?

Ⓐ $\frac{2}{6} = \frac{4}{6}$

Ⓑ $\frac{2}{6} < \frac{4}{6}$

Ⓒ $\frac{4}{6} < \frac{2}{6}$

Ⓓ $\frac{2}{6} > \frac{4}{6}$

5. Kevin and Trevor each have a small pizza. Kevin eats $\frac{5}{6}$ of his pizza and Trevor eats $\frac{4}{6}$ of his pizza. Who eats the lesser amount? Explain how to use fraction circles to compare the fractions.

____

____

____

© Houghton Mifflin Harcourt Publishing Company

Name ______________________________

COMMON CORE STANDARD CC.3.NF.3d

Lesson Objective: Compare fractions with the same numerator by using models and reasoning strategies.

Compare Fractions with the Same Numerator

Ryan takes a survey of his class. $\frac{1}{8}$ of the class has dogs, and $\frac{1}{3}$ of the class has cats. Are there more dog owners or cat owners in Ryan's class?

Compare the fractions. $\frac{1}{8}$ ● $\frac{1}{3}$

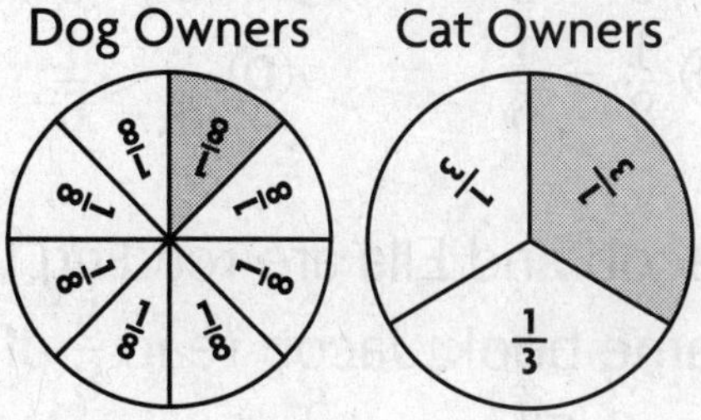

Step 1 Divide the first circle into 8 equal parts. Shade $\frac{1}{8}$ of the circle to show dog owners.

Step 2 Divide the second circle into 3 equal parts. Shade $\frac{1}{3}$ of the circle to show cat owners.

Step 3 Compare the shaded parts of the circles. Which shaded part is larger?

$\frac{1}{3}$ **is larger than** $\frac{1}{8}$. $\frac{1}{8} < \frac{1}{3}$

So, there are more **cat owners** than **dog owners** in Ryan's class.

Compare. Write <, >, or =.

1. $\frac{3}{4}$ ○ $\frac{3}{6}$
2. $\frac{1}{8}$ ○ $\frac{1}{6}$
3. $\frac{2}{4}$ ○ $\frac{2}{6}$
4. $\frac{2}{3}$ ○ $\frac{2}{6}$
5. $\frac{4}{6}$ ○ $\frac{4}{8}$
6. $\frac{2}{8}$ ○ $\frac{2}{4}$
7. $\frac{5}{6}$ ○ $\frac{5}{8}$
8. $\frac{1}{3}$ ○ $\frac{1}{4}$
9. $\frac{3}{6}$ ○ $\frac{3}{4}$
10. $\frac{1}{3}$ ○ $\frac{1}{3}$
11. $\frac{3}{3}$ ○ $\frac{3}{4}$
12. $\frac{2}{4}$ ○ $\frac{2}{6}$

© Houghton Mifflin Harcourt Publishing Company

Name ____________________

1. Jenna ate $\frac{1}{8}$ of one pizza. Mark ate $\frac{1}{6}$ of another pizza. The pizzas are the same size. Which statement correctly compares the amount of pizza that was eaten?

   (A) $\frac{1}{6} < \frac{1}{8}$
   (B) $\frac{1}{8} = \frac{1}{6}$
   (C) $\frac{1}{8} > \frac{1}{6}$
   (D) $\frac{1}{8} < \frac{1}{6}$

2. Jacob and Ella are reading the same book. Jacob read $\frac{5}{8}$ of the book. Ella read $\frac{5}{6}$ of the book. Which statement is correct?

   (A) Jacob read more of the book than Ella.
   (B) Ella read less of the book than Jacob.
   (C) Jacob read less of the book than Ella.
   (D) Ella and Jacob read the same amount of the book.

3. In a survey, $\frac{1}{3}$ of the students chose soccer as their favorite sport and $\frac{1}{4}$ chose basketball. Which statement correctly compares the fractions?

   (A) $\frac{1}{3} < \frac{1}{4}$
   (B) $\frac{1}{3} = \frac{1}{4}$
   (C) $\frac{1}{3} > \frac{1}{4}$
   (D) $\frac{1}{4} > \frac{1}{3}$

4. Maria put $\frac{3}{4}$ yard of fringe around the pillow she made. Nancy put $\frac{3}{8}$ yard of fringe around her pillow. Which statement correctly compares the fractions?

   (A) $\frac{3}{4} > \frac{3}{8}$
   (B) $\frac{3}{4} < \frac{3}{8}$
   (C) $\frac{3}{4} = \frac{3}{8}$
   (D) $\frac{3}{8} > \frac{3}{4}$

Problem Solving REAL WORLD

5. Javier is buying food in the lunch line. The tray of salad plates is $\frac{3}{8}$ full. The tray of fruit plates is $\frac{3}{4}$ full. Which tray is more full?

   ____

6. Rachel bought some buttons. Of the buttons, $\frac{2}{4}$ are yellow and $\frac{2}{8}$ are red. Rachel bought more of which color buttons?

   ____

© Houghton Mifflin Harcourt Publishing Company

Name ______________________________

Lesson 69

COMMON CORE STANDARD CC.3.NF.3d

Lesson Objective: Compare fractions by using models and strategies involving the size of the pieces in the whole.

Compare Fractions

Mrs. Brown's recipe uses $\frac{2}{3}$ cup of flour. Mrs. Young's recipe uses $\frac{3}{4}$ cup of flour. Which recipe uses more flour?

Compare $\frac{2}{3}$ and $\frac{3}{4}$.

- You can compare fractions using fraction strips.

Step 1 Model each fraction.

Step 2 Compare the lengths of the models. The length of the $\frac{3}{4}$ model is greater than the length of the $\frac{2}{3}$ model.

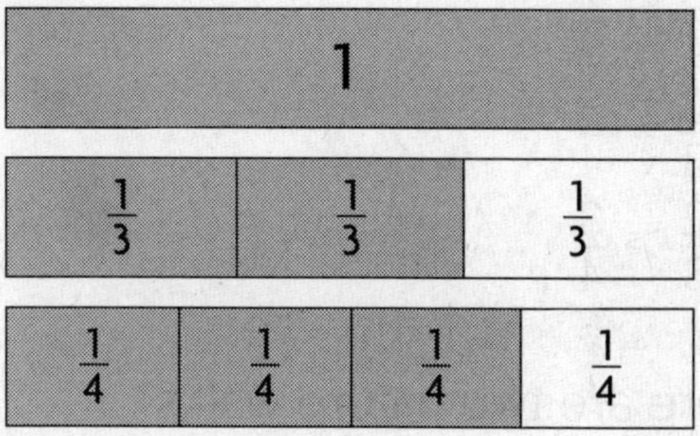

$\frac{3}{4}$ (>) $\frac{2}{3}$

So, Mrs. Young's recipe uses more flour.

Compare $\frac{3}{6}$ and $\frac{4}{6}$. Which is greater?

- The denominators are the same, so compare the numerators.

$3 < 4$, so $\frac{3}{6} < \frac{4}{6}$.

So, $\frac{4}{6}$ is greater than $\frac{3}{6}$. $\frac{4}{6}$ (>) $\frac{3}{6}$

Compare. Write $<$, $>$, or $=$. Write the strategy you used.

1. $\frac{2}{8}$ ◯ $\frac{3}{8}$

____

2. $\frac{7}{8}$ ◯ $\frac{5}{6}$

____

3. $\frac{3}{4}$ ◯ $\frac{3}{6}$

____

4. $\frac{3}{6}$ ◯ $\frac{5}{6}$

____

© Houghton Mifflin Harcourt Publishing Company

Name ______________________________

Lesson 69
CC.3.NF.3d

1. Floyd caught a fish that weighed $\frac{3}{4}$ pound. Kevin caught a fish that weighed $\frac{2}{3}$ pound. Which statement is correct?

   Ⓐ $\frac{3}{4} > \frac{2}{3}$
   Ⓑ $\frac{3}{4} < \frac{2}{3}$
   Ⓒ $\frac{2}{3} = \frac{3}{4}$
   Ⓓ $\frac{2}{3} > \frac{3}{4}$

2. There are two nature walks around the park. One trail is $\frac{7}{8}$ mile long. The other trail is $\frac{4}{8}$ mile long. Which statement is correct?

   Ⓐ $\frac{7}{8} < \frac{4}{8}$
   Ⓑ $\frac{7}{8} = \frac{4}{8}$
   Ⓒ $\frac{4}{8} < \frac{7}{8}$
   Ⓓ $\frac{4}{8} > \frac{7}{8}$

3. Olga is making play dough. She starts by mixing $\frac{1}{8}$ cup of salt with $\frac{1}{3}$ cup of water. Which statement is correct?

   Ⓐ $\frac{1}{8} = \frac{1}{3}$
   Ⓑ $\frac{1}{8} < \frac{1}{3}$
   Ⓒ $\frac{1}{8} > \frac{1}{3}$
   Ⓓ $\frac{1}{3} < \frac{1}{8}$

4. Kyle and Kelly planted seedlings. Kyle's plant is $\frac{5}{6}$ inch tall. Kelly's plant is $\frac{5}{8}$ inch tall. Which statement is correct?

   Ⓐ $\frac{5}{8} > \frac{5}{6}$
   Ⓑ $\frac{5}{8} = \frac{5}{6}$
   Ⓒ $\frac{5}{6} < \frac{5}{8}$
   Ⓓ $\frac{5}{6} > \frac{5}{8}$

Problem Solving REAL WORLD

5. At the third-grade party, two groups each had their own pizza. The blue group ate $\frac{7}{8}$ pizza. The green group ate $\frac{2}{8}$ pizza. Which group ate more of their pizza?

   ____

6. Ben and Antonio both take the same bus to school. Ben's ride is $\frac{7}{8}$ mile. Antonio's ride is $\frac{3}{4}$ mile. Who has a longer bus ride?

   ____

© Houghton Mifflin Harcourt Publishing Company

Name ______________________________

Lesson 70

COMMON CORE STANDARD CC.3.NF.3d

Lesson Objective: Compare and order fractions by using models and reasoning strategies.

Compare and Order Fractions

You can use a number line to compare and order fractions.

Order $\frac{5}{8}$, $\frac{2}{8}$, and $\frac{7}{8}$ from least to greatest.

Since you are comparing eighths, use a number line divided into eighths.

Step 1 Draw a point on the number line to show $\frac{5}{8}$.

Step 2 Repeat for $\frac{2}{8}$ and $\frac{7}{8}$.

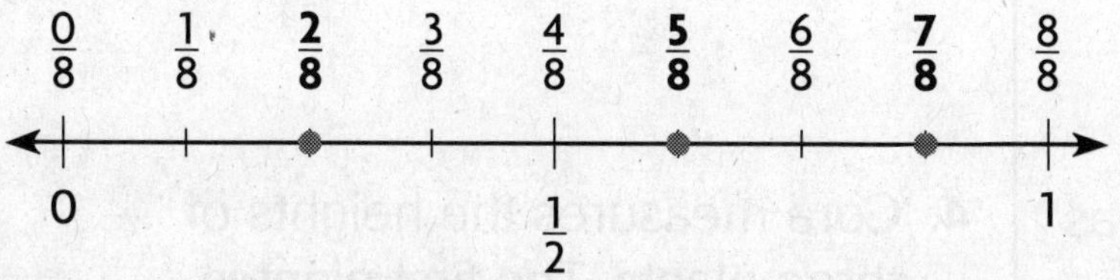

Step 3 Fractions increase in size as you move right on the number line. Write the fractions in order from left to right.

So, the order from least to greatest is $\frac{2}{8}$, $\frac{5}{8}$, $\frac{7}{8}$.

Write the fractions in order from least to greatest.

1. $\frac{4}{6}, \frac{6}{6}, \frac{3}{6}$

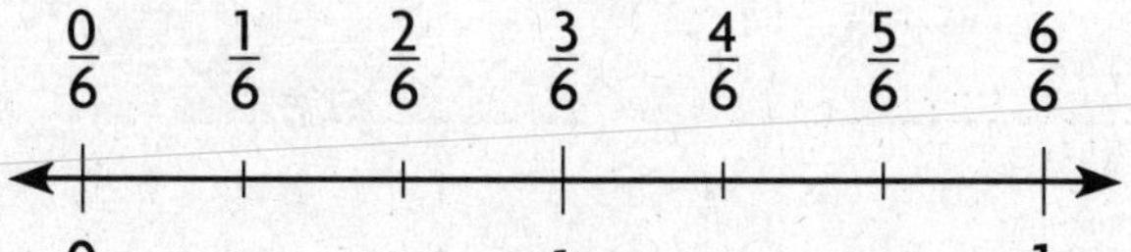

____

2. $\frac{2}{3}, \frac{2}{6}, \frac{2}{4}$

Think: When the numerators are the same, look at the denominators to compare the size of the pieces.

____

3. $\frac{1}{4}, \frac{1}{8}, \frac{1}{2}$

____

4. $\frac{3}{4}, \frac{0}{4}, \frac{2}{4}$

____

© Houghton Mifflin Harcourt Publishing Company

1. Pat, Elina, and Mike are meeting at the library. Pat lives $\frac{3}{4}$ mile from the library. Elina lives $\frac{1}{4}$ mile from the library. Mike lives $\frac{2}{4}$ mile from the library. Which list orders the fractions from **least** to **greatest**?

Ⓐ $\frac{2}{4}, \frac{1}{4}, \frac{3}{4}$
Ⓑ $\frac{1}{4}, \frac{3}{4}, \frac{2}{4}$
Ⓒ $\frac{1}{4}, \frac{2}{4}, \frac{3}{4}$
Ⓓ $\frac{3}{4}, \frac{2}{4}, \frac{1}{4}$

2. Ming is painting a picture. He has $\frac{2}{3}$ pint of red paint, $\frac{2}{8}$ pint of yellow paint, and $\frac{2}{6}$ pint of green paint. Which list orders the fractions from **greatest** to **least**?

Ⓐ $\frac{2}{3}, \frac{2}{8}, \frac{2}{6}$
Ⓑ $\frac{2}{3}, \frac{2}{6}, \frac{2}{8}$
Ⓒ $\frac{2}{8}, \frac{2}{6}, \frac{2}{3}$
Ⓓ $\frac{2}{6}, \frac{2}{3}, \frac{2}{8}$

3. Brian is making coconut bars. He needs $\frac{1}{3}$ cup coconut flakes, $\frac{1}{4}$ cup milk, and $\frac{1}{2}$ cup flour. Which list orders the fractions from **least** to **greatest**?

Ⓐ $\frac{1}{4}, \frac{1}{3}, \frac{1}{2}$
Ⓑ $\frac{1}{2}, \frac{1}{3}, \frac{1}{4}$
Ⓒ $\frac{1}{4}, \frac{1}{2}, \frac{1}{3}$
Ⓓ $\frac{1}{3}, \frac{1}{4}, \frac{1}{2}$

4. Cora measures the heights of three plants. The first plant is $\frac{4}{4}$ foot tall. The second plant is $\frac{4}{8}$ foot tall. The third plant is $\frac{4}{6}$ foot tall. Which list orders the fractions from **greatest** to **least**?

Ⓐ $\frac{4}{4}, \frac{4}{6}, \frac{4}{8}$
Ⓑ $\frac{4}{6}, \frac{4}{8}, \frac{4}{4}$
Ⓒ $\frac{4}{8}, \frac{4}{6}, \frac{4}{4}$
Ⓓ $\frac{4}{4}, \frac{4}{8}, \frac{4}{6}$

Problem Solving REAL WORLD

5. Mr. Jackson ran $\frac{7}{8}$ mile on Monday. He ran $\frac{3}{8}$ mile on Wednesday and $\frac{5}{8}$ mile on Friday. On which day did Mr. Jackson run the shortest distance?

____

6. Delia has three pieces of ribbon. Her red ribbon is $\frac{2}{4}$ foot long. Her green ribbon is $\frac{2}{3}$ foot long. Her yellow ribbon is $\frac{2}{6}$ foot long. She wants to use the longest piece for a project. Which color ribbon should Delia use?

____

© Houghton Mifflin Harcourt Publishing Company

Name ______________________________

Lesson 71

COMMON CORE STANDARD CC.3.MD.1

Lesson Objective: Read, write, and tell time on analog and digital clocks to the nearest minute.

Time to the Minute

Tommy wants to know what time the clock shows. He also wants to know one way to write the time.

Step 1 Where is the hour hand pointing? What is the hour?

It points just after the 6, so the hour is 6.

Step 2 Where is the minute hand pointing?

It points just after the 3.

Count the minutes. Count zero at the 12. Count on by fives: **5, 10, 15.**

Then count on by ones: **16, 17.**

So, the time is **6:17**, or **seventeen minutes after six.**

Write the time. Write one way you can read the time.

1.

____

____

____

2.

____

____

____

3.

____

____

____

4.

____

____

____

© Houghton Mifflin Harcourt Publishing Company

1. Brad looked at the clock on his way to football practice.

What time is shown on Brad's clock?

Ⓐ thirteen minutes before nine

Ⓑ thirteen minutes after nine

Ⓒ nine forty-five

Ⓓ thirteen minutes before ten

2. Sarah looked at her watch before she began mowing the grass. The hour hand was between the 9 and the 10. The minute hand was on the 7. At what time did Sarah begin mowing the grass?

Ⓐ 7:09 Ⓒ 9:07

Ⓑ 7:10 Ⓓ 9:35

3. Chris looked at his watch before he began raking the leaves. The hour hand was between the 10 and the 11. The minute hand was on the 5. At what time did Chris begin raking the leaves?

Ⓐ 10:25 Ⓒ 5:11

Ⓑ 10:05 Ⓓ 5:10

4. Jillian checked the clock before she began piano practice.

What time is shown on Jillian's clock?

Ⓐ four twenty-five

Ⓑ twenty-seven minutes after four

Ⓒ three minutes before five

Ⓓ twenty-seven minutes before five

Problem Solving REAL WORLD

5. What time is it when the hour hand is a little past the 3 and the minute hand is pointing to the 3?

____

6. Pete began practicing at twenty-five minutes before eight. What is another way to write this time?

____

© Houghton Mifflin Harcourt Publishing Company

Name ______________________________

Lesson 72

COMMON CORE STANDARD CC.3.MD.1

Lesson Objective: Decide when to use A.M. and P.M. when telling time to the nearest minute.

A.M. and P.M.

Lori and her father went shopping at the time shown on the clock at the right. How should Lori write the time?

Use A.M. or P.M.

Step 1 Read the time on the clock. **11:30**

Step 2 Decide if the time is A.M. or P.M.

Write P.M. for times after noon and before midnight.

Write A.M. for times after midnight and before noon.

Think: Most people go shopping **during the day**.

So, Lori should write the time as **11:30 A.M.**

REMEMBER

Noon is 12:00 in the daytime.

Midnight is 12:00 at night.

Write the time for the activity. Use A.M. or P.M.

1. leave school

____

2. eat dinner

____

3. arrive at school

____

4. Mackenzie's violin lesson starts at the time shown on the clock. Write the time using A.M. or P.M.

____

5. The diner opens for breakfast at the time shown on the clock. Write the time using A.M. or P.M.

____

© Houghton Mifflin Harcourt Publishing Company

Name ______________________

Lesson 72

CC.3.MD.1

1. Keisha is eating dinner at quarter after 6:00. At what time is Keisha eating dinner?

   Ⓐ 5:45 A.M.

   Ⓑ 6:15 A.M.

   Ⓒ 5:45 P.M.

   Ⓓ 6:15 P.M.

2. Terry went fishing at 6 minutes past 7:00 in the morning. At what time did Terry go fishing?

   Ⓐ 6:07 A.M.

   Ⓑ 7:06 A.M.

   Ⓒ 6:07 P.M.

   Ⓓ 7:06 P.M.

3. Ricardo wakes up at quarter to 7:00 in the morning. At what time does Ricardo wake up?

   Ⓐ 6:45 A.M.

   Ⓑ 7:15 A.M.

   Ⓒ 6:45 P.M.

   Ⓓ 7:15 P.M.

4. Makati's class begins social studies at 10 minutes after 1:00 in the afternoon. At what time does social studies begin?

   Ⓐ 1:10 A.M.

   Ⓑ 10:01 A.M.

   Ⓒ 1:10 P.M.

   Ⓓ 10:01 P.M.

Problem Solving REAL WORLD

5. Jaime is in math class. What time is it? Use A.M. or P.M.

____

6. Pete began practicing his trumpet at fifteen minutes past three. Write this time using A.M. or P.M.

____

© Houghton Mifflin Harcourt Publishing Company

Name ______________________________

Lesson 73

COMMON CORE STANDARD CC.3.MD.1

Lesson Objective: Use a number line or an analog clock to measure time intervals in minutes.

Measure Time Intervals

Julia starts her homework at 4:20 P.M. She finishes at 5:00 P.M. How much time does Julia spend doing homework?

Elapsed time is the amount of time that passes from the start of an activity to the end of the activity.

Use a number line to find elapsed time.

Step 1 Begin with the start time, **4:20**.

Step 2 Skip count **by tens** to count the minutes from 4:20 to 5:00.

Step 3 Label the number line. Draw jumps for every 10 minutes until you get to 5:00.

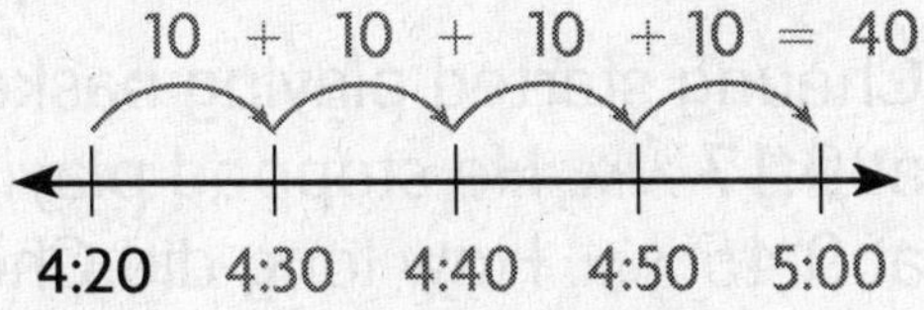

Step 4 Add the minutes that have elapsed. **40 minutes**

So, Julia spends **40 minutes** doing homework.

Use the number line to find the elapsed time.

1. Start: 3:15 P.M. End: 3:45 P.M.

____

2. Start: 11:05 A.M. End: 11:56 A.M.

____

Find the elapsed time.

3. Start: 4:10 P.M. End: 4:46 P.M.

____

4. Start: 10:30 A.M. End: 10:59 A.M.

____

© Houghton Mifflin Harcourt Publishing Company

Name ______________________________

Lesson 73
CC.3.MD.1

1. Arianna started reading her book at 11:20 A.M. and stopped reading her book at 11:43 A.M. For how long did Arianna read her book?

Ⓐ 23 minutes

Ⓑ 28 minutes

Ⓒ 33 minutes

Ⓓ 63 minutes

2. Hector left to take a walk at 6:25 P.M. He returned home at 6:51 P.M. How long was Hector's walk?

Ⓐ 16 minutes

Ⓑ 21 minutes

Ⓒ 26 minutes

Ⓓ 76 minutes

3. Victoria started her spelling homework at 4:25 P.M. and finished at 4:37 P.M. How long did it take Victoria to complete her spelling homework?

Ⓐ 27 minutes

Ⓑ 22 minutes

Ⓒ 17 minutes

Ⓓ 12 minutes

4. Cheung started playing basketball at 9:17 A.M. He stopped playing at 9:45 A.M. How long did Cheung play basketball?

Ⓐ 28 minutes Ⓒ 38 minutes

Ⓑ 32 minutes Ⓓ 42 minutes

Problem Solving REAL WORLD

5. A show at the museum starts at 7:40 P.M. and ends at 7:57 P.M. How long is the show?

____

6. The first train leaves the station at 6:15 A.M. The second train leaves at 6:55 A.M. How much later does the second train leave the station?

____

© Houghton Mifflin Harcourt Publishing Company

Name ______________________________

Lesson 74

COMMON CORE STANDARD CC.3.MD.1

Lesson Objective: Use a number line or an analog clock to add or subtract time intervals to find starting times or ending times.

Use Time Intervals

You can use a number line to find the starting time when you know the ending time and the elapsed time.

The ending time is 4:05 P.M. Use the number line to find the starting time if the elapsed time is 35 minutes.

Step 1

Find the ending time on the number line.

Think: The ending time is 4:05 P.M.

Step 2

Jump back 5 minutes.

Think: Jump back 5 minutes to get to the hour.

You jump back to **4:00** P.M.

Step 3

Jump back 30 minutes.

Think: Jump back 30 minutes to get to a total of 35 minutes.

You jump back to **3:30** P.M.

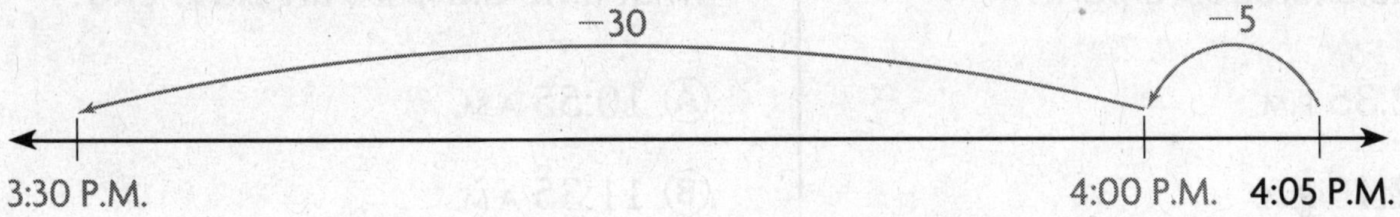

So, the starting time is **3:30** P.M.

1. Use the number line to find the starting time if the elapsed time is 25 minutes. ____________

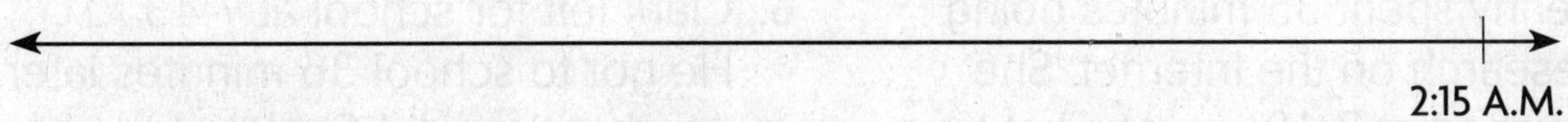

2. Use the number line to find the starting time if the elapsed time is 45 minutes. ____________

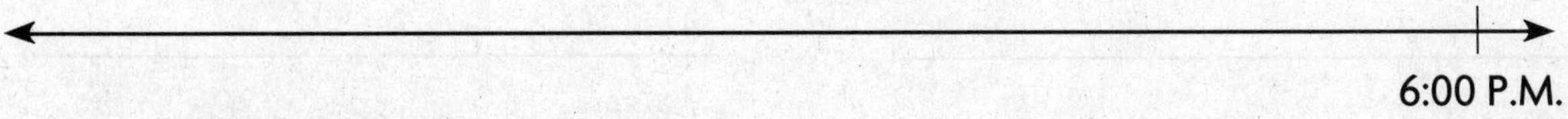

© Houghton Mifflin Harcourt Publishing Company

1. Jai's piano lesson started at 4:35 P.M. The lesson lasted 45 minutes. What time did Jai's piano lesson end?

Ⓐ 3:50 P.M.

Ⓑ 5:10 P.M.

Ⓒ 5:20 P.M.

Ⓓ 5:35 P.M.

2. Ky was at the skateboard park for 35 minutes. He left the park at 3:10 P.M. What time did Ky arrive at the skateboard park?

Ⓐ 2:35 P.M.

Ⓑ 2:40 P.M.

Ⓒ 2:45 P.M.

Ⓓ 3:45 P.M.

3. A batch of muffins needs to bake for 22 minutes. Wade puts the muffins in the oven at 10:17 A.M. At what time should Wade take the muffins out of the oven?

Ⓐ 10:29 A.M.

Ⓑ 10:39 A.M.

Ⓒ 10:49 A.M.

Ⓓ 10:55 A.M.

4. Yul's art class started at 11:25 A.M. The class lasted 30 minutes. At what time did Yul's art class end?

Ⓐ 10:55 A.M.

Ⓑ 11:35 A.M.

Ⓒ 11:50 A.M.

Ⓓ 11:55 A.M.

Problem Solving REAL WORLD

5. Jenny spent 35 minutes doing research on the Internet. She finished at 7:10 P.M. At what time did Jenny start her research?

____

6. Clark left for school at 7:43 A.M. He got to school 36 minutes later. At what time did Clark get to school?

____

© Houghton Mifflin Harcourt Publishing Company

Name ______________________________

Lesson 75

COMMON CORE STANDARD CC.3.MD.1

Lesson Objective: Solve problems involving addition and subtraction of time intervals by using the strategy *draw a diagram*.

Problem Solving • Time Intervals

As soon as Carter got home, he worked on his book report for 45 minutes. Then he did chores for 30 minutes. He finished at 5:15 P.M. At what time did Carter get home?

Read the Problem

What do I need to find?

I need to find what <u>time</u> Carter got <u>home</u>.

What information do I need to use?

Carter worked for <u>45 minutes</u> on his report. He did chores for <u>30 minutes</u>. He finished at <u>5:15 P.M.</u>.

How will I use the information?

I will use a number line and count back to find the time Carter got home.

Solve the Problem

- Find Carter's 5:15 P.M. finishing time on the number line.
- Count back 30 minutes using two 15-minute jumps to find the time Carter started his chores. <u>4:45 P.M.</u>

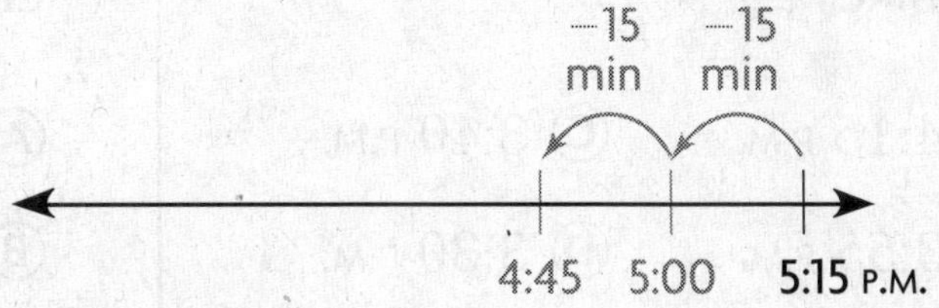

- Count back 45 minutes for the time Carter worked on his report. The jumps end at <u>4:00 P.M.</u>

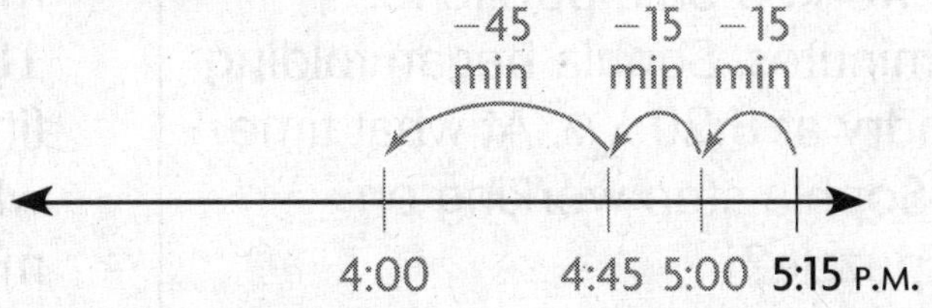

So, Carter got home at <u>4:00 P.M.</u>.

1. Kiera must be at school at 7:45 A.M. The ride to school takes 15 minutes. She needs 45 minutes to eat breakfast and get ready. At what time should Kiera get up?

____

2. Jack and his family go to the movies. First, they eat lunch at 1:30 P.M. It takes them 40 minutes to eat. Then they drive 25 minutes to get to the movie theater. At what time do Jack and his family get to the theater?

____

© Houghton Mifflin Harcourt Publishing Company

Name ______________________________

1. Omar rode his bike in the park for 45 minutes and rode in his neighborhood for 25 minutes. Omar stopped riding his bike at 4:40 P.M.

At what time did Omar start riding his bike?

Ⓐ 4:15 P.M. Ⓒ 3:40 P.M.

Ⓑ 3:55 P.M. Ⓓ 3:30 P.M.

2. Sophia folded laundry for 25 minutes. After folding laundry, she worked on a puzzle for 42 minutes. Sophia began folding laundry at 8:20 A.M. At what time did Sophia stop working on the puzzle?

Ⓐ 7:13 A.M. Ⓒ 9:27 A.M.

Ⓑ 9:02 A.M. Ⓓ 9:32 A.M.

3. Cheerleading practice started at 3:10 P.M. During practice, Dina practiced tumbling for 15 minutes. Then she practiced cheers for 35 minutes.

At what time did Dina's cheerleading practice end?

Ⓐ 3:25 P.M. Ⓒ 4:00 P.M.

Ⓑ 3:45 P.M. Ⓓ 4:15 P.M.

4. Mr. Carver spent 45 minutes making dinner. Then, he spent 18 minutes eating dinner. He finished eating at 6:15 P.M. At what time did Mr. Carver start making dinner?

Ⓐ 5:12 P.M. Ⓒ 5:30 P.M.

Ⓑ 5:22 P.M. Ⓓ 6:12 P.M.

5. Karl did his chores for 25 minutes. Then he read for 15 minutes. He finished reading at 5:20 P.M. Explain how you can find the time he began his chores.

____

____

____

© Houghton Mifflin Harcourt Publishing Company

Name ____________________________________

Lesson 76

COMMON CORE STANDARD CC.3.MD.2

Lesson Objective: Estimate and measure liquid volume in liters.

Estimate and Measure Liquid Volume

Liquid volume is the amount of liquid in a container. You can measure liquid volume using the metric unit **liter** (L).

A water bottle holds about 1 liter. Estimate how much liquid a plastic cup and a fish bowl will hold. Then write the containers in order from the greatest to least liquid volume.

A plastic cup holds **less than 1 liter.**

A water bottle holds about 1 liter.

A fish bowl holds **more than 1 liter.**

Think: A plastic cup is *smaller* than a water bottle.

Think: A fish bowl is *larger* than a water bottle.

So, the order of the containers from greatest to least liquid volume is **fish bowl, water bottle, plastic cup.**

1. A wading pool is filled with water. Is the amount *more than 1 liter, about 1 liter,* or *less than 1 liter?*

____

Estimate how much liquid volume there will be when the container is filled. Write *more than 1 liter, about 1 liter,* or *less than 1 liter.*

2. vase

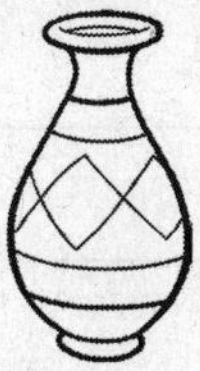

____

3. mug

____

4. bathtub

____

© Houghton Mifflin Harcourt Publishing Company

Name ______________________________

1. There are four bottles of punch on a shelf. The bottles are all the same size. Which bottle has the least amount of punch?

Q *R* *S* *T*

(A) Bottle *Q*
(B) Bottle *R*
(C) Bottle *S*
(D) Bottle *T*

2. Meiki fills a mug with hot cocoa. Which is the best estimate of how much she poured into the mug?

(A) about 1 liter
(B) less than 1 liter
(C) more than 1 liter
(D) about 5 liters

3. There are four bottles of juice on the counter. The bottles are all the same size. Which bottle has the greatest amount of juice?

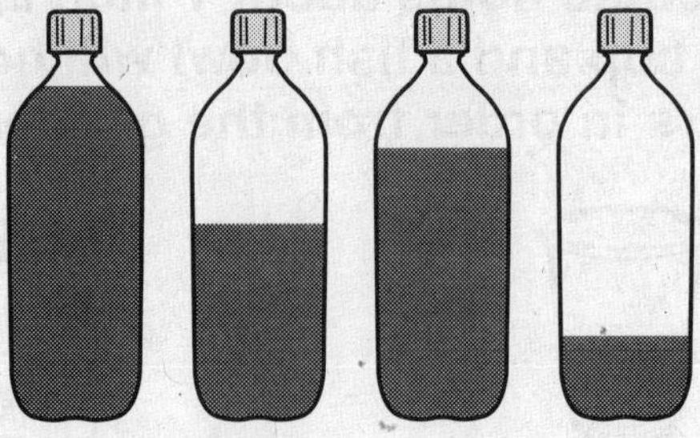

A *B* *C* *D*

(A) Bottle *A*
(B) Bottle *B*
(C) Bottle *C*
(D) Bottle *D*

4. Jed fills a bucket with water to wash the floor. Which is the best estimate of how much water he put in the bucket?

(A) a lot less than a liter
(B) a little less than a liter
(C) about a liter
(D) more than a liter

5. A soup pot and a water bottle are the same height. Which one will hold more liquid? Explain.

____

____

____

____

© Houghton Mifflin Harcourt Publishing Company

Name ________________________________

COMMON CORE STANDARD CC.3.MD.2

Lesson Objective: Estimate and measure mass in grams and kilograms.

Estimate and Measure Mass

Mass is the amount of matter in an object. You can measure mass using the metric units **gram** (g) and **kilogram** (kg).

Should you use gram or kilogram to measure the mass of a penny?

The mass of one grape is about 1 gram.

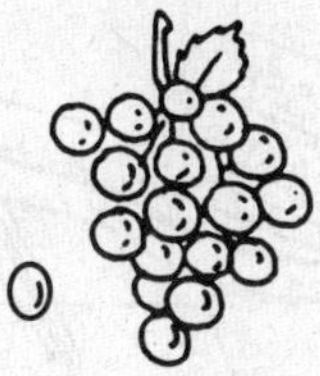

The mass of a book is about 1 kilogram.

Think: The mass of a penny is closer to the mass of a grape than to the mass of a book. So, use **grams** to measure the mass of a penny.

You can use a pan balance to compare the masses of an eraser and a stapler.

Think: The pan with the stapler is lower.

So, the mass of a stapler **is more than** the mass of an eraser.

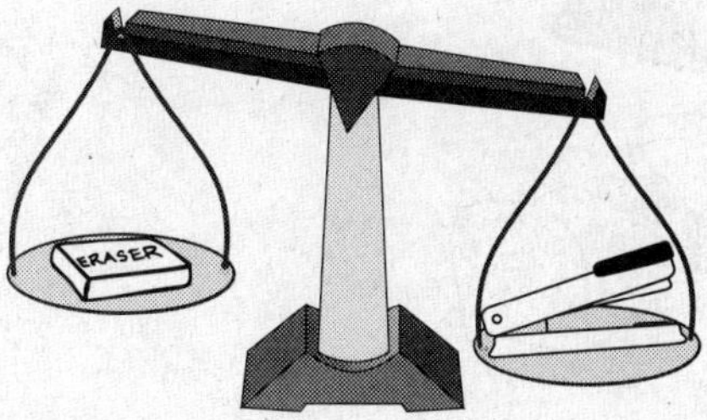

Choose the unit you would use to measure the mass. Write *gram* or *kilogram*.

1. cherry

____

2. cat

____

3. pencil

____

4. Compare the masses of the objects. Write *is less than, is the same as,* or *is more than.*

The mass of the pencil ____________ the mass of the apple.

© Houghton Mifflin Harcourt Publishing Company

Name ______________________________

1. Ling uses grams to measure the mass of an object in her room. Which object would be **best** measured using grams?

Ⓐ 

Ⓑ 

Ⓒ 

Ⓓ 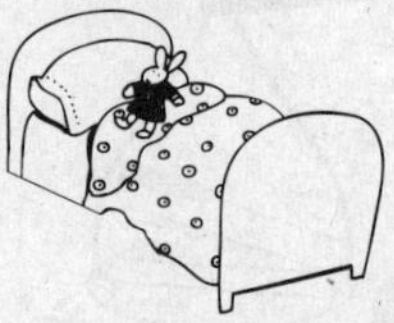

2. Kylie wants to find the mass of a pair of her sneakers. Which unit should she use?

Ⓐ liter
Ⓑ kilogram
Ⓒ inch
Ⓓ gram

3. Jason uses a balance to compare the masses of the objects shown. What is true about the objects?

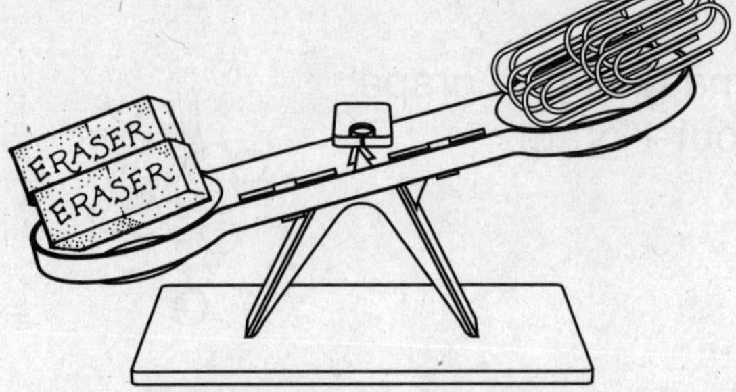

Ⓐ The mass of the erasers is the same as the mass of the paper clips.

Ⓑ The mass of the erasers is less than the mass of the paper clips.

Ⓒ The mass of the paper clips is less than the mass of the erasers.

Ⓓ The mass of the paper clips is greater than the mass of the erasers.

Problem Solving REAL WORLD

4. A red ball has a mass that is less than 1 kilogram. A blue ball has a mass of 1 kilogram. Is the mass of the blue ball more than or less than the mass of the red ball?

____

5. Brock's dog is a collie. To find the mass of his dog, should Brock use *grams* or *kilograms*?

____

© Houghton Mifflin Harcourt Publishing Company

Name ______________________________

Lesson 78

COMMON CORE STANDARD CC.3.MD.2

Lesson Objective: Add, subtract, multiply, or divide to solve problems involving liquid volumes or masses.

Solve Problems About Liquid Volume and Mass

You can use a model or write an equation to solve problems about liquid volume and mass.

Tina's watering can holds 4 liters of water. Todd's watering can holds 6 liters of water. What is the total liquid volume of both watering cans?

Tina's Watering Can

Todd's Watering Can

Use a bar model.

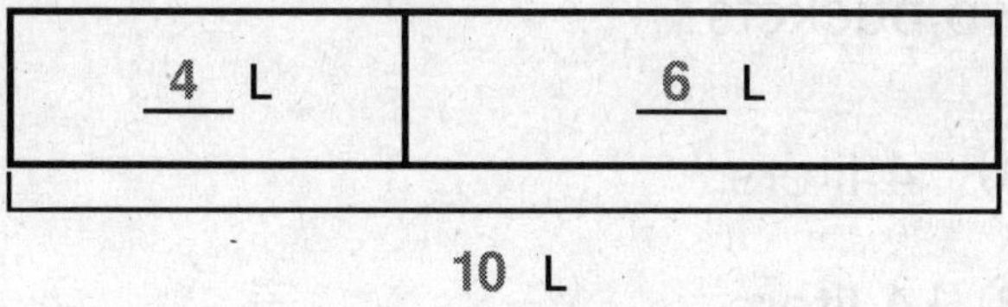

Think: Add to find the total.

4 L + 6 L = **10 L**

So, the total liquid volume is **10** L.

Write an equation.

Think: I can write an addition equation to find the sum of the liquid volumes.

4 (+) **6** = **10**

So, the total liquid volume is **10** L.

Write an equation and solve the problem.

1. Kyra has a small bucket that holds 3 liters of water and a large bucket that holds 5 liters of water. Altogether, how many liters of water do the two buckets hold?

___ ◯ ___ = ___ ________

2. Rick's recipe calls for 25 grams of raisins and 40 grams of nuts. How many more grams of nuts than raisins does the recipe call for?

___ ◯ ___ = ___ ________

© Houghton Mifflin Harcourt Publishing Company

Name ____________________

1. Bryce has a container completely filled with 13 liters of water. Ben has a container completely filled with 8 liters of water. What is the total liquid volume of the containers?

Ⓐ 5 liters
Ⓑ 11 liters
Ⓒ 21 liters
Ⓓ 24 liters

2. An online company shipped three packages. The packages had masses of 8 kilograms, 15 kilograms, and 9 kilograms. What is the total mass of the three packages?

Ⓐ 23 kilograms
Ⓑ 24 kilograms
Ⓒ 32 kilograms
Ⓓ 34 kilograms

3. Mama's Restaurant sold a total of 15 liters of orange juice in 3 hours. The same amount of orange juice was sold each hour. How many liters of orange juice were sold each hour?

Ⓐ 5 liters
Ⓑ 12 liters
Ⓒ 18 liters
Ⓓ 45 liters

4. Simon pours 19 liters of water into one bucket and 15 liters of water into another bucket. Each bucket is filled completely. What is the total liquid volume of the two buckets?

Ⓐ 4 liters
Ⓑ 14 liters
Ⓒ 24 liters
Ⓓ 34 liters

Problem Solving REAL WORLD

5. Zoe's fish tank holds 27 liters of water. She uses a 3-liter container to fill the tank. How many times does she have to fill the 3-liter container in order to fill her fish tank?

____

6. Adrian's backpack has a mass of 15 kilograms. Theresa's backpack has a mass of 8 kilograms. What is the total mass of both backpacks?

____

© Houghton Mifflin Harcourt Publishing Company

Name ______________________________

Lesson 79

COMMON CORE STANDARD CC.3.MD.3

Lesson Objective: Organize data in tables and solve problems using the strategy *make a table.*

Problem Solving • Organize Data

One way to show data is in a tally table. Another way to show data is in a frequency table. A **frequency table** uses numbers to record data.

The students in Jake's class voted for their favorite sport. How many more students chose soccer than chose baseball?

Favorite Sport	
Sport	**Tally**
Soccer	卌 ||||
Baseball	卌 |
Football	||||

Read the Problem

What do I need to find?

How many more students chose soccer than chose baseball?

What information do I need to use?

the data about favorite sport from the tally table

How will I use the information?

I will count the tally marks. Then I will write the number of tally marks for each sport in the frequency table.

Next, I will subtract to compare the votes for soccer and the votes for baseball.

Solve the Problem

Count the tally marks for each sport. Write the numbers in the frequency table.

Think: | = 1 vote

卌 = 5 votes

Soccer has **1** 卌 and **4** |, so write 9 in the frequency table.

Favorite Sport	
Sport	**Number**
Soccer	9
Baseball	6
Football	4

Subtract to find how many more students chose soccer than chose baseball.

$9 - 6 = 3$

So, **3** more students chose soccer than chose baseball as their favorite sport.

1. How many students chose football and baseball combined?

____

2. How many fewer students chose football than chose soccer?

____

© Houghton Mifflin Harcourt Publishing Company

Name ____________________

Use the table for 1–2.

Mike asked people what season they liked best. The tally table shows the results.

Favorite Season	
Winter	𝍸 |||
Spring	𝍸 𝍸 |
Summer	||||
Fall	𝍸

1. How many people chose Winter or Summer?

Ⓐ 4 Ⓒ 11

Ⓑ 10 Ⓓ 12

2. How many **more** students chose Spring than Fall?

Ⓐ 4 Ⓒ 6

Ⓑ 5 Ⓓ 11

Use the table for 3–4.

Rory and his classmates voted for a favorite class activity. They organized the data in a tally table.

Favorite Class Activity	
Science Fair	𝍸 𝍸
Bake Sale	||||
Fitness Fun Day	𝍸 𝍸 ||
Class Play	𝍸 ||||

3. How many students chose the Science Fair or Fitness Fun Day?

Ⓐ 6 Ⓒ 20

Ⓑ 12 Ⓓ 22

4. How many **fewer** students chose a Bake Sale than Fitness Fun Day?

Ⓐ 4 Ⓒ 10

Ⓑ 8 Ⓓ 12

5. Dan asked 24 members of his class how they traveled to their last vacation spot. The frequency table shows the results. Complete the table and explain how you did it.

Travel Vehicle		
	Boys	**Girls**
Car		4
Airplane	6	5
Bus	2	3

____

____

____

© Houghton Mifflin Harcourt Publishing Company

Name ______________________________

Lesson 80

COMMON CORE STANDARD CC.3.MD.3

Lesson Objective: Read and interpret data in a scaled picture graph.

Use Picture Graphs

A **picture graph** shows information using small pictures or symbols.

A **key** tells what the symbol stands for. A symbol can stand for more than 1.

Which state in the picture graph below has 9 national park areas?

The key for the picture graph shows that each (tree) = **6** national park areas.

Count the number of (tree) next to each state.

Oregon has one tree picture and half of a tree picture.

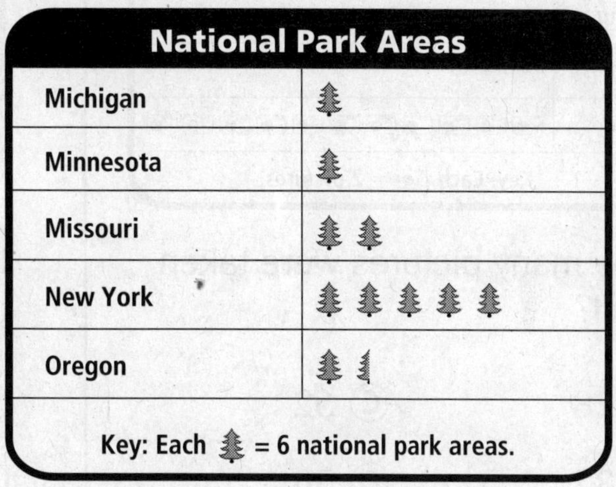

Think:
(tree) = 6 park areas
(half tree) = 3 park areas

So, **Oregon** has 9 national park areas.

Use the Favorite Ice Pop Flavor picture graph for 1–4.

1. How many people chose orange?

____

2. How many people chose lemon?

____

3. How many fewer people chose lemon than chose strawberry?

____

4. How many people in all were surveyed?

____

© Houghton Mifflin Harcourt Publishing Company

Name ______________________________

1. Ms. Sanchez's class took pictures of a lighthouse during a field trip. The picture graph shows how many pictures each student took.

How many pictures were taken in all?

Ⓐ 28 Ⓒ 52

Ⓑ 32 Ⓓ 56

2. The picture graph shows the number of bottles Mr. Tao's class recycled each week for an Earth Day project.

How many bottles were recycled during Week 2 and Week 3?

Ⓐ 9 Ⓒ 85

Ⓑ 14 Ⓓ 140

3. Mrs. Hampton's class made a picture graph to show the type of material used to make each picture at an art show.

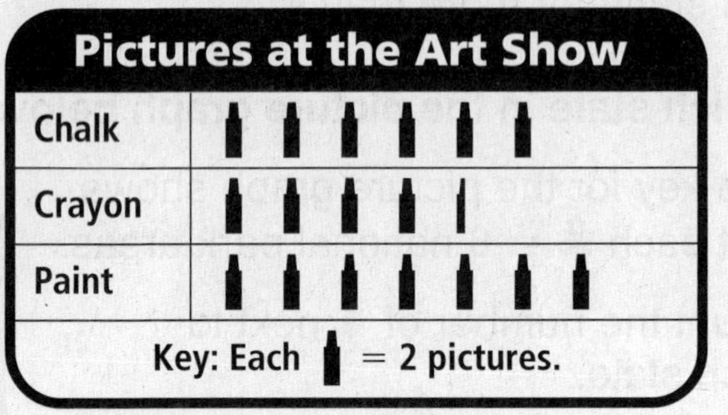

How many **fewer** pictures were made with crayon than with paint?

Ⓐ 4 Ⓒ 9

Ⓑ 5 Ⓓ 12

4. Pam tossed a coin 20 times and made a picture graph of her data.

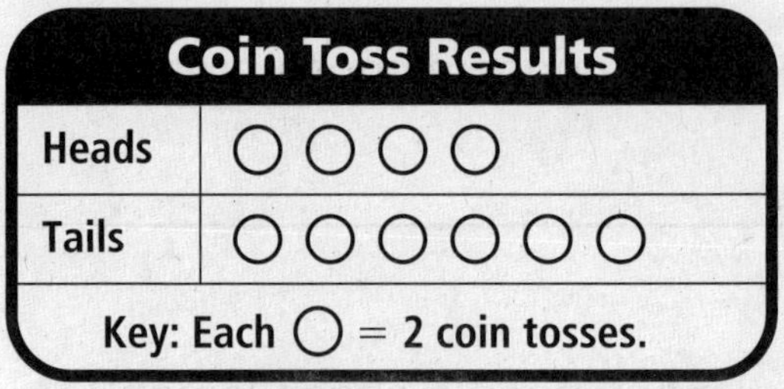

Explain how the picture graph would be different if each circle represented 4 coin tosses.

____

____

____

____

© Houghton Mifflin Harcourt Publishing Company

Name ______________________________

Lesson 81
COMMON CORE STANDARD CC.3.MD.3
Lesson Objective: Draw a scaled picture graph to show data in a table.

Make Picture Graphs

Use the data in this table to make a picture graph.

Number of Ball Caps Sold

Basketball Game	Caps
Falcons and Mustangs	20
Sharks and Bulldogs	30
Hawks and Comets	5
Rams and Cardinals	15

Step 1 Write the title.

Step 2 Write the names of the games.

Step 3 Decide what number each picture will represent. You can count by fives to find the number of caps sold, so let each cap represent 5 caps.

Step 4 Draw one cap for every 5 caps sold during each game. There were 20 caps sold during the Falcons and Mustangs game. Count to 20 by fives. 5, 10, 15, 20. So, 4 caps should be drawn. Draw the caps for the rest of the games.

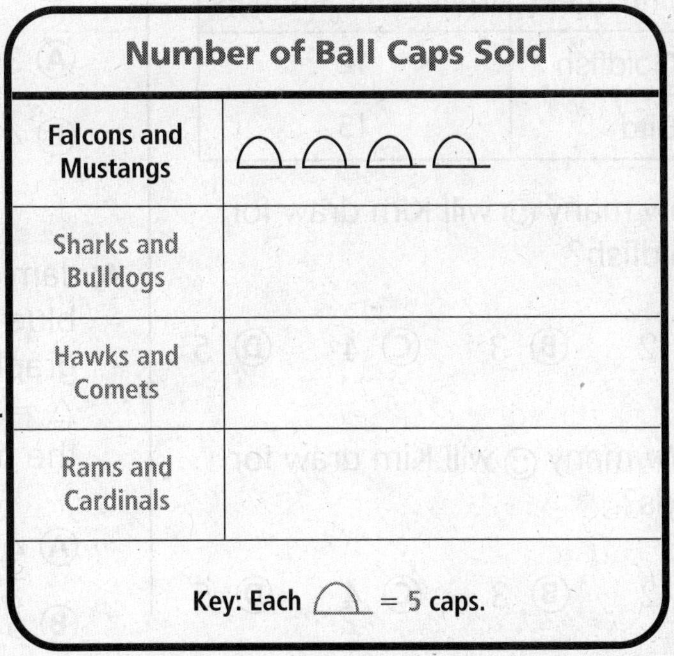

Number of Ball Caps Sold
Falcons and Mustangs
Sharks and Bulldogs
Hawks and Comets
Rams and Cardinals
Key: Each = 5 caps.

Use your picture graph above for 1–3.

1. During which game were the most ball caps sold?

____

2. How many pictures would you draw if 45 ball caps were sold in a game?

____

3. During which two games were a total of 25 caps sold?

____

© Houghton Mifflin Harcourt Publishing Company

Name ______________________________

Lesson 81
CC.3.MD.3

Use the table for 1–2.

Kim did a survey to learn which pet her classmates liked best. She wrote the results in a table and will use the data to make a picture graph with a key of ☺ = 3 students.

Favorite Pet

Kind of Pet	Number of Students
Goldfish	12
Bird	15

1. How many ☺ will Kim draw for Goldfish?

Ⓐ 2 Ⓑ 3 Ⓒ 4 Ⓓ 5

2. How many ☺ will Kim draw for Birds?

Ⓐ 2 Ⓑ 3 Ⓒ 4 Ⓓ 5

3. Jerel made a picture graph to show the number of sunny days his city had in June and July. This is the key to Jerel's picture graph.

Key: Each  **= 10 days.**

How many sunny days do  stand for?

Ⓐ 3 Ⓒ 30

Ⓑ 4 Ⓓ 35

4. Jamie saw 24 red cars and 16 blue cars. She made a picture graph to show her results. If △ = 4 cars, how many △s show the number of blue cars she saw?

Ⓐ 4 Ⓒ 8

Ⓑ 5 Ⓓ 16

5. Jeff took a survey about the snack his 26 classmates liked best. He used the data to begin making a picture graph. Complete Jeff's picture graph. Explain your work.

Favorite Snack

Crackers	☺ ☺ ☺ ☺
Fruit	
Key: Each ☺ = 4 students.	

____

____

____

© Houghton Mifflin Harcourt Publishing Company

Name ______________________

Lesson 82

COMMON CORE STANDARD CC.3.MD.3

Lesson Objective: Read and interpret data in a scaled bar graph.

Use Bar Graphs

How many Olympic medals did Norway win in the 2008 Summer Olympics?

- Both bar graphs show the same data about Olympic medals. The top graph is a **vertical bar graph**. The bottom graph is a **horizontal bar graph**.
- Find Norway on the vertical bar graph and follow the bar to its end. Then follow the end across to the scale to find the number of medals. **10** medals.
- Find Norway on the horizontal bar graph and follow the bar to its end. Then follow the end down to the scale to find the number of medals. **10** medals.

So, Norway won **10** medals.

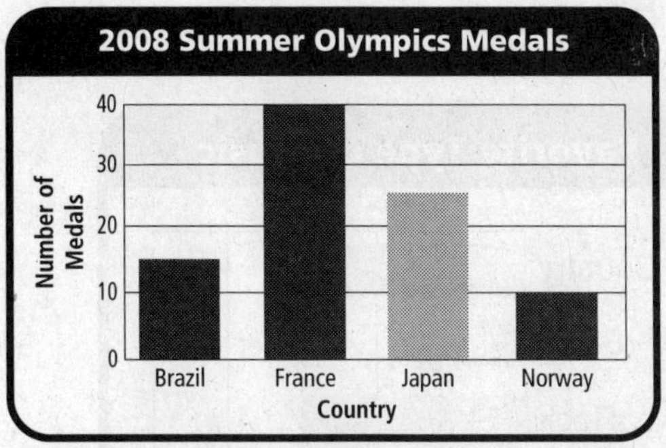

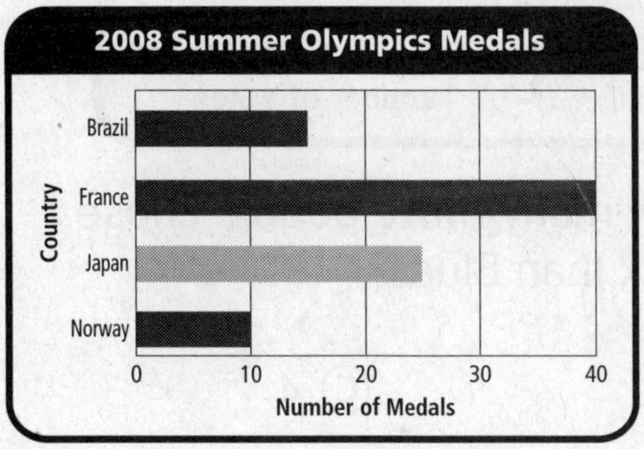

Use the Favorite Type of Book bar graph for 1–4.

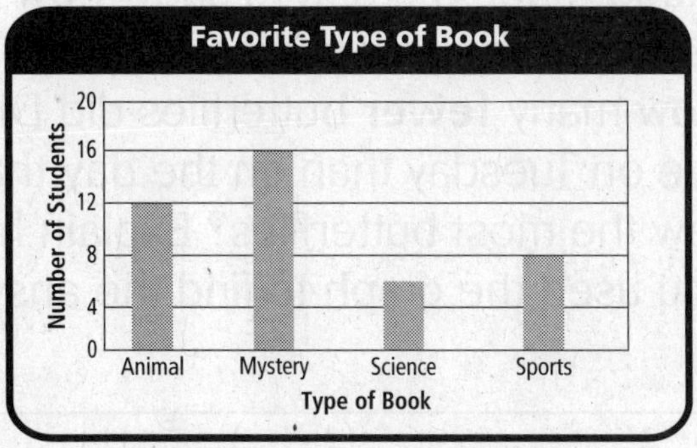

1. Which type of book did the most students choose?

____

2. Which type of book received 4 fewer votes than mystery?

____

3. Did more students choose books about mystery or books about science and sports together?

____

4. How many students in all answered the survey?

____

© Houghton Mifflin Harcourt Publishing Company

Name ______________________________

Lesson 82
CC.3.MD.3

Use the graph for 1–3.

Carrie asked people at the mall to choose a favorite type of music. The bar graph shows the results.

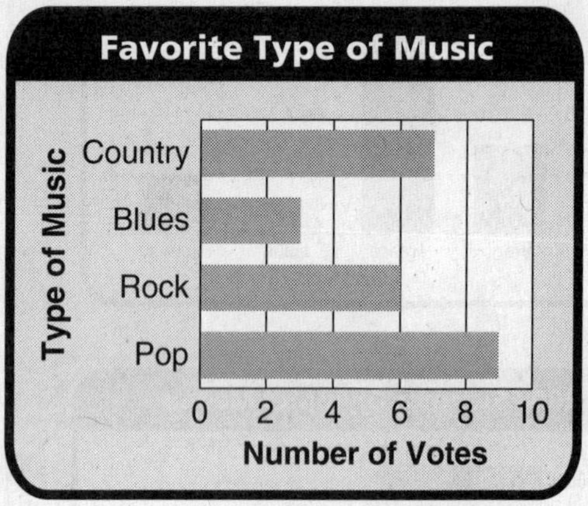

1. How many **more** people chose Rock than Blues?

(A) 2 (C) 4

(B) 3 (D) 9

2. How many people in all chose a type of music?

(A) 4 (C) 22

(B) 16 (D) 25

3. How many **more** people would have to choose Blues to have the same number of people choose Blues and Country?

(A) 3 (C) 6

(B) 4 (D) 7

4. Diego made a graph to show how many butterflies he saw in his yard each day. How many **fewer** butterflies did Diego see on Tuesday than on the day that he saw the most butterflies? Explain how you used the graph to find the answer.

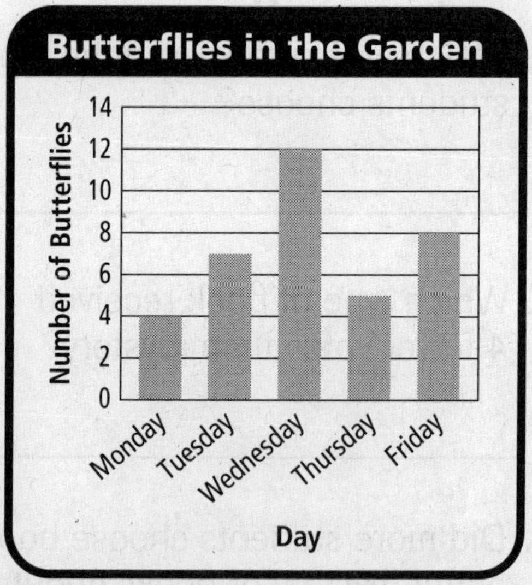

____

____

____

____

____

____

© Houghton Mifflin Harcourt Publishing Company

Name ______________________________

Lesson 83

COMMON CORE STANDARD CC.3.MD.3

Lesson Objective: Draw a scaled bar graph to show data in a table or picture graph.

Make Bar Graphs

Use data in a table to make a bar graph.

Favorite Winter Activity	
Sport	**Number of Votes**
Ice Skating	17
Skiing	14
Sledding	12
Snowboarding	3

Step 1 Write the title for the bar graph.

Step 2 Label the side and the bottom.

Step 3 Write the names of the sports.

Step 4 Choose a scale for your graph.

- The scale must be able to show the least number, 3, and the greatest number, 17.
- The numbers must be equally spaced. Start with 0 and count by twos until you reach 18.

Step 5 Draw the bar for ice skating. The bar will end halfway between 16 and 18 at 17.

Step 6 Then use the results in the table to draw the rest of the bars.

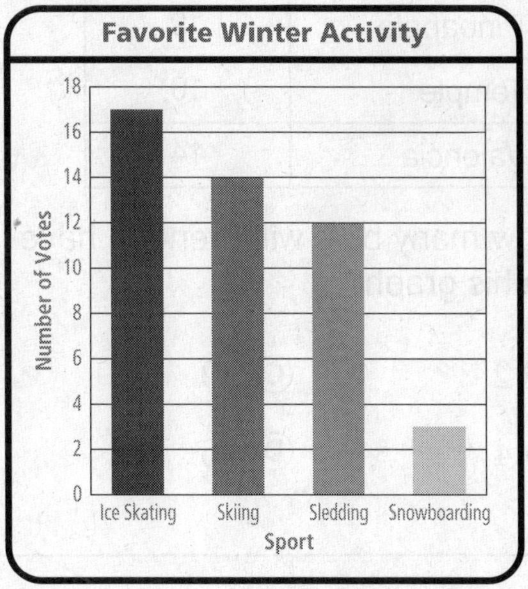

Use the results in the table to make a bar graph.

Favorite Summer Sport	
Sport	**Number of Votes**
Swimming	15
Inline Skating	10
Cycling	20

© Houghton Mifflin Harcourt Publishing Company

Name ______________________________

Lesson 83
CC.3.MD.3

Use the table for 1–2.

Brendon wants to use a table with data about the number of oranges picked to make a bar graph.

Oranges Picked

Type of Orange	Bushels
Navel	15
Pineapple	12
Temple	10
Valencia	14

1. How many bars will Brendon have on his graph?

Ⓐ 2
Ⓑ 4
Ⓒ 9
Ⓓ 16

2. Which type of orange will have the longest bar?

Ⓐ Navel
Ⓑ Pineapple
Ⓒ Temple
Ⓓ Valencia

3. Joey is making a bar graph to show how many pets his classmates have. Which pet will have the shortest bar in his graph?

Ⓐ 8 cats
Ⓑ 6 hamsters
Ⓒ 4 dogs
Ⓓ 3 horses

4. Martina is making a bar graph to show the 37 finches she saw in her garden from Monday through Friday. How tall should Martina make the bar to show how many finches she saw on Wednesday? Explain your answer and complete the graph.

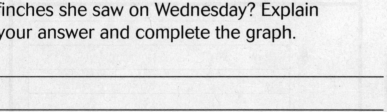

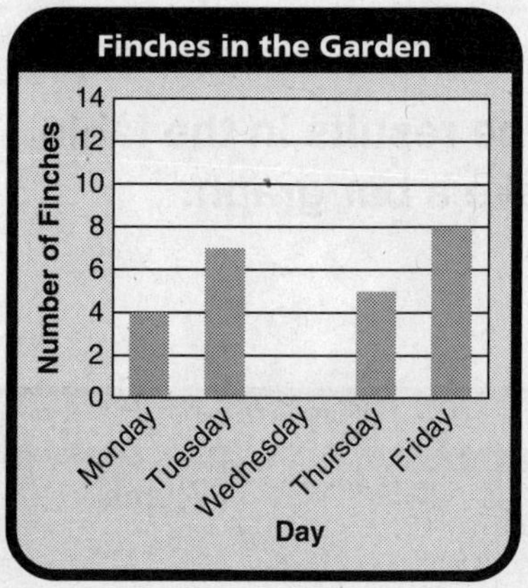

____

____

____

____

____

____

© Houghton Mifflin Harcourt Publishing Company

Name ______________________________ **Lesson 84**

COMMON CORE STANDARD CC.3.MD.3

Lesson Objective: Solve one- and two-step compare problems using data represented in scaled bar graphs.

Solve Problems Using Data

You can use a model or write a number sentence to help you answer questions about data.

The bar graph shows the different ways students use the computer center after school. How many more students use the computer center for projects than for games?

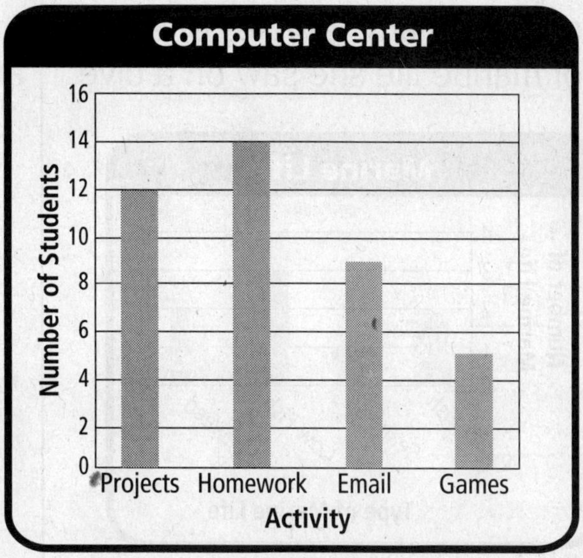

One Way Use a model.

Find the bar for projects. The bar ends at 12. So, **12** students use the computer center for projects.

Find the bar for games. The bar ends halfway between 4 and 6. So, **5** students use the computer center for games. Count back along the scale from 12 to 5 to find the difference. The difference is <u>7</u> students.

Another Way Write a number sentence.

Subtract to compare the number of students.
Think: There are 12 students who work on projects.
There are 5 students who play games.

$12 - 5 = 7$

So, **7** more students use the computer center for projects than for games.

Use the Computer Center bar graph for 1–3.

1. How many more students use the computer center for homework than for email? _____ more students

2. How many fewer students use the computer center for games than for homework? _____ fewer students

3. Do more students use the computer center for projects or for email and games combined? **Explain.** ________________________________

© Houghton Mifflin Harcourt Publishing Company

Name ______________________________

Use the graph for 1–2.

A biologist made a bar graph to show how many samples of each type of marine life she saw on a dive.

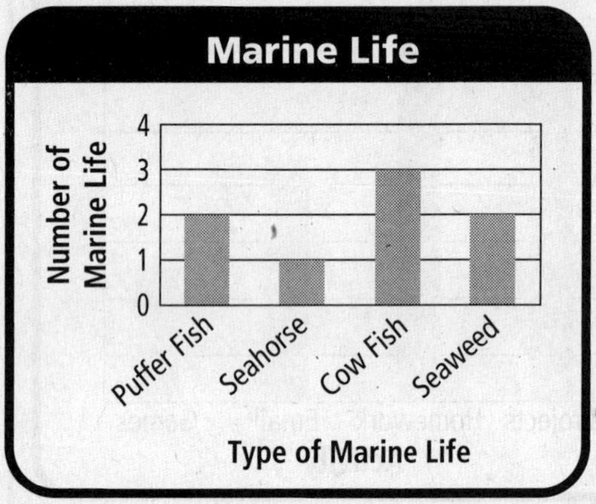

1. Of which type of marine life did the marine biologist see the **fewest**?

Ⓐ Cow Fish
Ⓑ Puffer Fish
Ⓒ Seahorse
Ⓓ Seaweed

2. How many more Cow Fish did the biologist see than Seahorses?

Ⓐ 1 Ⓑ 2 Ⓒ 3 Ⓓ 4

Use the graph for 3–4.

Nigel made a bar graph to show how many bushels of each type of orange are for sale at a fruit stand.

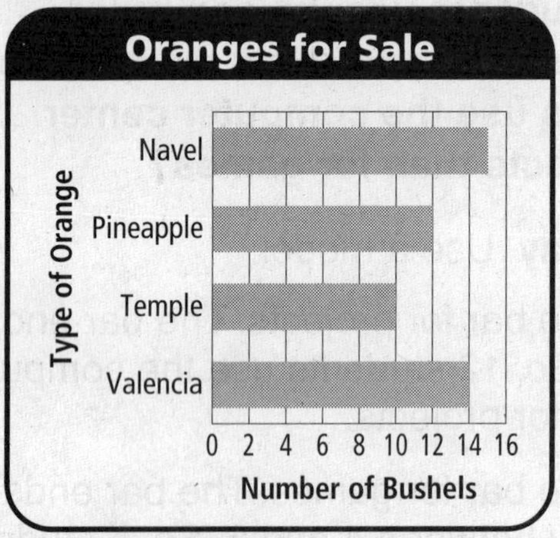

3. How many **more** bushels of Pineapple oranges and Navel oranges are there than Temple oranges and Valencia oranges?

Ⓐ 1 bushel
Ⓑ 3 bushels
Ⓒ 7 bushels
Ⓓ 24 bushels

4. How would you use the graph to find out if there were more Navel and Pineapple oranges for sale or more Temple and Valencia oranges for sale?

____

____

____

____

____

© Houghton Mifflin Harcourt Publishing Company

Name ________________________________

Lesson 85

COMMON CORE STANDARD CC.3.MD.4

Lesson Objective: Read and interpret data in a line plot and use data to make a line plot.

Use and Make Line Plots

A **line plot** uses marks to record each piece of data above a number line.

Louise measured the heights of tomato plants in her garden. She recorded the height of each plant.

How many tomato plants are there?

Each ✗ stands for 1 **plant**.

Count all the ✗s. There are **19** in all.

This tells the total number of **plants**.

How many plants are taller than 13 inches?

Add the number of ✗s for 14 and 15.

3 plants are 14 inches tall. 1 plant is 15 inches tall.

3 + 1 = 4 So, **4** plants are taller than 13 inches.

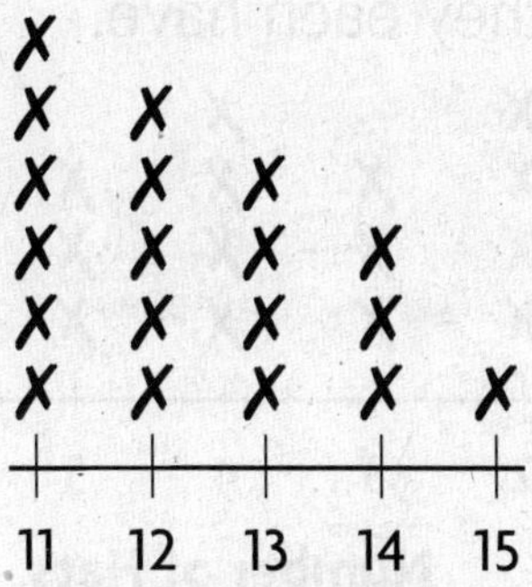

Heights of Tomato Plants (inches)

Use the Spelling Test Scores line plot for 1–3.

1. Which test score did the most students receive?

____

2. How many more students scored 90 than 100?

____

3. How many students in all took the spelling test?

____

Spelling Test Scores

© Houghton Mifflin Harcourt Publishing Company

Name ______________________

Lesson 85
CC.3.MD.4

Use the line plot for 1–2.

Mr. Robinson's students made a line plot to show the number of hats they each have.

1. How many students have 4 or fewer hats?

Ⓐ 3 Ⓒ 7

Ⓑ 4 Ⓓ 11

2. How many students were included in the line plot?

Ⓐ 13 Ⓒ 15

Ⓑ 14 Ⓓ 16

Use the line plot for 3–4.

Anna made a line plot to show the number of books each student in her class read for a reading contest.

3. How many students read 9 books?

Ⓐ 4 Ⓒ 2

Ⓑ 3 Ⓓ 1

4. How many students read **fewer** than 8 books?

Ⓐ 4 Ⓒ 6

Ⓑ 5 Ⓓ 7

5. Lewis made a line plot to show the number of hours students in his class spend at practice each week. Find the total number of students and the total number of hours. Explain how you found your answers.

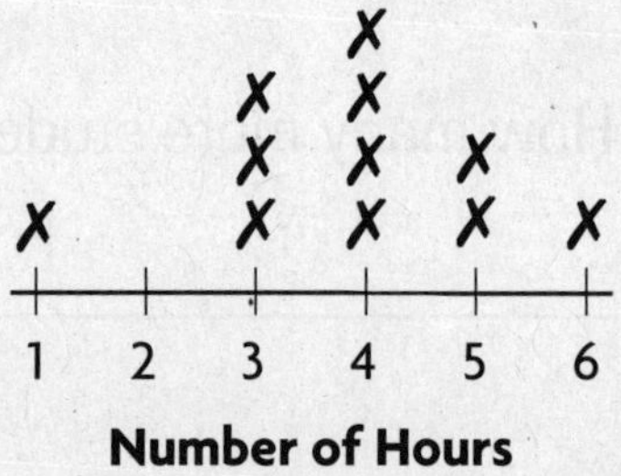

____

____

____

____

© Houghton Mifflin Harcourt Publishing Company

Name ____________________

Lesson 86

COMMON CORE STANDARD CC.3.MD.4

Lesson Objective: Measure length to the nearest half or fourth inch and use measurement data to make a line plot.

Measure Length

You can measure length to the nearest half or fourth inch.

Use a ruler to measure lines A–C to the nearest half inch.

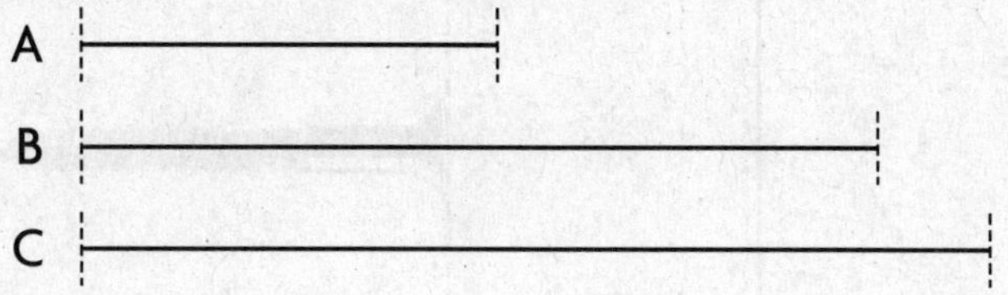

Step 1 Line up the left end of Line A with the zero mark on the ruler.

Step 2 The right end of Line A is between the half-inch marks for __1__ and __$1\frac{1}{2}$__.

The mark that is closest to the right end is for __$1\frac{1}{2}$__ inches.

So, the length of Line A to the nearest half inch is __$1\frac{1}{2}$__ inches.

Repeat Steps 1 and 2 for lines B and C.

The length of Line B to the nearest half inch is __$2\frac{1}{2}$__ inches.

The length of Line C to the nearest half inch is __3__ inches.

Measure the length to the nearest half inch. Is the crayon closest to $1\frac{1}{2}$ inches, 2 inches, or $2\frac{1}{2}$ inches?

1.

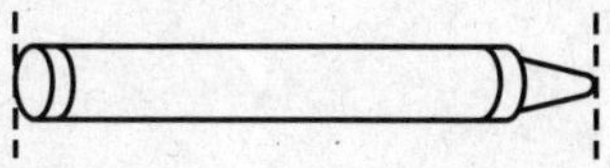

____ inches

2.

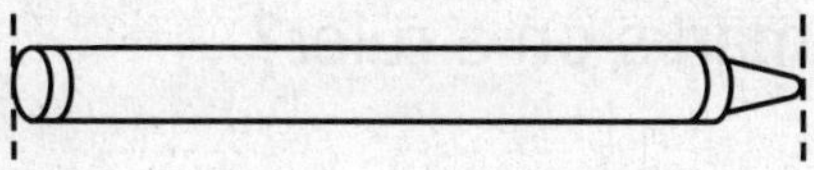

____ inches

© Houghton Mifflin Harcourt Publishing Company

Name ______________________________

Lesson 86
CC.3.MD.4

1. Mrs. Williams uses an inch ruler to measure a flower in a picture. How tall is the flower to the nearest fourth inch?

Ⓐ 2 inches
Ⓑ $2\frac{1}{4}$ inches
Ⓒ $2\frac{3}{4}$ inches
Ⓓ 3 inches

2. Hector uses an inch ruler to measure a screw. What is the length of the screw to the nearest half inch?

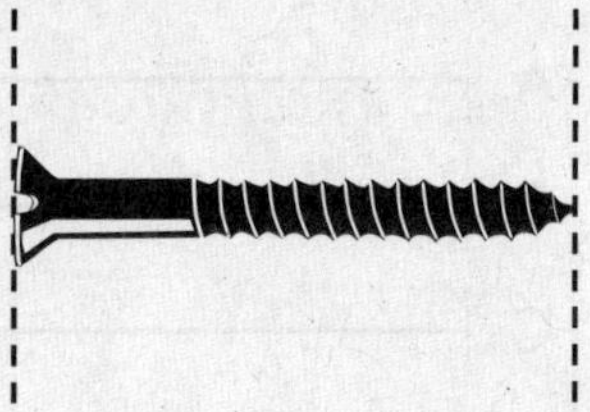

Ⓐ $1\frac{1}{2}$ inches
Ⓑ 2 inches
Ⓒ $2\frac{1}{2}$ inches
Ⓓ 3 inches

3. Julio uses an inch ruler to measure a pencil sharpener. What is the length of the pencil sharpener to the nearest fourth inch?

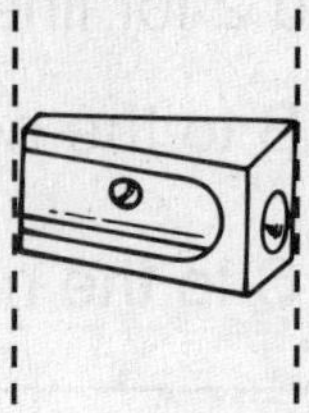

Ⓐ $\frac{1}{4}$ inch
Ⓑ $\frac{3}{4}$ inch
Ⓒ 1 inch
Ⓓ $1\frac{3}{4}$ inches

Problem Solving REAL WORLD

Use a separate sheet of paper for 4.

4. Draw 8 lines that are between 1 inch and 3 inches long. Measure each line to the nearest fourth inch, and make a line plot.

____

5. The tail on Alex's dog is $5\frac{1}{4}$ inches long. This length is between which two inch-marks on a ruler?

____

© Houghton Mifflin Harcourt Publishing Company

Name ______________________________

Lesson 87

COMMON CORE STANDARDS
CC.3.MD.5, CC.3.MD.5a

Understand Area

Lesson Objective: Explore perimeter and area as attributes of polygons.

A **unit square** is a square with a side length of 1 unit. **Area** is the measure of the number of unit squares needed to cover a surface. A **square unit** is used to measure area.

What is the area of the shape?

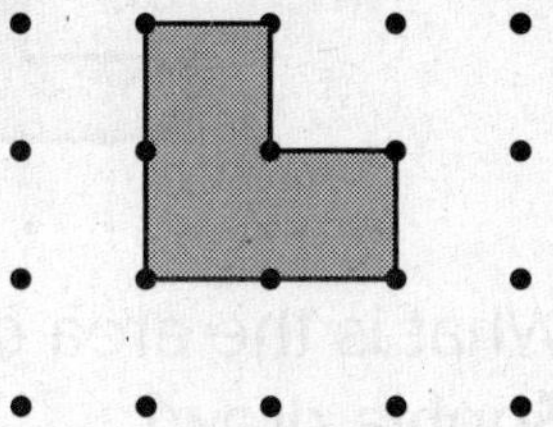

Step 1 Draw lines to show each unit square in the shape.

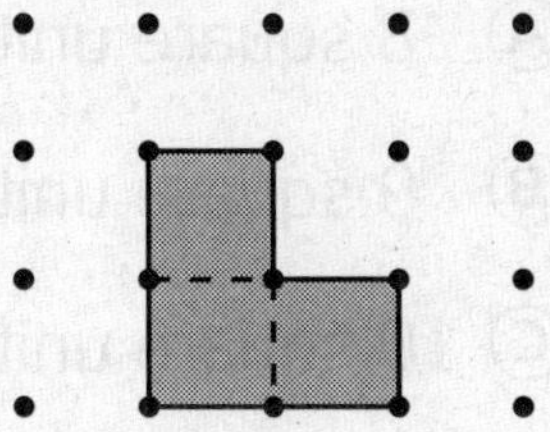

Step 2 Count the number of unit squares to find the area.

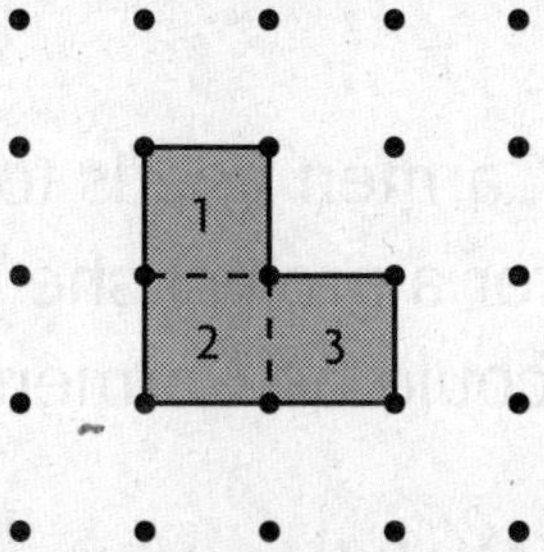

The area of the shape is **3** square units.

Count to find the area of the shape.

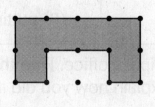

1. 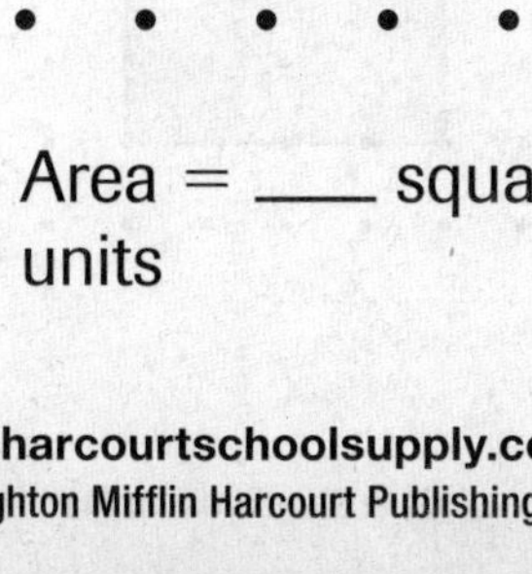

Area = ____ square units

2. 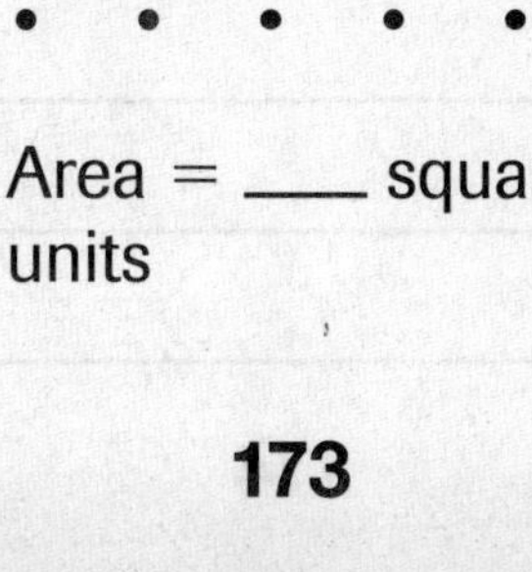

Area = ____ square units

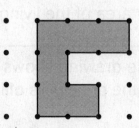

3. 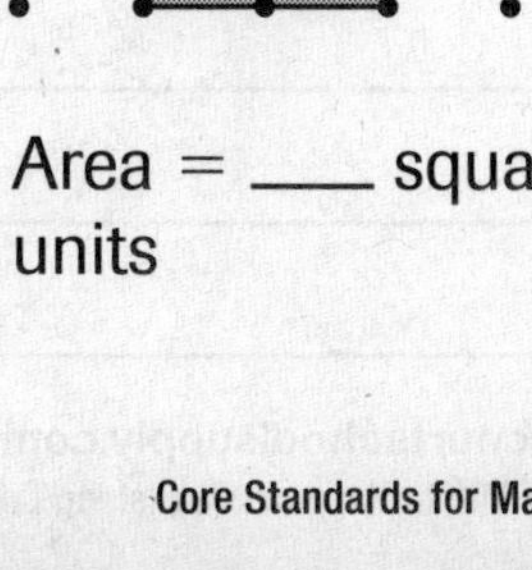

Area = ____ square units

© Houghton Mifflin Harcourt Publishing Company

Name ______________________________

Lesson 87
CC.3.MD.5, CC.3.MD.5a

1. Greg drew the shape of the parking lot at school.

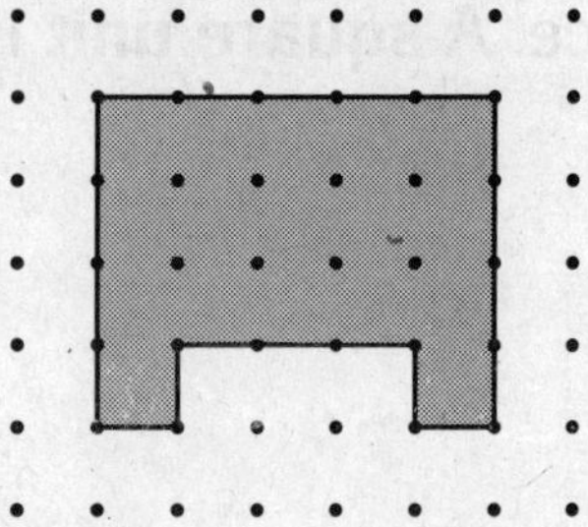

What is the area of the parking lot?

Ⓐ 15 square units

Ⓑ 17 square units

Ⓒ 20 square units

Ⓓ 22 square units

2. Mr. Chang wants to buy a rug for his living room. Which of the following does Mr. Chang need to find to know how much rug he will need?

Ⓐ height of the living room

Ⓑ length of the living room

Ⓒ perimeter of the living room

Ⓓ area of the living room

3. Sophia drew the shape of a path on dot paper.

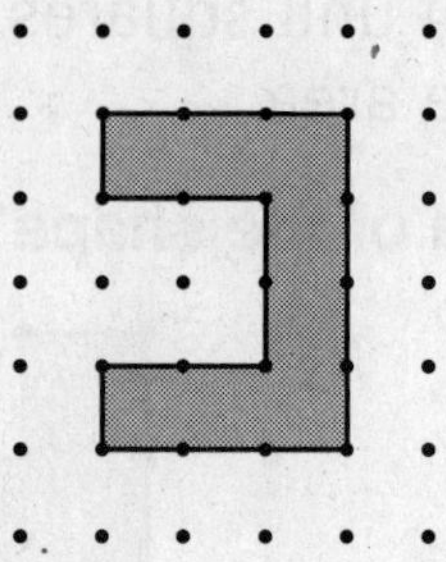

What is the area of the path Sophia drew?

Ⓐ 8 square units

Ⓑ 9 square units

Ⓒ 10 square units

Ⓓ 12 square units

4. Carmen needs to find the area for a project she is doing. Which could be Carmen's project?

Ⓐ gluing string around a picture

Ⓑ using wood to make a frame

Ⓒ painting a wall

Ⓓ putting a fence around a pool

5. The drawing shows the principal's office. Find the area of the principal's office and explain how you did it.

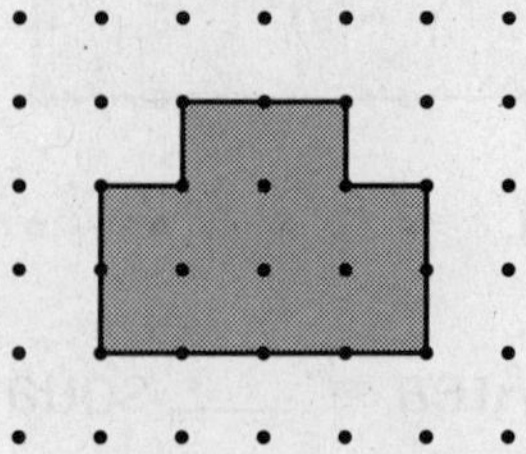

____

____

____

© Houghton Mifflin Harcourt Publishing Company

Name ______________________

COMMON CORE STANDARDS CC.3.MD.5b, CC.3.MD.6

Measure Area

Lesson Objective: Estimate and measure area of plane shapes by counting unit squares.

Find the area of the shape. Each unit square is 1 square inch.

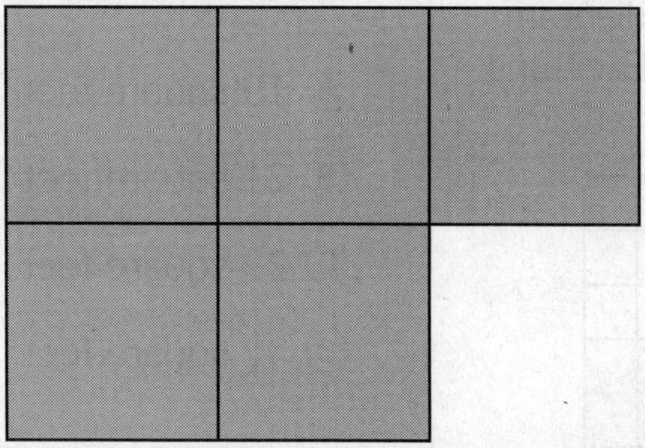

Think: How many unit squares are needed to cover this flat surface?

Step 1 Use 1-inch square tiles. Cover the surface of the shape with the tiles. Make sure there are no gaps (space between the tiles). Do not overlap the tiles.

Step 2 Count the tiles you used.
5 tiles are needed to cover the shape.

So, the area of the shape is **5** square inches.

Count to find the area of the shape.
Each square is 1 square inch.

1.

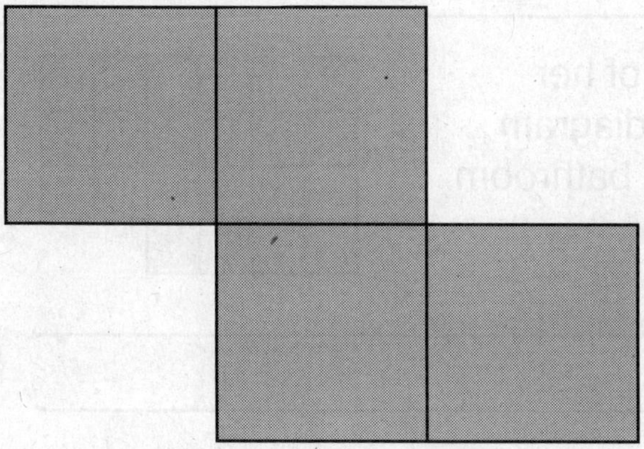

Area = _____ square inches

2.

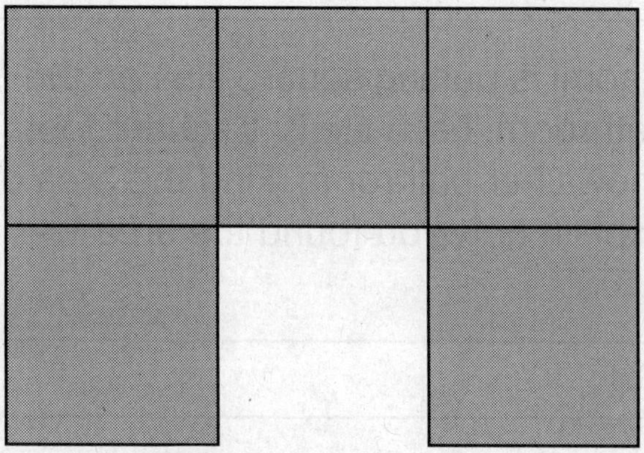

Area = _____ square inches

© Houghton Mifflin Harcourt Publishing Company

Name ______________________________

Use the information for 1–3.

Billy is painting the background for the school play. The diagram shows the background. Each unit square is 1 square foot.

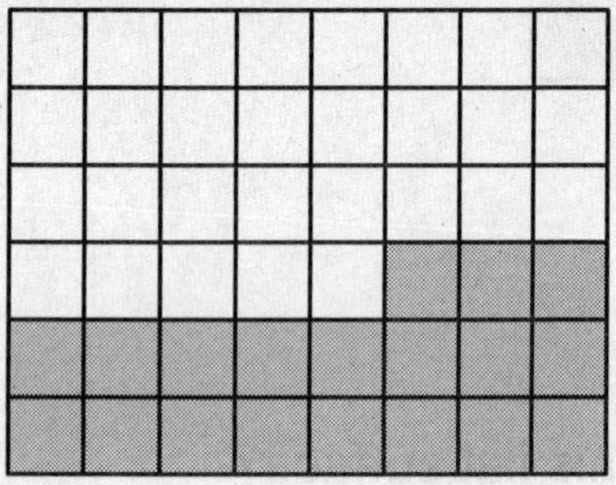

1. The shaded part shows the part Billy has already painted. What is the area of the background that Billy has already painted?

Ⓐ 16 square feet

Ⓑ 19 square feet

Ⓒ 22 square feet

Ⓓ 48 square feet

2. The white part shows the part Billy has left to paint. What is the area of the part Billy has left to paint?

Ⓐ 19 square feet

Ⓑ 21 square feet

Ⓒ 29 square feet

Ⓓ 32 square feet

3. What is the total area of the background that Billy is painting for the school play?

Ⓐ 28 square feet

Ⓑ 36 square feet

Ⓒ 40 square feet

Ⓓ 48 square feet

4. Naomi is putting square tiles on the floor of her bathroom. Each tile is 1 square foot. The diagram shows her bathroom. Find the area of the bathroom. Explain how you found the area.

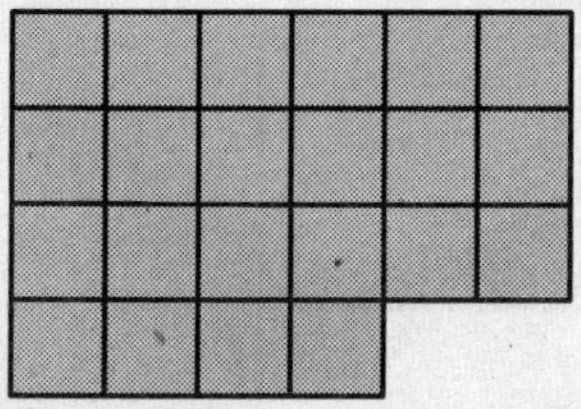

____

____

____

____

© Houghton Mifflin Harcourt Publishing Company

Name ______________________________

Lesson 89

COMMON CORE STANDARD CC.3.MD.7a

Lesson Objective: Relate area to addition and multiplication by using area models.

Use Area Models

Use multiplication to find the area of the shape.
Each unit square is 1 square meter.

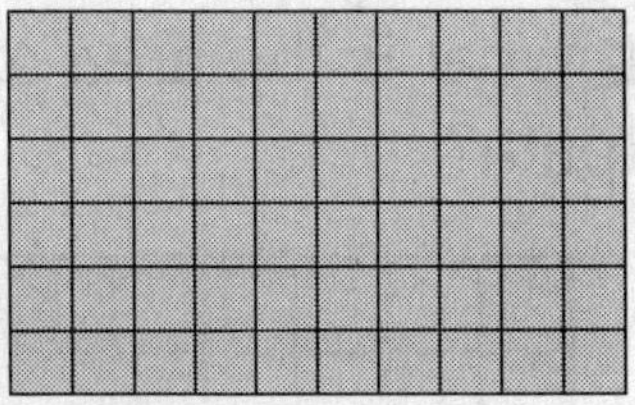

Step 1 Count the number of rows.
There are **6** rows.

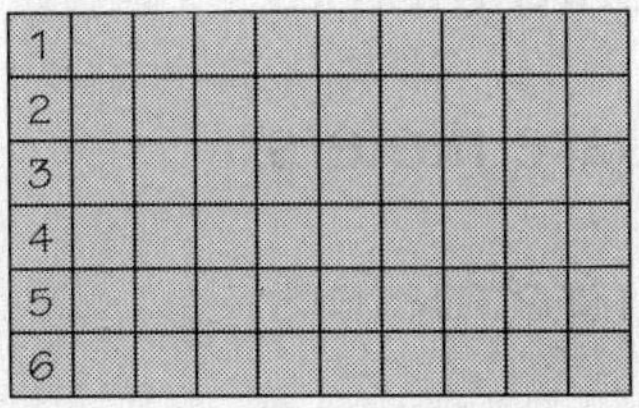

Step 2 Count the number of unit squares in each row.
There are **10** unit squares.

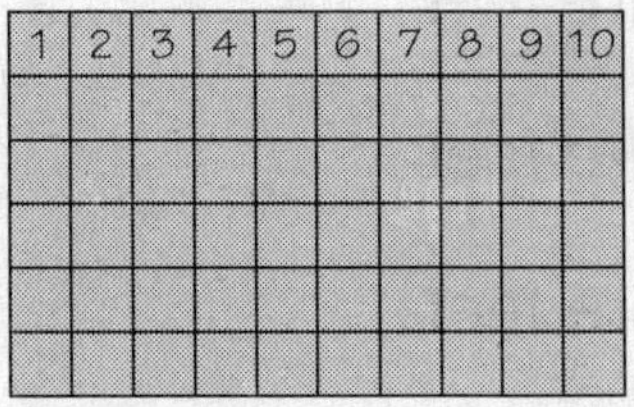

Step 3 Multiply the number of rows by the number in each row to find the area.

number of rows × number in each row = area

6 × 10 = **60**

So, the area of the shape is **60** square meters.

Find the area of the shape.
Each unit square is 1 square meter.

1.

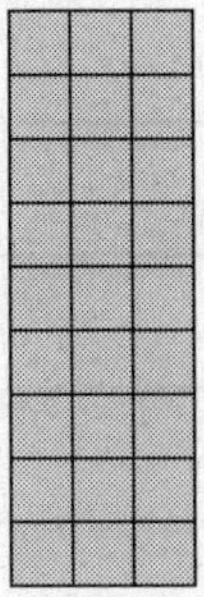

____

2.

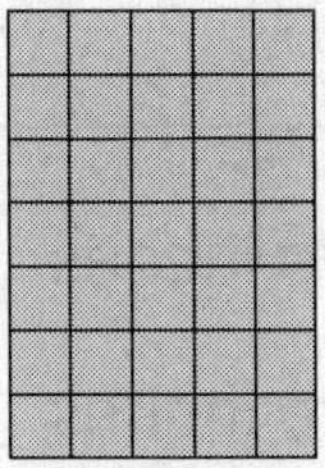

____

© Houghton Mifflin Harcourt Publishing Company

Name ______________________

Lesson 89
CC.3.MD.7a

1. The drawing shows Seth's plan for a footpath through his garden. Each unit square is 1 square foot. What is the area of Seth's footpath?

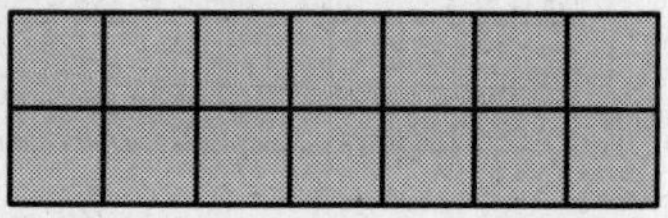

Ⓐ 14 square feet

Ⓑ 16 square feet

Ⓒ 18 square feet

Ⓓ 21 square feet

2. Keisha draws a sketch of a tile mosaic she wants to make on grid paper. Each unit square is 1 square inch. What is the area of Keisha's mosaic?

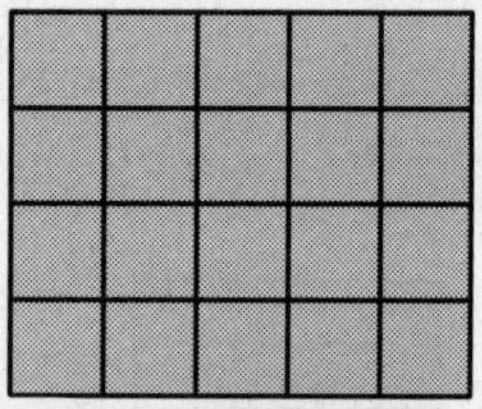

Ⓐ 9 square inches

Ⓑ 18 square inches

Ⓒ 20 square inches

Ⓓ 25 square inches

3. The drawing represents a vegetable garden in the Wilsons' backyard. Each unit square is 1 square meter. What is the area of the Wilsons' vegetable garden?

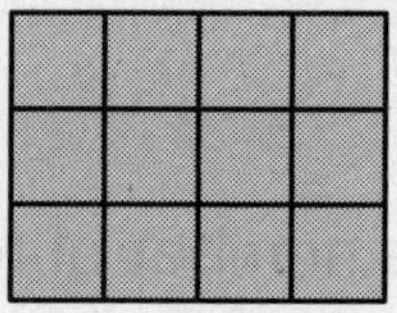

Ⓐ 7 square meters

Ⓑ 12 square meters

Ⓒ 14 square meters

Ⓓ 24 square meters

4. Roberto put square tiles down in the entryway. Each tile is 1 square foot. Write the area of the entryway floor. Explain how you found the area.

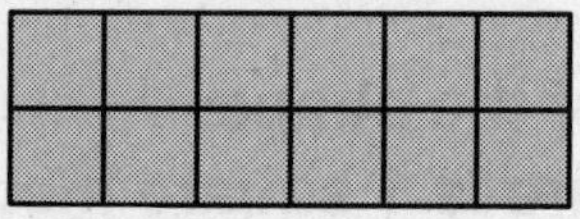

© Houghton Mifflin Harcourt Publishing Company

Name ______________________

Lesson 90

COMMON CORE STANDARD CC.3.MD.7b

Lesson Objective: Solve area problems by using the strategy *find a pattern.*

Problem Solving • Area of Rectangles

Mrs. Wilson wants to plant a garden, so she drew plans for some sample gardens. She wants to know how the areas of the gardens are related. How will the areas of Gardens A and B change? How will the areas of Gardens C and D change?

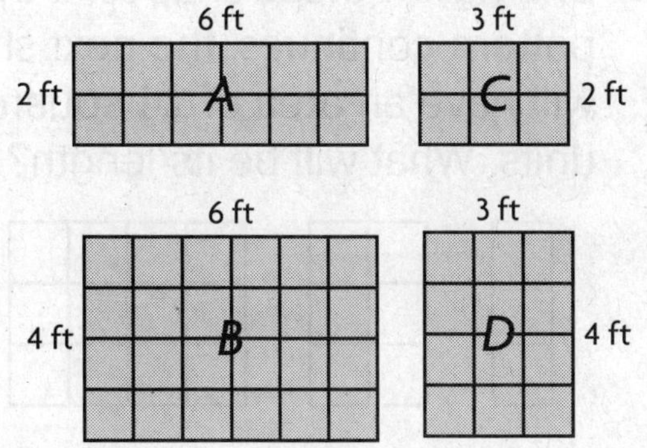

Use the graphic organizer to help you solve the problem.

Read the Problem

What do I need to find?	What information do I need to use?	How will I use the information?
I need to know how the areas will change from *A* to *B* and from **C** to **D**.	I need to use the **length** and **width** of each garden to find its area.	I will record the areas in a table. Then I will look for a pattern to see how the **areas** will change.

Solve the Problem

	Length	Width	Area		Length	Width	Area
Garden A	2 ft	6 ft	12 sq ft	Garden C	2 ft	3 ft	6 sq ft
Garden B	4 ft	6 ft	24 sq ft	Garden D	4 ft	3 ft	12 sq ft

From the table, I see that the lengths will be doubled and the widths will be the same.

The areas in square feet will change from **12** to **24** and from **6** to **12**.

So, the area will be **doubled**.

Solve.

1. Mrs. Rios made a flower garden that is 8 feet long and 2 feet wide. She made a vegetable garden that is 4 feet long and 2 feet wide. How do the areas change?

____

____

© Houghton Mifflin Harcourt Publishing Company

1. Brian drew these shapes. If the pattern continues, the next shape will have an area of 24 square units. What will be its length?

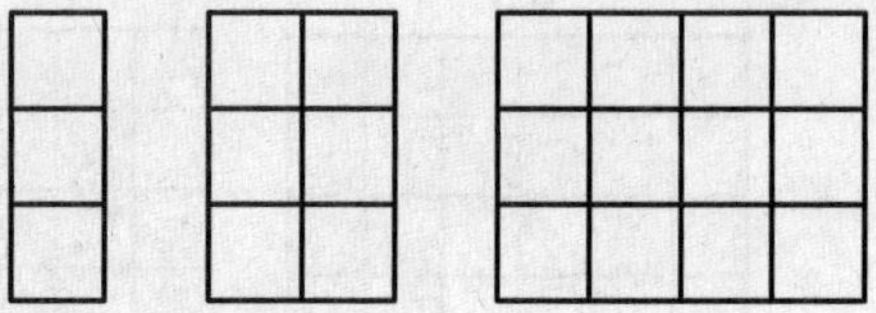

Ⓐ 4 units

Ⓑ 6 units

Ⓒ 8 units

Ⓓ 16 units

2. Brent uses carpet squares to make the pattern. Each unit square is 1 square foot. If the pattern continues, what will be the area of the fourth shape?

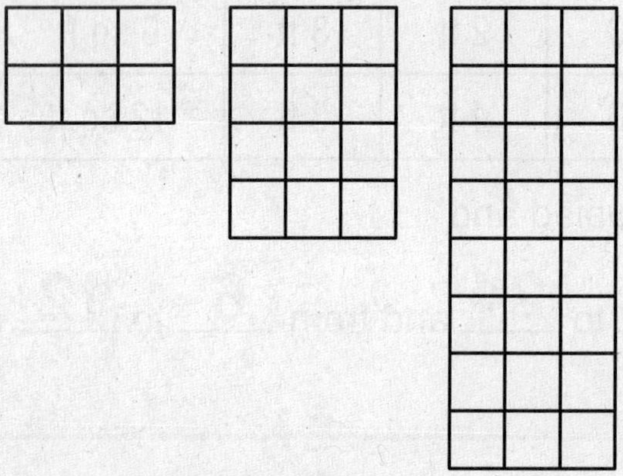

Ⓐ 27 square feet

Ⓑ 30 square feet

Ⓒ 42 square feet

Ⓓ 48 square feet

3. Julia uses tiles to make the pattern below. Each unit square is 1 square inch. If the pattern continues, what will be the area of the fourth shape?

Ⓐ 6 square inches

Ⓑ 8 square inches

Ⓒ 10 square inches

Ⓓ 12 square inches

4. Amy measured two rooms at her school.The first room is 8 feet wide and 10 feet long. The second room is 16 feet wide and 10 feet long. Describe how the lengths and widths of the rooms are related. Then use this information to explain how the areas of the two rooms are related.

____

____

____

____

____

____

____

____

© Houghton Mifflin Harcourt Publishing Company

Name ______________________________ **Lesson 91**

COMMON CORE STANDARDS CC.3.MD.7c, CC.3.MD.7d

Lesson Objective: Apply the Distributive Property to area models and to find the area of combined rectangles.

Area of Combined Rectangles

You can break apart a shape into rectangles to find the total area of the shape.

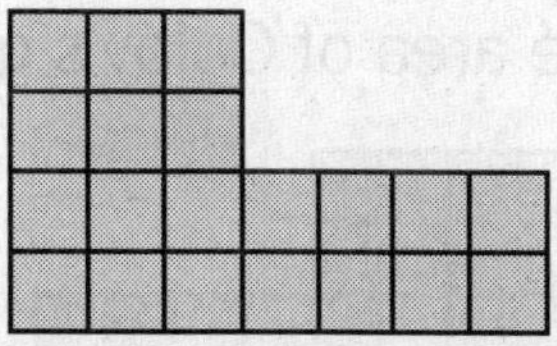

Step 1 Draw a line to break apart the shape into two rectangles.

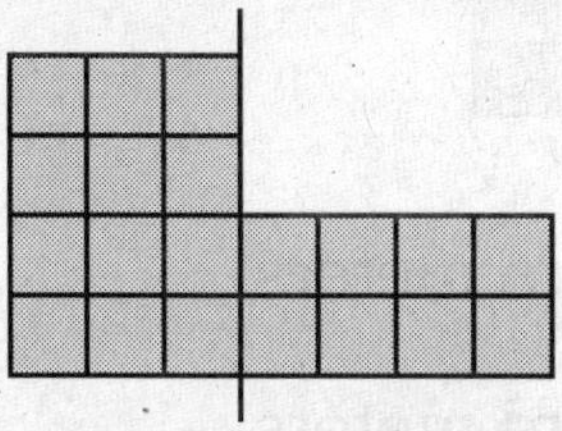

Step 2 Count the number of unit squares in each rectangle.

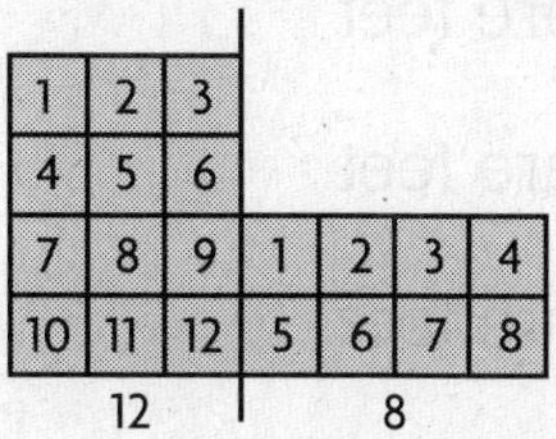

Step 3 Add the number of unit squares in each rectangle to find the total area.

12 + **8** = **20** unit squares

So, the area of the shape is **20** square units.

Draw a line to break apart the shape into rectangles. Find the area of the shape.

1.

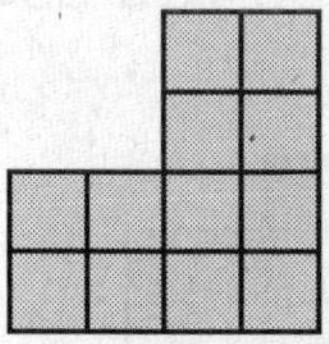

____

2.

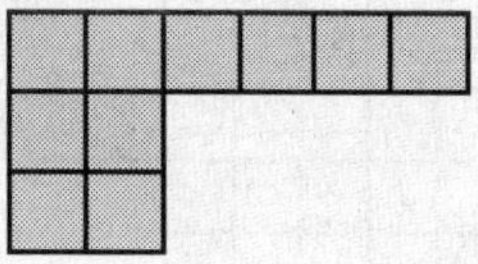

____

3.

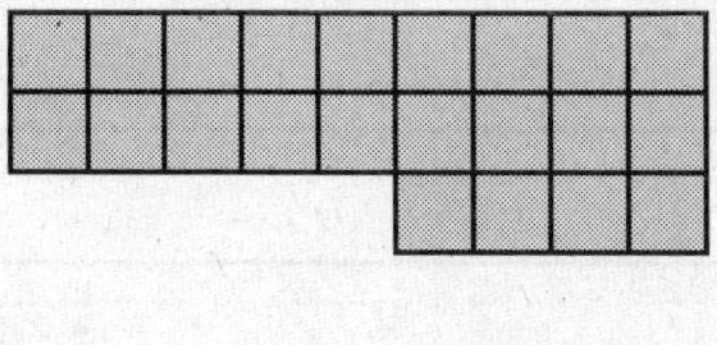

____

4.

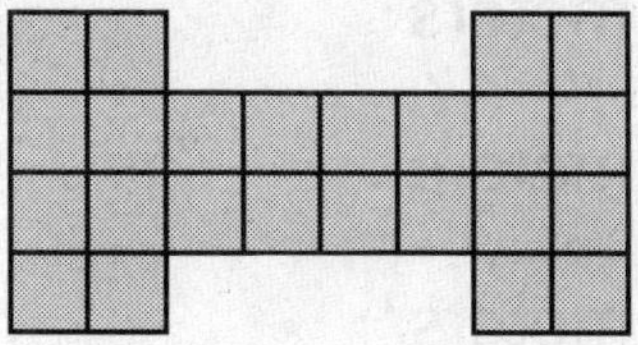

____

© Houghton Mifflin Harcourt Publishing Company

Name ______________________

1. Colby drew a diagram of his garden. Each unit square is 1 square foot. What is the area of Colby's garden?

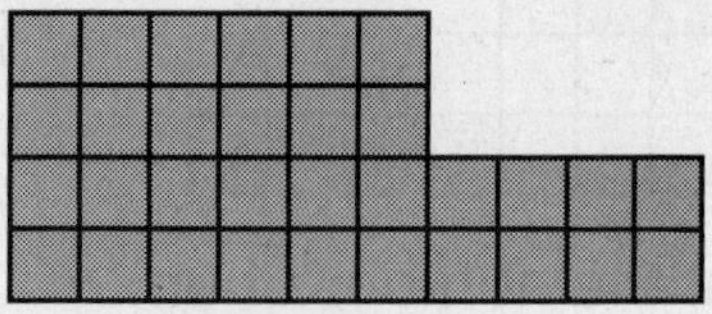

Ⓐ 32 square feet

Ⓑ 30 square feet

Ⓒ 24 square feet

Ⓓ 20 square feet

2. The school office is shown. Each unit square is equal to 1 square meter. What is the total area of the school office?

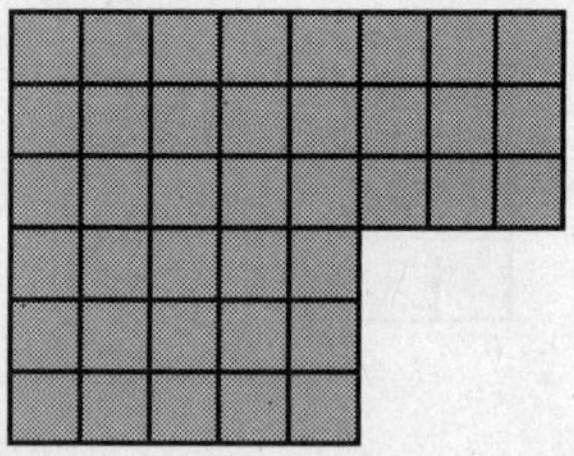

Ⓐ 24 square meters

Ⓑ 30 square meters

Ⓒ 39 square meters

Ⓓ 48 square meters

3. Mrs. McCarthy's art studio is shown. Each unit square is equal to 1 square meter. What is the total area of Mrs. McCarthy's art studio?

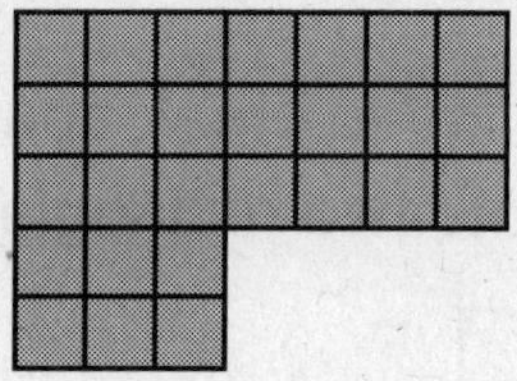

Ⓐ 35 square meters

Ⓑ 27 square meters

Ⓒ 25 square meters

Ⓓ 21 square meters

4. Jake drew the diagram of his bedroom shown. Each unit square is equal to 1 square meter. Write the area of Jake's bedroom. Explain the steps you used to find the area.

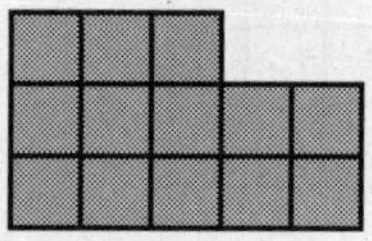

© Houghton Mifflin Harcourt Publishing Company

Name ______________________________

Lesson 92

COMMON CORE STANDARD CC.3.MD.8

Lesson Objective: Explore perimeter of polygons by counting units on grid paper.

Model Perimeter

Perimeter is the distance around a shape.

Find the perimeter of the shape.

Step 1 Choose a unit to begin counting and label it 1.

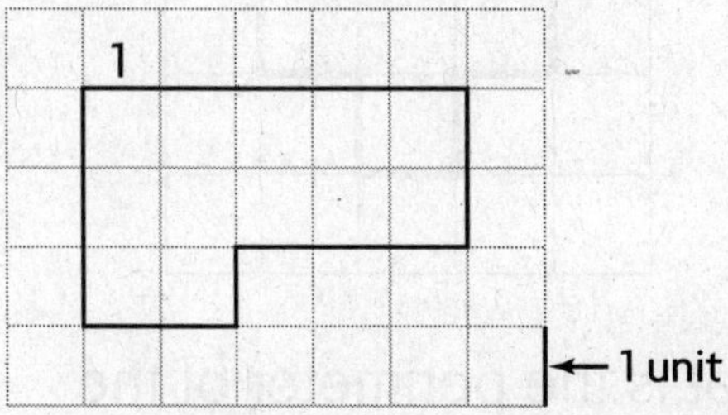

Step 2 Count each unit around the shape to find the perimeter.
16 units

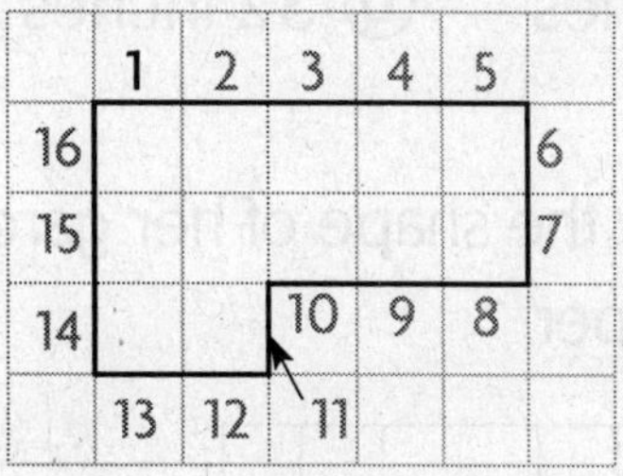

So, the perimeter of the shape is **16** units.

Find the perimeter of the shape. Each unit is 1 centimeter.

1.

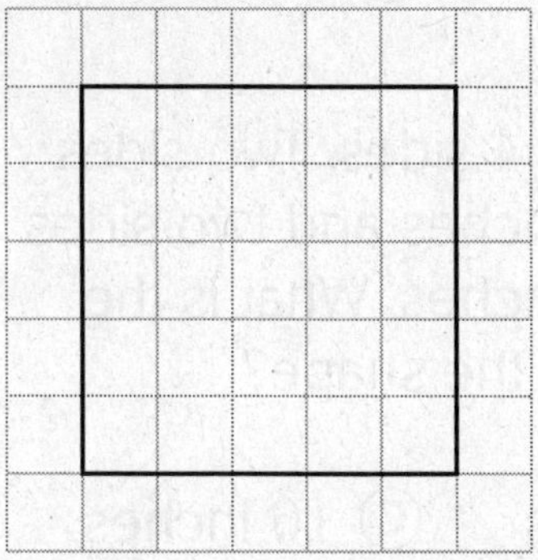

__________ centimeters

2.

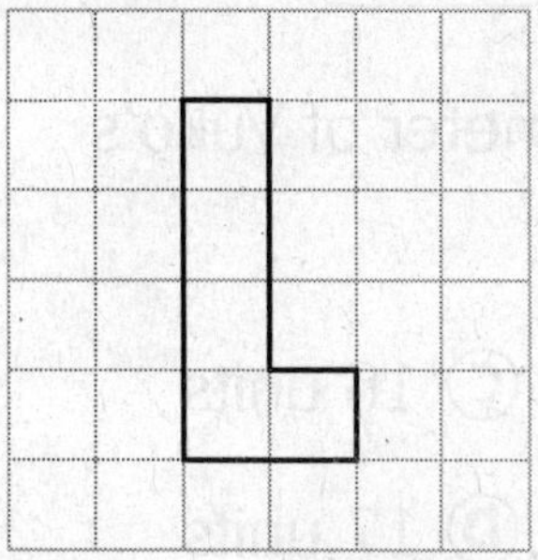

__________ centimeters

3.

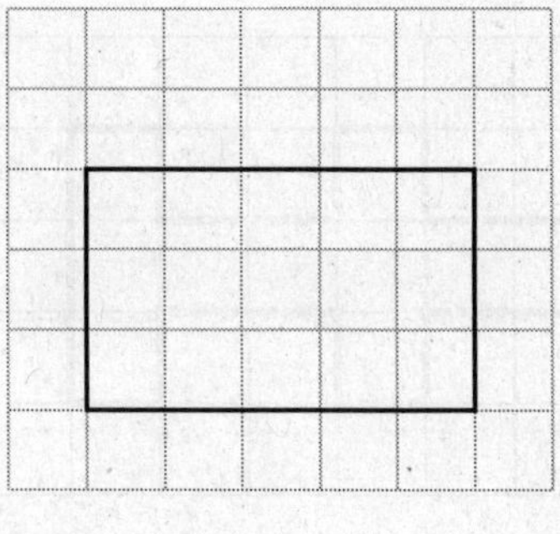

__________ centimeters

4.

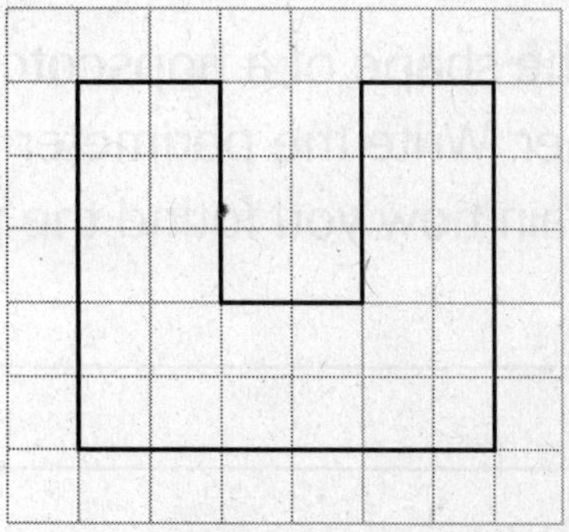

__________ centimeters

www.harcourtschoolsupply.com
© Houghton Mifflin Harcourt Publishing Company

1. Irie draws a 4-sided shape on his paper that measures 8 inches on each side. What is the perimeter of the shape?

Ⓐ 8 inches　Ⓒ 24 inches

Ⓑ 16 inches　Ⓓ 32 inches

2. Yuko drew the shape of her garden on grid paper.

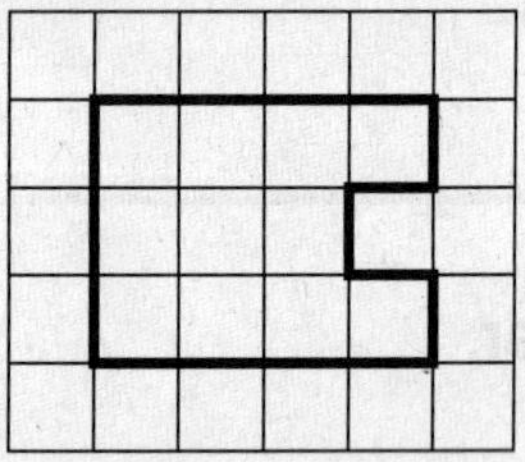

What is the perimeter of Yuko's garden?

Ⓐ 14 units　Ⓒ 16 units

Ⓑ 15 units　Ⓓ 17 units

3. Adam drew this shape on grid paper.

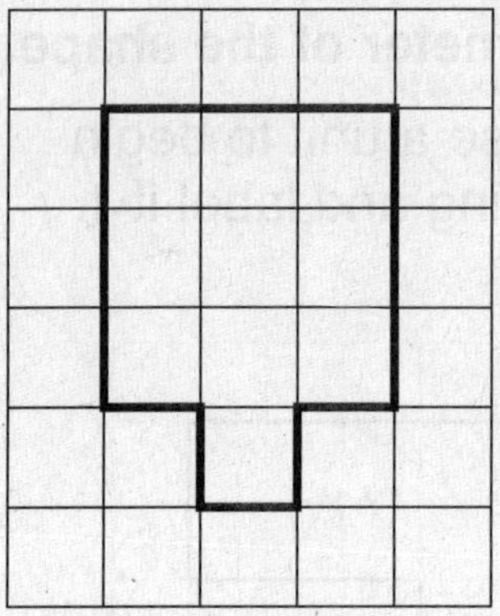

What is the perimeter of the shape?

Ⓐ 14 units　Ⓒ 10 units

Ⓑ 12 units　Ⓓ 9 units

4. A shape has 4 sides. Two sides measure 5 inches and two sides measure 8 inches. What is the perimeter of the shape?

Ⓐ 40 inches　Ⓒ 16 inches

Ⓑ 26 inches　Ⓓ 10 inches

5. Ling drew the shape of a hopscotch game on grid paper. Write the perimeter of the shape. Explain how you found the perimeter.

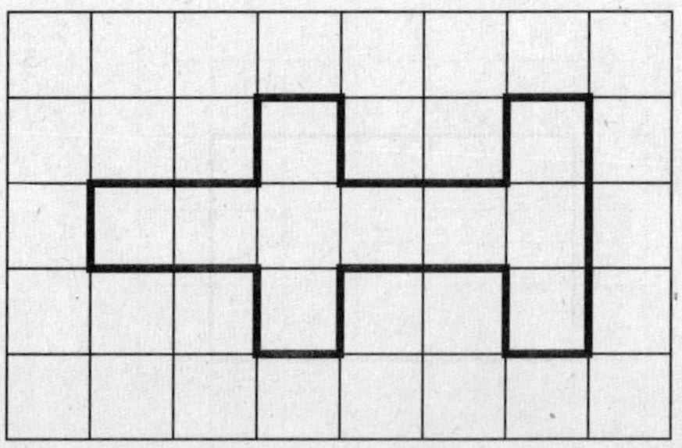

____

____

____

____

© Houghton Mifflin Harcourt Publishing Company

Lesson Objective: Estimate and measure perimeter of polygons using inch and centimeter rulers.

Find Perimeter

Kelsey wants to know the perimeter of the shape below. She can use an inch ruler to find the perimeter.

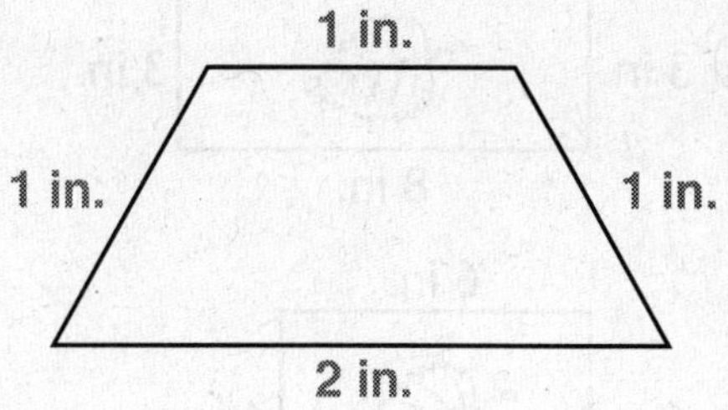

Step 1 Choose one side of the shape to measure. Place the zero mark of the ruler on the end of the side. Measure to the nearest inch. Write the length.

Step 2 Use the ruler to measure the other three sides. Write the lengths.

Step 3 Add the lengths of all the sides.
$1 + 1 + 2 + 1 = 5$

So, the perimeter of the shape is **5** inches.

Use an inch ruler to find the perimeter.

1.

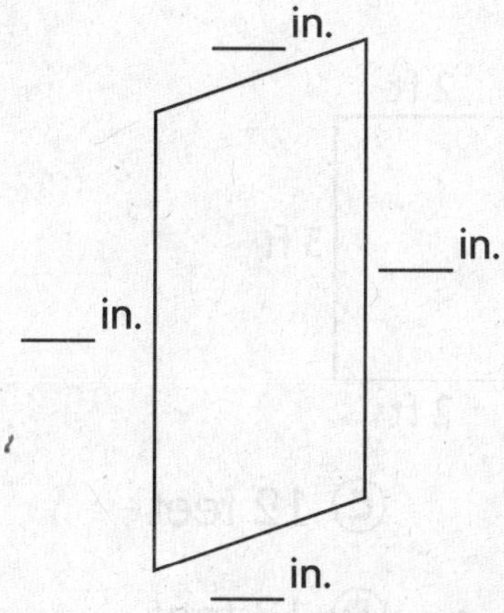

______________ inches

2.

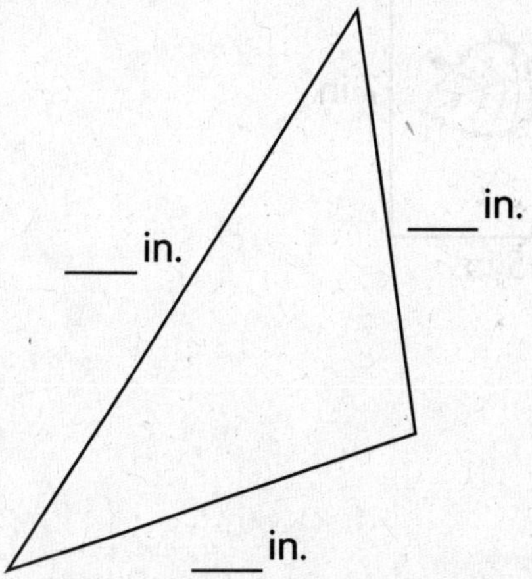

______________ inches

© Houghton Mifflin Harcourt Publishing Company

Name ______________________________

Lesson 93
CC.3.MD.8

1. Fiona bought a picture with a perimeter of 24 inches. Which picture did she buy?

Ⓐ 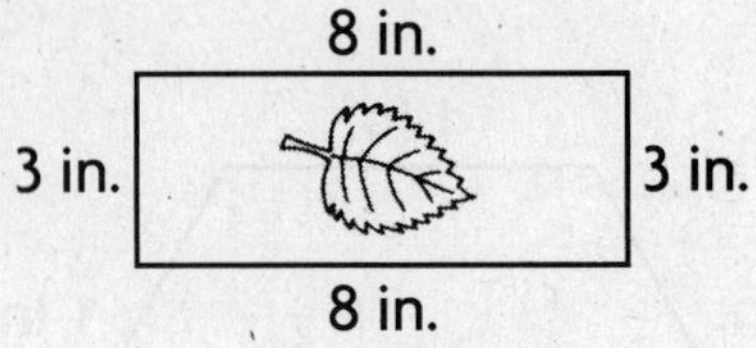

Ⓑ 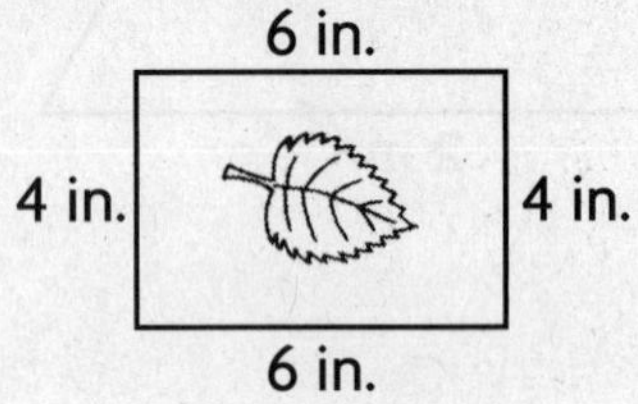

Ⓒ 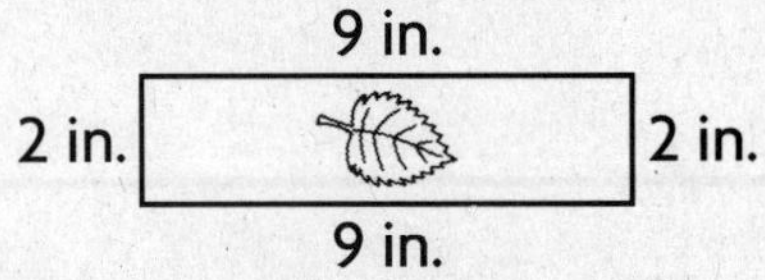

Ⓓ 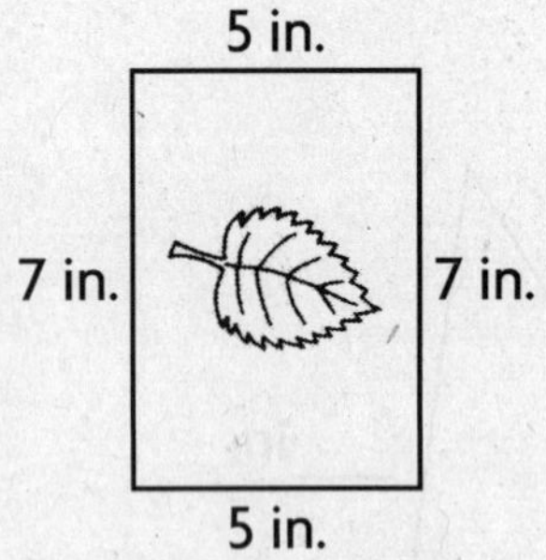

2. Kim wants to put trim around a picture she drew. How many centimeters of trim does Kim need for the perimeter of the picture?

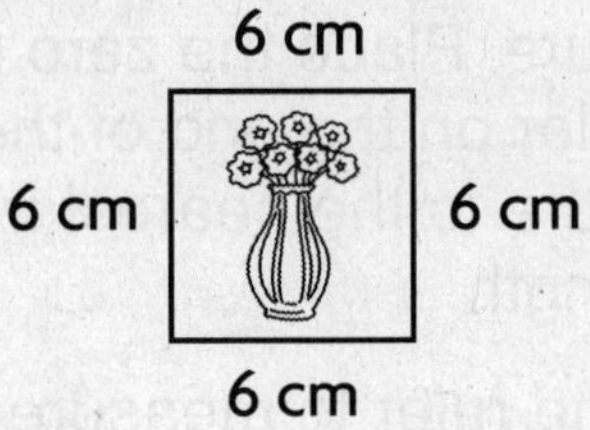

Ⓐ 6 cm Ⓒ 24 cm

Ⓑ 12 cm Ⓓ 36 cm

3. Mr. Gasper is putting wood trim around this window. How many feet of wood trim does Mr. Gasper need for the perimeter of the window?

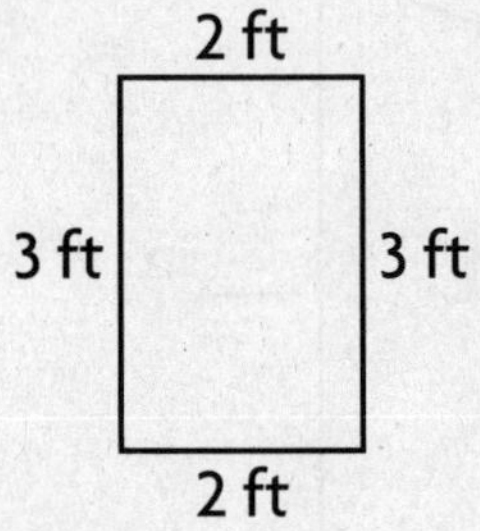

Ⓐ 6 feet Ⓒ 12 feet

Ⓑ 10 feet Ⓓ 13 feet

4. Dylan used a centimeter ruler to draw this square. Find the perimeter of Dylan's square and explain how you did it.

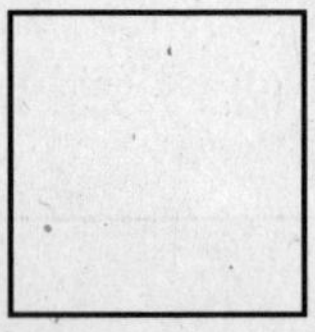

____

____

____

© Houghton Mifflin Harcourt Publishing Company

Name ______________________________

Lesson 94

COMMON CORE STANDARD CC.3.MD.8

Lesson Objective: Find the unknown length of a side of a polygon when you know its perimeter.

Algebra • Find Unknown Side Lengths

An unknown side length is a side that does not have its length labeled with a number. Instead the side is labeled with a symbol or letter, such as *a*.

The perimeter of the shape is 20 meters.
Find the length of side *a*.

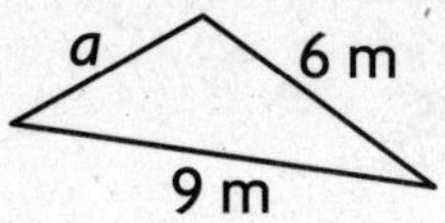

Think: There is only one unknown side length.

Step 1 Add the *known* side lengths.
$6 + 9 = 15$

Step 2 Subtract the sum of the known side lengths from the perimeter.
$20 - 15 = 5$

Step 3 Add to check your work.
$6 + 9 + 5 = 20$ ✓

So, the unknown side length, *a*, is **5** meters.

The perimeter of the square is 12 feet.
What is the length of each side of the square?

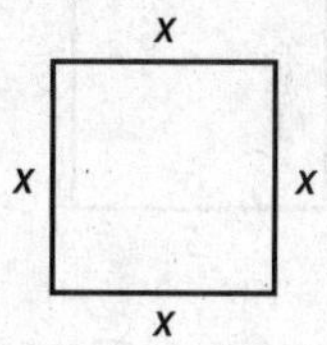

Think: A square has four sides of equal length.

Step 1 Divide the perimeter by the number of sides.
$12 \div 4 = 3$

Step 2 Multiply to check your work.
$4 \times 3 = 12$ ✓

So, the length of each side, *x*, is **3** feet.

Find the unknown side lengths.

1. Perimeter = 18 centimeters

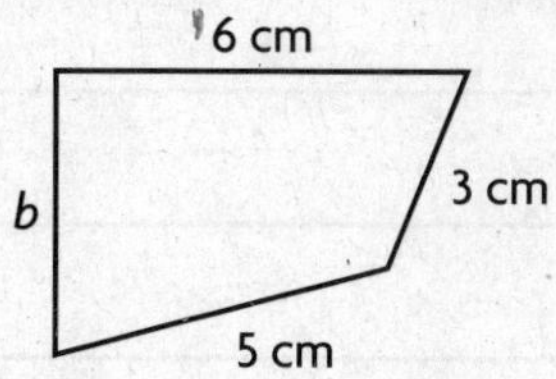

b = ______ centimeters

2. Perimeter = 20 yards

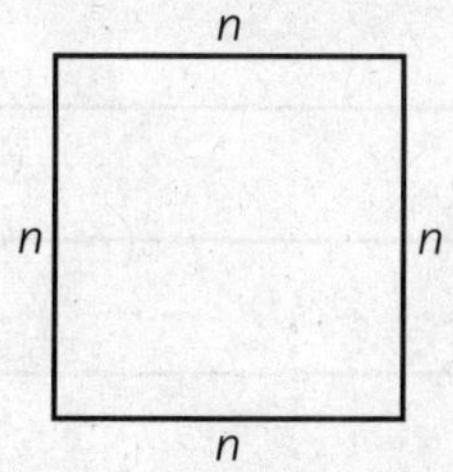

n = ______ yards

© Houghton Mifflin Harcourt Publishing Company

Name ______________________________

Lesson 94
CC.3.MD.8

1. Natasha cut out a rectangle that has a perimeter of 34 centimeters. The width of the rectangle is 7 centimeters. What is the length of the rectangle?

Ⓐ 5 centimeters

Ⓑ 10 centimeters

Ⓒ 20 centimeters

Ⓓ 27 centimeters

2. Vanessa uses a ruler to draw a square. The perimeter of the square is 12 centimeters. What is the length of each side of the square?

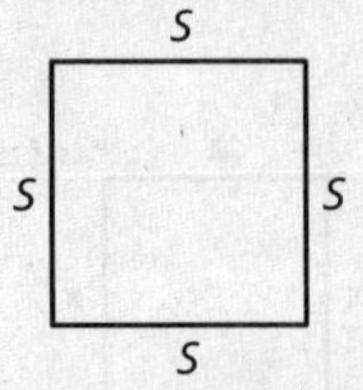

Ⓐ 3 cm Ⓒ 6 cm

Ⓑ 4 cm Ⓓ 48 cm

3. Mrs. Rios wants to put a wallpaper border around the room shown. She will use 36 feet of wallpaper border. What is the unknown side length?

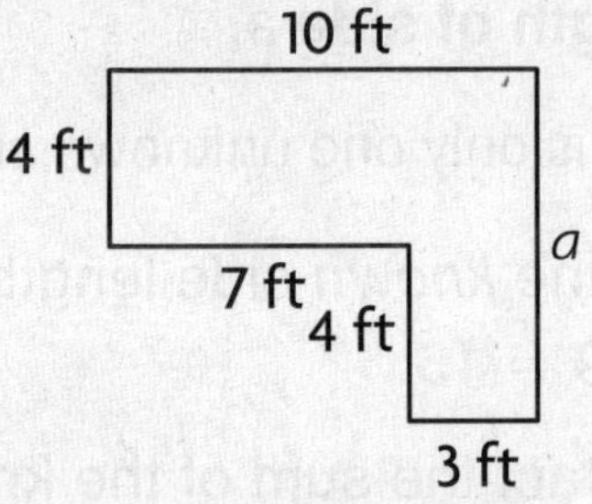

Ⓐ 6 feet Ⓒ 14 feet

Ⓑ 8 feet Ⓓ 28 feet

4. Frank uses 16 feet of fencing around the perimeter of a rectangular garden. The garden is 5 feet long. What is the width of the garden?

Ⓐ 11 feet Ⓒ 3 feet

Ⓑ 6 feet Ⓓ 2 feet

---

5. Mr. Rios has a rectangular rug. The perimeter of the rug is 28 feet. The width of the rug is 6 feet. Find the length of the rug. Explain the steps you used to find the missing length.

____

____

____

© Houghton Mifflin Harcourt Publishing Company

Name ___________________________

Lesson 95

COMMON CORE STANDARD CC.3.MD.8

Lesson Objective: Compare areas of rectangles that have the same perimeter.

Same Perimeter, Different Areas

You can use perimeter and area to compare rectangles.

Compare the perimeters of Rectangle *A* and Rectangle *B*.

A

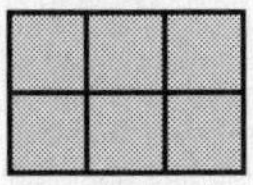

B

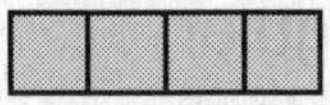

Find the number of units around each rectangle.

Rectangle *A*: 3 + 2 + 3 + 2 = **10** units

Rectangle *B*: 4 + 1 + 4 + 1 = **10** units

Compare: **10** units = **10** units

So, Rectangle *A* has the same perimeter as Rectangle *B*.

Compare the areas of Rectangle *A* and Rectangle *B*.

A

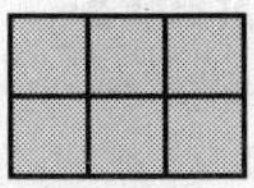

B

Find the number of unit squares needed to cover each rectangle.

Rectangle *A*: **2** rows of **3** = 2 × 3, or **6** square units

Rectangle *B*: **1** row of **4** = 1 × 4, or **4** square units

Compare: **6** square units > **4** square units

So, Rectangle *A* has a greater area than Rectangle *B*.

Find the perimeter and the area. Tell which rectangle has a greater area.

1. *A*

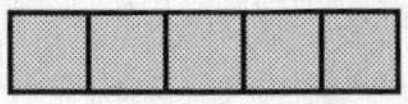

B

A: Perimeter = __________;

Area = __________

B: Perimeter = __________;

Area = __________

Rectangle ____ has a greater area.

2. *A*

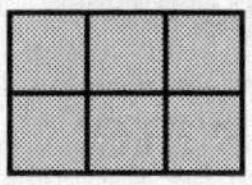

B

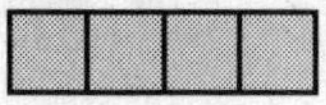

A: Perimeter = __________;

Area = __________

B: Perimeter = __________;

Area = __________

Rectangle ____ has a greater area.

© Houghton Mifflin Harcourt Publishing Company

Name ______________________________

Lesson 95
CC.3.MD.8

Use the information for 1–3.

Sarah is building a garden in the backyard. She drew a diagram of one way to lay out the garden.

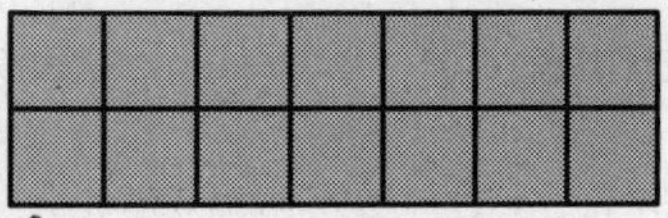

1. What is the perimeter of the garden?

Ⓐ 9 units

Ⓑ 12 units

Ⓒ 14 units

Ⓓ 18 units

2. What is the area of the garden?

Ⓐ 6 square units

Ⓑ 12 square units

Ⓒ 14 square units

Ⓓ 18 square units

3. Sarah wants her rectangular garden to have the greatest possible area, but she wants the same perimeter as shown in her diagram. Which could be the length and width of Sarah's garden?

Ⓐ 5 units by 4 units

Ⓑ 6 units by 3 units

Ⓒ 8 units by 1 unit

Ⓓ 5 units by 2 units

Problem Solving REAL WORLD

4. Tara's and Jody's bedrooms are shaped like rectangles. Tara's bedroom is 9 feet long and 8 feet wide. Jody's bedroom is 7 feet long and 10 feet wide. Whose bedroom has the greater area? **Explain**.

____

____

5. Mr. Sanchez has 16 feet of fencing to put around a rectangular garden. He wants the garden to have the greatest possible area. How long should the sides of the garden be?

____

____

© Houghton Mifflin Harcourt Publishing Company

Name ______________________________

Lesson 96

COMMON CORE STANDARD CC.3.MD.8

Lesson Objective: Compare perimeters of rectangles that have the same area.

Same Area, Different Perimeters

Find the perimeter and area of Rectangles *A* and *B*. Tell which rectangle has a greater perimeter.

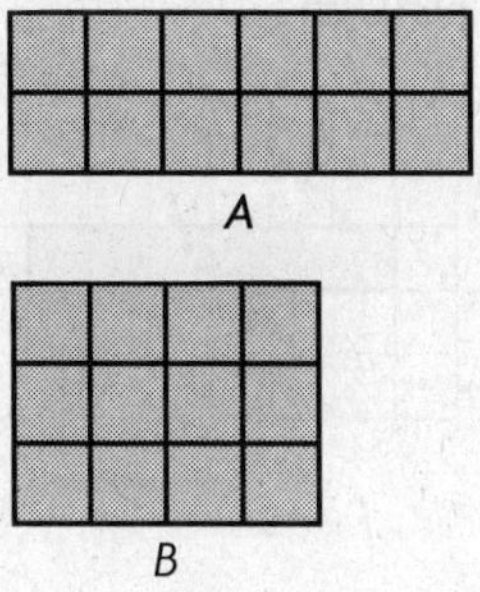

Step 1 Find the area of each rectangle. You can multiply the number of unit squares in each row by the number of rows.

Rectangle *A*: 2 × 6 = **12** square units

Rectangle *B*: **3** × **4** = **12** square units

Step 2 Find the perimeter of each rectangle. You can add the sides.

Rectangle *A*: **6** + **2** + **6** + **2** = **16** units

Rectangle *B*: **4** + **3** + **4** + **3** = **14** units

Step 3 Compare the perimeters. **16** units > **14** units.

So, Rectangle ***A*** has a greater perimeter.

Find the perimeter and the area. Tell which rectangle has a greater perimeter.

1.

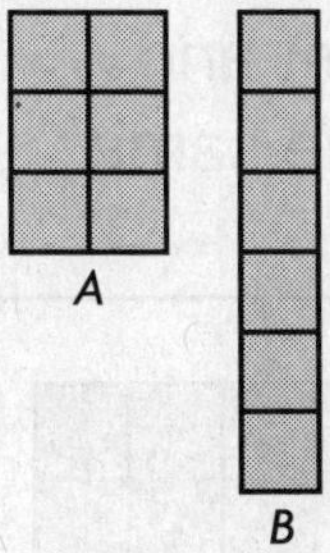

A: Area = ______________________;

Perimeter = ____________

B: Area = ______________________;

Perimeter = ____________

Rectangle ____ has a greater perimeter.

2.

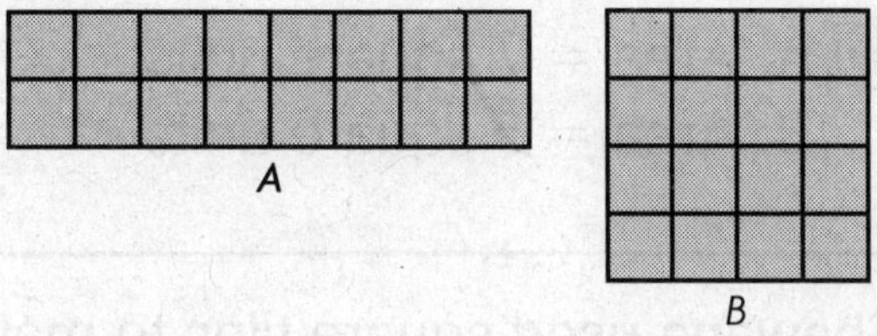

A: Area = ______________________;

Perimeter = ____________

B: Area = ______________________;

Perimeter = ____________

Rectangle ____ has a greater perimeter.

© Houghton Mifflin Harcourt Publishing Company

Use the information for 1–3.

Cheung drew two rectangles on grid paper.

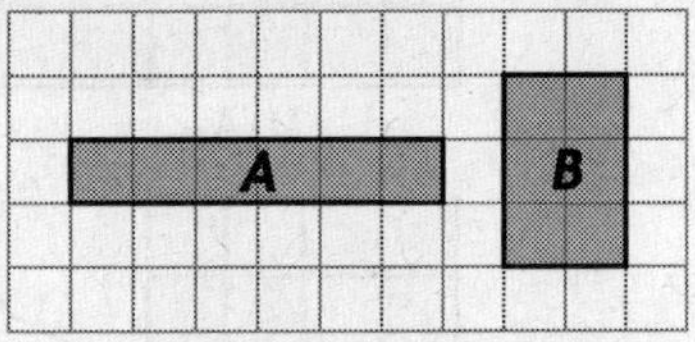

1. What is the area of each rectangle?

Ⓐ *A*: Area = 6 square units;
B: Area = 6 square units

Ⓑ *A*: Area = 6 square units;
B: Area = 3 square units

Ⓒ *A*: Area = 14 square units;
B: Area = 10 square units

Ⓓ *A*: Area = 7 square units;
B: Area = 5 square units

2. What is the perimeter of rectangle *B*?

Ⓐ 5 units

Ⓑ 6 units

Ⓒ 8 units

Ⓓ 10 units

3. Which statement about the perimeters and areas of Cheung's rectangles is true?

Ⓐ The areas are the same and the perimeters are the same.

Ⓑ The areas are the same and the perimeters are different.

Ⓒ The areas are different and the perimeters are different.

Ⓓ The areas are different and the perimeters are the same.

---

4. Shawana used square tiles to make the rectangles shown. Compare and contrast the areas and perimeters of her two rectangles.

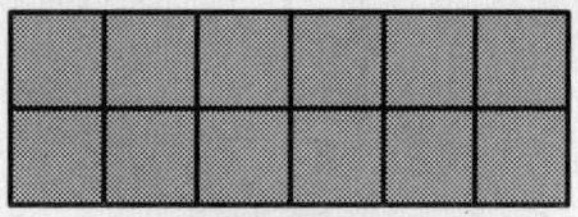

A

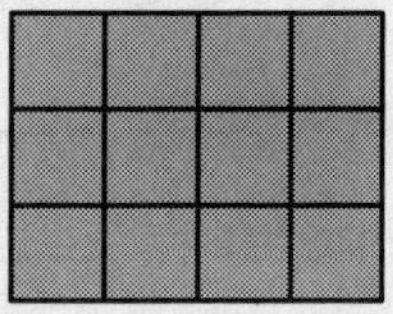

B

____

____

____

____

____

© Houghton Mifflin Harcourt Publishing Company

Name ____________________________________

Lesson 97

COMMON CORE STANDARD CC.3.G.1

Lesson Objective: Identify and describe attributes of plane shapes.

Describe Plane Shapes

You can use math words to describe plane shapes.

point

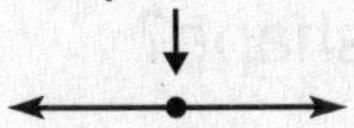

an exact position or location

line

a straight path that goes in two directions without end

endpoints

points that are used to show segments of lines

line segment

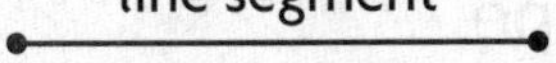

part of a straight line and has 2 endpoints

ray

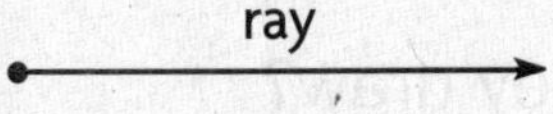

part of a straight line that has 1 endpoint and continues in one direction

A **plane shape** is a shape on a flat surface. It is formed by points that make curved paths, line segments, or both. Plane shapes can be open or closed.

A **closed shape** starts and ends at the same point.

An **open shape** does not start and end at the same point.

Look at this plane shape called a triangle.

It is a **closed shape.**

It has **3 line segments.**

The line segments meet at the **endpoints.**

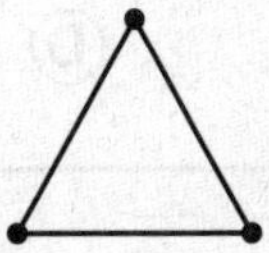

Circle all the words that describe the shape.

1.

line
line segment

2.

point
ray

3.

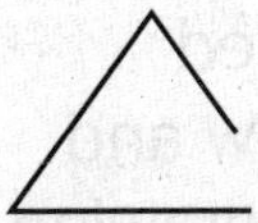

closed shape
open shape

4.

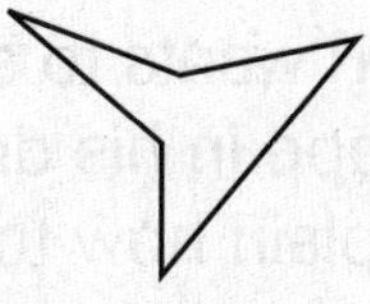

closed shape
open shape

Write whether the shape is *open* or *closed*.

5.

____

6.

____

7.

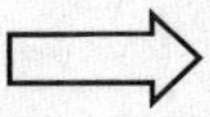

____

8.

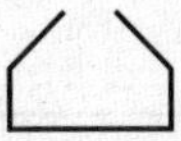

____

© Houghton Mifflin Harcourt Publishing Company

1. Abby drew a point. Which shows a point?

Ⓐ

Ⓑ

Ⓒ

Ⓓ

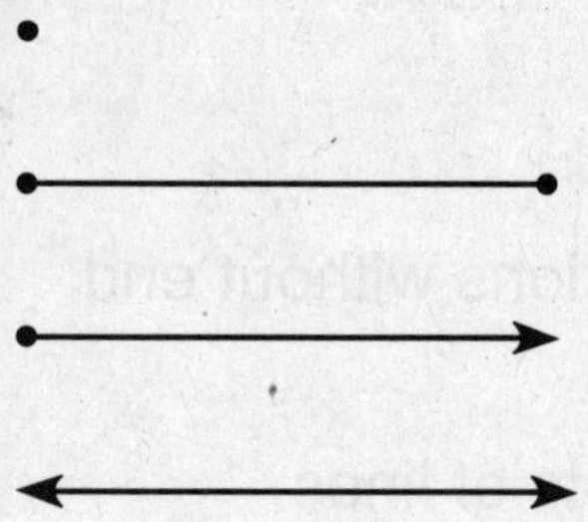

2. Cyrus uses line segments to draw a shape.

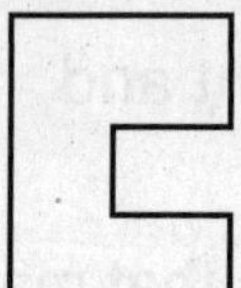

How many line segments does Cyrus's shape have?

Ⓐ 6 Ⓒ 8

Ⓑ 7 Ⓓ 9

3. Four friends draw shapes. Rachel, Zoe, and Jorge draw closed shapes. Andy draws an open shape. Which is Andy's shape?

Ⓐ 

Ⓑ 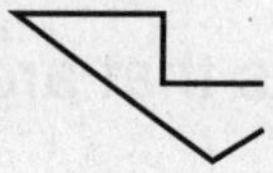

Ⓒ 

Ⓓ 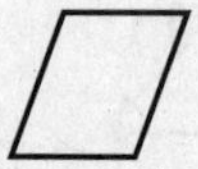

4. Jamey drew this shape.

What shape did Jamey draw?

Ⓐ line

Ⓑ line segment

Ⓒ point

Ⓓ ray

Problem Solving REAL WORLD

5. Carl wants to show a closed shape in his drawing. Show and explain how to make the drawing a closed shape.

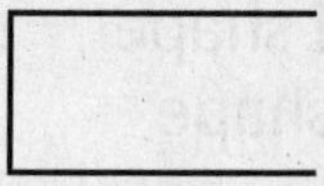

____

____

____

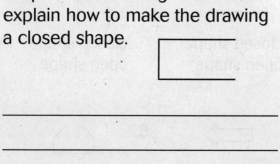

6. The shape of a fish pond at a park is shown below. Is the shape open or closed?

____

© Houghton Mifflin Harcourt Publishing Company

Name ______________________________

Lesson 98

COMMON CORE STANDARD CC.3.G.1

Lesson Objective: Describe angles in plane shapes.

Describe Angles in Plane Shapes

There are different types of angles.

A **right angle** forms a square corner.

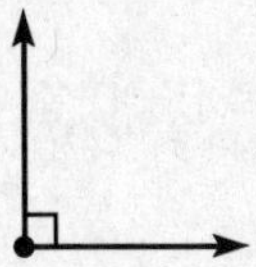

Some angles are less than a right angle.

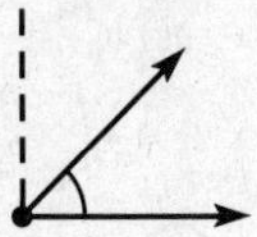

Some angles are greater than a right angle.

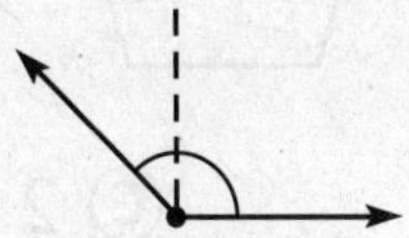

Look at this shape. Describe the angles.

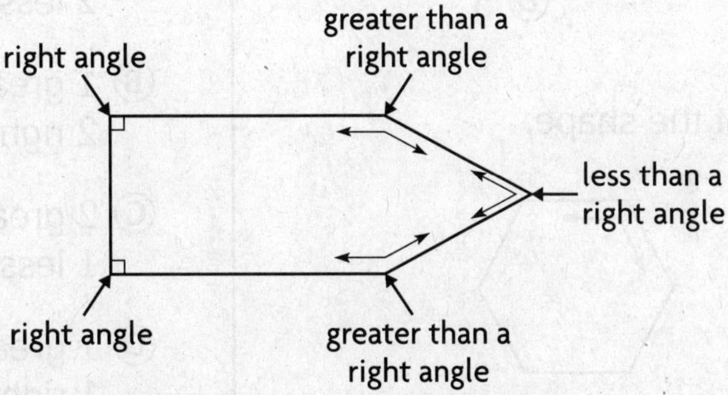

There are **2** right angles.

There are **2** angles greater than a right angle.

There is **1** angle less than a right angle.

Use the corner of a sheet of paper to tell whether the angle is a *right angle, less than a right angle,* or *greater than a right angle.*

1. 

____

2. 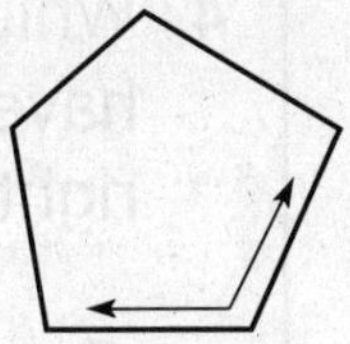

____

3. 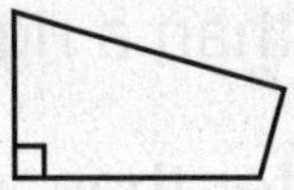

____

Write how many of each type of angle the shape has.

4. 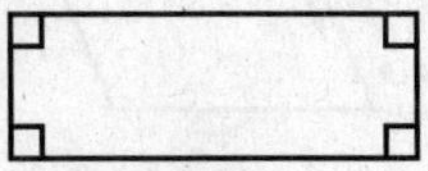

____ right

____ less than a right

____ greater than a right

5. 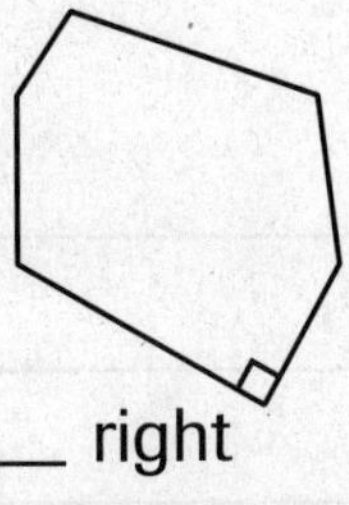

____ right

____ less than a right

____ greater than a right

6. 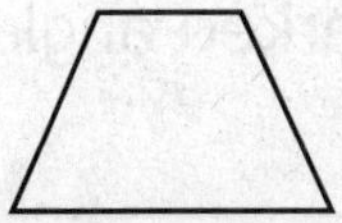

____ right

____ less than a right

____ greater than a right

© Houghton Mifflin Harcourt Publishing Company

Name ______________________________

Lesson 98
CC.3.G.1

1. How many right angles does this shape appear to have?

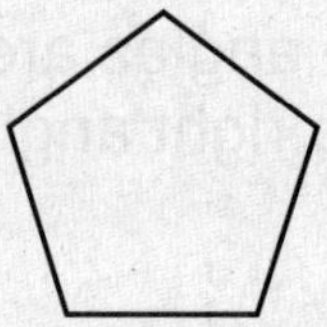

Ⓐ 0
Ⓑ 1
Ⓒ 2
Ⓓ 5

2. Look at the shape.

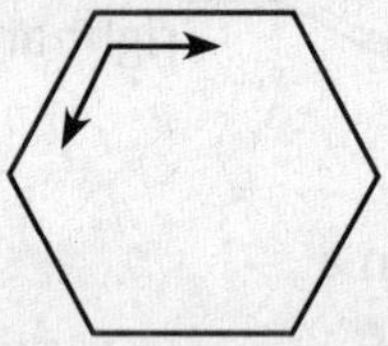

Which **best** describes the marked angle?

Ⓐ less than a right angle

Ⓑ greater than a right angle

Ⓒ a right angle

Ⓓ a straight angle

3. Which describes the angles of this triangle?

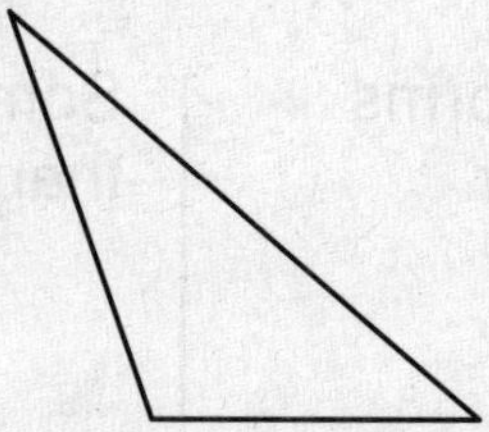

Ⓐ 1 greater than a right angle; 2 less than a right angle

Ⓑ 1 greater than a right angle; 2 right angles

Ⓒ 2 greater than a right angle; 1 less than a right angle

Ⓓ 1 greater than a right angle; 1 right angle; 1 less than a right angle

4. Which capital letter appears to have an angle that is less than a right angle?

Ⓐ H
Ⓑ L
Ⓒ T
Ⓓ Z

5. Mrs. Simpson drew this shape. Explain how to classify the marked angle.

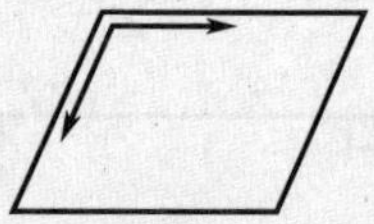

____

____

____

____

© Houghton Mifflin Harcourt Publishing Company

Name ______________________________

Lesson 99

COMMON CORE STANDARD CC.3.G.1

Lesson Objective: Identify polygons by the number of sides they have.

Identify Polygons

You can identify and name polygons by the number of sides and angles they have.

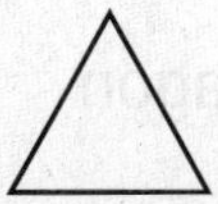

3 sides
3 angles
triangle

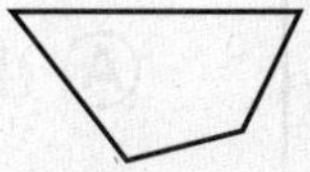

4 sides
4 angles
quadrilateral

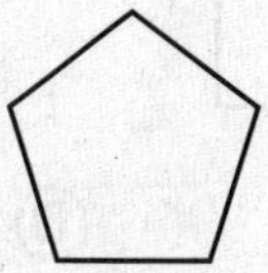

5 sides
5 angles
pentagon

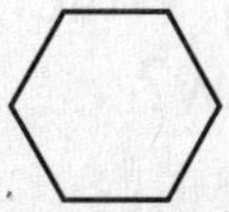

6 sides
6 angles
hexagon

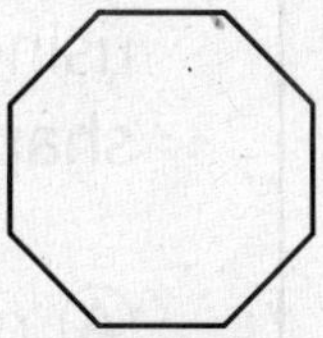

8 sides
8 angles
octagon

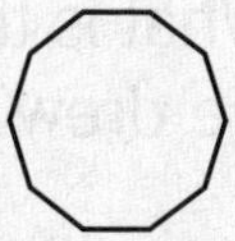

10 sides
10 angles
decagon

Describe and name this shape.

It has **4** sides.

It has **4** angles.

It is a **quadrilateral**.

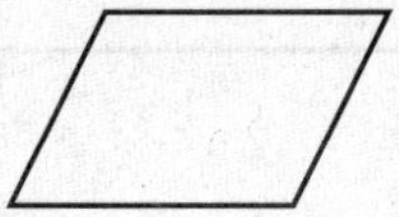

Describe and name this shape.

It has **6** sides.

It has **6** angles.

It is a **hexagon**.

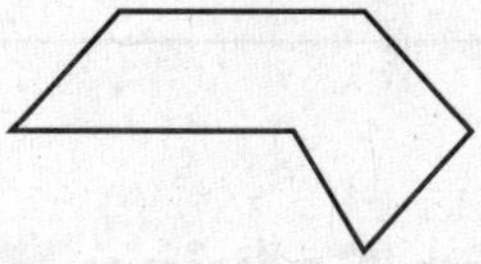

Write the number of sides and the number of angles. Then name the polygon.

1.

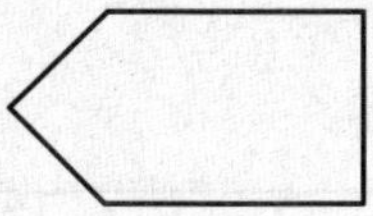

__________ sides

__________ angles

____

2.

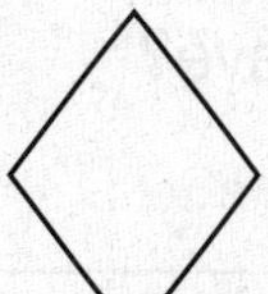

__________ sides

__________ angles

____

© Houghton Mifflin Harcourt Publishing Company

Name ______________________________

Lesson 99
CC.3.G.1

1. Which shape is **not** a polygon?

Ⓐ 

Ⓒ 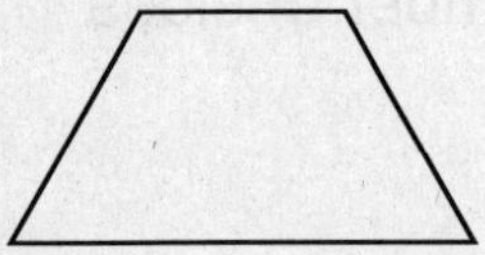

Ⓑ 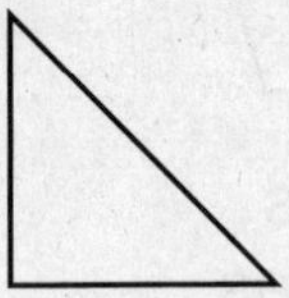

Ⓓ 

2. Vance drew a polygon with 6 sides. What is the name of the polygon he drew?

Ⓐ triangle

Ⓑ pentagon

Ⓒ hexagon

Ⓓ decagon

3. A builder is using tiles on a bathroom floor. Each tile has 8 angles. What type of polygon are the tiles?

Ⓐ decagon

Ⓒ octagon

Ⓑ hexagon

Ⓓ quadrilateral

4. Kendall drew one closed shape using 5 line segments. Which shape did Kendall draw?

Ⓐ quadrilateral

Ⓑ pentagon

Ⓒ hexagon

Ⓓ octagon

Problem Solving REAL WORLD

5. Mr. Murphy has an old coin that has ten sides. If its shape is a polygon, how many angles does the old coin have?

____

6. Lin says that an octagon has six sides. Chris says that it has eight sides. Whose statement is correct?

____

© Houghton Mifflin Harcourt Publishing Company

Name ______________________

Lesson 100

COMMON CORE STANDARD CC.3.G.1

Lesson Objective: Determine if lines or line segments are intersecting, perpendicular, or parallel.

Describe Sides of Polygons

There are different types of line segments in polygons.

- **Intersecting lines** are lines that cross or meet. Intersecting lines form angles.

- **Perpendicular lines** are intersecting lines that cross or meet to form right angles.

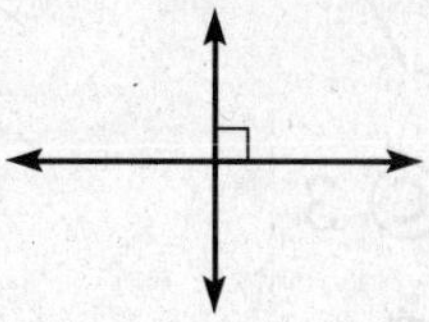

- Lines that appear never to cross or meet and are always the same distance apart are **parallel lines**. They never form angles.

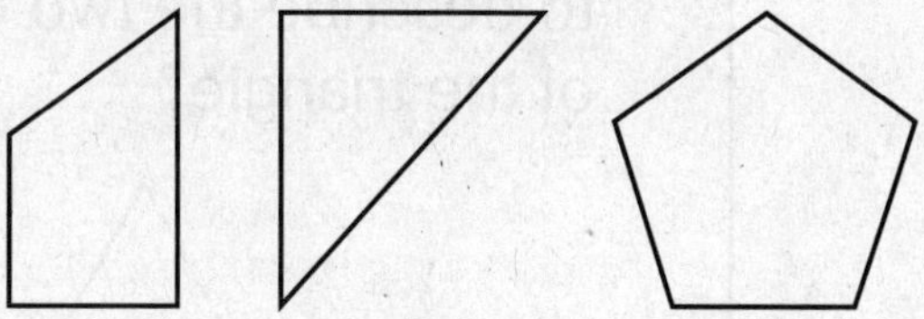

Which shape or shapes appear to have parallel sides? *A*

Which shape or shapes appear to have perpendicular sides? *A, B*

Which shape or shapes appear to have intersecting sides? *A, B, C*

Look at the dashed sides of the polygon. Tell if they appear to be *intersecting*, *perpendicular*, or *parallel*. Write all the words that describe the sides.

1.

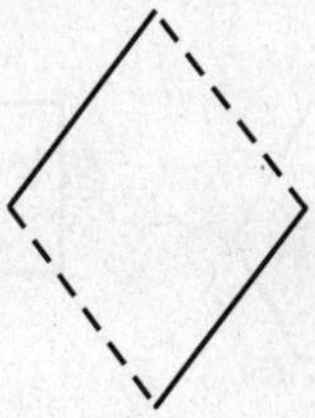

____

2.

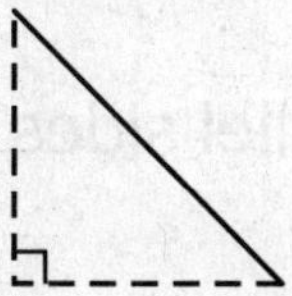

____

3.

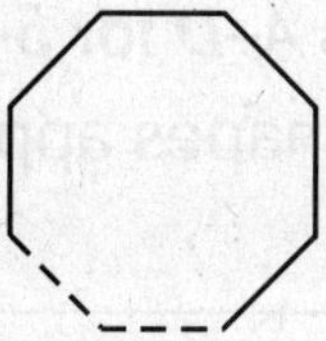

____

© Houghton Mifflin Harcourt Publishing Company

Name ______________________________________

1. How many pairs of parallel sides does this hexagon appear to have?

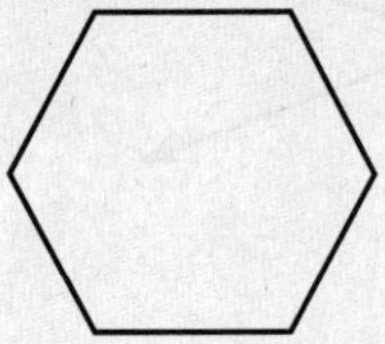

Ⓐ 0 Ⓒ 3

Ⓑ 1 Ⓓ 6

2. Brad drew a quadrilateral. Which sides of the quadrilateral appear to be parallel?

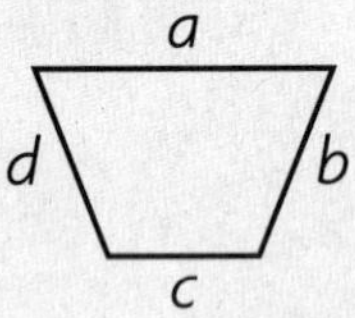

Ⓐ *a* and *b* Ⓒ *b* and *d*

Ⓑ *a* and *c* Ⓓ *c* and *d*

3. Which word can be used to describe the dashed sides of the triangle?

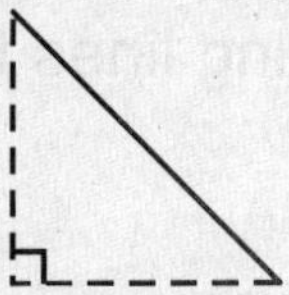

Ⓐ parallel Ⓒ point

Ⓑ perpendicular Ⓓ quadrilateral

4. Sami uses straws to model a triangle. Which word can be used to describe the two dashed sides of the triangle?

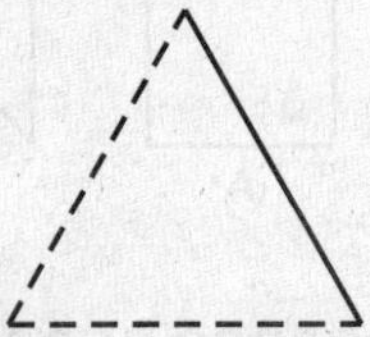

Ⓐ intersecting Ⓒ perpendicular

Ⓑ parallel Ⓓ right

Problem Solving REAL WORLD

Use shapes *A–D* for 5–6.

5. Which shapes appear to have parallel sides?

____

6. Which shapes appear to have perpendicular sides?

____

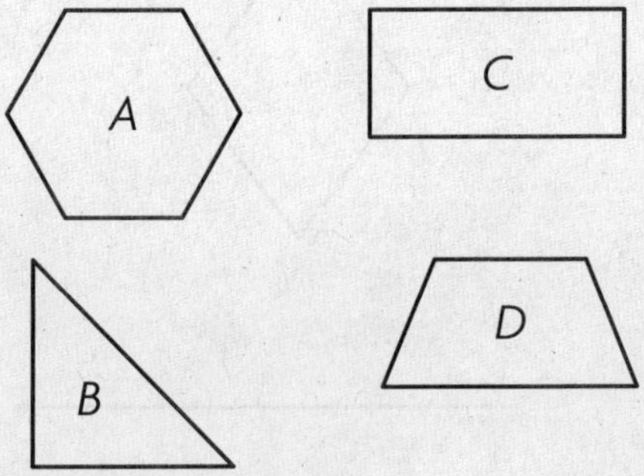

© Houghton Mifflin Harcourt Publishing Company

Name ______________________________

Lesson 101

COMMON CORE STANDARD CC.3.G.1

Lesson Objective: Describe, classify, and compare quadrilaterals based on their sides and angles.

Classify Quadrilaterals

You can classify quadrilaterals by their sides and by their angles.

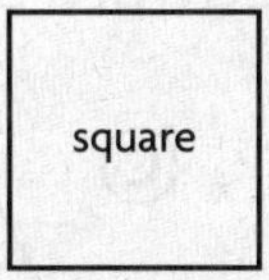

2 pairs of opposite sides that are parallel

4 sides that are of equal length

4 right angles

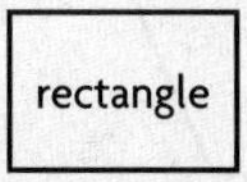

2 pairs of opposite sides that are parallel

2 pairs of sides that are of equal length

4 right angles

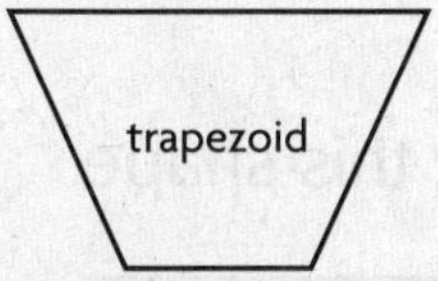

1 pair of opposite sides that are parallel

lengths of sides could be the same

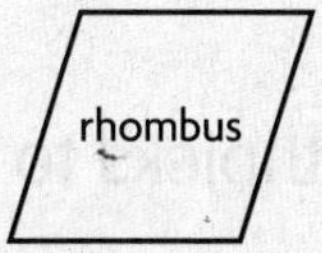

2 pairs of opposite sides that are parallel

4 sides that are of equal length

How can you classify the quadrilateral?

It has only 1 pair of opposite sides that are **parallel**.

The lengths of all 4 sides are **not equal**.

So, the quadrilateral is a **trapezoid**.

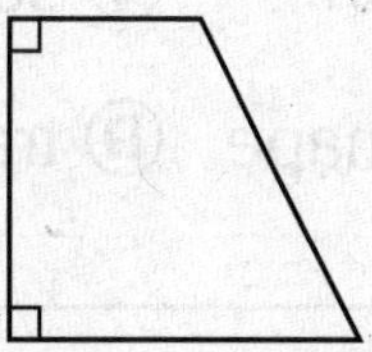

Circle all the words that describe the quadrilateral.

1.

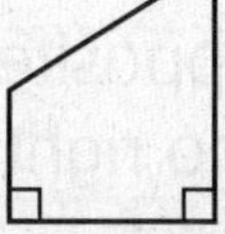

square

rhombus

trapezoid

2.

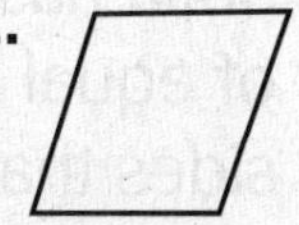

square

rectangle

quadrilateral

3.

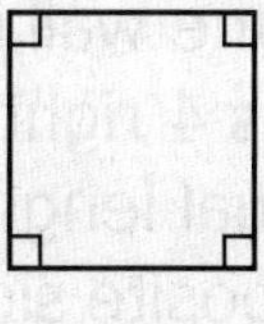

square

rectangle

rhombus

© Houghton Mifflin Harcourt Publishing Company

Name ______________________

Lesson 101
CC.3.G.1

1. Hillary drew this shape.

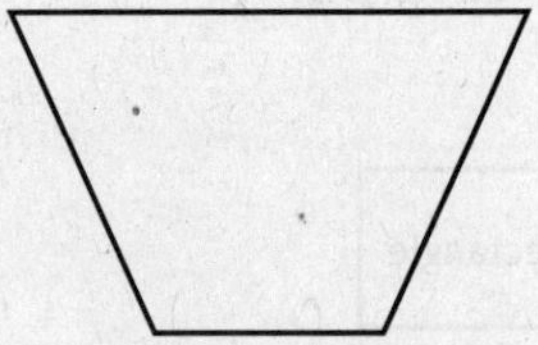

Which word **best** describes the shape Hillary drew?

Ⓐ square
Ⓑ rectangle
Ⓒ rhombus
Ⓓ trapezoid

2. Cooper used toothpicks to make a shape.

Which **best** describes the shape Cooper made?

Ⓐ decagon
Ⓑ open shape
Ⓒ square
Ⓓ trapezoid

3. Edward says he drew a quadrilateral. Which of these could **not** be Edward's shape?

Ⓐ 

Ⓑ 

Ⓒ 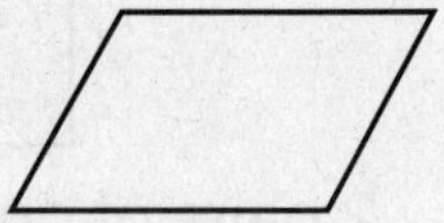

Ⓓ 

4. Helen drew this shape.

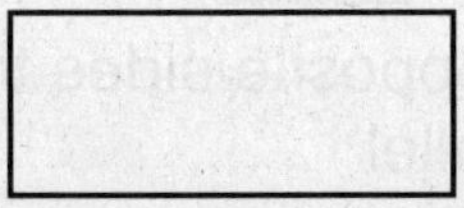

Which word **best** describes the shape Helen drew?

Ⓐ rectangle
Ⓑ rhombus
Ⓒ square
Ⓓ trapezoid

Problem Solving REAL WORLD

5. A picture on the wall in Jeremy's classroom has 4 right angles, 4 sides of equal length, and 2 pairs of opposite sides that are parallel. What quadrilateral best describes the picture?

____

6. Sofia has a plate that has 4 sides of equal length, 2 pairs of opposite sides that are parallel, and no right angles. What quadrilateral best describes the plate?

____

© Houghton Mifflin Harcourt Publishing Company

Name ______________________________

Lesson 102

COMMON CORE STANDARD CC.3.G.1

Lesson Objective: Draw quadrilaterals.

Draw Quadrilaterals

Use grid paper to draw a quadrilateral.

Step 1 Use a ruler to draw line segments. Connect *A* to *B*.

Step 2 Connect *B* to *C*.

Step 3 Connect *C* to *D*.

Step 4 Connect *D* to *A*.

Write the name of your quadrilateral.

rhombus

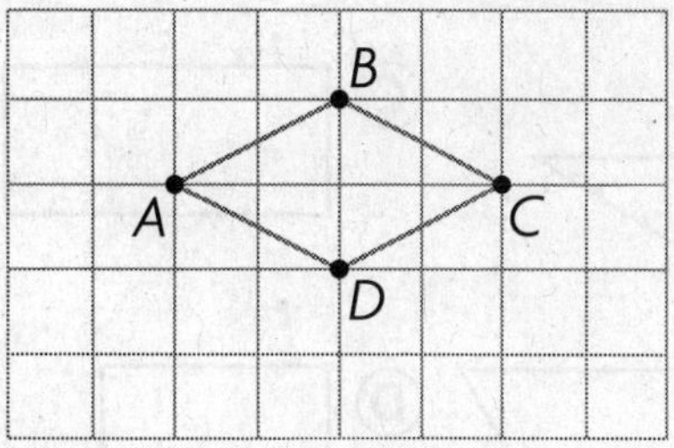

1. Choose four endpoints that connect to make a square.

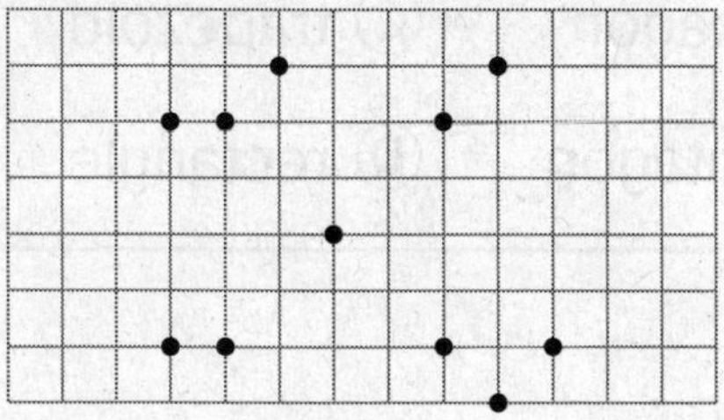

2. Choose four endpoints that connect to make a trapezoid.

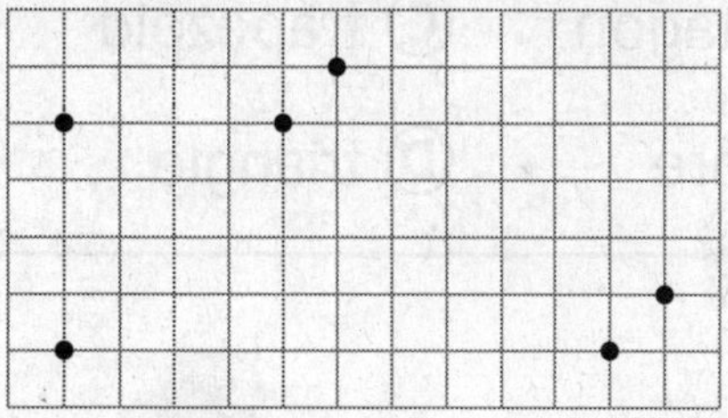

Use grid paper to draw a quadrilateral that is described. Name the quadrilateral you drew.

3. 4 right angles

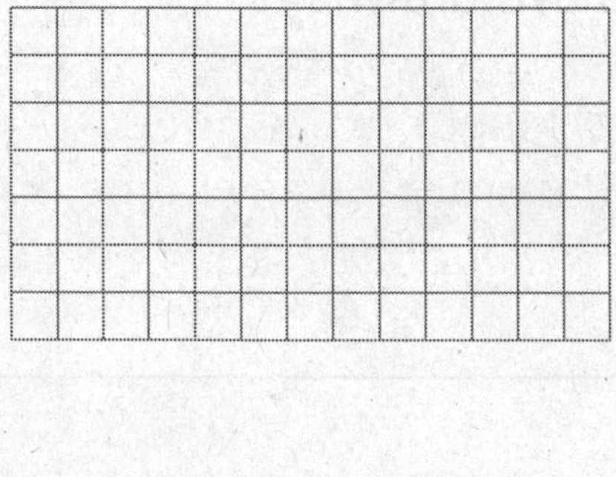

____

4. 2 pairs of opposite sides that are parallel

____

© Houghton Mifflin Harcourt Publishing Company

Name ________________________

1. Melody draws a quadrilateral with 2 pairs of opposite sides that are parallel. Which could be the quadrilateral Melody draws?

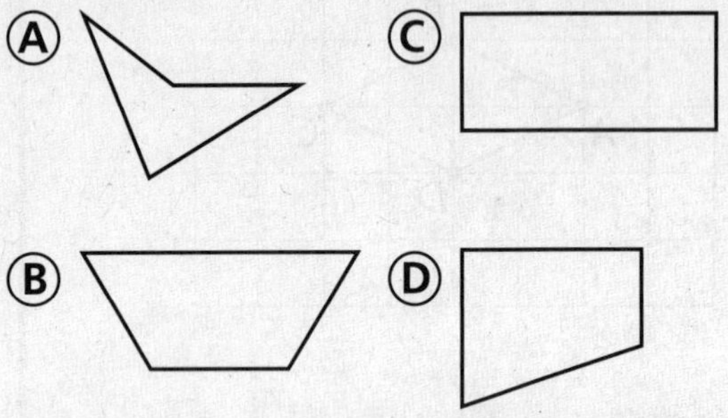

2. Gina drew a quadrilateral that has 4 sides of equal length and 4 right angles. Which shape did she draw?

Ⓐ pentagon
Ⓑ square
Ⓒ trapezoid
Ⓓ triangle

3. Hannah drew a quadrilateral with exactly 1 pair of opposite sides that are parallel. Which shows a shape Hannah could have drawn?

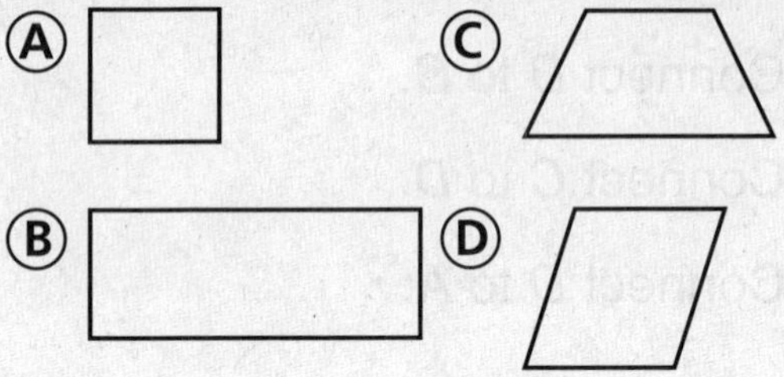

4. Henry drew a quadrilateral that has 2 pairs of sides of equal length and 4 right angles. Which shape did he draw?

Ⓐ hexagon
Ⓑ pentagon
Ⓒ trapezoid
Ⓓ rectangle

Problem Solving REAL WORLD

5. Layla drew a quadrilateral with 4 right angles and 2 pairs of opposite sides that are parallel. Name the quadrilateral she could have drawn.

____

6. Victor drew a quadrilateral with no right angles and 4 sides of equal length. What quadrilateral could Victor have drawn?

____

© Houghton Mifflin Harcourt Publishing Company

Name ______________________________

Lesson 103

COMMON CORE STANDARD CC.3.G.1

Lesson Objective: Describe and compare triangles based on the number of sides that have equal length and by their angles.

Describe Triangles

You can describe a triangle by its types of angles.	**You can describe a triangle by the number of sides of equal length.**
This triangle has **1** right angle. 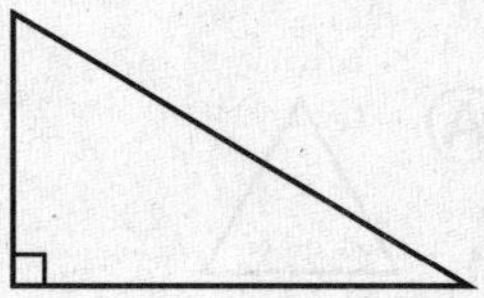	This triangle has **0** sides of the same length. 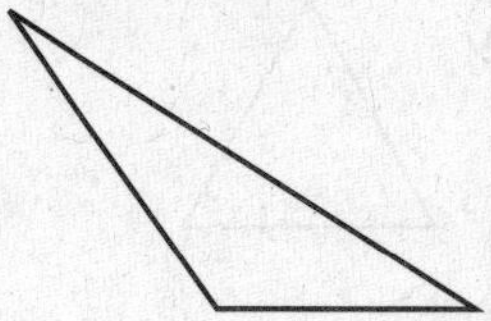
This triangle has **1** angle greater than a right angle. 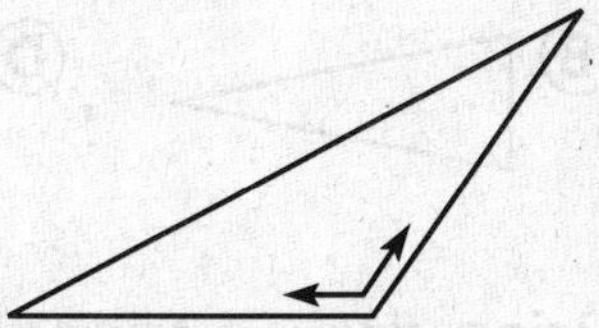	This triangle has **2** sides of the same length. 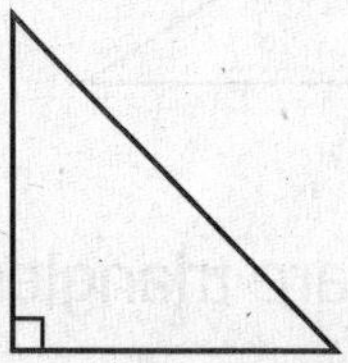
This triangle has **3** angles less than a right angle. 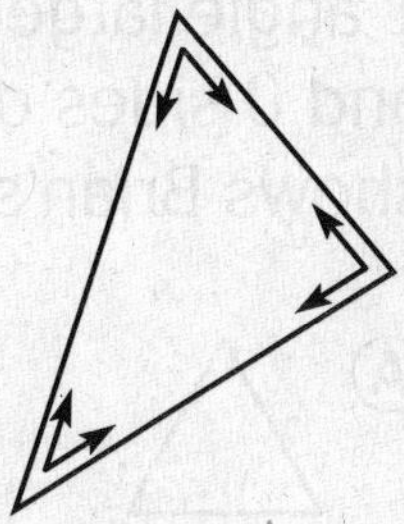	This triangle has **3** sides of the same length. 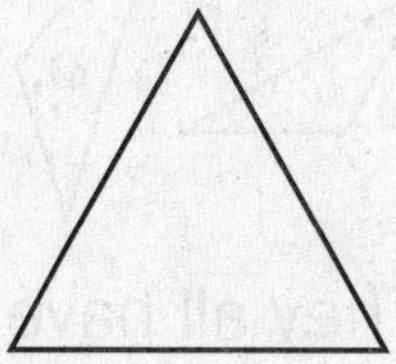

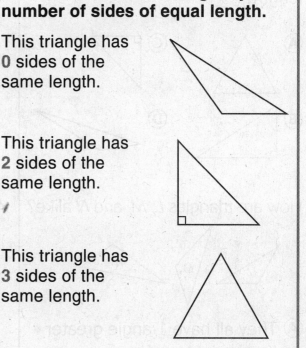

Draw a line to match the description of the triangle(s).

1. One angle is a right angle.

2. One angle is greater than a right angle.

3. Three angles are less than a right angle.

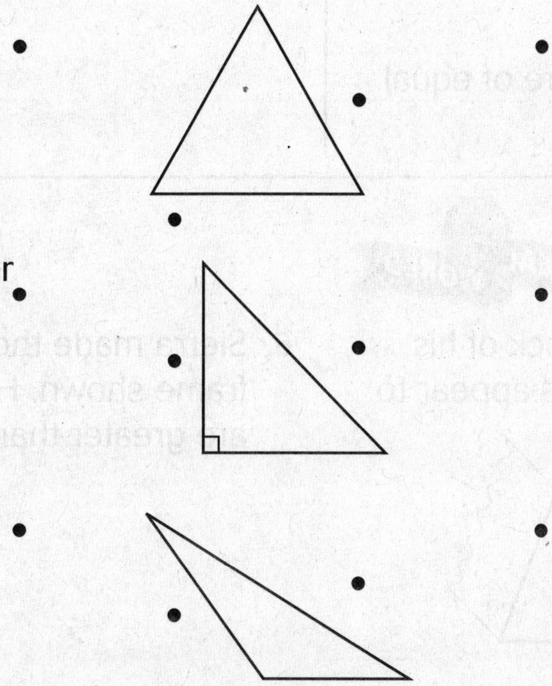

4. No sides are equal in length.

5. Two sides are equal in length.

6. Three sides are equal in length.

© Houghton Mifflin Harcourt Publishing Company

Name ______________________________

Lesson 103
CC.3.G.1

1. Which triangle appears to have 1 right angle and 0 sides of equal length?

Ⓐ 

Ⓒ 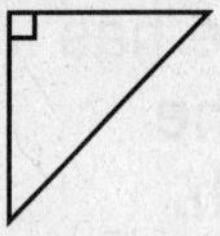

Ⓑ 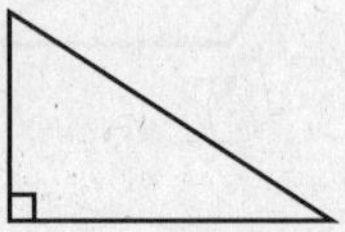

Ⓓ 

2. How are triangles *L, M,* and *N* alike?

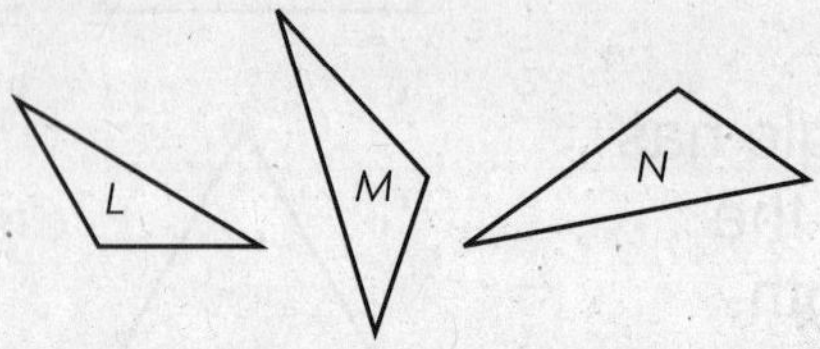

Ⓐ They all have 1 angle greater than a right angle.

Ⓑ They all have 1 right angle.

Ⓒ They all have 3 angles less than a right angle.

Ⓓ All of their sides are of equal length.

3. Ping drew a triangle that has 3 angles smaller than a right angle and 3 sides of equal length. Which shows Ping's triangle?

Ⓐ 

Ⓒ 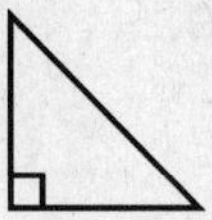

Ⓑ 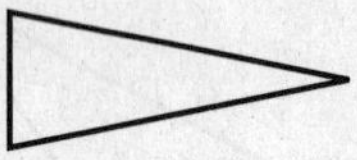

Ⓓ 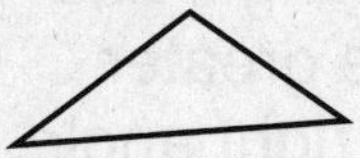

4. Brian drew a triangle that has 1 angle larger than a right angle and 0 sides of equal length. Which shows Brian's triangle?

Ⓐ 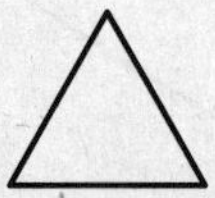

Ⓒ 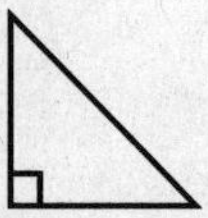

Ⓑ 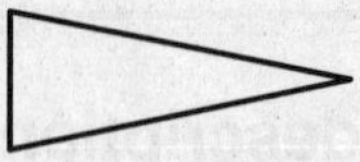

Ⓓ 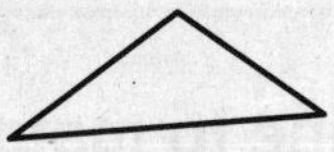

Problem Solving REAL WORLD

5. Matthew drew the back of his tent. How many sides appear to be of equal length?

____

6. Sierra made the triangular picture frame shown. How many angles are greater than a right angle?

____

© Houghton Mifflin Harcourt Publishing Company

Name ______________________________

Lesson 104

COMMON CORE STANDARD CC.3.G.1

Lesson Objective: Solve problems by using the strategy *draw a diagram* to classify plane shapes.

Problem Solving • Classify Plane Shapes

A **Venn diagram** shows how sets of things are related. This Venn diagram shows how quadrilaterals and polygons with all sides of equal length are related. The shapes in the section where the circles overlap show shapes that belong to both groups.

What types of polygons are in both circles?

Read the Problem	Solve the Problem
What do I need to find? what types of polygons are in both circles	What is true about all polygons in the circle labeled Quadrilaterals? They all have 4 sides. What is true about all polygons in the other circle? They all have sides of equal length.
What information do I need to use? The circles are labeled Quadrilaterals and Polygons with All Sides of Equal Length.	Which polygons are in the section where the circles overlap? shapes that are quadrilaterals and that have 4 sides that are of equal length
How will I use the information? I will describe the shapes in the section where the circles overlap.	So, a square and a rhombus are in the section where the circles overlap.

1. Brad drew the Venn diagram at the right. What type of shapes are in the section where the circles overlap?

____

© Houghton Mifflin Harcourt Publishing Company

Name ______________________________

Lesson 104
CC.3.G.1

Use the Venn diagram for 1–3.

Polygons with Right Angles **A**

2. Patrick found some more shapes to sort. Which shape should he place into the overlap section of the Venn diagram?

Ⓐ 

Ⓒ 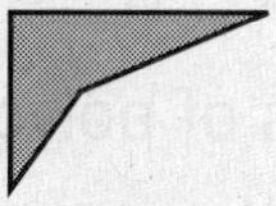

Ⓑ 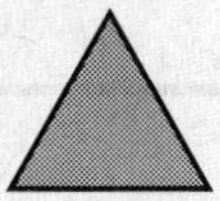

Ⓓ 

1. Patrick used the Venn diagram to sort shapes. Which label could he use for part A?

Ⓐ Open Shapes

Ⓑ Quadrilaterals

Ⓒ Shapes with Sides of Equal Length

Ⓓ Shapes with 1 Right Angle

3. Patrick has the shape shown below. Where should he place the shape in the diagram?

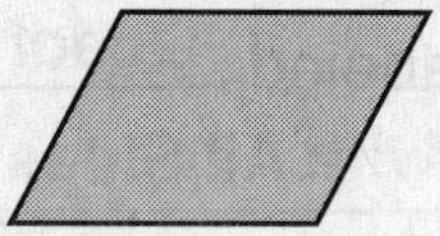

Ⓐ part A

Ⓑ Polygons with Right Angles

Ⓒ overlap section

Ⓓ outside the Venn diagram

4. Kendra used a Venn diagram to sort shapes. Write a label she could use for circle A. Explain your reasoning.

Quadrilaterals **A**

____

____

____

____

____

© Houghton Mifflin Harcourt Publishing Company

Name ______________________

Lesson 105

COMMON CORE STANDARD CC.3.G.2

Lesson Objective: Partition shapes into parts with equal areas and express the area as a unit fraction of the whole.

Relate Shapes, Fractions, and Area

You can separate a plane shape into equal parts to explore the relationship between fractions and area.

Divide the rectangle into 6 parts with equal area. Write the fraction that names the area of each part of the whole.

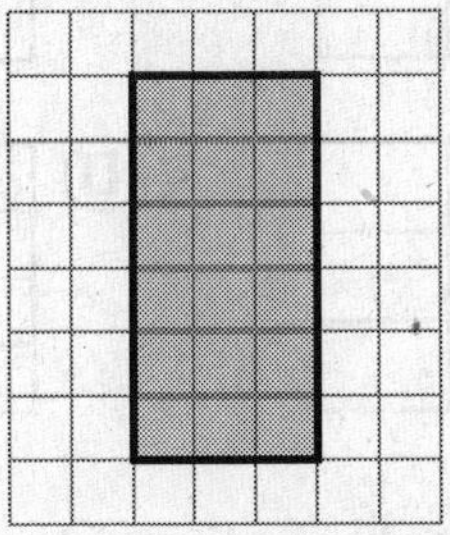

Step 1 Draw lines to divide the rectangle into 6 parts with equal area. Use the grid to help you.

Step 2 Write the fraction that names each part of the divided whole.

Think: Each part is 1 part out of 6 equal parts.

Each part is $\frac{1}{6}$ of the whole shape's area.

Step 3 Write the fraction that names the whole area.

Think: There are 6 equal parts.

The fraction that names the whole area is $\frac{6}{6}$.

Draw lines to divide the shape into parts with equal area. Write the area of each part as a unit fraction.

1. 4 equal parts

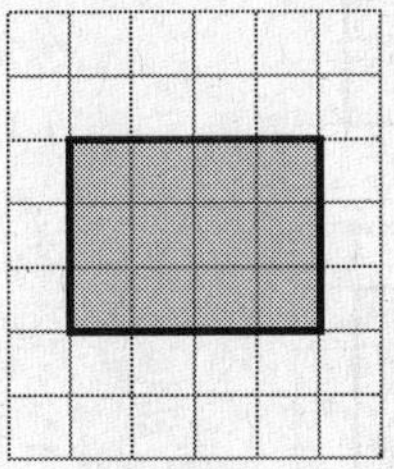

Each part is ______ of the whole shape's area.

2. 8 equal parts

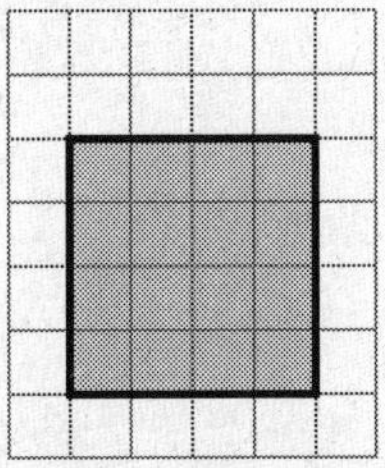

Each part is ______ of the whole shape's area.

© Houghton Mifflin Harcourt Publishing Company

1. Talon divides a square into equal parts that each show $\frac{1}{6}$. Which could be Talon's square?

Ⓐ 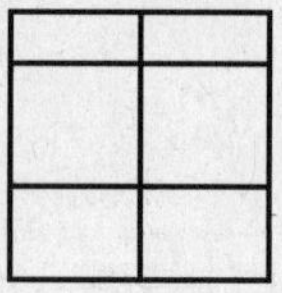

Ⓑ 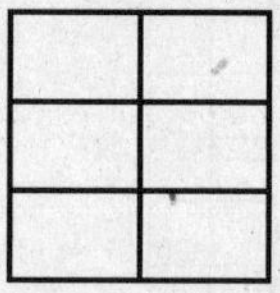

Ⓒ 

Ⓓ 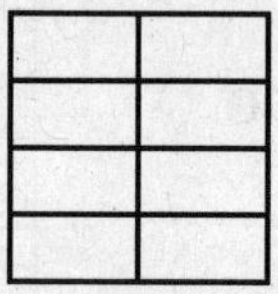

2. Colleen drew lines to divide a trapezoid into equal parts that each represent $\frac{1}{3}$ of the whole area. Which could be Colleen's trapezoid?

Ⓐ 

Ⓑ 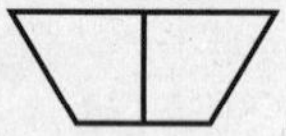

Ⓒ 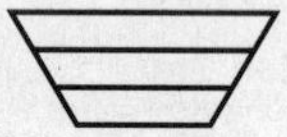

Ⓓ 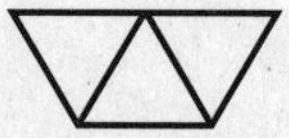

3. Tad divides a rhombus into equal parts that each show $\frac{1}{2}$. Which could be Tad's rhombus?

Ⓐ 

Ⓑ 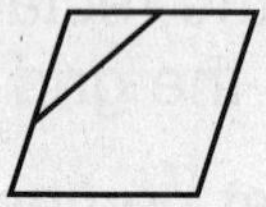

Ⓒ 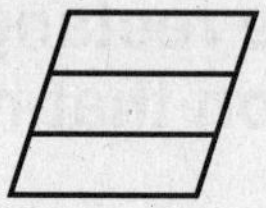

Ⓓ 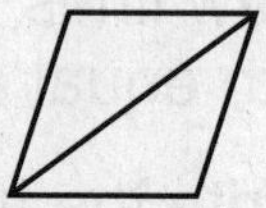

4. Dennie drew lines to divide a shape into 3 parts each with equal area. Which could be Dennie's shape?

Ⓐ 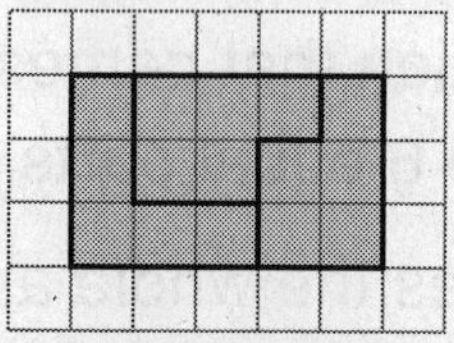

Ⓑ 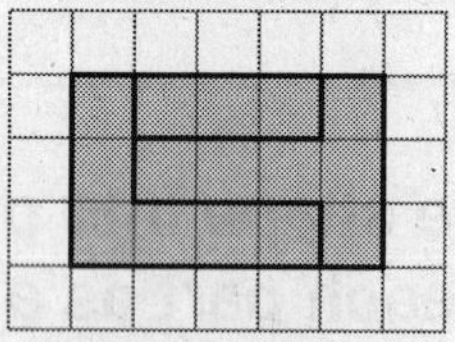

Ⓒ 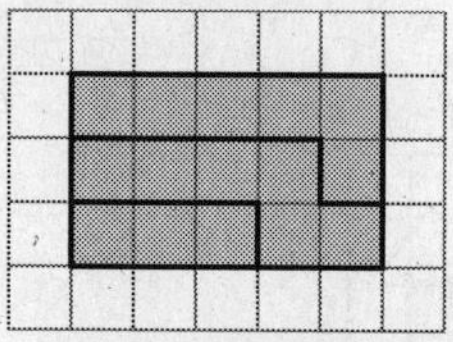

Ⓓ 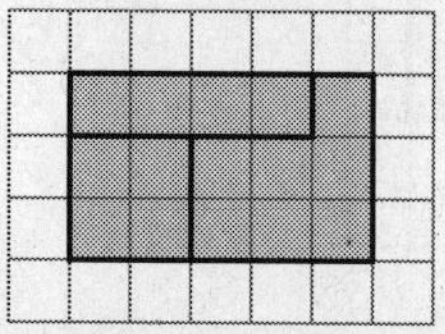

5. Reese divided the shaded shape into equal parts. Write the unit fraction that names each part of the divided whole. Explain your reasoning.

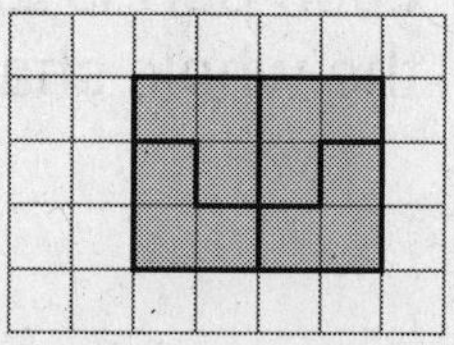

____

____

© Houghton Mifflin Harcourt Publishing Company

Name ____________________

Lesson 1
COMMON CORE STANDARD CC.3.OA.1
Lesson Objective: Model and skip count objects in equal groups to find how many there are.

Count Equal Groups

Equal groups have the same number in each group.

There are 3 tulips in each of 4 vases. How many tulips are there in all?

Step 1 Think: there are 4 vases, so draw 4 circles to show 4 equal groups.

Step 2 Think: there are 3 tulips in each vase, so draw 3 dots in each group.

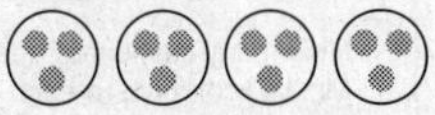

Step 3 Skip count by 3s to find how many in all: 3, 6, 9, 12

There are 4 equal groups with 3 tulips in each group.

So, there are 12 tulips in all.

1. Draw 3 groups of 5. Skip count to find how many.

Check students' drawings.

15 in all

Count equal groups to find how many.

2. 

2 groups of 5

10 in all

3. 

4 groups of 2

8 in all

Name ____________________

Lesson 1
CC.3.OA.1

1. There are 5 tables in the library. Four students are sitting at each table.

How many students are sitting in the library?

Ⓐ 9 Ⓑ 16 **Ⓒ 20** Ⓓ 24

2. Alondra made 3 bracelets. There are 7 beads on each bracelet.

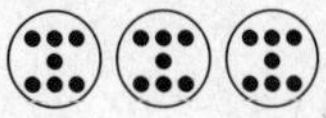

How many beads did Alondra use to make the bracelets?

Ⓐ 10 Ⓑ 14 **Ⓒ 21** Ⓓ 24

3. Stella decorated using 4 groups of balloons. She drew this model to show the number of balloons.

How many balloons did Stella use to decorate?

Ⓐ 3 Ⓑ 6 Ⓒ 9 **Ⓓ 12**

4. Mrs. Bennett sorted spools of thread into 3 containers. Each container held 3 spools.

How many spools of thread does Mrs. Bennett have in all?

Ⓐ 6 **Ⓑ 9** Ⓒ 10 Ⓓ 12

Problem Solving REAL WORLD

5. Marcia puts 2 slices of cheese on each sandwich. She makes 4 cheese sandwiches. How many slices of cheese does Marcia use in all?

8 slices

6. Tomas works in a cafeteria kitchen. He puts 3 cherry tomatoes on each of 5 salads. How many tomatoes does he use?

15 tomatoes

Name ____________________

Lesson 2
COMMON CORE STANDARD CC.3.OA.1
Lesson Objective: Write an addition sentence and a multiplication sentence for a model.

Algebra • Relate Addition and Multiplication

You can add to find how many in all.

You can also multiply to find how many in all when you have equal groups.

$3 \times 2 = 6$

The **factors** are 3 and 2.
The **product** is 6.

So, $2 + 2 + 2 = 6$ and $3 \times 2 = 6$.

Write related addition and multiplication sentences for the model.

1. 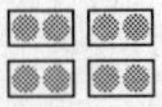

$2 + 2 + 2 + 2 = 8$

$4 \times 2 = 8$

2. 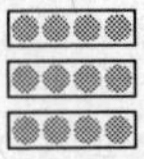

$4 + 4 + 4 = 12$

$3 \times 4 = 12$

Draw a quick picture to show the equal groups. Then write related addition and multiplication sentences.

Check students' drawings.

3. 4 groups of 3 

$3 + 3 + 3 + 3 = 12$

$4 \times 3 = 12$

4. 2 groups of 3 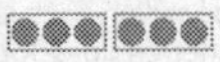

$3 + 3 = 6$

$2 \times 3 = 6$

Name ____________________

Lesson 2
CC.3.OA.1

1. Eric was doing his math homework. Eric wrote:

$$2 + 2 + 2 + 2 + 2$$

Which is another way to show what Eric wrote?

Ⓐ 2×2 **Ⓑ 5×2** Ⓒ 10×2 Ⓓ $5 + 2$

2. Dallas and Mark each sharpened 4 pencils before school.

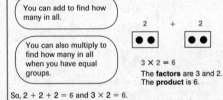

Which sentence shows the number of pencils sharpened in all?

Ⓐ $2 + 2 = 4$ Ⓑ $4 + 2 = 6$ Ⓒ $4 \times 4 = 16$ **Ⓓ $2 \times 4 = 8$**

3. A pet store has some fish bowls on display. There are 3 fish in each of 5 bowls. Which number sentence shows how many fish there are in all?

Ⓐ $5 \times 3 = 15$ Ⓑ $5 \times 5 = 25$ Ⓒ $5 + 3 = 8$ Ⓓ $3 \times 3 = 9$

4. Carlos spent 5 minutes working on each of 8 math problems. He can use 8×5 to find the total number of minutes he spent on the problems. Which is equal to 8×5?

Ⓐ $8 + 5$

Ⓑ $8 + 8 + 8$

Ⓒ $5 + 5 + 5 + 5 + 5$

Ⓓ $5 + 5 + 5 + 5 + 5 + 5 + 5 + 5$

Problem Solving REAL WORLD

5. There are 6 jars of pickles in a box. Ed has 3 boxes of pickles. How many jars of pickles does he have in all? Write a multiplication sentence to find the answer.

$3 \times 6 = 18$ jars

6. Each day, Jani rides her bike 5 miles. How many miles does Jani ride in all in 4 days? Write a multiplication sentence to find the answer.

$4 \times 5 = 20$ miles

Answer Key

Name ____________ **Lesson 3**

COMMON CORE STANDARD CC.3.OA.2
Lesson Objective: Use models to explore the meaning of partitive (sharing) division.

Size of Equal Groups

When you **divide**, you separate into equal groups.

Use counters or draw a quick picture. Make equal groups. Complete the table.

Counters	Number of Equal Groups	Number in Each Group
24	6	■

The number in each group is unknown, so divide.

Place 1 counter at a time in each group until all 24 counters are used.

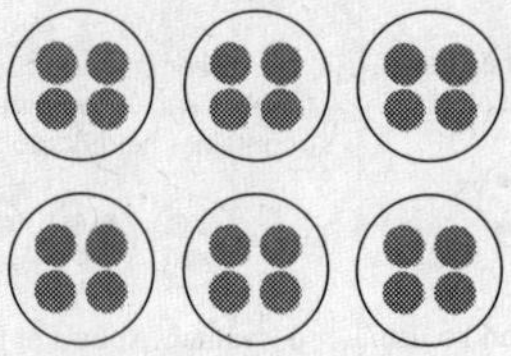

There are 4 counters in each of 6 groups.

Use counters or draw a quick picture. Make equal groups. Complete the table.

	Counters	Number of Equal Groups	Number in Each Group
1.	12	2	6
2.	10	5	2
3.	16	4	4
4.	24	3	8
5.	15	5	3

Name ____________ **Lesson 3**
CC.3.OA.2

1. Derek has 12 sweaters. He places an equal number of sweaters into 2 drawers.

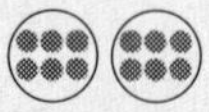

How many sweaters are in each drawer?

Ⓐ 2 Ⓒ **6** (filled)
Ⓑ 4 Ⓓ 8

2. Megan found 36 seashells. She put an equal number of shells in each of 4 piles. How many seashells are in each pile?

Ⓐ 32
Ⓑ **9** (filled)
Ⓒ 6
Ⓓ 4

3. Mr. Jackson has 16 flashcards. He gives an equal number of flashcards to 4 groups.

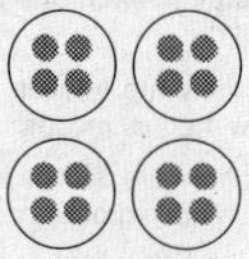

How many flashcards does Mr. Jackson give to each group?

Ⓐ **4** (filled) Ⓒ 12
Ⓑ 8 Ⓓ 16

4. Linda picked 48 flowers. She placed them equally into 8 vases. How many flowers are in each vase?

Ⓐ 4 Ⓒ **6** (filled)
Ⓑ 5 Ⓓ 7

Problem Solving REAL WORLD

5. Alicia has 12 eggs that she will use to make 4 different cookie recipes. If each recipe calls for the same number of eggs, how many eggs will she use in each recipe?

3 eggs

6. Brett picked 27 flowers from the garden. He plans to give an equal number of flowers to each of 3 people. How many flowers will each person get?

9 flowers

Name ____________ **Lesson 4**

COMMON CORE STANDARD CC.3.OA.2
Lesson Objective: Use models to explore the meaning of quotative (measurement) division.

Number of Equal Groups

Complete the table. Use counters to help find the number of equal groups.

Counters	Number of Equal Groups	Number in Each Group
18	■	3

The number of equal groups is unknown, so divide.
Circle groups of 3 counters until all 18 counters are in a group.

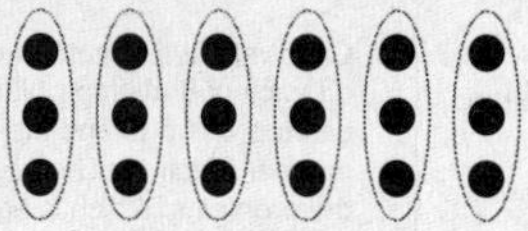

There are 6 groups of 3 counters each.

Draw counters. Then circle equal groups. Complete the table.

	Counters	Number of Equal Groups	Number in Each Group
1.	24	6	4
2.	20	4	5
3.	21	3	7
4.	36	9	4

Name ____________ **Lesson 4**
CC.3.OA.2

1. Elle puts 24 charms into groups of 4. How many groups of charms are there?

Ⓐ 4
Ⓑ **6** (filled)
Ⓒ 20
Ⓓ 28

2. A sporting goods store has 72 baseball caps in stacks of 8 caps each. How many stacks of baseball caps are there?

Ⓐ 7
Ⓑ 8
Ⓒ **9** (filled)
Ⓓ 11

3. Heather places 32 stamps into groups of 8. How many groups of stamps are there?

Ⓐ 12
Ⓑ 8
Ⓒ 6
Ⓓ **4** (filled)

4. Mr. Smith wants to divide his students into groups of 6 for the planetarium tour. How many groups of 6 can be made with 18 students?

Ⓐ 2
Ⓑ **3** (filled)
Ⓒ 6
Ⓓ 9

Problem Solving REAL WORLD

5. In his bookstore, Toby places 21 books on shelves, with 7 books on each shelf. How many shelves does Toby need?

3 shelves

6. Mr. Holden has 32 quarters in stacks of 4 on his desk. How many stacks of quarters are on his desk?

8 stacks

Name ______________

Lesson 5

COMMON CORE STANDARD CC.3.OA.2

Lesson Objective: Model division by using equal groups and bar models.

Model with Bar Models

Use counters to find 15 ÷ 5.

Step 1 Use 15 counters. Draw 5 circles to show the number of equal groups.

Step 2 Place 1 counter at a time in each circle.

Step 3 Continue until you have placed all 15 counters.

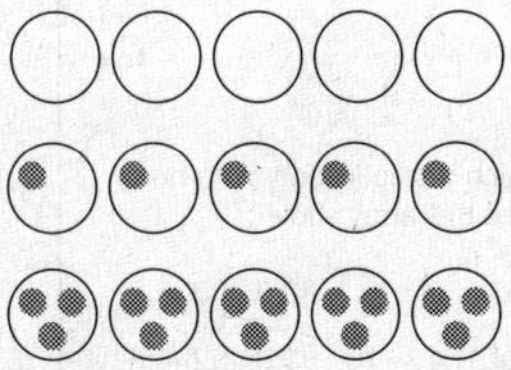

Step 4 Count the number of counters in each circle.

There are 3 counters in each of the 5 groups.

You can use a bar model to show how the parts of a problem are related.

- There are 15 counters.
- There are 5 equal groups.
- There are 3 counters in each group.

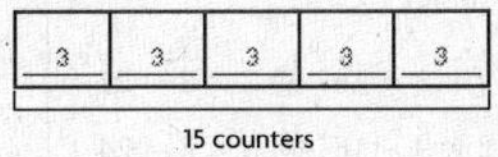

Write a division equation for the model.

15 ÷ 5 = 3

Write a division equation for the picture.

1. 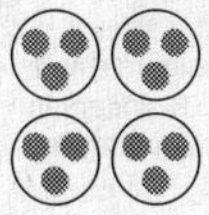

12 ÷ 4 = 3 or 12 ÷ 3 = 4

2. 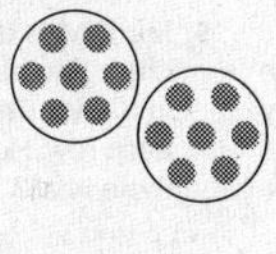

14 ÷ 2 = 7 or 14 ÷ 7 = 2

3. 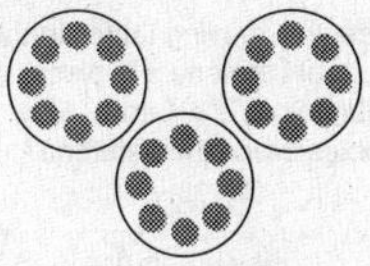

24 ÷ 3 = 8 or 24 ÷ 8 = 3

Name ______________

Lesson 5

CC.3.OA.2

1. The Bike Shack displays 45 bikes grouped by color. There are 5 bikes in each group. How many colors of bikes are on display?

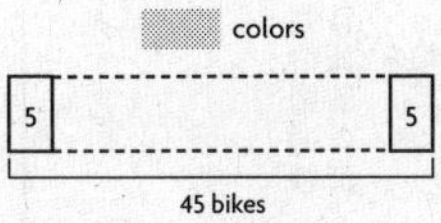

Ⓐ 5 Ⓒ 8 Ⓑ 7 Ⓓ 9

2. Rico went for a 12 mile bike ride. He stopped every 3 miles to take pictures. How many times did Rico stop during his bike ride?

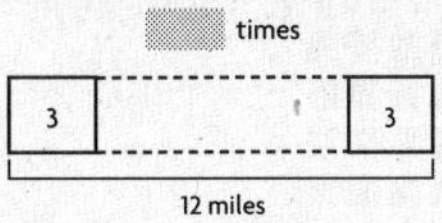

Ⓐ 3 Ⓒ 9 Ⓑ 4 Ⓓ 15

3. Amber divided her marbles evenly among 3 friends.

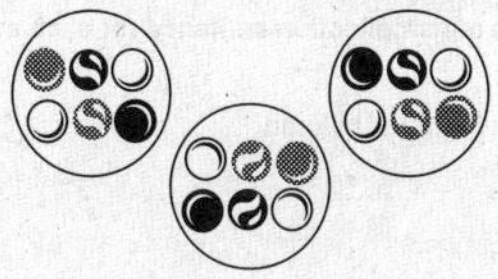

Which division equation is represented by the picture?

Ⓐ 3 ÷ 3 = 1
Ⓑ 18 ÷ 3 = 6
Ⓒ 18 ÷ 2 = 9
Ⓓ 21 ÷ 3 = 7

Problem Solving REAL WORLD

4. Jalyn collected 24 stones. She put them in 4 equal piles. How many stones are in each pile?

6 stones

5. Tanner has 30 stickers. He puts 6 stickers on each page. On how many pages does he put stickers?

5 pages

Name ______________

Lesson 6

COMMON CORE STANDARD CC.3.OA.3

Lesson Objective: Model and skip count on a number line to find how many there are.

Skip Count on a Number Line

When you have **equal groups**, you can skip count on a number line to find how many in all.

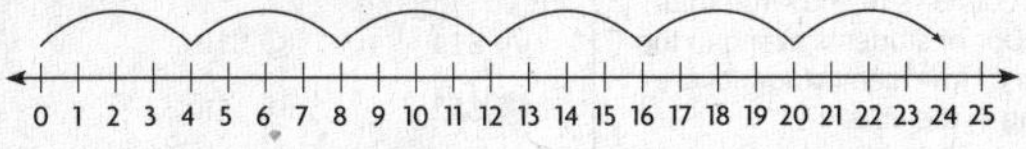

How many jumps are there? 6

How long is each jump? 4 spaces

Think: 6 jumps of 4 shows 6 groups of 4.

Multiply. 6 × 4

6 × 4 = 24

1. Skip count by drawing jumps on the number line. Find how many in 4 jumps of 4. Then write the product. Check students' drawings.

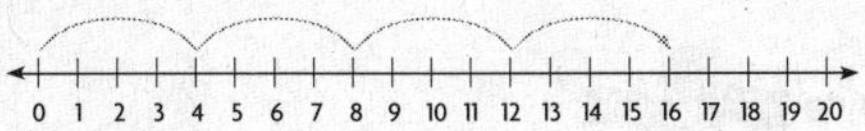

4 × 4 = 16

2. Draw jumps on the number line to show 6 groups of 3. Then find the product.

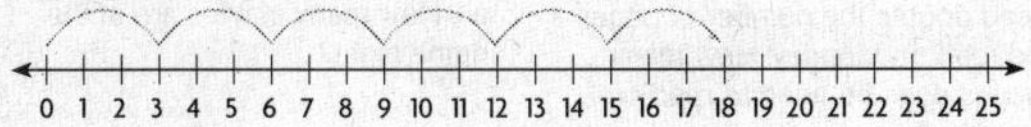

6 × 3 = 18

3. Write the multiplication sentence the number line shows.

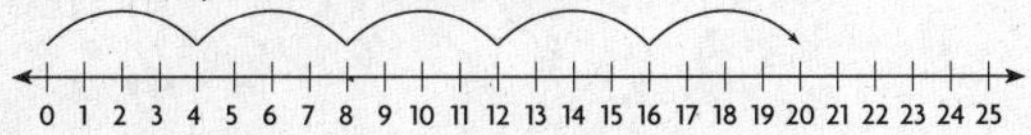

5 × 4 = 20

Name ______________

Lesson 6

CC.3.OA.3

1. Julio has a collection of coins. He puts the coins in 2 equal groups. There are 7 coins in each group.

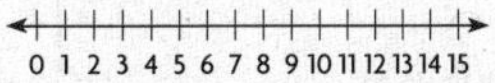

How many coins does Julio have in all?

Ⓐ 7 Ⓑ 9 Ⓒ 14 Ⓓ 15

2. Mrs. Riley buys 3 packages of mangos to make a large fruit salad. Each package contains 2 mangos.

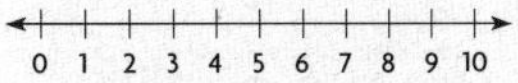

How many mangos does Mrs. Riley have in all?

Ⓐ 4 Ⓑ 5 Ⓒ 6 Ⓓ 8

3. Mr. Walters was cleaning his closet. He packed 2 shoes in each of 5 shoeboxes to donate to charity.

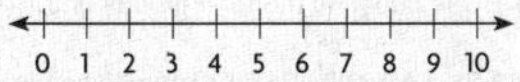

How many shoes did he pack in all?

Ⓐ 3 Ⓑ 7 Ⓒ 9 Ⓓ 10

4. Luis has 3 boxes of cars. There are 3 cars in each box.

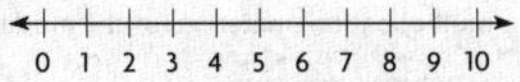

How many cars does Luis have in all?

Ⓐ 10 Ⓑ 9 Ⓒ 8 Ⓓ 6

Problem Solving REAL WORLD

5. Allie is baking muffins for students in her class. There are 6 muffins in each baking tray. She bakes 5 trays of muffins. How many muffins is she baking in all?

30 muffins

6. A snack package has 4 cheese sticks. How many cheese sticks are in 4 packages?

16 cheese sticks

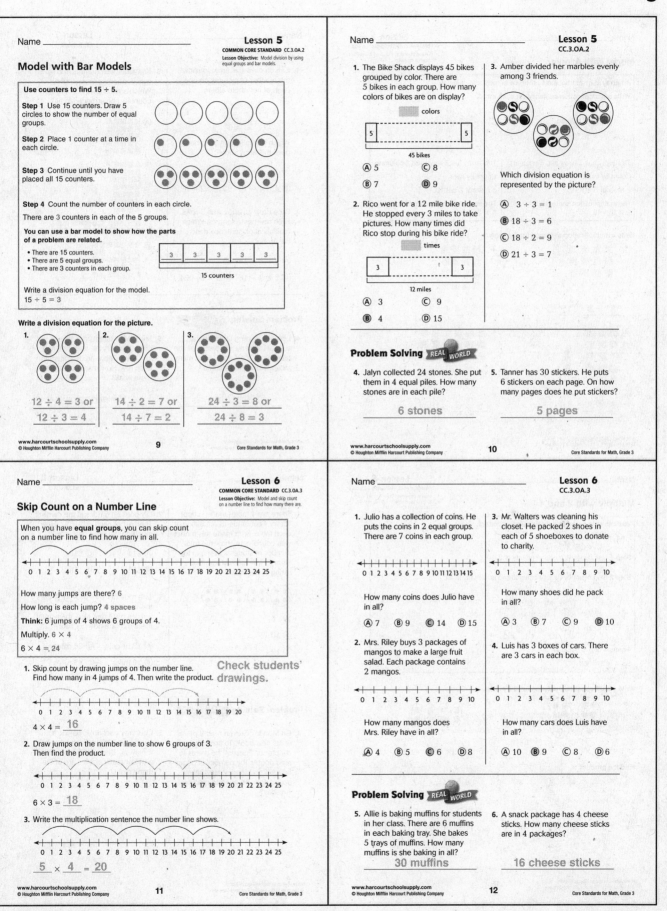

© Houghton Mifflin Harcourt Publishing Company

Name ____________________

Lesson 7
COMMON CORE STANDARD CC.3.OA.3
Lesson Objective: Use arrays to model products and factors.

Model with Arrays

An **array** is a set of objects arranged in rows and columns.

Write a multiplication sentence for each array.

This array has 2 rows and 5 columns.	This array has 5 rows and 2 columns.
Count by fives.	Count by twos.
2 rows of 5 are 10.	5 rows of 2 are 10.
The multiplication sentence is $2 \times 5 = 10$.	The multiplication sentence is $5 \times 2 = 10$.

Write a multiplication sentence for the array.

1. 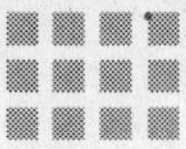

3 × 4 = 12

2. 

4 × 4 = 16

3. 

5 × 3 = 15

4. 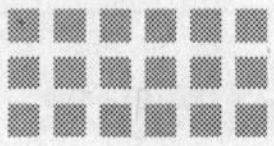

3 × 6 = 18

Name ____________________

Lesson 7
CC.3.OA.3

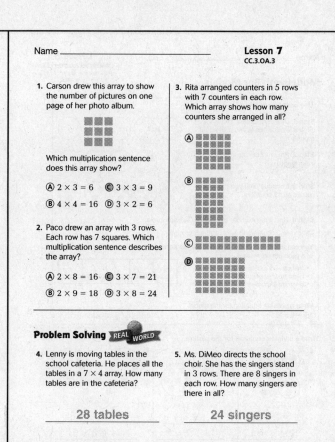

1. Carson drew this array to show the number of pictures on one page of her photo album.

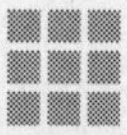

Which multiplication sentence does this array show?

Ⓐ $2 \times 3 = 6$ Ⓒ $3 \times 3 = 9$
Ⓑ $4 \times 4 = 16$ Ⓓ $3 \times 2 = 6$

2. Paco drew an array with 3 rows. Each row has 7 squares. Which multiplication sentence describes the array?

Ⓐ $2 \times 8 = 16$ Ⓒ $3 \times 7 = 21$
Ⓑ $2 \times 9 = 18$ Ⓓ $3 \times 8 = 24$

3. Rita arranged counters in 5 rows with 7 counters in each row. Which array shows how many counters she arranged in all?

Ⓐ 

Ⓑ 

Ⓒ 

Ⓓ 

Problem Solving REAL WORLD

4. Lenny is moving tables in the school cafeteria. He places all the tables in a 7 × 4 array. How many tables are in the cafeteria?

28 tables

5. Ms. DiMeo directs the school choir. She has the singers stand in 3 rows. There are 8 singers in each row. How many singers are there in all?

24 singers

Name ____________________

Lesson 8
COMMON CORE STANDARD CC.3.OA.3
Lesson Objective: Draw a picture, count by 2s, or use doubles to multiply with the factors 2 and 4.

Multiply with 2 and 4

You can skip count to help you find a product.

Find the product. 4 × 3

Step 1 Use cubes to model 4 groups of 3.

Step 2 Skip count by 3s four times to find how many in all.

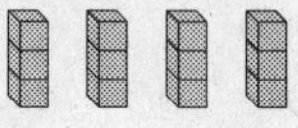

3, 6, 9, 12

4 groups of 3 is equal to 12.

So, 4 × 3 = 12.

Write a multiplication sentence for the model.

1. 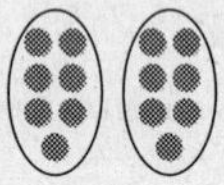

2 × 7 = 14

2. 

4 × 2 = 8

Find the product.

3. $2 \times 3 = 6$
4. $4 \times 8 = 32$
5. $2 \times 6 = 12$
6. $4 \times 1 = 4$
7. $2 \times 9 = 18$
8. $2 \times 2 = 4$
9. $4 \times 9 = 36$
10. $2 \times 5 = 10$
11. $4 \times 5 = 20$
12. $4 \times 7 = 28$

Name ____________________

Lesson 8
CC.3.OA.3

1. There are 4 tables in the school library. Four students are sitting at each table. Brett made this model with counters to show the total number of students sitting in the library. How many students are sitting in the library?

Ⓐ 8
Ⓑ 10
Ⓒ 12
Ⓓ 16

2. Lily goes on 6 rides at the carnival. The cost of each ride is $2. How much do the rides cost in all?

Ⓐ $14 Ⓒ $10
Ⓑ $12 Ⓓ $8

3. Tara rode her bike to work 4 days this week. She rode a total of 9 miles each day. How many total miles did Tara ride her bike?

Ⓐ 13 miles Ⓒ 36 miles
Ⓑ 18 miles Ⓓ 45 miles

Problem Solving REAL WORLD

4. On Monday, Steven read 9 pages of his new book. To finish the first chapter on Tuesday, he needs to read double the number of pages he read on Monday. How many pages does he need to read on Tuesday?

18 pages

5. Courtney's school is having a family game night. Each table has 4 players. There are 7 tables in all. How many players are at the game night?

28 players

Name ____________

Lesson 9

COMMON CORE STANDARD CC.3.OA.3

Lesson Objective: Use skip counting, a number line, or a bar model to multiply with the factors 5 and 10.

Multiply with 5 and 10

You can use an array to multiply with 5.

Find the product. 5 × 4

Step 1 Make an array to show 5 × 4.
Show 5 rows of 4 tiles.

Step 2 Count the tiles.
5 rows of 4 tiles = 20 tiles

So, 5 × 4 = 20.

You can use doubles to multiply with 10.

Find the product. 6 × 10

Think: 5 + 5 = 10

Multiply with 5. 6 × 5 = 30

Then double the product. 30 + 30 = 60

So, 6 × 10 = 60.

Find the product.

1. 2 × 5 = 10
2. 10 × 2 = 20
3. 5 × 5 = 25
4. 5 × 1 = 5
5. 10 × 1 = 10
6. 10 × 5 = 50
7. 3 × 5 = 15
8. 10 × 7 = 70
9. 10 × 4 = 40
10. 6 × 5 = 30
11. 9 × 5 = 45
12. 10 × 3 = 30
13. 5 × 2 = 10
14. 10 × 6 = 60
15. 8 × 5 = 40
16. 10 × 8 = 80

Name ____________

Lesson 9
CC.3.OA.3

1. Kyle bought 4 erasers at the school store. Each eraser cost 10¢.

10¢	10¢	10¢	10¢

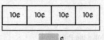

▢ ¢

How much did the erasers cost in all?

(A) 14¢ **(C) 40¢**
(B) 20¢ (D) 44¢

2. Mrs. Howard's students stack their chairs at the end of the day. Each stack contains 5 chairs. If there are 6 stacks of chairs, how many chairs are stacked?

(A) 15 (C) 25
(B) 20 **(D) 30**

3. Aleesha has 10 packages of beads. There are 6 beads in each package. How many beads does Aleesha have altogether?

(A) 16 **(C) 60**
(B) 30 (D) 66

4. Tran buys an apple. He gives the store clerk 9 nickels. Each nickel has a value of 5 cents. How many cents does Tran give the store clerk?

(A) 45 cents
(B) 35 cents
(C) 14 cents
(D) 10 cents

Problem Solving REAL WORLD

5. Ginger takes 10 nickels to buy some pencils at the school store. How many cents does Ginger have to spend?

50 cents

6. The gym at Evergreen School has three basketball courts. There are 5 players on each of the courts. How many players are there in all?

15 players

Name ____________

Lesson 10

COMMON CORE STANDARD CC.3.OA.3

Lesson Objective: Draw a picture, use 5s facts and addition, doubles, or a multiplication table to multiply with the factors 3 and 6.

Multiply with 3 and 6

You can use a number line to multiply with 3 or 6.

Find the product. 6 × 3

The factor 6 tells you to make **6 jumps**.

The factor 3 tells you each jump should be **3 spaces**.

Step 1 Start at 0.
Make 6 jumps of 3 spaces.

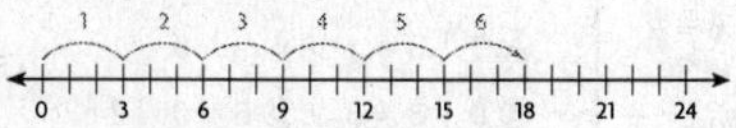

Step 2 The number you land on is the product.

So, 6 × 3 = 18.

Find the product.

1. 3 × 1 = 3
2. 12 = 2 × 6
3. 8 × 3 = 24
4. 6 × 6 = 36
5. 3 × 0 = 0
6. 5 × 6 = 30
7. 15 = 3 × 5
8. 9 × 6 = 54
9. 3 × 9 = 27
10. 6 × 4 = 24
11. 7 × 3 = 21
12. 1 × 6 = 6
13. 10 × 6 = 60
14. 3 × 6 = 18
15. 6 × 7 = 42
16. 4 × 3 = 12

Name ____________

Lesson 10
CC.3.OA.3

1. Jason has 6 bookshelves in his room. There are 6 books on each shelf. How many books are there in all?

(A) 12 **(C) 36**
(B) 24 (D) 42

2. Madison makes 4 types of hair ribbons. She makes each type of ribbon using 3 different colors. How many hair ribbons does Madison make?

(A) 12
(B) 10
(C) 9
(D) 7

3. Dora is making hexagons with straws. She uses 6 straws for each hexagon. If she makes 3 hexagons, how many straws does Dora use?

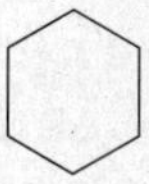

(A) 9 **(C) 18**
(B) 12 (D) 24

4. Elvira bought 4 packages of stickers. There are 6 stickers in each package. How many stickers did Elvira buy?

(A) 12 (C) 30
(B) 24 (D) 36

Problem Solving REAL WORLD

5. James got 3 hits in each of his baseball games. He has played 4 baseball games. How many hits has he had in all?

12 hits

6. Mrs. Burns is buying muffins. There are 6 muffins in each box. If she buys 5 boxes, how many muffins will she buy?

30 muffins

Answer Key

Name ____________ **Lesson 11**

COMMON CORE STANDARD CC.3.OA.3

Lesson Objective: Solve division problems by using the strategy *act it out.*

Problem Solving • Model Division

There are 35 people going to the amusement park. They will all travel in 5 vans with the same number of people in each van. How many people will travel in each van?

Read the Problem	Solve the Problem
What do I need to find? I need to find the number of people who will travel in each van.	**Describe how to act out the problem to solve.** **Step 1** Start with 35 counters.
What information do I need to use? There are 35 people. 5 vans are taking all the people to the amusement park.	**Step 2** Make 5 equal groups. Place 1 counter at a time in each group until all 35 counters are used.
How will I use the information? I can act out the problem by making equal groups with counters.	**Step 3** Count the number of counters in each group. 7 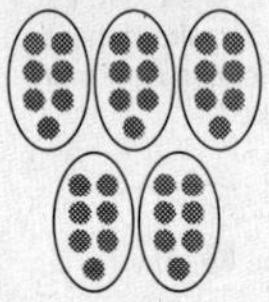 So, 7 people will travel in each van.

1. José packs 54 CDs into small boxes. Each box holds 9 CDs. How many boxes does José pack to hold all 54 CDs?

   6 boxes

2. Mary volunteers at the library. She has 36 books to put on 4 empty shelves. If Mary puts an equal number of books on each shelf, how many books will be on each shelf?

   9 books

Name ____________ **Lesson 11**

CC.3.OA.3

1. During a field trip, 30 students in Mrs. Beckman's class were placed into groups of 6 students each for a tour of the museum. How many groups were there?

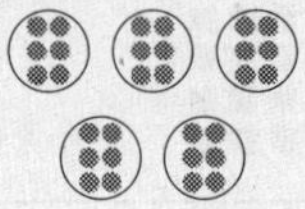

Ⓐ 5 Ⓒ 7
Ⓑ 6 Ⓓ 8

2. Tao has 8 sand dollars in his collection. He makes a model to show how he shares his collection equally with his friend, Yom.

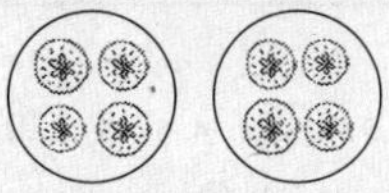

How many sand dollars does each boy get?

Ⓐ 2 Ⓒ 6
Ⓑ 4 Ⓓ 8

3. Barry has 15 comic books. He wants to place his books in 3 equal piles. Which model shows how many comic books Barry should put in each pile?

Ⓐ 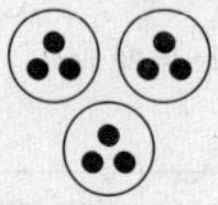

Ⓑ 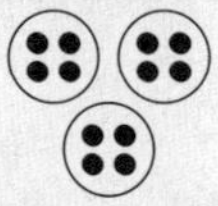

Ⓒ 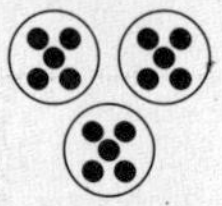

Ⓓ 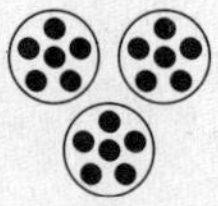

4. There are 54 party favors. Each of 6 tables will have the same number of party favors. How many party favors will go on each table? Explain how you can act out the problem with counters.

   9 party favors; Possible explanation: I can draw 6 circles and put one counter in each circle until I use up all 54 counters. I find that each circle gets 9 counters so each table gets 9 favors.

Name ____________ **Lesson 12**

COMMON CORE STANDARD CC.3.OA.3

Lesson Objective: Use repeated subtraction and a number line to relate subtraction to division.

Algebra • Relate Subtraction and Division

Find 18 ÷ 6.

	Use base-ten blocks.	**Use repeated subtraction.**
Step 1 Start with the number you are dividing, 18.		
Step 2 Subtract the number you are dividing by, 6.		18 − 6 = 12
Step 3 There are more than 6 left. Subtract 6 again.	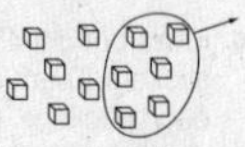	18 − 6 = 12; 12 − 6 = 6
Step 4 There are 6 left. Subtract 6 again.	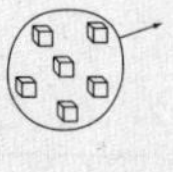	18 − 6 = 12; 12 − 6 = 6; 6 − 6 = 0

Step 5 Count the number of times you subtract 6.

You subtract 6 three times, so there are 3 groups of 6 in 18.

Write: 18 ÷ 6 = 3

Write a division equation.

1. 27 − 9 = 18; 18 − 9 = 9; 9 − 9 = 0

   27 ÷ 9 = 3

2. 16 − 4 = 12; 12 − 4 = 8; 8 − 4 = 4; 4 − 4 = 0

   16 ÷ 4 = 4

Name ____________ **Lesson 12**

CC.3.OA.3

1. Mr. Burt shared 12 olives equally with each person in his family.

Which division equation is represented by the number line?

Ⓐ 12 ÷ 3 = 4 Ⓒ 12 ÷ 2 = 6
Ⓑ 3 ÷ 3 = 1 Ⓓ 12 ÷ 6 = 2

2. Lionel bought a bag of favors for his party guests. He used repeated subtraction to help him divide the favors equally among his guests.

   16 − 4 = 12; 12 − 4 = 8; 8 − 4 = 4; 4 − 4 = 0

   Which division equation matches the repeated subtraction?

   Ⓐ 16 ÷ 2 = 8 Ⓒ 12 ÷ 3 = 4
   Ⓑ 4 ÷ 4 = 1 Ⓓ 16 ÷ 4 = 4

3. Marco's mother bought 9 toy cars. She asked Marco to share the cars equally among his friends. Marco used a number line to help.

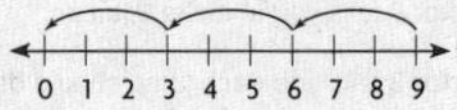

Which division equation is represented by the number line?

Ⓐ 3 ÷ 3 = 1 Ⓒ 9 ÷ 9 = 1
Ⓑ 9 ÷ 3 = 3 Ⓓ 6 ÷ 3 = 2

4. Lola bought a bag of 15 apples for her friends. She used repeated subtraction to help her divide the apples equally among her friends.

   15 − 5 = 10; 10 − 5 = 5; 5 − 5 = 0

   Which division equation matches the repeated subtraction?

   Ⓐ 15 ÷ 15 = 1 Ⓒ 15 ÷ 5 = 3
   Ⓑ 10 ÷ 5 = 2 Ⓓ 15 ÷ 1 = 15

5. How is repeated subtraction like counting back on a number line? Explain how both methods help you divide.

   Possible explanation: they both start with the number you are dividing. Then they both subtract equal groups of the number you are dividing by. The number line shows the groups subtracted by counting back. The quotient is the number of jumps or the number of subtractions made.

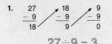

Name ______________________ **Lesson 13**

COMMON CORE STANDARD CC.3.OA.3

Lesson Objective: Model division by using arrays.

Model with Arrays

You can use arrays to model division.

How many rows of 6 tiles each can you make with 24 tiles?

Use square tiles to make an array. Solve.

Step 1 Use 24 tiles.

Step 2 Make as many rows of 6 as you can.

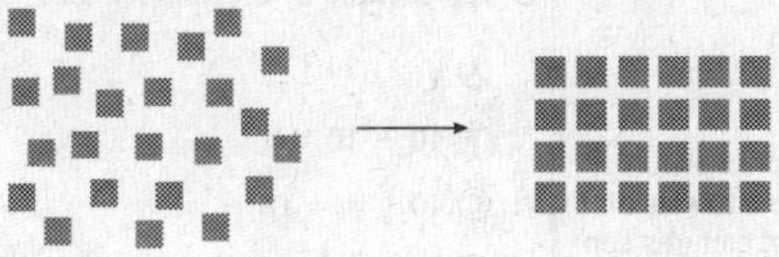

You can make 4 rows of 6.

So, there are 4 rows of 6 tiles in 24.

Use square tiles to make an array. Solve. Check students' arrays.

1. How many rows of 7 are in 28? 4 rows
2. How many rows of 5 are in 15? 3 rows

Make an array. Then write a division equation. Check students' arrays.

3. 18 tiles in 3 rows $18 \div 3 = 6$
4. 20 tiles in 4 rows $20 \div 4 = 5$
5. 14 tiles in 2 rows $14 \div 2 = 7$
6. 36 tiles in 4 rows $36 \div 4 = 9$

Name ______________________ **Lesson 13**

CC.3.OA.3

1. Which division sentence best fits the array?

Ⓐ $16 \div 16 = 1$
Ⓑ $16 \div 8 = 2$
Ⓒ $16 \div 4 = 4$
Ⓓ $16 \div 1 = 16$

2. Damian has 30 tiles. How many rows of 10 tiles can he make?

Ⓐ 27
Ⓑ 15
Ⓒ 10
Ⓓ 3

3. Which division sentence best fits the array?

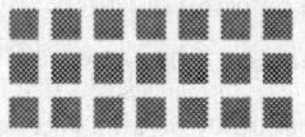

Ⓐ $21 \div 1 = 21$
Ⓑ $21 \div 3 = 7$
Ⓒ $20 \div 5 = 4$
Ⓓ $20 \div 10 = 2$

4. The 24 mailboxes in a building are in an array with 6 rows. How many mailboxes are in each row?

Ⓐ 4 Ⓒ 8
Ⓑ 6 Ⓓ 12

Problem Solving REAL WORLD

5. A dressmaker has 24 buttons. He needs 3 buttons to make one dress. How many dresses can he make with 24 buttons? 8 dresses
6. Liana buys 36 party favors for her 9 guests. She gives an equal number of favors to each guest. How many party favors does each guest get? 4 party favors

Name ______________________ **Lesson 14**

COMMON CORE STANDARD CC.3.OA.3

Lesson Objective: Use models to represent division by 2.

Divide by 2

You can draw a picture to show how to divide.

Find the quotient. $16 \div 2$

Step 1 Draw 16 counters.

Step 2 Circle groups of 2. Continue circling groups of 2 until all 16 counters are in groups.

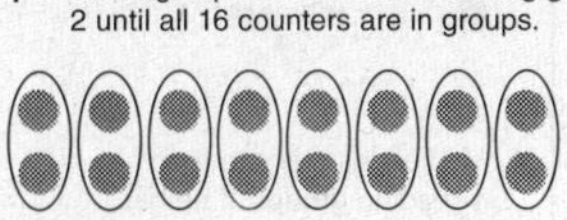

There are 8 groups of 2.

So, $16 \div 2 = 8$.

Write a division equation for the picture.

1. 

$6 \div 2 = 3$ or $6 \div 3 = 2$

2. 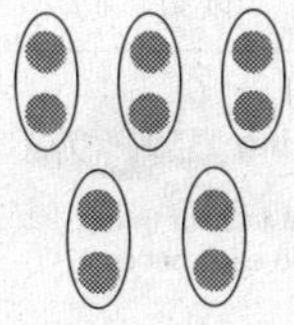

$10 \div 2 = 5$ or $10 \div 5 = 2$

Name ______________________ **Lesson 14**

CC.3.OA.3

1. Lionel has 14 mittens.

Which division equation is represented by the picture?

Ⓐ $7 \div 7 = 1$
Ⓑ $2 \div 2 = 1$
Ⓒ $14 \div 14 = 1$
Ⓓ $14 \div 2 = 7$

2. Garret practiced on the piano for the same amount of time each day for 2 days. He practiced a total of 4 hours. How many hours did Garret practice each day?

Ⓐ 1 hour Ⓒ 6 hours
Ⓑ 2 hours Ⓓ 8 hours

3. Ben needs 2 oranges to make a glass of orange juice. If oranges come in bags of 10, how many glasses of orange juice can he make using one bag of oranges?

Ⓐ 4 Ⓒ 6
Ⓑ 5 Ⓓ 8

4. Mrs. Conner has 16 shoes.

What division sentence is represented by the picture?

Ⓐ $80 \div 8 = 1$
Ⓑ $16 \div 16 = 1$
Ⓒ $16 \div 2 = 8$
Ⓓ $2 \div 2 = 1$

Problem Solving REAL WORLD

5. Mr. Reynolds, the gym teacher, divided a class of 16 students into 2 equal teams. How many students were on each team? 8 students
6. Sandra has 10 books. She divides them into groups of 2 each. How many groups can she make? 5 groups

Answer Key

Name ______________________ **Lesson 15**

COMMON CORE STANDARD CC.3.OA.3

Lesson Objective: Count up by 5s, count back on a number line, or use 10s facts and doubles to divide by 5.

Divide by 5

You can use a hundred chart and count up to help you divide.

Find the quotient. $30 \div 5$

Step 1 Count up by 5s until you reach 30. Circle the numbers you say in the count.

Step 2 Count the number of times you count up.

5, 10, 15, 20, 25, 30

1, 2, 3, 4, 5, 6

Step 3 Use the number of times you count up to complete the equation.

You counted up by 5 six times.

So, $30 \div 5 =$ 6.

1	2	3	4	(5)	6	7	8	9	(10)
11	12	13	14	(15)	16	17	18	19	(20)
21	22	23	24	(25)	26	27	28	29	(30)
31	32	33	34	35	36	37	38	39	40
41	42	43	44	45	46	47	48	49	50
51	52	53	54	55	56	57	58	59	60
61	62	63	64	65	66	67	68	69	70
71	72	73	74	75	76	77	78	79	80
81	82	83	84	85	86	87	88	89	90
91	92	93	94	95	96	97	98	99	100

Use the hundred chart and count up to solve.

1. $20 \div 5 =$ 4
2. $35 \div 5 =$ 7
3. $40 \div 5 =$ 8

Find the quotient.

4. $25 \div 5 =$ 5
5. 9 $= 45 \div 5$
6. $10 \div 5 =$ 2
7. 3 $= 15 \div 5$
8. $50 \div 5 =$ 10
9. 1 $= 5 \div 5$

Name ______________________ **Lesson 15**

CC.3.OA.3

1. The Bike Shack displays 45 bikes grouped by color. There are 5 bikes in each group. How many colors of bikes does the store have?

   Ⓐ 7
   Ⓑ 9 (marked)
   Ⓒ 20
   Ⓓ 40

2. Mrs. Alvarez printed 35 pictures. She will group them into sets of 5. How many sets of pictures can she make?

   Ⓐ 40
   Ⓑ 30
   Ⓒ 7 (marked)
   Ⓓ 6

3. Hannah made $40 selling hats. Each hat costs $5. She wants to know how many hats she sold. Hannah used a number line to help her.

   Which division equation is represented by the number line?

   Ⓐ $6 \div 6 = 1$
   Ⓑ $40 \div 10 = 4$
   Ⓒ $40 \div 4 = 10$
   Ⓓ $40 \div 5 = 8$ (marked)

Problem Solving REAL WORLD

4. A model car maker puts 5 wheels in each kit. A machine makes 30 wheels at a time. How many packages of 5 wheels can be made from the 30 wheels?

   6 packages

5. A doll maker puts a small bag with 5 hair ribbons inside each box with a doll. How many bags of 5 hair ribbons can be made from 45 hair ribbons?

   9 bags

Name ______________________ **Lesson 16**

COMMON CORE STANDARD CC.3.OA.4

Lesson Objective: Use an array or a multiplication table to find an unknown factor.

Algebra • Find Unknown Factors

Lily has 20 stuffed animals. She wants to put the same number of stuffed animals on each of 5 shelves. How many stuffed animals will Lily put on each shelf?

Find the unknown factor. $5 \times c = 20$

You can use counters to find the unknown factor.

Step 1 Use 20 counters.

Step 2 Make 5 equal groups. Place 1 counter in each of the groups until you have placed all 20 counters.

Step 3 Count the number of counters in each group.
4 counters

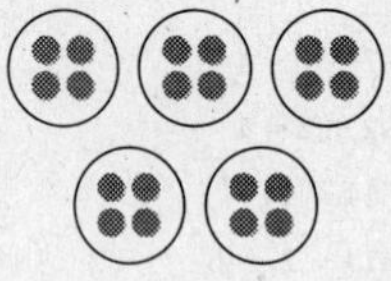

$c = 4$

So, Lily will put 4 stuffed animals on each of the 5 shelves. $5 \times 4 = 20$

Find the unknown factor.

1. $3 \times b = 24$ — $b =$ 8
2. $n \times 7 = 21$ — $n =$ 3
3. $36 = 4 \times z$ — $z =$ 9
4. $s \times 8 = 56$ — $s =$ 7
5. $r \times 5 = 45$ — $r =$ 9
6. ▩ $\times 4 = 40$ — ▩ $=$ 10
7. $12 = 3 \times p$ — $p =$ 4
8. $m \times 6 = 42$ — $m =$ 7
9. $6 \times h = 36$ — $h =$ 6
10. $63 = 7 \times d$ — $d =$ 9
11. $3 \times y = 6$ — $y =$ 2
12. $32 = 4 \times$ ▲ — ▲ $=$ 8

Name ______________________ **Lesson 16**

CC.3.OA.4

1. The volleyball club plans to have 7 teams. There were 42 students who signed up to play. How many students will be on each team?

   $7 \times$ ▩ $= 42$

   Ⓐ 5
   Ⓑ 6 (marked)
   Ⓒ 7
   Ⓓ 8

2. Duane needs 36 hats for a party. There are 6 hats in each package. How many packages of hats does Duane need to buy?

   $p \times 6 = 36$

   Ⓐ 2
   Ⓑ 6 (marked)
   Ⓒ 18
   Ⓓ 30

3. Pilar spent $48 on 6 books. The cost of each book was the same. Which equation can be used to find the cost of one book?

   Ⓐ $48 × ▩ = 6
   Ⓑ 3 × ▩ = 6
   Ⓒ $48 × ▩ = 8
   Ⓓ 6 × ▩ = $48 (marked)

4. Mr. Perkins plans to teach 4 reading groups. If he has 28 students, how many students will be in each reading group?

   $4 \times$ ▩ $= 28$

   Ⓐ 24
   Ⓑ 8
   Ⓒ 7 (marked)
   Ⓓ 6

Problem Solving REAL WORLD

5. Carmen spent $42 for 6 hats. How much did each hat cost?

   $7

6. Mark has a baking tray with 24 cupcakes. The cupcakes are arranged in 4 equal rows. How many cupcakes are in each row?

   6 cupcakes

Answer Key

Name ______________________ **Lesson 17**

COMMON CORE STANDARD CC.3.OA.4

Lesson Objective: Use repeated subtraction, a related multiplication fact, or a multiplication table to divide by 8.

Divide by 8

You can use a number line to divide by 8.

Find the quotient. 24 ÷ 8

Step 1 Start at 24. Count back by 8s as many times as you can until you reach 0. Draw the jumps on the number line.

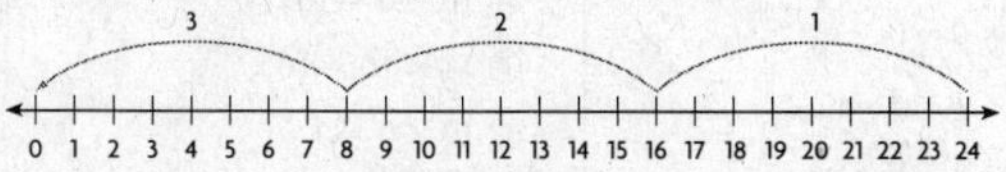

Step 2 Count the number of times you jumped back 8.

You jumped back by 8 three times.

So, 24 ÷ 8 = 3.

Find the unknown factor and quotient.

1. 9 × 8 = 72 72 ÷ 8 = 9
2. 8 × 6 = 48 48 ÷ 8 = 6
3. 8 × 5 = 40 40 ÷ 8 = 5
4. 2 × 8 = 16 16 ÷ 8 = 2

Find the quotient.

5. 32 ÷ 8 = 4
6. 1 = 8 ÷ 8
7. 64 ÷ 8 = 8
8. 56 ÷ 8 = 7
9. 2 = 16 ÷ 8
10. 40 ÷ 8 = 5
11. 24 ÷ 8 = 3
12. 9 = 72 ÷ 8
13. 48 ÷ 8 = 6

www.harcourtschoolsupply.com
© Houghton Mifflin Harcourt Publishing Company

Name ______________________ **Lesson 17**

CC.3.OA.4

1. Brian is dividing 64 baseball cards equally among 8 friends. How many baseball cards will each friend get?

   Ⓐ 7
   Ⓑ 8 (filled)
   Ⓒ 9
   Ⓓ 10

2. Adam and his friends raked enough leaves to fill 48 bags. Each person filled 8 bags. How many people raked leaves?

   Ⓐ 6 (filled)
   Ⓑ 5
   Ⓒ 4
   Ⓓ 3

3. Students celebrated Earth Day by planting 24 seedlings at 8 different locations in town. They planted the same number of seedlings at each location. How many seedlings did they plant at each location?

   Ⓐ 6 Ⓒ 4
   Ⓑ 5 Ⓓ 3 (filled)

4. Keith arranged 40 toy cars in 8 equal rows. How many toy cars are in each row?

   Ⓐ 4
   Ⓑ 5 (filled)
   Ⓒ 6
   Ⓓ 32

Problem Solving REAL WORLD

5. Sixty-four students are going on a field trip. There is 1 adult for every 8 students. How many adults are there?

   8 adults

6. Mr. Chen spends $32 for tickets to a play. If the tickets cost $8 each, how many tickets does Mr. Chen buy?

   4 tickets

www.harcourtschoolsupply.com
© Houghton Mifflin Harcourt Publishing Company

Name ______________________ **Lesson 18**

COMMON CORE STANDARD CC.3.OA.5

Lesson Objective: Model the Commutative Property of Multiplication and use it to find products.

Algebra • Commutative Property of Multiplication

The **Commutative Property of Multiplication** states that you can change the order of the factors and the product stays the same.

There are 4 rows of 5 tiles.

Think: 4 equal groups of 5

5 + 5 + 5 + 5 = 20

Multiply. 4 × 5 = 20

There are 5 rows of 4 tiles.

Think: 5 equal groups of 4

4 + 4 + 4 + 4 + 4 = 20

Multiply. 5 × 4 = 20

The factors are 4 and 5. The product is 20.

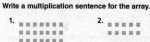

Write a multiplication sentence for the array. Possible sentences are shown.

1. 
   3 × 7 = 21
2. 
   2 × 5 = 10
3. 
   1 × 8 = 8

Write a multiplication sentence for the model. Then use the Commutative Property of Multiplication to write a related multiplication sentence.

4. 
   4 × 2 = 8
   2 × 4 = 8
5. 
   4 × 3 = 12
   3 × 4 = 12
6. 
   4 × 6 = 24
   6 × 4 = 24

www.harcourtschoolsupply.com
© Houghton Mifflin Harcourt Publishing Company

Name ______________________ **Lesson 18**

CC.3.OA.5

1. Donna wrote 5 × 9 = 45. Which is a related number sentence?

   Ⓐ 5 + 4 = 9 Ⓒ 5 × 5 = 25
   Ⓑ 9 × 5 = 45 (filled) Ⓓ 4 × 5 = 20

2. Matthew made arrays with counters to show the Commutative Property of Multiplication.

   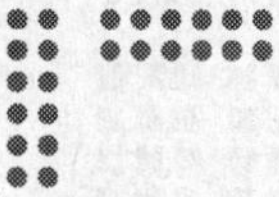

   Which multiplication sentences are shown by his arrays?

   Ⓐ 3 × 4 = 12 and 4 × 3 = 12
   Ⓑ 6 × 4 = 24 and 4 × 6 = 24
   Ⓒ 6 × 2 = 12 and 2 × 6 = 12 (filled)
   Ⓓ 2 × 7 = 14 and 7 × 2 = 14

3. Greta put 6 coins into each of 3 stacks. She wrote 3 × 6 = 18. Which is a related number sentence?

   Ⓐ 6 × 3 = 18 (filled)
   Ⓑ 6 + 3 = 9
   Ⓒ 3 + 3 + 3 = 9
   Ⓓ 6 × 6 = 36

4. Ben put 10 color pencils into each of 6 bags. He wrote 6 × 10 = 60 to represent the total. Which is a related multiplication sentence?

   Ⓐ 10 × 10 = 100
   Ⓑ 5 × 12 = 60
   Ⓒ 6 × 6 = 36
   Ⓓ 10 × 6 = 60 (filled)

Problem Solving REAL WORLD

5. A garden store sells trays of plants. Each tray holds 2 rows of 8 plants. How many plants are in one tray?

   16 plants

6. Jeff collects toy cars. They are displayed in a case that has 4 rows. There are 6 cars in each row. How many cars does Jeff have?

   24 cars

www.harcourtschoolsupply.com
© Houghton Mifflin Harcourt Publishing Company

© Houghton Mifflin Harcourt Publishing Company

Answer Key

Name ____________________

Lesson 19
COMMON CORE STANDARD CC.3.OA.5
Lesson Objective: Model multiplication with the factors 1 and 0.

Algebra • Multiply with 1 and 0

Find the product.

4 × 0 = ▦

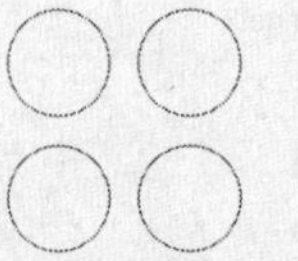

Model 4 × 0.
Each circle contains 0 counters.

4 circles × 0 counters = 0 counters

Zero Property of Multiplication
The product of zero and any number is zero.

So, 4 × 0 = 0 and 0 × 4 = 0.

Find the product.

6 × 1 = ▦

Model 6 × 1.
Each circle contains 1 star.

6 circles × 1 star = 6 stars

Identity Property of Multiplication
The product of any number and 1 is that number.

So, 6 × 1 = 6 and 1 × 6 = 6.

Find the product.

1. 9 × 0 = 0
2. 1 × 5 = 5
3. 0 × 10 = 0
4. 8 × 1 = 8
5. 0 × 3 = 0
6. 7 × 1 = 7
7. 5 × 0 = 0
8. 1 × 2 = 2

Name ____________________

Lesson 19
CC.3.OA.5

1. Sierra looked in 4 jars for marbles. In each jar she found 0 marbles. Which number sentence represents the total number of marbles Sierra found?
   - Ⓐ 4 + 0 = 4
   - **Ⓑ 4 × 0 = 0**
   - Ⓒ 4 × 1 = 4
   - Ⓓ 4 − 4 = 0

2. Robin found 1 pinecone under each of 3 trees. Which number sentence shows how many pinecones Robin found?
   - Ⓐ 3 − 3 = 0
   - Ⓑ 3 + 0 = 3
   - Ⓒ 3 × 0 = 0
   - **Ⓓ 3 × 1 = 3**

3. Juan bought a golf ball display case with 10 shelves. There are 0 golf balls on each shelf. Which number sentence shows how many golf balls Juan has in the display case now?
   - Ⓐ 10 − 0 = 10
   - Ⓑ 1 × 10 = 10
   - **Ⓒ 10 × 0 = 0**
   - Ⓓ 10 + 0 = 10

4. Aiden saw 4 lifeguard towers at the beach. Each tower had 1 lifeguard. Which number sentence represents the total number of lifeguards Aiden saw?
   - Ⓐ 4 × 4 = 16
   - **Ⓑ 4 × 1 = 4**
   - Ⓒ 1 × 1 = 1
   - Ⓓ 4 + 1 = 5

Problem Solving REAL WORLD

5. Peter is in the school play. His teacher gave 1 copy of the play to each of 6 students. How many copies of the play did the teacher hand out?
   6 copies

6. There are 4 egg cartons on the table. There are 0 eggs in each carton. How many eggs are there in all?
   0 eggs

Name ____________________

Lesson 20
COMMON CORE STANDARD CC.3.OA.5
Lesson Objective: Use the Distributive Property to find products by breaking apart arrays.

Algebra • Distributive Property

A garden has 4 rows of 7 corn stalks. How many corn stalks in all are in the garden?

You can use the **Distributive Property** to break an array into smaller arrays to help you find the answer.

Find 4 × 7.

Step 1 Make an array to show 4 rows of 7.

4 rows of 7, or 4 × 7

Step 2 Break apart the array to make two smaller arrays for facts you know.

4 × 4 + 4 × 3
16 + 12 = 28

Step 3 Write the multiplication for the new arrays. Multiply and then add the products to find the answer.

4 × 7 = (4 × 4) + (4 × 3)
4 × 7 = 16 + 12
4 × 7 = 28

So, there are 28 corn stalks in all in the garden.

Write one way to break apart the array. Then find the product. Possible answers are given.

1.

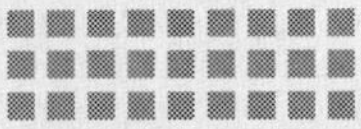

(3 × 4) + (3 × 5); or
(1 × 9) + (2 × 9); 27

2.

(6 × 1) + (6 × 2); or
(3 × 3) + (3 × 3); 18

Name ____________________

Lesson 20
CC.3.OA.5

1. Henry and 5 friends are going to the movies. Tickets cost $8 each. Henry used this model to help him find the total cost of tickets.

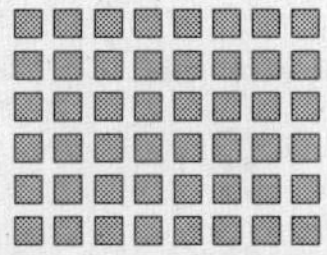

   Which shows one way to break apart the array to find the product?
   - **Ⓐ (6 × 5) + (6 × 3)**
   - Ⓑ (3 × 8) + (6 × 8)
   - Ⓒ (6 × 6) + (6 × 4)
   - Ⓓ 6 + (4 × 4)

2. Which number sentence is an example of the Distributive Property of Multiplication?
   - Ⓐ 7 × 8 = 50 + 6
   - Ⓑ 7 × 8 = 7 × (2 × 4)
   - Ⓒ 7 × 8 = 8 × 7
   - **Ⓓ 7 × 8 = (7 × 4) + (7 × 4)**

3. Which is equal to 7 × 9?
   - Ⓐ (7 × 3) + (7 × 3)
   - Ⓑ (7 × 3) × (7 × 3)
   - **Ⓒ (7 × 3) + (7 × 6)**
   - Ⓓ (7 × 3) × (7 × 6)

Problem Solving REAL WORLD

4. There are 2 rows of 8 chairs set up in the library for a puppet show. How many chairs are there in all? Use the Distributive Property to solve.
   16 chairs

5. A marching band has 4 rows of trumpeters with 10 trumpeters in each row. How many trumpeters are in the marching band? Use the Distributive Property to solve.
   40 trumpeters

Name ______________________

Lesson 21
COMMON CORE STANDARD CC.3.OA.5
Lesson Objective: Use the Associative Property of Multiplication to multiply with three factors.

Algebra • Associative Property of Multiplication

You can use the **Associative Property of Multiplication** to multiply 3 factors. If you change the grouping of factors, the product remains the same.

Find 4 × (3 × 1).

Step 1 Start inside the parentheses. Make 3 groups of 1 counter.

(3 × 1) 

Step 2 Multiply by 4, the number outside the parentheses. Make 4 groups of the counters in Step 1.

4 × (3 × 1)

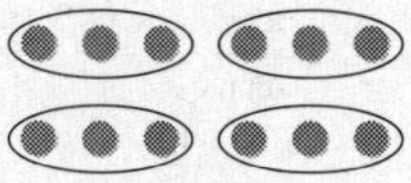

Step 3 Count the total number of counters. 12 counters

Find (4 × 3) × 1.

Step 1 Start inside the parentheses. Make 4 groups of 3 counters.

(4 × 3) 

Step 2 Multiply by 1, the number outside the parentheses. Make 1 group of the counters in Step 1.

(4 × 3) × 1

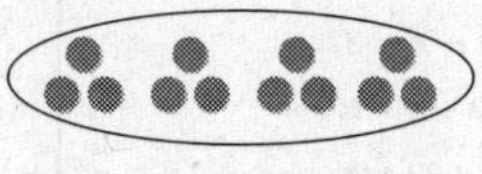

Step 3 Count the total number of counters. 12 counters

So, 4 × (3 × 1) = 12 and (4 × 3) × 1 = 12.

Possible groupings are given.

Write another way to group the factors. Then find the product.

1. (2 × 3) × 2 — 2 × (3 × 2); 12
2. 2 × (4 × 2) — (2 × 4) × 2; 16
3. 2 × (3 × 1) — (2 × 3) × 1; 6
4. 5 × (7 × 1) — (5 × 7) × 1; 35
5. 8 × (4 × 1) — (8 × 4) × 1; 32
6. 2 × (2 × 6) — (2 × 2) × 6; 24

Name ______________________

Lesson 21
CC.3.OA.5

1. Which number sentence is an example of the Associative Property of Multiplication?
   - Ⓐ 4 × 2 = 2 × 4
   - **Ⓑ (4 × 2) × 2 = 4 × (2 × 2)**
   - Ⓒ 4 × 2 = (4 × 1) + (4 × 1)
   - Ⓓ 4 × (2 + 2) = (4 × 2) + (4 × 2)

2. Which is equal to (2 × 2) × 5?
   - Ⓐ 2 × (2 + 5)
   - **Ⓑ 2 × (2 × 5)**
   - Ⓒ (2 × 2) × (2 × 5)
   - Ⓓ (2 + 5) × (2 + 5)

3. Corey has 3 stacks of boxes. In each stack are 3 boxes with 2 trains in each box. How many trains does he have in all?
   - Ⓐ 6
   - Ⓑ 9
   - **Ⓒ 18**
   - Ⓓ 27

4. There are 2 walls in Yolanda's classroom that each have 2 rows of pictures. Each row has 3 pictures. How many pictures are on these walls in Yolanda's classroom?
   - **Ⓐ 12**
   - Ⓑ 7
   - Ⓒ 6
   - Ⓓ 4

Problem Solving REAL WORLD

5. Beth and Maria are going to the county fair. Admission costs $4 per person for each day. They plan to go for 3 days. How much will the girls pay in all?

   $24

6. Randy's garden has 3 rows of carrots with 3 plants in each row. Next year he plans to plant 4 times the number of rows of 3 plants. How many plants will he have next year?

   36 plants

Name ______________________

Lesson 22
COMMON CORE STANDARD CC.3.OA.5
Lesson Objective: Divide using the rules for 1 and 0.

Algebra • Division Rules for 1 and 0

Division rules can help you understand how to divide with 1 and 0.

Rule A: Any number divided by 1 equals that number.

5 ÷ 1 = 5 or $\begin{array}{r}5\\1\overline{)5}\end{array}$

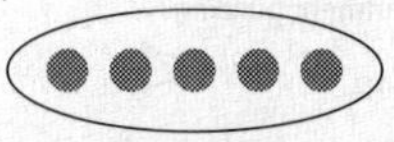

One group of 5

Rule B: Any number (except 0) divided by itself equals 1.

5 ÷ 5 = 1 or $\begin{array}{r}1\\5\overline{)5}\end{array}$

Five groups of 1

Rule C: Zero divided by any number (except 0) equals 0.

0 ÷ 5 = 0 or $\begin{array}{r}0\\5\overline{)0}\end{array}$

Five groups of 0

Rule D: You cannot divide by 0.

Find the quotient.

1. 4 ÷ 1 = 4
2. 2 ÷ 2 = 1
3. 8 ÷ 1 = 8
4. 7 ÷ 7 = 1
5. 0 ÷ 8 = 0
6. 0 ÷ 9 = 0
7. 4 ÷ 4 = 1
8. 6 ÷ 1 = 6
9. 6 ÷ 6 = 1
10. 0 ÷ 4 = 0
11. 0 ÷ 2 = 0
12. 3 ÷ 1 = 3

Name ______________________

Lesson 22
CC.3.OA.5

1. There are 0 books and 4 bookshelves. How many books are on each bookshelf?

   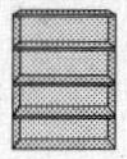

   - **Ⓐ 0**
   - Ⓑ 1
   - Ⓒ 3
   - Ⓓ 4

2. Percy paid $9 for some notebooks for school. Each notebook cost $1. How many notebooks did Percy buy?
   - Ⓐ 0
   - Ⓑ 1
   - Ⓒ 8
   - **Ⓓ 9**

3. Otis paid $7 for some markers for school. Each marker cost $1. How many markers did Otis buy?
   - Ⓐ 0
   - Ⓑ 1
   - Ⓒ 6
   - **Ⓓ 7**

4. Norma made 8 cat treats. She gave an equal number of cat treats to each of 8 cats. How many cat treats did Norma give to each cat?
   - Ⓐ 0
   - **Ⓑ 1**
   - Ⓒ 4
   - Ⓓ 8

Problem Solving REAL WORLD

5. There are no horses in the stables. There are 3 stables in all. How many horses are in each stable?

   0 horses

6. Jon has 6 kites. He and his friends will each fly 1 kite. How many people in all will fly a kite?

   6 people

Answer Key

Name ____________________

Lesson 23
COMMON CORE STANDARD CC.3.OA.6
Lesson Objective: Use bar models and arrays to relate multiplication and division as inverse operations.

Algebra • Relate Multiplication and Division

You can use an array to complete 21 ÷ 3 = ____.

Use 21 counters.
Make 3 equal rows.

●●●●●●● There are 7 counters in each row.
●●●●●●● 3 rows of 7 = 21
●●●●●●● So, 21 ÷ 3 = 7

The 21 tells the total number of counters in the array.
The 3 stands for the number of equal rows.
The 7 stands for the number of counters in each row.

You can use a related multiplication fact to check your answer.

21 ÷ 3 = 7   3 × 7 = 21

So, 3 rows of 7 represents 21 ÷ 3 = 7 or 3 × 7 = 21.

Complete.

1. 

6 rows of 4 = 24
6 × 4 = 24
24 ÷ 6 = 4

2. 

3 rows of 9 = 27
3 × 9 = 27
27 ÷ 3 = 9

3. 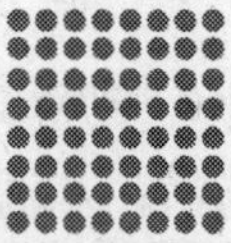

8 rows of 8 = 64
8 × 8 = 64
64 ÷ 8 = 8

Complete the equations.

4. 6 × 7 = 42   42 ÷ 7 = 6

5. 9 × 6 = 54   54 ÷ 6 = 9

Name ____________________

Lesson 23
CC.3.OA.6

1. Cindy made 24 bracelets using 8 different colors. She made the same number of bracelets of each color. How many bracelets of each color did she make?

8 × ■ = 24   24 ÷ 8 = ■

Ⓐ 2   Ⓒ 4
Ⓑ 3   Ⓓ 8

2. There are 32 chairs in Mr. Owen's art room. There are 4 chairs at each table. Which equation can be used to find the number of tables in the art room?

Ⓐ 4 + ■ = 32
Ⓑ 32 + 4 = ■
Ⓒ 4 × 32 = ■
Ⓓ ■ × 4 = 32

3. Yolanda knitted 15 scarves in 3 different colors. She knitted the same number of scarves of each color. How many scarves of each color did she make?

3 × ■ = 15   15 ÷ 3 = ■

Ⓐ 5   Ⓒ 9
Ⓑ 8   Ⓓ 12

4. Mike wrote these related equations. Which number completes both equations?

6 × ■ = 48   48 ÷ 6 = ■

Ⓐ 9   Ⓒ 7
Ⓑ 8   Ⓓ 6

Problem Solving REAL WORLD

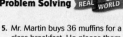

5. Mr. Martin buys 36 muffins for a class breakfast. He places them on plates for his students. If he places 9 muffins on each plate, how many plates does Mr. Martin use?

4 plates

6. Ralph read 18 books during his summer vacation. He read the same number of books each month for 3 months. How many books did he read each month?

6 books

Name ____________________

Lesson 24
COMMON CORE STANDARD CC.3.OA.7
Lesson Objective: Use the Commutative or Distributive Property or known facts to multiply with the factor 7.

Multiply with 7

Pablo is making gift bags for his party. He puts 7 pencils in each bag. How many pencils will he need for 3 gift bags?

Find 3 × 7.

You can use a number line to find the product.

Step 1 Draw a number line.

Step 2 Start at 0. Draw 3 jumps of 7.

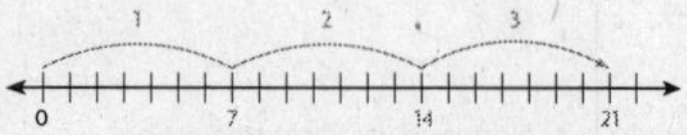

3 × 7 = 21

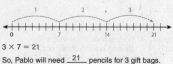

So, Pablo will need 21 pencils for 3 gift bags.

Find the product.

1. 0 = 0 × 7
2. 5 × 7 = 35
3. 4 × 7 = 28
4. 42 = 6 × 7
5. 7 × 7 = 49
6. 63 = 7 × 9
7. 1 × 7 = 7
8. 14 = 7 × 2
9. 10 × 7 = 70
10. 7 × 8 = 56
11. 7 × 0 = 0
12. 7 × 3 = 21
13. 9 × 7 = 63
14. 6 × 7 = 42
15. 7 × 5 = 35
16. 1 × 7 = 7
17. 7 × 7 = 49
18. 4 × 7 = 28

Name ____________________

Lesson 24
CC.3.OA.7

1. There are 7 apartments on every floor of Sean's apartment building. The building has 5 floors. How many apartments are in Sean's apartment building?

Ⓐ 12
Ⓑ 21
Ⓒ 35
Ⓓ 42

2. Sandy made greeting cards for a craft show. She put 7 greeting cards in each of 7 boxes. How many greeting cards did Sandy make altogether?

Ⓐ 56
Ⓑ 49
Ⓒ 28
Ⓓ 14

3. Mike sent 7 postcards to each of 4 friends when he was on vacation. How many postcards did Mike send altogether?

Ⓐ 11
Ⓑ 14
Ⓒ 21
Ⓓ 28

4. There are 9 vans taking students to the museum. Each van is carrying 7 students. How many students are in the vans?

Ⓐ 16
Ⓑ 63
Ⓒ 70
Ⓓ 77

Problem Solving REAL WORLD

5. Julie buys a pair of earrings for \$7. Now she would like to buy the same earrings for 2 of her friends. How much will she spend for all 3 pairs of earrings?

\$21

6. Owen and his family will go camping in 8 weeks. There are 7 days in 1 week. How many days are in 8 weeks?

56 days

Answer Key

Name ____________________

Lesson 25
COMMON CORE STANDARD CC.3.OA.7
Lesson Objective: Use doubles, a number line, or the Associative Property of Multiplication to multiply with the factor 8.

Multiply with 8

You can break apart arrays to multiply with 8.

Candace works at a candle shop.
She places candles in a box for display.
The box has 7 rows of 8 candles.
How many candles are in the box in all?

You can break apart an array to find 7 × 8.

Step 1 Draw 7 rows of 8 squares.

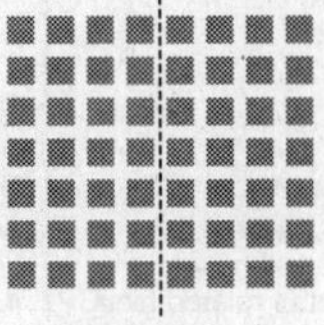

Step 2 Draw a dashed line to break apart the array into two smaller arrays to show facts you know.

7 × 8 = (7 × 4) + (7 × 4)

7 × 8 = 28 + 28

7 × 8 = 56

So, there are 56 candles in the box.

Find the product.

1. 3 × 8 = 24
2. 0 = 0 × 8
3. 2 × 8 = 16
4. 4 × 8 = 32
5. 72 = 9 × 8
6. 5 × 8 = 40
7. 8 × 10 = 80
8. 64 = 8 × 8
9. 7 × 8 = 56
10. 10 × 8 = 80
11. 8 × 4 = 32
12. 8 × 3 = 24
13. 1 × 8 = 8

Name ____________________

Lesson 25
CC.3.OA.7

1. Ashley buys 8 fishbowls. There are 2 goldfish in each bowl. How many goldfish did Ashley buy?
   - Ⓐ 4
   - Ⓑ 8
   - **Ⓒ 16**
   - Ⓓ 24

2. There are 8 teams setting up booths for the school fair. There are 7 people on each team. How many people are setting up booths?
   - Ⓐ 28
   - Ⓑ 48
   - **Ⓒ 56**
   - Ⓓ 64

3. Students' exhibits at a science fair are judged in 5 categories. Akio's exhibit received 8 points in each category. How many total points did Akio's exhibit receive?
   - Ⓐ 20
   - **Ⓑ 40**
   - Ⓒ 48
   - Ⓓ 56

4. Liz buys 6 flowerpots. There are 8 flowers in each pot. How many flowers did Liz buy?
   - Ⓐ 4
   - Ⓑ 14
   - Ⓒ 40
   - **Ⓓ 48**

Problem Solving REAL WORLD

5. There are 6 teams in the basketball league. Each team has 8 players. How many players are there in all?
   48 players

6. Lynn has 4 stacks of quarters. There are 8 quarters in each stack. How many quarters does Lynn have in all?
   32 quarters

7. Tomas is packing 7 baskets for a fair. He is placing 8 apples in each basket. How many apples are there in all?
   56 apples

8. There are 10 pencils in each box. If Jenna buys 8 boxes, how many pencils will she buy?
   80 pencils

Name ____________________

Lesson 26
COMMON CORE STANDARD CC.3.OA.7
Lesson Objective: Use the Distributive Property with addition or subtraction or patterns to multiply with the factor 9.

Multiply with 9

Ana goes to the pet store to buy a fish. The store has 3 fish tanks. Each tank has 9 fish. How many fish in all are in the tanks?

You can use counters to find the product.

Find 3 × 9.

Step 1 Make 3 groups of 9 counters.

Step 2 Skip count by 9s to find the total number of counters.

9, 18, 27 counters

3 × 9 = 27

So, there are 27 fish in all in the tanks.

Find the product.

1. 4 × 9 = 36
2. 6 × 9 = 54
3. 3 × 9 = 27
4. 7 × 9 = 63
5. 1 × 9 = 9
6. 72 = 8 × 9
7. 9 × 5 = 45
8. 0 = 0 × 9
9. 2 × 9 = 18
10. 9 × 9 = 81
11. 9 × 3 = 27
12. 9 × 4 = 36
13. 10 × 9 = 90

Name ____________________

Lesson 26
CC.3.OA.7

1. Mika bought 3 boxes of bouncy balls. Each box contains 9 bouncy balls. How many bouncy balls did Mika buy in all?
   - Ⓐ 12
   - Ⓑ 18
   - Ⓒ 24
   - **Ⓓ 27**

2. There are 8 students in the camera club. Each student took 9 pictures. How many pictures did the students take altogether?
   - Ⓐ 81
   - **Ⓑ 72**
   - Ⓒ 64
   - Ⓓ 17

3. Shana bought 5 bags of hard pretzels. Each bag contains 9 pretzels. How many hard pretzels did Shana buy in all?
   - Ⓐ 14
   - Ⓑ 40
   - **Ⓒ 45**
   - Ⓓ 50

4. Raul has 6 shoeboxes on his bookshelf. If he has 9 toy robots in each shoebox, how many toy robots does Raul have?
   - Ⓐ 63
   - **Ⓑ 54**
   - Ⓒ 36
   - Ⓓ 15

Problem Solving REAL WORLD

5. There are 9 positions on the softball team. Three people are trying out for each position. How many people in all are trying out?
   27 people

6. Carlos bought a book for $9. Now he would like to buy 4 other books for the same price. How much will he have to pay in all for the other 4 books?
   $36

Answer Key

Name ______________________

Lesson 27
COMMON CORE STANDARD CC.3.OA.7
Lesson Objective: Write related multiplication and division facts.

Algebra • Write Related Facts

Related facts are a set of related multiplication and division equations.

Write the related facts for the array.

There are 4 equal rows of tiles.
There are 6 tiles in each row.
There are 24 tiles.
Write 2 multiplication equations and 2 division equations for the array.

factor × factor = product	dividend ÷ divisor = quotient
4 × 6 = 24	24 ÷ 4 = 6
6 × 4 = 24	24 ÷ 6 = 4

The equations show how the numbers 4, 6, and 24 are related.

So, the related facts are 4 × 6 = 24, 6 × 4 = 24, 24 ÷ 4 = 6, and 24 ÷ 6 = 4.

Write the related facts for the array.

1. 

2 × 9 = 18   9 × 2 = 18
18 ÷ 2 = 9   18 ÷ 9 = 2

2. 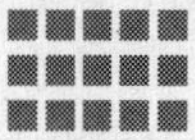

3 × 5 = 15   5 × 3 = 15
15 ÷ 3 = 5   15 ÷ 5 = 3

3. 

4 × 9 = 36   9 × 4 = 36
36 ÷ 4 = 9   36 ÷ 9 = 4

4. 

5 × 8 = 40   8 × 5 = 40
40 ÷ 5 = 8   40 ÷ 8 = 5

Name ______________________

Lesson 27
CC.3.OA.7

1. Han wrote a set of related facts for the array below. Which equation is **not** related to this array?

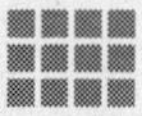

Ⓐ 3 × 4 = 12
Ⓑ 6 × 2 = 12
Ⓒ 12 ÷ 4 = 3
Ⓓ 12 ÷ 3 = 4

2. Lucy writes a set of related facts. One of the facts she writes is 24 ÷ 6 = 4. Which equation is related to this fact?

Ⓐ 8 × 3 = 24
Ⓑ 24 ÷ 8 = 3
Ⓒ 6 × 4 = 24
Ⓓ 24 ÷ 3 = 8

3. Fritz wrote a set of related facts for the array below. Which equation is **not** related to this array?

Ⓐ 6 × 3 = 18
Ⓑ 6 ÷ 2 = 3
Ⓒ 3 × 2 = 6
Ⓓ 2 × 3 = 6

4. Alex uses the numbers 3, 4, and 12 to write multiplication and division related facts. Which equation is one of the related facts that Alex writes?

Ⓐ 3 + 4 = 7
Ⓑ 12 − 8 = 4
Ⓒ 12 ÷ 6 = 2
Ⓓ 4 × 3 = 12

Problem Solving REAL WORLD

5. CDs are on sale for $5 each. Jennifer has $45 and wants to buy as many as she can. How many CDs can Jennifer buy?

9 CDs

6. Mr. Moore has 21 feet of wallpaper. He cuts it into sections that are each 3 feet long. How many sections does Mr. Moore have?

7 sections

Name ______________________

Lesson 28
COMMON CORE STANDARD CC.3.OA.7
Lesson Objective: Use repeated subtraction, a number line, or a multiplication table to divide by 10.

Divide by 10

You can use a multiplication table to divide by 10.

Find the quotient. 30 ÷ 10

Think of a related multiplication fact.

10 × ■ = 30

Step 1 Find the row for the factor, 10. This number is the divisor.

Step 2 Look across the row to find the product, 30. This number is the dividend.

Step 3 Look up to the top row to find the unknown factor, 3. This is the quotient.

Since 10 × 3 = 30, then 30 ÷ 10 = 3.

So, 30 ÷ 10 = 3.

×	0	1	2	3	4	5	6	7	8	9	10
0	0	0	0	0	0	0	0	0	0	0	0
1	0	1	2	3	4	5	6	7	8	9	10
2	0	2	4	6	8	10	12	14	16	18	20
3	0	3	6	9	12	15	18	21	24	27	30
4	0	4	8	12	16	20	24	28	32	36	40
5	0	5	10	15	20	25	30	35	40	45	50
6	0	6	12	18	24	30	36	42	48	54	60
7	0	7	14	21	28	35	42	49	56	63	70
8	0	8	16	24	32	40	48	56	64	72	80
9	0	9	18	27	36	45	54	63	72	81	90
10	0	10	20	30	40	50	60	70	80	90	100

Find the unknown factor and quotient.

1. 10 × 7 = 70   7 = 70 ÷ 10

2. 10 × 2 = 20   20 ÷ 10 = 2

Find the quotient.

3. 60 ÷ 10 = 6
4. 80 ÷ 10 = 8
5. 100 ÷ 10 = 10
6. $10\overline{)50}$ = 5
7. $10\overline{)90}$ = 9
8. $10\overline{)30}$ = 3

Name ______________________

Lesson 28
CC.3.OA.7

1. Larah found 50 pinecones. She put 10 pinecones in each bag. How many bags did Larah use?

Ⓐ 5
Ⓑ 6
Ⓒ 9
Ⓓ 10

2. Michael wants to display his model car collection on shelves. He has 60 model cars. He puts 10 cars on each shelf. How many shelves does Michael use?

Ⓐ 6
Ⓑ 8
Ⓒ 10
Ⓓ 70

3. There are 20 students in science class. There are 10 students sitting at each table. Which division sentence shows how many tables have students at them?

Ⓐ 20 ÷ 4 = 5
Ⓑ 20 ÷ 10 = 2
Ⓒ 10 ÷ 5 = 2
Ⓓ 10 ÷ 10 = 1

4. Stickers cost 10¢ each. How many stickers can Todd buy with 80¢?

Ⓐ 10
Ⓑ 9
Ⓒ 8
Ⓓ 7

Problem Solving REAL WORLD

5. Pencils cost 10¢ each. How many pencils can Brent buy with 90¢?

9 pencils

6. Mrs. Marks wants to buy 80 pens. If the pens come in packs of 10, how many packs does she need to buy?

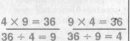

8 packs

Name ______________________ **Lesson 29**

COMMON CORE STANDARD CC.3.OA.7

Lesson Objective: Use equal groups, a number line, or a related multiplication fact to divide by 3.

Divide by 3

You can draw a picture to show how to divide.

Find the quotient.

21 ÷ 3

Step 1 Draw 21 counters to show the dividend.

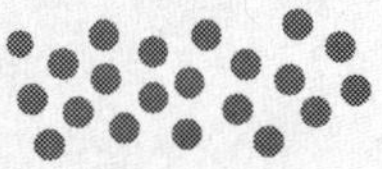

Step 2 Circle groups of 3 to show the divisor.

Step 3 Count the groups.

There are 7 groups of 3. So, the quotient is 7.

You can use a related multiplication fact to check your answer.

Think: 7 × 3 = 21

So, 21 ÷ 3 = 7.

Circle groups of 3 to find the quotient. Check students' drawings.

1. 9 ÷ 3 = 3

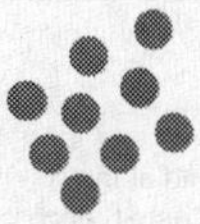

2. 15 ÷ 3 = 5

3. 2 = 6 ÷ 3

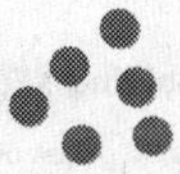

Find the quotient.

4. 12 ÷ 3 = 4
5. 18 ÷ 3 = 6
6. 24 ÷ 3 = 8
7. 27 ÷ 3 = 9

Name ______________________ **Lesson 29**

CC.3.OA.7

1. Steve and his family traveled 12 miles on a sunset cruise. Every 3 miles, the boat stopped for people to take pictures. How many times did the boat stop for pictures?

   Ⓐ 4 (marked)
   Ⓑ 6
   Ⓒ 9
   Ⓓ 15

2. Martina plays tennis. She gets 21 new tennis balls. They come in cans of 3. How many cans of tennis balls did Martina get?

   Ⓐ 18
   Ⓑ 8
   Ⓒ 7 (marked)
   Ⓓ 6

3. Jake walked 15 miles in a walk-a-thon. Every 3 miles, he stopped for a rest. How many times did Jake stop for a rest?

   Ⓐ 4
   Ⓑ 5 (marked)
   Ⓒ 6
   Ⓓ 12

4. There are 27 students in Mr. Garcia's class. The class is going on a field trip to a water park. Mr. Garcia separates the students into groups of 3. How many groups will Mr. Garcia make?

   Ⓐ 30
   Ⓑ 24
   Ⓒ 14
   Ⓓ 9 (marked)

Problem Solving REAL WORLD

5. The principal at Miller Street School has 12 packs of new pencils. She will give 3 packs to each third-grade class. How many third-grade classes are there?

   4 classes

6. Mike has $21 to spend at the mall. He spends all of his money on bracelets for his sisters. Bracelets cost $3 each. How many bracelets does he buy?

   7 bracelets

Name ______________________ **Lesson 30**

COMMON CORE STANDARD CC.3.OA.7

Lesson Objective: Use an array, equal groups, factors, or a related multiplication fact to divide by 4.

Divide by 4

One way to divide is to count back on a number line.

Find the quotient.

12 ÷ 4

Start at 12.

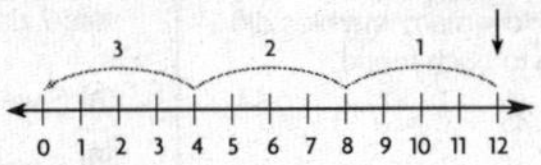

Count back by 4s as many times as you can until you reach 0.

Count the number of times you jumped back 4. 3 times

So, 12 ÷ 4 = 3.

Find the quotient.

32 ÷ 4

Start at 32.

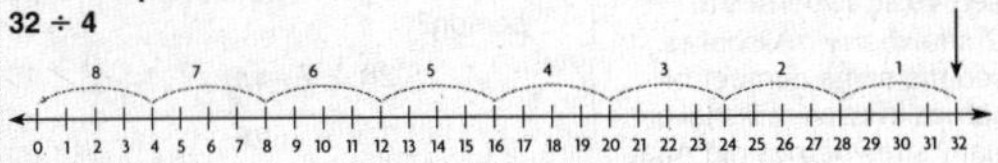

Count back by 4s as many times as you can until you reach 0.

Count the number of times you jumped back 4. 8 times

So, 32 ÷ 4 = 8.

Find the quotient.

1. 24 ÷ 4 = 6
2. 4 = 12 ÷ 3
3. 16 ÷ 4 = 4
4. 2 = 8 ÷ 4
5. 4 ÷ 2 = 2
6. 7 = 28 ÷ 4
7. 36 ÷ 4 = 9
8. 20 ÷ 4 = 5

Find the unknown number.

9. 4 ÷ 4 = ▲   ▲ = 1
10. 40 ÷ 10 = *t*   *t* = 4
11. 8 ÷ 2 = *g*   *g* = 4
12. 21 ÷ 7 = *m*   *m* = 3

Name ______________________ **Lesson 30**

CC.3.OA.7

1. Ellen is making 4 gift baskets for her friends. She has 16 prizes she wants to divide equally among the baskets. How many prizes should she put in each basket?

   Ⓐ 4 (marked)
   Ⓑ 8
   Ⓒ 12
   Ⓓ 20

2. Casey has 20 coins. She places them in equal stacks. There are 4 coins in each stack. How many stacks of coins are there?

   Ⓐ 5 (marked)
   Ⓑ 6
   Ⓒ 7
   Ⓓ 8

3. Jim collected 28 seashells at the beach. He arranged them in equal rows. There are 4 seashells in each row. How many rows of seashells are there?

   Ⓐ 6
   Ⓑ 7 (marked)
   Ⓒ 24
   Ⓓ 30

4. Holly is making 4 veggie trays for a party. She wants to divide 36 carrot sticks equally among the trays. How many carrot sticks will she put on each tray?

   Ⓐ 7
   Ⓑ 8
   Ⓒ 9 (marked)
   Ⓓ 32

Problem Solving REAL WORLD

5. Ms. Higgins has 28 students in her gym class. She puts them in 4 equal groups. How many students are in each group?

   7 students

6. Andy has 36 CDs. He buys a case that holds 4 CDs in each section. How many sections can he fill?

   9 sections

Answer Key

Name ____________

Lesson 31

COMMON CORE STANDARD CC.3.OA.7

Lesson Objective: Use equal groups, a related multiplication fact, or factors to divide by 6.

Divide by 6

You can use a multiplication table to divide by 6.

Find the quotient. 42 ÷ 6

Think of a related multiplication fact.
6 × ■ = 42

Find the row for the factor, 6.

Look right to find the product, 42.

Look up to find the unknown factor, 7.

7 is the factor you multiply by 6 to get the product, 42.

So, 6 × 7 = 42.

Use this related multiplication fact to find the quotient.

Since 6 × 7 = 42, then 42 ÷ 6 = 7.

So, 42 ÷ 6 = 7.

×	0	1	2	3	4	5	6	7	8	9	10
0	0	0	0	0	0	0	0	0	0	0	0
1	0	1	2	3	4	5	6	7	8	9	10
2	0	2	4	6	8	10	12	14	16	18	20
3	0	3	6	9	12	15	18	21	24	27	30
4	0	4	8	12	16	20	24	28	32	36	40
5	0	5	10	15	20	25	30	35	40	45	50
6	0	6	12	18	24	30	36	42	48	54	60
7	0	7	14	21	28	35	42	49	56	63	70
8	0	8	16	24	32	40	48	56	64	72	80
9	0	9	18	27	36	45	54	63	72	81	90
10	0	10	20	30	40	50	60	70	80	90	100

Find the unknown factor and quotient.

1. 6 × <u>5</u> = 30 30 ÷ 6 = <u>5</u>
2. 6 × <u>8</u> = 48 48 ÷ 6 = <u>8</u>
3. 6 × <u>3</u> = 18 18 ÷ 6 = <u>3</u>
4. 6 × <u>4</u> = 24 24 ÷ 6 = <u>4</u>

Find the quotient.

5. 6 ÷ 6 = <u>1</u>
6. 48 ÷ 6 = <u>8</u>
7. 54 ÷ 6 = <u>9</u>
8. 12 ÷ 6 = <u>2</u>
9. 0 ÷ 6 = <u>0</u>
10. 36 ÷ 6 = <u>6</u>
11. 6 ÷ 1 = <u>6</u>
12. 18 ÷ 6 = <u>3</u>

Name ____________

Lesson 31

CC.3.OA.7

1. Pedro uses 30 game pieces to play a game. He gives 6 players the same number of game pieces. How many game pieces does each player get?

   Ⓐ 4 Ⓒ 10
   Ⓑ 5 Ⓓ 15

2. Each team at a hockey tournament has 6 players. How many teams are there if 42 players are at the tournament?

   Ⓐ 5
   Ⓑ 6
   Ⓒ 7
   Ⓓ 8

3. There are picnic tables at the park. Each picnic table seats 6 people. How many picnic tables are needed to seat 24 people?

   Ⓐ 3
   Ⓑ 4
   Ⓒ 5
   Ⓓ 6

4. Luis uses 36 marbles to play a game. There are 6 players in the game. If each player gets the same number of marbles, how many marbles does each player get?

   Ⓐ 30 Ⓒ 12
   Ⓑ 18 **Ⓓ 6**

Problem Solving REAL WORLD

5. Lucas has 36 pages of a book left to read. If he reads 6 pages a day, how many days will it take Lucas to finish the book?

   <u>6 days</u>

6. Juan has $24 to spend at the bookstore. If books cost $6 each, how many books can he buy?

   <u>4 books</u>

Name ____________

Lesson 32

COMMON CORE STANDARD CC.3.OA.7

Lesson Objective: Use an array, a related multiplication fact, or equal groups to divide by 7.

Divide by 7

You can use counters to divide by 7.

Find the quotient. 35 ÷ 7

Step 1 Draw 7 circles to show 7 groups. Place 1 counter in each group.

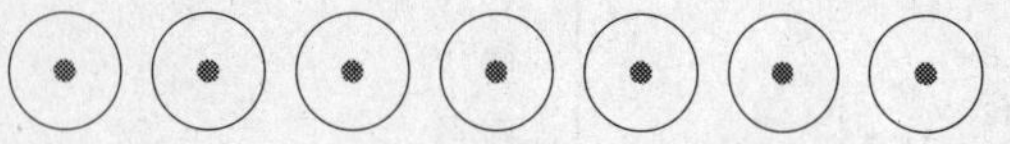

Step 2 Continue placing 1 counter at a time in each group until all 35 counters are placed.

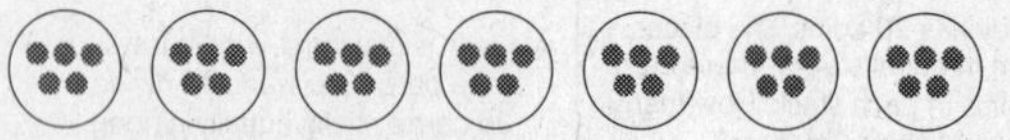

There are 5 counters in each group.

So, 35 ÷ 7 = 5.

Find the unknown factor and quotient.

1. 7 × <u>9</u> = 63 63 ÷ 7 = <u>9</u>
2. 7 × <u>1</u> = 7 7 ÷ 7 = <u>1</u>
3. 7 × <u>2</u> = 14 14 ÷ 7 = <u>2</u>
4. 7 × <u>4</u> = 28 28 ÷ 7 = <u>4</u>

Find the quotient.

5. <u>8</u> = 56 ÷ 7
6. 21 ÷ 7 = <u>3</u>
7. 42 ÷ 7 = <u>6</u>
8. 28 ÷ 7 = <u>4</u>
9. <u>5</u> = 35 ÷ 7
10. 63 ÷ 7 = <u>9</u>
11. 49 ÷ 7 = <u>7</u>
12. 70 ÷ 7 = <u>10</u>

Name ____________

Lesson 32

CC.3.OA.7

1. Ming divided 35 marbles among 7 different friends. Each friend received the same number of marbles. How many marbles did Ming give to each friend?

   $35 \div 7 = a$

   $7 \times a = 35$

   Ⓐ 4 Ⓒ 6
   Ⓑ 5 Ⓓ 7

2. Ana used 49 strawberries to make 7 strawberry milkshakes. She used the same number of strawberries in each milkshake. How many strawberries did Ana use in each milkshake?

   Ⓐ 4 Ⓒ 6
   Ⓑ 5 **Ⓓ 7**

3. Joni texted her dad every day for 42 days. How many weeks did Joni text her dad? [Hint: 1 week has 7 days.]

   Ⓐ 5 weeks Ⓒ 7 weeks
   Ⓑ 6 weeks Ⓓ 8 weeks

4. Shang divided 28 postcards among 7 different people. Each person received the same number of postcards. How many postcards did Shang give to each person?

   $28 \div 7 = n$

   $7 \times n = 28$

   Ⓐ 4 Ⓒ 6
   Ⓑ 5 Ⓓ 21

Problem Solving REAL WORLD

5. Twenty-eight players sign up for basketball. The coach puts 7 players on each team. How many teams are there?

   <u>4 teams</u>

6. Roberto read 42 books over 7 months. He read the same number of books each month. How many books did Roberto read each month?

   <u>6 books</u>

Name ____________________ **Lesson 33**

COMMON CORE STANDARD CC.3.OA.7

Lesson Objective: Use equal groups, factors, or a related multiplication fact to divide by 9.

Divide by 9

You can use repeated subtraction to divide by 9.

Find the quotient.
36 ÷ 9

Step 1 Start with 36. Subtract 9 as many times as you can until you reach 0. Write the answers.

$36 - 9 = 27 \rightarrow 27 - 9 = 18 \rightarrow 18 - 9 = 9 \rightarrow 9 - 9 = 0$

Step 2 Count the number of times you subtract 9.

You subtracted 9 four times.

So, 36 ÷ 9 = 4.

Find the quotient.

1. 9 ÷ 9 = 1
2. 27 ÷ 9 = 3
3. 18 ÷ 9 = 2
4. 36 ÷ 9 = 4
5. 8 = 72 ÷ 9
6. 7 = 63 ÷ 9
7. 45 ÷ 9 = 5
8. 2 = 18 ÷ 9
9. 6 = 54 ÷ 9
10. 9)63 — 7
11. 9)81 — 9
12. 9)36 — 4
13. 8)48 — 6
14. 4)36 — 9
15. 7)28 — 4

Name ____________________ **Lesson 33**

CC.3.OA.7

1. Mrs. Torres separates 45 students into 9 equal groups for a field trip. How many students are in each group?
   Ⓐ 4 Ⓒ 6
   Ⓑ 5 Ⓓ 7

2. Carla sells homemade pretzels in bags with 9 pretzels in each bag. She sells 54 pretzels in all. How many bags of pretzels does she sell?
   Ⓐ 6 Ⓒ 4
   Ⓑ 5 Ⓓ 3

3. A flower shop sells tulips in bunches of 9. It sells 27 tulips. How many bunches of tulips does the shop sell?
   Ⓐ 2 Ⓒ 4
   Ⓑ 3 Ⓓ 9

4. There are 36 athletes at a baseball workshop. A baseball team has 9 players. How many teams can be formed?
   Ⓐ 7 Ⓒ 5
   Ⓑ 6 **Ⓓ 4**

Problem Solving REAL WORLD

5. A crate of oranges has trays inside that hold 9 oranges each. There are 72 oranges in the crate. If all trays are filled, how many trays are there?

   8 trays

6. Van has 45 new baseball cards. He puts them in a binder that holds 9 cards on each page. How many pages does he fill?

   5 pages

Name ____________________ **Lesson 34**

COMMON CORE STANDARD CC.3.OA.8

Lesson Objective: Solve addition and subtraction problems by using the strategy *draw a diagram.*

Problem Solving • Model Addition and Subtraction

Kim sold 127 tickets to the school play. Jon sold 89 tickets. How many more tickets did Kim sell than Jon?

Read the Problem	Solve the Problem
What do I need to find? I need to find how many more tickets Kim sold than Jon	Complete the bar model. Kim: 127 tickets; Jon: 89 tickets, ■ tickets
What information do I need to use? I know that Kim sold 127 tickets and Jon sold 89 tickets.	Subtract to find the unknown part. 127 − 89 = 38; ■ = 38 tickets
How will I use the information? I will draw a bar model to help me see what operation to use to solve the problem.	So, Kim sold 38 more tickets than Jon.

1. Kasha collected 76 fall leaves. She collects 58 more leaves. How many leaves does she have now?

   134 leaves

2. Max has 96 stamps. Pat has 79 stamps. How many more stamps does Max have than Pat?

   17 more stamps

Name ____________________ **Lesson 34**

CC.3.OA.8

1. During the first week of school, 345 students bought their lunch. During the second week of school, 23 fewer students bought their lunch than the week before. How many students bought their lunch in those two weeks?
   Ⓐ 322 **Ⓒ 667**
   Ⓑ 368 Ⓓ 713

2. On Monday, 117 students signed up to plant trees in the park. On Tuesday, 16 fewer students signed up than on Monday. How many students signed up to plant trees on Monday and Tuesday?
   Ⓐ 218 Ⓒ 118
   Ⓑ 158 Ⓓ 101

3. In one week, 103 students were absent. The next week, 17 fewer students were absent than the week before. How many students were absent in those two weeks?
   Ⓐ 86 **Ⓒ 189**
   Ⓑ 120 Ⓓ 223

4. For two days, Imani counted taxis that passed her house from 4:30 to 4:45 P.M. She counted 33 taxis on Monday. That was 19 fewer than the number of taxis she counted on Tuesday. How many taxis did Imani count on both days?
   Ⓐ 14 Ⓒ 52
   Ⓑ 33 **Ⓓ 85**

5. Draw bar models to solve 45 + 92 = ■ and 92 − ■ = 45. Explain how the models are alike and how they are different.

   Check students' drawings.

   Possible explanation: for the addition problem, you know the 2 smaller parts and find the whole. In the subtraction problem, you know the whole and one part. You need to find the other part.

Answer Key

Name ______________________ **Lesson 35**

COMMON CORE STANDARD CC.3.OA.8

Lesson Objective: Solve one- and two-step problems by using the strategy *draw a diagram.*

Problem Solving • Model Multiplication

There are 2 rows of flute players in a marching band. Each row has 7 students. How many flute players are there in all?

Read the Problem	Solve the Problem
What do I need to find? I need to find how many flute players are in the marching band.	Complete the bar model to show the flute players. Write 7 in each box to show the 7 students in each of the 2 groups. [7 | 7] 14 students
What information do I need to use? I know there are 2 rows. There are 7 students in each row.	
How will I use the information? I will draw a bar model to help me see what operation I need to use to solve the problem.	Since there are equal groups, I can multiply to find the number of flute players in the band. 2 × 7 = 14. So, there are 14 flute players in all.

1. The Coopers put a new floor in the bathroom. There are 5 rows of 6 red tiles. How many tiles did they use?

30 tiles

2. Tommy has a jar of coins. He makes 8 piles of 4 quarters. How many quarters does Tommy have in all?

32 quarters

Name ______________________ **Lesson 35**

CC.3.OA.8

1. Edith sorts buttons into 4 groups. Each group contains 3 buttons. How many buttons does Edith sort?

[ ] buttons

Ⓐ 4 Ⓑ 11 Ⓒ 12 (circled) Ⓓ 16

2. Hector has 4 groups of blocks with 2 blocks in each group. He uses 3 of the blocks for a project. How many blocks does Hector have left?

Ⓐ 3 Ⓑ 5 (circled) Ⓒ 9 Ⓓ 11

3. John sold 3 baskets of peaches at the market. Each basket contained 6 peaches. How many peaches did John sell?

[ ] peaches

Ⓐ 36 Ⓑ 30 Ⓒ 18 (circled) Ⓓ 9

4. Sophia buys 3 baskets of apples to make applesauce. Each basket has 9 apples in it. How many apples does Sophia buy in all?

Ⓐ 27 (circled) Ⓑ 24 Ⓒ 18 Ⓓ 9

5. Landon sorted his trading cards into 3 groups. Each group had 7 cards. How many trading cards does he have in all? Use the bar model to solve. Explain your answer.

[7 | 7 | 7] 21 trading cards

Possible answer: I wrote 7 in each box to show the 7 cards in each group. I multiplied to solve: 3 × 7 = 21.

Name ______________________ **Lesson 36**

COMMON CORE STANDARD CC.3.OA.8

Lesson Objective: Solve multiplication problems by using the strategy *make a table.*

Problem Solving • Multiplication

Lucy's mother is making punch for the students. For each pitcher, she uses 1 can of fruit juice, 1 bottle of ginger ale, and 6 scoops of sherbet. How much of each ingredient will she need to make 5 pitchers of punch?

Read the Problem

What do I need to find?

I need to find how much of each ingredient Lucy's mother needs to make 5 pitchers of punch.

What information do I need to use?

Lucy's mother uses 1 can of fruit juice, 1 bottle of ginger ale, and 6 scoops of sherbet for each pitcher.

How will I use the information?

I will make a table to show the total amounts of each ingredient Lucy's mother needs.

Solve the Problem

First, make a table with the information.

Number of Pitchers	1	2	3	4	5
Cans of Fruit Juice	1	2	3	4	5
Bottles of Ginger Ale	1	2	3	4	5
Scoops of Sherbet	6	12	18	24	30

Next, look for information in the table that will help you solve the problem.

Look for a pattern. The cans of fruit juice and the bottles of ginger ale increase by 1. The scoops of sherbet increase by 6. Complete the table.

So, Lucy's mother will need 5 cans of fruit juice, 5 bottles of ginger ale, and 30 scoops of sherbet.

1. Suppose Lucy's mother decides to make 2 more pitchers of punch. How many scoops of sherbet would she need for 7 pitchers of punch? **Explain** your answer.

42 scoops; possible explanation: the table shows that 6 scoops are needed for 1 pitcher. Multiply 7 × 6 to find the number of scoops needed for 7 pitchers.

2. Jake gives his dog 4 chew bones and 1 dog toy each month. How many chew bones and how many toys will Jake give his dog in 5 months?

20 chew bones and 5 toys

Name ______________________ **Lesson 36**

CC.3.OA.8

1. Bella is planning to write in her journal. Some pages will have two journal entries on them, and other pages will have three journal entries on them. If Bella wants to make 18 entries, how many different ways can she write them in her journal?

Ⓐ 2 (circled) Ⓑ 4 Ⓒ 5 Ⓓ 10

2. Jayme wants to make $1.50 using dollars, half dollars, and quarters. How many different ways can she make $1.50?

Ⓐ 4 Ⓑ 5 Ⓒ 6 (circled) Ⓓ 7

3. Toddrick has a photo album. Some pages have one photo on them, and other pages have two photos on them. If Toddrick has 9 photos, how many different ways can he put them in the album?

Ⓐ 2 Ⓑ 3 Ⓒ 4 (circled) Ⓓ 5

4. Myra has 30 cousins. Each month for the past 5 months, she has seen 2 different cousins. How many more cousins does she have to see before she has seen all 30 cousins?

Ⓐ 18 Ⓑ 20 (circled) Ⓒ 25 Ⓓ 28

5. Erin wants to arrange flower bouquets in rows for a reception. Each row can have 4 or 6 bouquets. She has a total of 22 bouquets and wants to know how many different ways she can arrange them. Explain how Erin could make a table to find how many different ways she can arrange the bouquets.

Erin can make a table with three rows. The top row of the table would show rows with 4 bouquets. The second row of the table would show rows with 6 bouquets. The bottom row of the table would show the total number of bouquets, which is 22. She could fill in the different combinations of numbers for 4 or 6 bouquets in the table to find all the different ways.

Name ______________ **Lesson 37**

COMMON CORE STANDARD CC.3.OA.8

Lesson Objective: Solve two-step problems by using the strategy *act it out.*

Problem Solving • Two-Step Problems

Chloe bought 5 sets of books. Each set had the same number of books. She donated 9 books to her school. Now she has 26 books left. How many books were in each set that Chloe bought?

Read the Problem	Solve the Problem
What do I need to find? I need to find how many books were in each set.	First, begin with the number of books left. Add the number of books donated. books left + books donated = t, total number of books 26 + 9 = t 35 = t
What information do I need to use? I need to use the information given: Chloe bought 5 sets of books. She donated 9 books. She has 26 books left.	Then divide to find the number of books in each set. t, total number of books ÷ sets of books = s, books in each set 35 ÷ 5 = s 7 = s
How will I use the information? I will use the information to act out the problem.	So, 7 books were in each set.

Solve the problem.

1. Jackie had 6 equal packs of pencils. Her friend gave her 4 more pencils. Now she has 52 pencils. How many pencils were in each pack?

   8 pencils

2. Tony had 4 equal sets of sports cards. He gave his friends 5 cards. Now he has 31 cards. How many cards were in each set?

   9 cards

Name ______________ **Lesson 37**

CC.3.OA.8

1. Gary bought 4 packs of cards. Each pack had the same number of cards. A friend gave him 3 more cards. Now he has 35 cards in all. How many cards were in each pack?

   Ⓐ 42 Ⓒ 8 (circled)
   Ⓑ 28 Ⓓ 7

2. Mrs. Jackson bought 5 packages of juice boxes. Each package had the same number of juice boxes. She opened one package and gave 3 juice boxes away. Now she has 27 juice boxes. How many juice boxes were in each package?

   Ⓐ 6 (circled) Ⓒ 24
   Ⓑ 8 Ⓓ 35

3. Ms. King bought 7 packages of raisin boxes. Each package had the same number of raisin boxes. She opened one package and gave 5 raisin boxes away. Now she has 51 raisin boxes. How many raisin boxes were in each package?

   Ⓐ 56 Ⓒ 8 (circled)
   Ⓑ 12 Ⓓ 7

4. George had 6 sheets of animal stickers. Each sheet had the same number of stickers. A friend gave him 4 more animal stickers. Now he has 40 animal stickers. How many animal stickers were on each sheet?

   Ⓐ 50 Ⓒ 10
   Ⓑ 24 Ⓓ 6 (circled)

5. Ruby saved $12 to buy cat toys. Her uncle gives her $3 more. Each cat toy costs $5. Explain the steps needed to find how many cat toys Ruby can buy.

   Possible answer: first, add the money Ruby saved ($12) to the $3 her uncle gave her. She has $15. Then, divide to see how many $5 toys Ruby can buy with $15. Since 3 × $5 = $15, I know that $15 can buy 3 $5 cat toys.

Name ______________ **Lesson 38**

COMMON CORE STANDARD CC.3.OA.8

Lesson Objective: Perform operations in order when there are no parentheses.

Order of Operations

Danny buys a marker for $4. He also buys 5 pens for $2 each. How much money does he spend?

You can write $4 + 5 \times 2 = c$ to describe and solve the problem.

Find $4 + 5 \times 2 = c$.

When there is more than one type of operation in an equation, use the **order of operations**, or the set of rules for the order in which to do operations.

Order of Operations

First: Multiply and divide from left to right.

Then: Add and subtract from left to right.

Step 1 Multiply from left to right.

$4 + 5 × $2 = c (multiply)

$4 + $10 = c

Step 2 Next, add from left to right.

$4 + $10 = c (add)

$14 = c

So, Danny spends $14.

Write *correct* if the operations are listed in the correct order. If not correct, write the correct order of operations.

1. 5 + 6 × 3 add, multiply

   multiply, add

2. 20 ÷ 4 − 3 divide, subtract

   correct

Follow the order of operations to find the unknown number.

3. $9 - 7 + 2 = k$ k = 4
4. $8 + 2 \times 5 = m$ m = 18
5. $7 \times 8 - 6 = g$ g = 50
6. $16 + 4 \div 2 = s$ s = 18
7. $12 - 6 \div 2 = y$ y = 9
8. $36 \div 6 + 13 = f$ f = 19

Name ______________ **Lesson 38**

CC.3.OA.8

1. Amber uses the order of operations to solve the equation below.

   $63 - 49 \div 7 = b$

   What is the unknown number?

   Ⓐ $b = 2$ Ⓒ $b = 55$
   Ⓑ $b = 14$ Ⓓ $b = 56$ (circled)

2. Aki uses the order of operations to solve the equation below.

   $3 + 12 \div 3 = c$

   What is the unknown number?

   Ⓐ $c = 7$ (circled) Ⓒ $c = 5$
   Ⓑ $c = 6$ Ⓓ $c = 4$

3. Kayla uses the order of operations to solve the equation below.

   $78 - 54 \div 6 = h$

   What is the unknown number?

   Ⓐ $h = 4$ Ⓒ $h = 69$ (circled)
   Ⓑ $h = 24$ Ⓓ $h = 70$

4. Deon uses the order of operations to solve the equation below.

   $3 + 7 \times 3 = x$

   What is the unknown number?

   Ⓐ $x = 13$ Ⓒ $x = 24$ (circled)
   Ⓑ $x = 21$ Ⓓ $x = 30$

Problem Solving REAL WORLD

5. Shelley bought 3 kites for $6 each. She gave the clerk $20. How much change should Shelley get?

   $2

6. Tim has 5 apples and 3 bags with 8 apples in each bag. How many apples does Tim have in all?

   29 apples

© Houghton Mifflin Harcourt Publishing Company

Name ______________________

Lesson 39
COMMON CORE STANDARD CC.3.OA.9
Lesson Objective: Identify and describe whole-number patterns and solve problems.

Algebra • Number Patterns

A **pattern** is an ordered set of numbers or objects. The order helps you predict what will come next.

Use the addition table to find patterns.

+	0	1	2	3	4
0	0	1	2	3	4
1	1	2	3	4	5
2	2	3	4	5	6
3	3	4	5	6	7
4	4	5	6	7	8

- Color the row that starts with 1. What pattern do you see?
  The numbers increase by 1.
- Color the column that starts with 1. What pattern do you see?
  The numbers increase by 1. The numbers are the same as in the row starting with 1.
- Circle the sum of 4 in the column you colored. Circle the addends for that sum. What two addition sentences can you write for that sum of 4?
  3 + 1 = 4 and 1 + 3 = 4

The addends are the same. The sum is the same.

The **Commutative Property of Addition** states that you can add two or more numbers in any order and get the same sum.

Use the addition table to find the sum.

1. 2 + 3 = 5 3 + 2 = 5
2. 2 + 0 = 2 0 + 2 = 2

Find the sum. Then use the Commutative Property of Addition to write the related addition sentence.

3. 3 + 0 = 3 0 + 3 = 3
4. 4 + 1 = 5 1 + 4 = 5
5. 2 + 3 = 5 3 + 2 = 5

Name ______________________

Lesson 39
CC.3.OA.9

1. Kara wrote this number sentence to show how many yellow stickers and green stickers she earned. Which describes Kara's number sentence?

   7 + 0 = 7

   Ⓐ Commutative Property of Addition
   Ⓑ Identity Property of Addition
   Ⓒ odd + odd = odd
   Ⓓ even + even = even

2. Pablo finds the sum of two addends. The sum is odd. Which statement is **true** about the addends?

   Ⓐ Both addends are odd.
   Ⓑ Both addends are even.
   Ⓒ The addends are both odd or both even.
   Ⓓ One addend is odd and one addend is even.

3. Maria wrote the number sentence 4 + 7 = 11. Which number sentence shows the Commutative Property of Addition?

   Ⓐ 11 − 4 = 7
   Ⓑ 3 + 4 = 7
   Ⓒ 4 + 7 = 11
   Ⓓ 7 + 4 = 11

4. Gregory finds the sum of two addends. The sum is even. Which could **not** be Gregory's addends?

   Ⓐ 3 + 10
   Ⓑ 7 + 1
   Ⓒ 7 + 7
   Ⓓ 10 + 12

5. Ruby says she has read an even number of books. She has read 9 fiction books and 8 nonfiction books. Is Ruby correct? Explain your answer.

   No. Possible explanation: Ruby has read an odd number of books because 9 + 8 = 17, and 17 is an odd number.

Name ______________________

Lesson 40
COMMON CORE STANDARD CC.3.OA.9
Lesson Objective: Identify and explain patterns on the multiplication table.

Algebra • Patterns on the Multiplication Table

You can use a multiplication table to explore number patterns.

Step 1 Shade the columns for 5 and 10 on the multiplication table.

Step 2 Look for patterns in the shaded numbers.

- The products in the 5s column end in 0 or 5.
- The products in the 5s column repeat—even, odd.
- All the products in the 10s column are even.

×	0	1	2	3	4	5	6	7	8	9	10
0	0	0	0	0	0	0	0	0	0	0	0
1	0	1	2	3	4	5	6	7	8	9	10
2	0	2	4	6	8	10	12	14	16	18	20
3	0	3	6	9	12	15	18	21	24	27	30
4	0	4	8	12	16	20	24	28	32	36	40
5	0	5	10	15	20	25	30	35	40	45	50
6	0	6	12	18	24	30	36	42	48	54	60
7	0	7	14	21	28	35	42	49	56	63	70
8	0	8	16	24	32	40	48	56	64	72	80
9	0	9	18	27	36	45	54	63	72	81	90
10	0	10	20	30	40	50	60	70	80	90	100

Is the product even or odd? Write *even* or *odd*.

1. 5 × 5 odd
2. 6 × 4 even
3. 7 × 1 odd
4. 8 × 6 even

Use the multiplication table. Describe a pattern you see. Possible patterns are given.

5. in the row for 2
   All the products are even.
6. in the column for 3
   The products repeat – even, odd; each number is 3 more than the number above it.

Name ______________________

Lesson 40
CC.3.OA.9

Use the multiplication table for 1–3.

×	0	1	2	3	4	5	6	7	8	9	10
0	0	0	0	0	0	0	0	0	0	0	0
1	0	1	2	3	4	5	6	7	8	9	10
2	0	2	4	6	8	10	12	14	16	18	20
3	0	3	6	9	12	15	18	21	24	27	30
4	0	4	8	12	16	20	24	28	32	36	40
5	0	5	10	15	20	25	30	35	40	45	50
6	0	6	12	18	24	30	36	42	48	54	60
7	0	7	14	21	28	35	42	49	56	63	70
8	0	8	16	24	32	40	48	56	64	72	80
9	0	9	18	27	36	45	54	63	72	81	90
10	0	10	20	30	40	50	60	70	80	90	100

1. Which row of the table has only even numbers?

   Ⓐ the row for 3
   Ⓑ the row for 4
   Ⓒ the row for 7
   Ⓓ the row for 9

2. Which describes a pattern in the column for 5?

   Ⓐ All the products are even.
   Ⓑ All the products are odd.
   Ⓒ Each product is twice the product above it.
   Ⓓ Each product is 5 more than the product above it.

3. Which product is even?

   Ⓐ 3 × 7
   Ⓑ 4 × 5
   Ⓒ 5 × 3
   Ⓓ 9 × 1

Problem Solving REAL WORLD

4. Carl shades a row in the multiplication table. The products in the row are all even. The ones digits in the products repeat 0, 4, 8, 2, 6. What row does Carl shade?

   the row for 4

5. Jenna says that no row or column contains products with only odd numbers. Do you agree? **Explain.**

   Yes. Possible explanation: either the products are all even, or there is an even and odd number pattern.

© Houghton Mifflin Harcourt Publishing Company

Answer Key

Name ____________ **Lesson 41**

COMMON CORE STANDARD CC.3.OA.9

Lesson Objective: Identify and describe a number pattern shown in a function table.

Algebra • Describe Patterns

The table shows the number of candles in different numbers of packs. How many candles will be in 4 packs?

Packs	1	2	3	4
Candles	2	4	6	■

Describe a pattern in the columns.

Step 1 Look for a pattern by comparing the columns in the table. You can multiply the number of packs by 2 to find the number of candles in all.

$1 \times 2 = 2$

$2 \times 2 = 4$

$3 \times 2 = 6$

Multiply by 2 candles for each pack.

Step 2 Use the pattern to find the number of candles in 4 packs.

$4 \times 2 = 8$

So, there are 8 candles in 4 packs.

Possible descriptions are given.

Describe a pattern for the table. Then complete the table.

1.

Tricycles	1	2	3	4	5
Wheels	3	6	9	12	15

Add 3 wheels for each tricycle; Multiply the number of tricycles by 3.

2.

Boxes	1	2	3	4	5
Baseballs	6	12	18	24	30

Add 6 baseballs for each box; Multiply the number of boxes by 6.

Name ____________ **Lesson 41**

CC.3.OA.9

1. Lori is making bracelets. The table shows how many beads she will need. Which two numbers come next?

Bracelets	2	3	4	5	6
Beads	10	15	20	■	■

Ⓐ 25 and 30 Ⓒ 30 and 35
Ⓑ 25 and 35 Ⓓ 30 and 40

2. Sofia is making omelets. The table shows how many eggs she will need. Which of the following describes a pattern in this table?

Omelets	2	3	4	5	6
Eggs	6	9	12	15	18

Ⓐ Add 4. **Ⓒ Multiply by 3.**
Ⓑ Subtract 3. Ⓓ Multiply by 4.

3. Stephanie and John made a table about spiders. Which of the following describes a pattern in this table?

Spiders	2	3	4	5	6
Legs	16	24	32	40	48

Ⓐ Add 14. Ⓒ Multiply by 6.
Ⓑ Subtract 35. **Ⓓ Multiply by 8.**

4. Bobby made a table about ants. Which number completes the pattern in this table?

Ants	3	4	5	6	7
Legs	18	24	30	■	42

Ⓐ 6 **Ⓒ 36**
Ⓑ 35 Ⓓ 40

Problem Solving REAL WORLD

5. Caleb buys 5 cartons of yogurt. Each carton has 8 yogurt cups. How many yogurt cups does Caleb buy?

40 cups

6. Libby bought 4 packages of pencils. Each package has 6 pencils. How many pencils did Libby buy?

24 pencils

Name ____________ **Lesson 42**

COMMON CORE STANDARD CC.3.NBT.1

Lesson Objective: Round 2- and 3-digit numbers to the nearest ten or hundred.

Round to the Nearest Ten or Hundred

When you **round** a number, you find a number that tells you *about* how much or *about* how many.

Use place value to round 76 to the nearest ten.

Step 1 Look for the digit to the right of the tens place.

- If the ones digit is 5 or more, the tens digit increases by one.
- If the ones digit is less than 5, the tens digit stays the same.

Step 2 Write zero for the ones digit.

76 ↑ ones place

The digit in the ones place is 6.

$6 > 5$

So, the digit 7 in the tens place increases to 8.

So, 76 rounded to the nearest ten is 80.

Think: To round to the nearest hundred, look at the tens digit. So, 128 rounded to the nearest hundred is 100.

128 ↑ tens place

Round to the nearest ten.

1. 24 20
2. 15 20
3. 47 50
4. 42 40
5. 81 80
6. 65 70

Round to the nearest hundred.

7. 176 200
8. 395 400
9. 431 400
10. 421 400
11. 692 700
12. 470 500

Name ____________ **Lesson 42**

CC.3.NBT.1

1. On Friday, 209 people attended a show. What is 209 rounded to the nearest ten?

Ⓐ 100
Ⓑ 200
Ⓒ 210
Ⓓ 220

2. There are 852 mystery books in the school library. What is 852 rounded to the nearest ten?

Ⓐ 800
Ⓑ 850
Ⓒ 860
Ⓓ 900

3. There are 487 books in the classroom library. What is 487 rounded to the nearest ten?

Ⓐ 480
Ⓑ 490
Ⓒ 500
Ⓓ 510

4. Pizza Place sold 581 pizzas on Friday night. What is 581 rounded to the nearest hundred?

Ⓐ 600
Ⓑ 590
Ⓒ 580
Ⓓ 500

Problem Solving REAL WORLD

5. The baby elephant weighs 435 pounds. What is its weight rounded to the nearest hundred pounds?

400 pounds

6. Jayce sold 218 cups of lemonade at his lemonade stand. What is 218 rounded to the nearest ten?

220

Answer Key

Name ______________________

Lesson 43
COMMON CORE STANDARD CC.3.NBT.1
Lesson Objective: Use compatible numbers and rounding to estimate sums.

Estimate Sums

An **estimate** is a number close to an exact amount.

You can use **compatible numbers** to estimate. Compatible numbers are easy to compute mentally and are close to the real numbers.

Estimate. Use compatible numbers.

73 + 21 = ▩

73 ⟶ 75
+ 21 ⟶ + 25
100

So, 73 + 21 is about 100.

Another way to estimate is to round numbers to the same place value.

Estimate. Round each number to the nearest hundred. 214 + 678 = ▩

Step 1 Look at the digit to the right of the hundreds place.

- 1 < 5, so the digit 2 stays the same.
- 7 > 5, so the digit 6 increases by 1 to become 7.

214 ⟶ 200
+ 678 ⟶ + 700
900

Step 2 Write zeros for the tens and ones places.

So, 214 + 678 is about 900.

Possible answers are given.

Use rounding or compatible numbers to estimate the sum.

1. 42 + 36: 40 + 40 = 80
2. 523 + 117: 525 + 100 = 625
3. 235 + 374: 225 + 375 = 600
4. 23 + 99: 20 + 100 = 120
5. 254 + 167: 250 + 150 = 400
6. 299 + 199: 300 + 200 = 500

Name ______________________

Lesson 43
CC.3.NBT.1

1. Amber and her friends collected shells. The table shows how many shells each person collected.

Shells Collected

Name	Number of Shells
Amber	372
Melba	455
Pablo	421
Tom	515

Which is the **best** estimate of the total number of shells Amber and Pablo collected?

Ⓐ 600 Ⓑ 700 **Ⓒ 800** Ⓓ 900

2. The parking lot at the grocery store had 574 parking spaces. Another 128 parking spaces were added to the parking lot. Which is the **best** estimate of the total number of parking spaces in the parking lot now?

Ⓐ 800 **Ⓑ 700** Ⓒ 600 Ⓓ 500

3. Mavis and her friends collected bottle caps. The table shows how many bottle caps each person collected.

Bottle Caps Collected

Name	Number of Bottle Caps
Karen	372
Mavis	255
Pedro	121
John	315

Which is the **best** estimate of the total number of bottle caps Mavis and Pedro collected?

Ⓐ 100 Ⓑ 200 Ⓒ 300 **Ⓓ 400**

4. Umiko made 47 origami birds last week and 62 origami birds this week. About how many origami birds did she make in the two weeks?

Ⓐ 10 Ⓑ 60 **Ⓒ 110** Ⓓ 200

5. Bruce wants to use compatible numbers to estimate 173 + 327. Suggest two compatible numbers he could use to estimate the sum. Explain your choices.

Possible answer: 175 + 325; Possible explanation: 173 is close to 175, 327 is close to 325, and 175 and 325 are easy for me to add in my head.

Name ______________________

Lesson 44
COMMON CORE STANDARD CC.3.NBT.1
Lesson Objective: Use compatible numbers and rounding to estimate differences.

Estimate Differences

You can use what you know about estimating sums to estimate differences.

Estimate. Use compatible numbers.
78 − 47 = ▩

Think: Compatible numbers are easy to subtract.

78 ⟶ 75
− 47 ⟶ − 50
25

So, 78 − 47 is about 25.

Another way to estimate is to round to the same place value.

Estimate. Round each number to the earest hundred. 687 − 516 = ▩

Step 1 Look at the digit to the right of the hundreds place.

- 8 > 5, so the digit in the hundreds place increases by 1.
- 1 < 5, so the digit in the hundreds place stays the same.

687 ⟶ 200
− 516 ⟶ − 700
900

Step 2 Write zeros for the tens and ones places.

So, 687 − 516 is about 200.

Possible answers are given.

Use rounding or compatible numbers to estimate the difference.

1. 92 − 43: 90 − 40 = 50
2. 271 − 152: 270 − 150 = 120
3. 517 − 249: 500 − 250 = 250
4. 445 − 112: 450 − 100 = 350
5. 92 − 65: 90 − 70 = 20
6. 776 − 384: 800 − 400 = 400

Name ______________________

Lesson 44
CC.3.NBT.1

1. Three classes had a reading contest. The table shows how many books the students in each class read.

Reading Contest

Class	Number of Books
Mr. Lopez	273
Ms. Martin	403
Mrs. Wang	147

Which is the **best** estimate of how many more books Ms. Martin's class read than Mr. Lopez's class?

Ⓐ 100 Ⓑ 200 Ⓒ 300 Ⓓ 400

2. Abby and Cruz are playing a game. Abby's score is 168 points less than Cruz's score. Cruz's score is 754. Which is the **best** estimate of Abby's score?

Ⓐ 300 Ⓑ 400 Ⓒ 500 **Ⓓ 600**

3. Three classes had a spelling contest. The table shows how many words the students in each class spelled correctly.

Spelling Contest

Class	Number of Words
Mr. Silva	719
Ms. Parker	660
Mrs. Cheng	847

Which is the **best** estimate of how many more words Mrs. Cheng's class spelled correctly than Mr. Silva's class?

Ⓐ 100 Ⓑ 200 Ⓒ 300 Ⓓ 400

4. Andre and Salma collect stamps. Andre has 287 stamps. Salma has 95 stamps. About how many more stamps does Andre have than Salma has?

Ⓐ 400 Ⓑ 300 **Ⓒ 200** Ⓓ 100

5. To estimate 512 − 87, Kim rounded the numbers to 510 − 90 and subtracted. What is another way that Kim could have estimated to subtract? Explain why it might be easier.

Possible explanation: Kim could have used the compatible numbers, 500 and 100. 500 − 100 is easier to subtract mentally than 510 − 90. The estimate would be 400.

Name ________________ **Lesson 45**

COMMON CORE STANDARD CC.3.NBT.2

Lesson Objective: Count by tens and ones, use a number line, make compatible numbers, or use friendly numbers to find sums mentally.

Mental Math Strategies for Addition

You can count by tens and ones to find a sum.

Find 58 + 15.

Step 1 Count on to the nearest ten. Start at 58. Count to 60.	**Step 2** Count by tens. Start at 60. Count to 70.	**Step 3** Then count by ones. Start at 70. Count to 73.

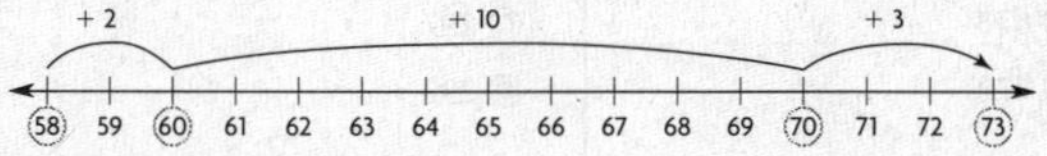

Think: 58 + 2 + 10 + 3 = 73

So, 58 + 15 = 73.

You can also count on by tens first and then by ones.

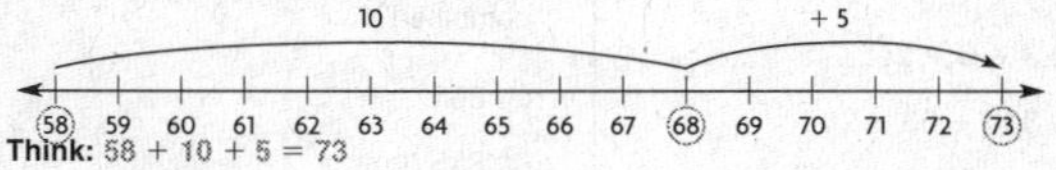

Think: 58 + 10 + 5 = 73

So, 58 + 15 = 73.

1. Count by tens and ones to find 54 + 26. Draw jumps and label the number line to show your thinking.

Possible drawing is given.

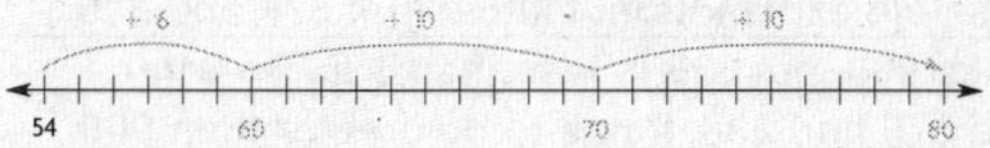

54 + 26 = 80

Name ________________ **Lesson 45**

CC.3.NBT.2

1. On Monday, 114 girls and 205 boys wore jeans to school. How many students wore jeans to school on Monday?

   Ⓐ 219
   Ⓑ 299
   Ⓒ 309
   Ⓓ 319

2. The snack stand has 28 honey granola bars and 42 maple granola bars. How many granola bars does the snack stand have in all?

   Ⓐ 60
   Ⓑ 68
   Ⓒ 70
   Ⓓ 78

3. The Smoothie Stop sold 216 banana smoothies and 132 peach smoothies for breakfast. How many banana smoothies and peach smoothies did the Smoothie Stop sell combined?

   Ⓐ 358
   Ⓑ 348
   Ⓒ 339
   Ⓓ 248

4. There are 37 second graders and 27 third graders in the soccer club. How many students are in the soccer club?

   Ⓐ 54
   Ⓑ 64
   Ⓒ 67
   Ⓓ 74

5. Aya has to find the sum of 67 + 34. Explain a mental math strategy she can use to find the sum.

   Possible explanation: she can use friendly numbers. She can add 3 to 67 to make 70. Next, she can subtract the 3 from 34 to get 31. Then, she can add 70 + 31 = 101.

Name ________________ **Lesson 46**

COMMON CORE STANDARD CC.3.NBT.2

Lesson Objective: Use the Commutative and Associative Properties of Addition to add more than two addends.

Algebra • Use Properties to Add

You can use addition properties and strategies to help you add.

Find 3 + 14 + 21.	**Find 7 + (3 + 22).**
The **Commutative Property of Addition** states that you can add numbers in any order and still get the same sum.	The **Associative Property of Addition** states that you can group addends in different ways and still get the same sum.
Step 1 Look for numbers that are easy to add. **Think:** Make doubles. 3 + 1 = 4 and 4 + 4 = 8.	**Step 1** Look for numbers that are easy to add. **Think:** Make a ten. 7 + 3 = 10
Step 2 Use the Commutative Property to change the order. 3 + 14 + 21 = 3 + 21 + 14	**Step 2** Use the Associative Property to change the grouping. 7 + (3 + 22) = (7 + 3) + 22
Step 3 Add. 3 + 21 + 14 = 24 + 14; 24 + 14 = 30 + 8	**Step 3** Add. (7 + 3) + 22 = 10 + 22; 10 + 22 = 32
So, 3 + 14 + 21 = 38.	So, 7 + (3 + 22) = 32.

Use addition properties and strategies to find the sum. Strategies will vary.

1. 2 + 15 + 8 = 25
2. 19 + 36 + 1 = 56
3. 25 + 44 + 5 = 74
4. 12 + 36 + 18 + 14 = 80
5. 23 + 14 + 23 = 60
6. 11 + 15 + 19 + 14 = 59

Name ________________ **Lesson 46**

CC.3.NBT.2

1. Amy writes a number sentence that shows the Commutative Property of Addition. Which could be Amy's number sentence?

   Ⓐ (53 + 9) + 41 = 53 + (9 + 41)
   Ⓑ 53 + 0 = 53
   Ⓒ 41 = 40 + 1
   Ⓓ 53 + 9 = 9 + 53

2. Mr. Rios bought 24 apples, 16 bananas, and 14 pears at the store. How many pieces of fruit did he buy?

   Ⓐ 64
   Ⓑ 54
   Ⓒ 40
   Ⓓ 38

3. Mario writes a number sentence that shows the Commutative Property of Addition. Which could be Mario's number sentence?

   Ⓐ 37 = 36 + 1
   Ⓑ 0 + 23 = 23
   Ⓒ 37 + 13 = 13 + 37
   Ⓓ (37 + 13) + 23 = 37 + (13 + 23)

4. John writes the following number sentences. Which shows the Associative Property of Addition?

   Ⓐ 7 + (13 + 8) = (7 + 13) + 8
   Ⓑ 44 + (56 + 13) = 44 + (13 + 56)
   Ⓒ 44 + 56 = 40 + 60
   Ⓓ 44 + 56 = 100

Problem Solving REAL WORLD

5. A pet shelter has 26 dogs, 37 cats, and 14 gerbils. How many of these animals are in the pet shelter in all?

   77 animals

6. The pet shelter bought 85 pounds of dog food, 50 pounds of cat food, and 15 pounds of gerbil food. How many pounds of animal food did the pet shelter buy?

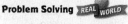

   150 pounds

Answer Key

Name ______________________ **Lesson 47**

COMMON CORE STANDARD CC.3.NBT.2

Lesson Objective: Use the break apart strategy to add 3-digit numbers.

Use the Break Apart Strategy to Add

You can use the break apart strategy to add.

Add. 263 + 215

Think and Record

Step 1 Estimate. Round to the nearest hundred.

300 + 200 = 500

Step 2 Start with the hundreds. Break apart the addends. Then add each place value.

263 = 200 + 60 + 3
215 = 200 + 10 + 5
400 + 70 + 8

Step 3 Add the sums.

400 + 70 + 8 = 478

So, 263 + 215 = 478.

Model

263 = 2 hundreds + 6 tens + 3 ones

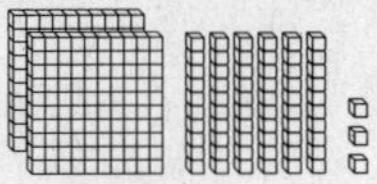

215 = 2 hundreds + 1 ten + 5 ones

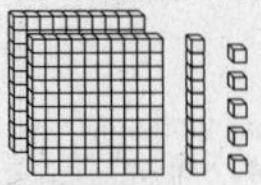

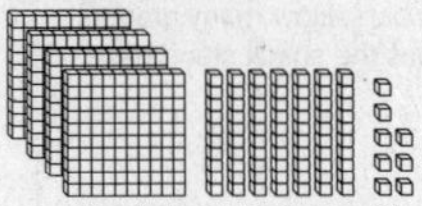

4 hundreds + 7 tens + 8 ones = 478

Estimate. Then use the break apart strategy to find the sum. Possible estimates are given.

1. Estimate: 700
   242 = 200 + 40 + 2
   + 536 = 500 + 30 + 6
   778 | 700 + 70 + 8

2. Estimate: 900
   469 = 400 + 60 + 9
   + 413 = 400 + 10 + 3
   882 | 800 + 70 + 12

3. Estimate: 900
   385 = 300 + 80 + 5
   + 519 = 500 + 10 + 9
   904 | 800 + 90 + 14

4. Estimate: 800
   527 = 500 + 20 + 7
   + 266 = 200 + 60 + 6
   793 | 700 + 80 + 13

Name ______________________ **Lesson 47**

CC.3.NBT.2

1. A Rent-A-Raft store rented 213 rafts in June and 455 rafts in July. How many rafts did the Rent-A-Raft store rent in June and July altogether?
   Ⓐ 658
   Ⓑ 668
   Ⓒ 678
   Ⓓ 778

2. Omar wants to break apart the addend 362 to complete an addition problem. Which shows a way to break apart the addend 362?
   Ⓐ 3 + 6 + 2
   Ⓑ 300 + 60 + 20
   Ⓒ 30 + 62
   Ⓓ 300 + 60 + 2

3. Marcus took 242 pictures with his new camera and 155 pictures with his camera phone. How many pictures did Marcus take in all?
   Ⓐ 397
   Ⓑ 387
   Ⓒ 297
   Ⓓ 292

4. The number of campers at Arrowhead Camp was 412 in July and 443 in August. How many campers were at Arrowhead Camp in July and August combined?
   Ⓐ 865
   Ⓑ 855
   Ⓒ 843
   Ⓓ 455

5. Explain how you can tell that the sum of 575 and 338 is greater than 900 without finding the exact sum.
   Possible explanation: I know that 575 and 325 make 900, but 325 is less than 338. So when I add 575 and 338, it has to be greater than 900.

Name ______________________ **Lesson 48**

COMMON CORE STANDARD CC.3.NBT.2

Lesson Objective: Use place value to add 3-digit numbers.

Use Place Value to Add

You can use place value to add 3-digit numbers.

Add. 268 + 195 **Estimate.** 300 + 200 = 500

Step 1 Add the ones. If there are 10 or more ones, regroup as tens and ones.

  1
 268
+ 195
   3

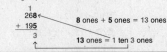

8 ones + **5** ones = 13 ones

13 ones = 1 ten 3 ones

Step 2 Add the tens. Regroup the tens as hundreds and tens.

 11
 268
+ 195
  63

1 ten + **6** tens + **9** tens = 16 tens

16 tens = 1 hundred 6 tens

Step 3 Add the hundreds.

 11
 268
+ 195
 463

1 hundred + **2** hundreds + **1** hundred = 4 hundreds

So, 268 + 195 = 463.

Estimate. Then find the sum. Possible estimates are given.

1. Estimate: 450 — 156 + 323 = 479
2. Estimate: 750 — 347 + 390 = 737
3. Estimate: 600 — 472 + 108 = 580
4. Estimate: 800 — 239 + 570 = 809
5. Estimate: 676 — 110 + 576 = 686
6. Estimate: 575 — 258 + 324 = 582
7. Estimate: 725 — 471 + 269 = 740
8. Estimate: 900 — 585 + 309 = 894

Name ______________________ **Lesson 48**

CC.3.NBT.2

1. The table shows the number of students visiting the zoo each day.

Field Trips This Week

Day	Number of Students
Monday	346
Tuesday	518
Wednesday	449
Thursday	608

How many students will visit the zoo on Monday and Tuesday combined?

Ⓐ 814 **Ⓒ 864**
Ⓑ 854 Ⓓ 964

2. Mr. Rodriguez drove 136 miles to Main City. Then he drove another 146 miles to Rock Town. How many miles did Mr. Rodriguez drive?

Ⓐ 212 miles Ⓒ 272 miles
Ⓑ 270 miles **Ⓓ 282 miles**

3. The table shows the number of students who bought lunch in the school cafeteria one week.

Bought Lunch in Cafeteria

Day	Number of Students
Monday	236
Tuesday	319
Wednesday	225
Thursday	284
Friday	306

How many students bought lunch in the cafeteria on Wednesday and Friday combined?

Ⓐ 261 **Ⓒ 531**
Ⓑ 521 Ⓓ 631

4. Mrs. Carlson drove 283 miles to Plant City. She then drove 128 miles to Bond Town. How far did Mrs. Carlson drive?

Ⓐ 411 miles Ⓒ 365 miles
Ⓑ 401 miles Ⓓ 311 miles

5. Bryce has 317 baseball cards. Elin has 168 baseball cards and Jeff has 425 baseball cards. Which two people together have fewer than 500 cards? Explain your answer.
   Bryce and Elin; Possible explanation: Jeff has about 400 cards; if I add 400 to either 317 or 168, the sum is greater than 500. So I know it is Bryce and Elin. 317 + 168 is less than 500.

Answer Key

Name ____________________

Lesson 49

COMMON CORE STANDARD CC.3.NBT.2

Lesson Objective: Use a number line, friendly numbers, or the break apart strategy to find differences mentally.

Mental Math Strategies for Subtraction

You can count up on a number line to find a difference.

Find 53 − 27.

Step 1 Count up by tens. Start at 27. Count up to 47.

Step 2 Count up by ones. Start at 47. Count up to 53.

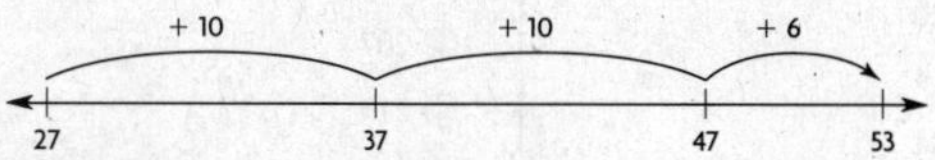

Think: 10 + 10 + 6 = 26.

So, 53 − 27 = 26.

You can take away tens and ones to find a difference.

Step 1 Take away tens. Start at 53.

Step 2 Take away ones. Start at 33.

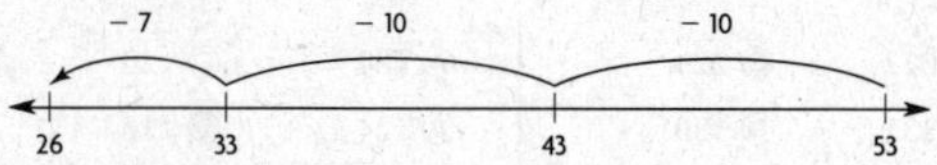

Think: 53 − 10 − 10 − 7 = 26.

So, 53 − 27 = 26.

Possible drawing is given.

1. Find 92 − 65. Draw jumps and label the number line to show your thinking.

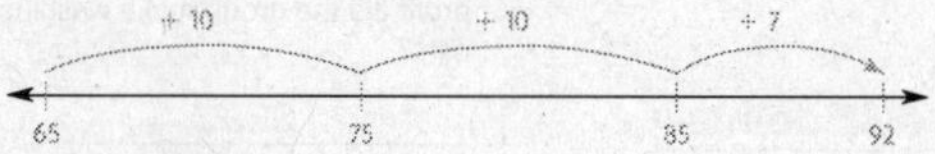

92 − 65 = 27

Name ____________________

Lesson 49

CC.3.NBT.2

1. Mikio drove a total of 267 miles in 2 days. He drove 125 miles the first day. How many miles did he drive the second day?
   - **Ⓐ 142 miles**
   - Ⓑ 162 miles
   - Ⓒ 242 miles
   - Ⓓ 392 miles

2. The Fruity Yogurt Company sold 86 banana yogurt bars and 47 strawberry yogurt bars. How many more banana yogurt bars were sold than strawberry yogurt bars?
   - Ⓐ 49
   - Ⓑ 41
   - **Ⓒ 39**
   - Ⓓ 31

3. The Party Popcorn Company sold 58 bags of cheese popcorn and 39 bags of nutty popcorn. How many more bags of cheese popcorn were sold than nutty popcorn?
   - Ⓐ 97
   - Ⓑ 41
   - Ⓒ 29
   - **Ⓓ 19**

4. Lin drove a total of 346 miles in 2 days. She drove 204 miles the first day. How many miles did she drive the second day?
   - **Ⓐ 142 miles**
   - Ⓑ 152 miles
   - Ⓒ 173 miles
   - Ⓓ 322 miles

Problem Solving REAL WORLD

5. Ruby has 78 books. Thirty-one of the books are on shelves. The rest are still packed in boxes. How many of Ruby's books are still in boxes?

   47 books

6. Kyle has 130 pins in his collection. He has 76 of the pins displayed on his wall. The rest are in a drawer. How many of Kyle's pins are in a drawer?

   54 pins

Name ____________________

Lesson 50

COMMON CORE STANDARD CC.3.NBT.2

Lesson Objective: Use place value to subtract 3-digit numbers.

Use Place Value to Subtract

You can use place value to subtract 3-digit numbers.

Subtract. 352 − 167 **Estimate.** 400 − 200 = 200

Step 1 Subtract the ones.

4 12
3~~5~~~~2~~
− 167
5

Are there enough ones to subtract 7?
There are not enough ones.
Regroup **5** tens **2** ones as 4 tens 12 ones.
12 ones − 7 ones = 5 ones

Step 2 Subtract the tens.

14
2 ~~4~~ 12
~~3~~~~5~~~~2~~
− 167
85

Are there enough tens to subtract 6?
There are not enough tens.
Regroup **3** hundreds **4** tens as 2 hundreds 14 tens.
14 tens − 6 tens = 8 tens

Step 3 Subtract the hundreds.

14
2 ~~4~~ 12
~~3~~~~5~~~~2~~
− 167
185

2 hundreds − **1** hundred = 1 hundred

So, 352 − 167 = 185.

Possible estimates are given.

Estimate. Then find the difference.

1. Estimate: 400	2. Estimate: 100	3. Estimate: 200	4. Estimate: 250
537 − 123 = 414	268 − 157 = 111	426 − 218 = 208	785 − 549 = 236
5. Estimate: 150	**6.** Estimate: 200	**7.** Estimate: 400	**8.** Estimate: 200
354 − 206 = 148	679 − 482 = 197	787 − 378 = 409	843 − 675 = 168

Name ____________________

Lesson 50

CC.3.NBT.2

1. The school store had 136 notepads. It sold 109 notepads. How many notepads are left?
   - **Ⓐ 27**
   - Ⓑ 33
   - Ⓒ 37
   - Ⓓ 43

2. Mr. Ruiz's art students used 159 green beads and 370 orange beads to make necklaces. How many more orange beads than green beads did they use?
   - Ⓐ 201
   - **Ⓑ 211**
   - Ⓒ 221
   - Ⓓ 229

3. The craft store had 151 bags of beads. It sold 128 bags. How many bags of beads are left?
   - Ⓐ 37
   - Ⓑ 33
   - Ⓒ 27
   - **Ⓓ 23**

4. A movie theater has 245 seats in the main section, and 78 seats up in the balcony. How many more seats are in the main section?
   - Ⓐ 137
   - **Ⓑ 167**
   - Ⓒ 187
   - Ⓓ 233

Problem Solving REAL WORLD

5. Mrs. Cohen has 427 buttons. She uses 195 buttons to make puppets. How many buttons does Mrs. Cohen have left?

   232 buttons

6. There were 625 ears of corn and 247 tomatoes sold at a farm stand. How many more ears of corn were sold than tomatoes?

   378 more ears of corn

Answer Key

Name ______________________ **Lesson 51**

COMMON CORE STANDARD CC.3.NBT.2

Lesson Objective: Use the combine place values strategy to subtract 3-digit numbers.

Combine Place Values to Subtract

You can combine place values to subtract. Think of two digits next to each other as one number.

Subtract. 354 − 248

Estimate. 350 − 250 = 100

Step 1 Look at the digits in the ones place.	**Step 2** Combine the tens and ones places.	**Step 3** Subtract the hundreds.
Think: 8 > 4, so combine place values.	**Think:** There are 54 ones and 48 ones. Subtract the ones. Write 0 for the tens.	
354 − 248	354 − 248 = 06	354 − 248 = 106

So, 354 − 248 = 106.

Remember: You can also combine hundreds and tens to subtract.

Possible estimates are given.

Estimate. Then find the difference.

1. Estimate: 100 — 485 − 376 = 109
2. Estimate: 250 — 657 − 424 = 233
3. Estimate: 150 — 347 − 198 = 149
4. Estimate: 200 — 623 − 397 = 226
5. Estimate: 250 — 443 − 207 = 236
6. Estimate: 150 — 500 − 338 = 162
7. Estimate: 300 — 835 − 548 = 287
8. Estimate: 400 — 712 − 289 = 423

www.harcourtschoolsupply.com
© Houghton Mifflin Harcourt Publishing Company 101 Core Standards for Math, Grade 3

Name ______________________ **Lesson 51**

CC.3.NBT.2

1. Students want to sell 420 tickets to the school fair. They have sold 214 tickets. How many more tickets do they need to sell to reach their goal?
   - Ⓐ 106
   - **Ⓑ 206**
   - Ⓒ 214
   - Ⓓ 634

2. A website received 724 visitors last month. This month, there were 953 visitors. How many more visitors did the website have this month than last month?
   - Ⓐ 1,677
   - Ⓑ 231
   - **Ⓒ 229**
   - Ⓓ 129

3. The owners of a new discount store expect 350 shoppers the day the store opens. By noon, there are 143 shoppers. How many more shoppers do they need to reach their goal?
   - Ⓐ 107
   - **Ⓑ 207**
   - Ⓒ 217
   - Ⓓ 223

4. A popular ride at a theme park has 200 seats. Only 84 people got tickets for the last ride of the day. How many empty seats were there?
   - Ⓐ 184
   - Ⓑ 124
   - Ⓒ 126
   - **Ⓓ 116**

Problem Solving REAL WORLD

5. Bev scored 540 points. This was 158 points more than Ike scored. How many points did Ike score?

   382 points

6. A youth group earned $285 washing cars. The group's expenses were $79. How much profit did the group make washing cars?

   $206

www.harcourtschoolsupply.com
© Houghton Mifflin Harcourt Publishing Company 102 Core Standards for Math, Grade 3

Name ______________________ **Lesson 52**

COMMON CORE STANDARD CC.3.NBT.3

Lesson Objective: Solve multiplication problems by using the strategy *draw a diagram.*

Problem Solving • Use the Distributive Property

There are 6 rows of singers in a performance. There are 20 singers in each row. How many singers are in the performance?

Read the Problem	Solve the Problem
What do I need to find? I need to find how many singers are in the performance.	**Record the steps you used to solve the problem.**
What information do I need to use? There are 6 rows of singers. Each row has 20 singers.	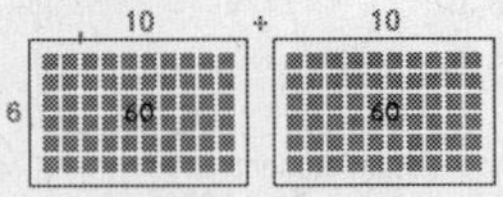 First, I draw and label a diagram to show 6 rows of 20 singers.
How will I use the information? I can draw a diagram and use the Distributive Property to break apart the factor 20 into 10 + 10 to use facts I know.	Next, I break apart 20 into 10 + 10 and find the products of the two smaller rectangles. 6 × 10 = 60 6 × 10 = 60. Then, I find the sum of the two products. 60 + 60 = 120. 6 × 20 = 120. So, there are 120 singers.

1. Eight teams play in a Little League series. Each team has 20 players. How many players are in the series?

   160 players

2. The assembly room has 6 rows with 30 chairs in each row. If third graders fill 3 rows, how many third graders are in the room?

   90 third graders

www.harcourtschoolsupply.com
© Houghton Mifflin Harcourt Publishing Company 103 Core Standards for Math, Grade 3

Name ______________________ **Lesson 52**

CC.3.NBT.3

1. Uncle Tito has 4 nephews. He gives each boy a $30 gift card to a hobby shop. What is the total cost of the 4 gift cards?
   - Ⓐ $34
   - Ⓑ $80
   - **Ⓒ $120**
   - Ⓓ $150

2. A toy store has 4 shelves of stuffed animals on display. Each shelf displays 20 stuffed animals. Which diagram shows a way to find the total number of stuffed animals on display?
   - Ⓐ 
   - **Ⓑ** 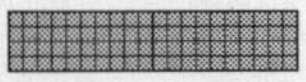
   - Ⓒ 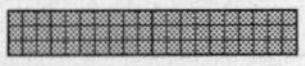
   - Ⓓ 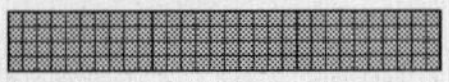

3. Wendy buys 7 boxes of envelopes. There are 80 envelopes in each box. How many envelopes does Wendy buy altogether?
   - Ⓐ 56
   - **Ⓑ 560**
   - Ⓒ 630
   - Ⓓ 640

4. Aunt Sonya has 5 nieces. She gives each girl a $40 gift card to the museum shop. What is the total cost of the 5 gift cards?
   - Ⓐ $45
   - Ⓑ $50
   - Ⓒ $160
   - **Ⓓ $200**

5. Corey sold 5 kites to each of 20 people. How many kites did Corey sell altogether? Explain your answer.

   100 kites; Possible explanation: I draw a diagram that shows 5 rows of 20. I know I can break up 5 × 20 into 5 × (10 + 10). So, I draw a vertical line to show 5 × 10 and another 5 × 10. 5 × 10 = 50, so the product is 50 + 50 or 100.

www.harcourtschoolsupply.com
© Houghton Mifflin Harcourt Publishing Company 104 Core Standards for Math, Grade 3

Answer Key

Name ____________ **Lesson 53**

COMMON CORE STANDARD CC.3.NBT.3

Lesson Objective: Use base-ten blocks, a number line, or place value to multiply with multiples of 10.

Multiplication Strategies with Multiples of 10

You can use place value to multiply with multiples of 10.

Find 5 × 20.

Step 1 Use a multiplication fact you know.

Think: 5 × 2 = 10, so 5 × 2 ones = 10 ones

Step 2 Use place value to find the product.

Think: 5 × 2 tens = 10 tens, or 100

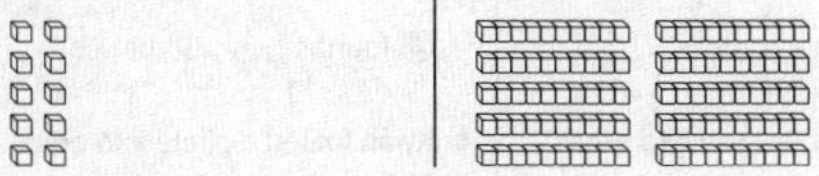

So, 5 × 20 = 100.

You can also use a number line to multiply with multiples of 10.

Find 4 × 30.

Think: There are 4 groups of 30. Draw 4 jumps of 30.

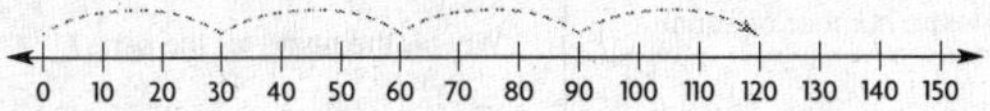

So, 4 × 30 = 120.

Use place value to find the product.

1. 6 × 40 = 6 × <u>4</u> tens = <u>24</u> tens = <u>240</u>
2. 50 × 7 = <u>5</u> tens × 7 = <u>35</u> tens = <u>350</u>
3. Use a number line to find the product. 3 × 50 = <u>150</u>

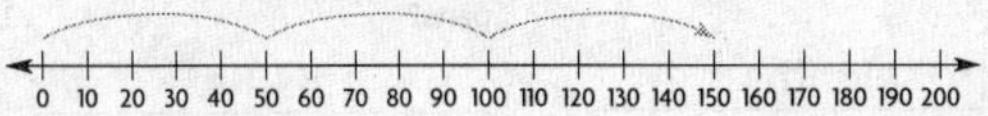

Name ____________ **Lesson 53**

CC.3.NBT.3

1. Lucia takes care of farm animals. She works 5 days each week. Last week she took care of 60 farm animals each day she worked. How many farm animals did Lucia take care of last week?
   - Ⓐ 360
   - Ⓒ 240
   - **Ⓑ 300**
   - Ⓓ 65
2. What multiplication sentence does the model show?

   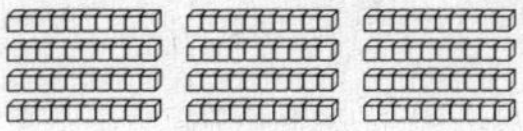

   - Ⓐ 3 × 4 = 12
   - Ⓑ 2 × 60 = 120
   - **Ⓒ 3 × 40 = 120**
   - Ⓓ 4 × 30 = 120
3. Each school bus has seats for 30 students. On a recent third-grade field trip, 7 buses were filled with students. How many students went on the field trip?
   - Ⓐ 21
   - Ⓒ 180
   - Ⓑ 37
   - **Ⓓ 210**
4. What multiplication sentence does the model show?

   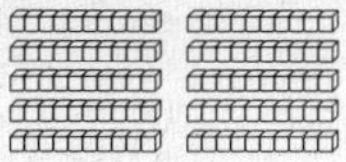

   - Ⓐ 2 × 5 = 10
   - Ⓑ 3 × 40 = 120
   - **Ⓒ 2 × 50 = 100**
   - Ⓓ 2 × 60 = 120

Problem Solving REAL WORLD

5. One exhibit at the aquarium has 5 fish tanks. Each fish tank holds 50 gallons of water. How much water do the 5 tanks hold in all?

   <u>250 gallons</u>
6. In another aquarium display, there are 40 fish in each of 7 large tanks. How many fish are in the display in all?

   <u>280 fish</u>

Name ____________ **Lesson 54**

COMMON CORE STANDARD CC.3.NBT.3

Lesson Objective: Model and record multiplication with multiples of 10.

Multiply Multiples of 10 by 1-Digit Numbers

You can use place value and regrouping to multiply multiples of 10.

Find 3 × 40.

	THINK	RECORD
Step 1 Use quick pictures to draw 3 groups of 40. 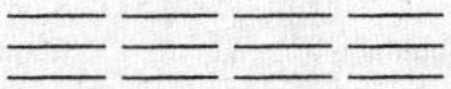	Multiply the ones. 3 × 0 ones = 0 ones.	40 × 3 0
Step 2 Regroup the 12 tens. 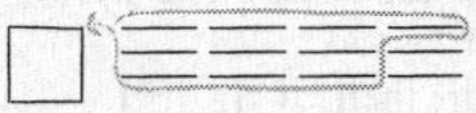	Multiply the tens. 3 × 4 tens = 12 tens Regroup the 12 tens as 1 hundred 2 tens	40 × 3 120

So, 3 × 40 = 120.

Find the product. Draw a quick picture.

Check students' quick pictures.

1. 4 × 50 = <u>200</u>
2. 7 × 30 = <u>210</u>
3. <u>180</u> = 9 × 20
4. 6 × 70 = <u>420</u>

Name ____________ **Lesson 54**

CC.3.NBT.3

1. A bank makes rolls of 40 nickels. How many nickels would there be in 8 rolls?
   - Ⓐ 640
   - **Ⓑ 320**
   - Ⓒ 80
   - Ⓓ 64
2. Claire bought 6 bags of beads. There are 80 beads in each bag. How many beads did Claire buy?
   - **Ⓐ 480**
   - Ⓑ 460
   - Ⓒ 400
   - Ⓓ 380
3. Mr. Chandler planted 5 rows of bean seedlings. He planted 50 seedlings in each row. How many seedlings did Mr. Chandler plant?
   - Ⓐ 55
   - Ⓑ 200
   - **Ⓒ 250**
   - Ⓓ 350
4. Mei-Ling baked 6 batches of rice cakes. There were 30 rice cakes in each batch. How many rice cakes did she bake in all?
   - Ⓐ 36
   - Ⓑ 120
   - Ⓒ 150
   - **Ⓓ 180**

Problem Solving REAL WORLD

5. Each model car in a set costs $4. There are 30 different model cars in the set. How much would it cost to buy all the model cars in the set?

   <u>$120</u>
6. Amanda exercises for 50 minutes each day. How many minutes will she exercise in 7 days?

   <u>350 minutes</u>

Answer Key

Name ______________________

Lesson 55

COMMON CORE STANDARD CC.3.NF.1

Lesson Objective: Explore and identify equal parts of a whole.

Equal Parts of a Whole

When you divide a shape into **equal parts**, each part must be exactly the same size.

This rectangle is divided into 2 equal parts, or **halves**.

This rectangle is divided into 3 equal parts, or **thirds**.

This rectangle is divided into 4 equal parts, or **fourths**.

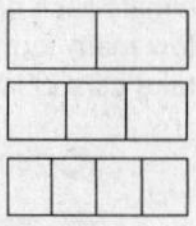

Write the number of equal parts. Then write the name for the parts.

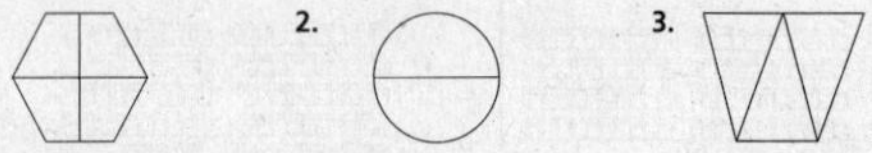

1. 4 equal parts — fourths
2. 2 equal parts — halves
3. 3 equal parts — thirds

Write whether each shape is divided into *equal* parts or *unequal* parts.

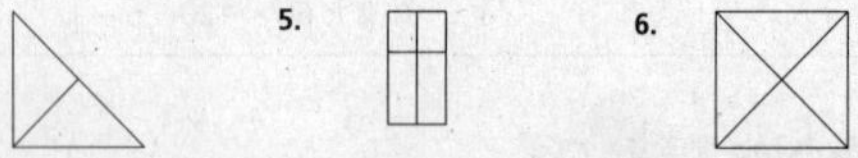

4. equal parts
5. unequal parts
6. equal parts

Draw lines to divide the squares into equal parts. Possible lines are shown.

7. 3 thirds
8. 6 sixths
9. 8 eighths

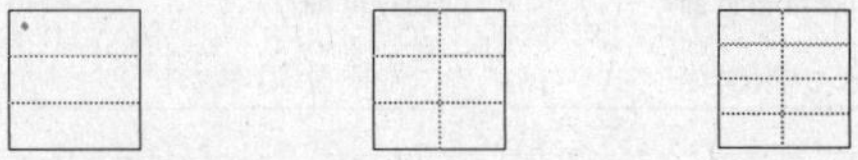

Name ______________________

Lesson 55

CC.3.NF.1

1. This shape is divided into equal parts.

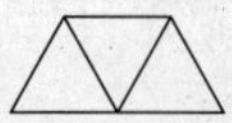

What is the name for the parts?

Ⓐ eighths Ⓒ halves
Ⓑ fourths **Ⓓ thirds**

2. This shape is divided into equal parts.

What is the number of equal parts?

Ⓐ 8 Ⓒ 3
Ⓑ 4 Ⓓ 2

3. Jamal folded a piece of cloth into equal parts.

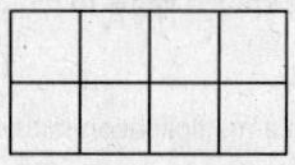

What is the name for the parts?

Ⓐ eighths Ⓒ thirds
Ⓑ fourths Ⓓ halves

4. Kwan folded a circle into equal parts.

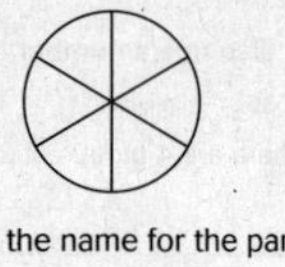

What is the name for the parts?

Ⓐ eighths Ⓒ fourths
Ⓑ sixths Ⓓ thirds

Problem Solving REAL WORLD

5. Diego cuts a round pizza into eight equal slices. What is the name for the parts?

eighths

6. Madison is making a place mat. She divides it into 6 equal parts to color. What is the name for the parts?

sixths

Name ______________________

Lesson 56

COMMON CORE STANDARD CC.3.NF.1

Lesson Objective: Divide models to make equal shares.

Equal Shares

Six brothers share 5 sandwiches equally. How much does each brother get? Draw to model the problem.

Step 1 Draw 5 squares for the sandwiches.

Step 2 There are 6 brothers. Draw lines to divide each sandwich into 6 equal parts.

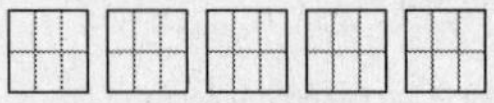

Step 3 Each brother will get 1 equal part from each sandwich.

So, each brother gets 5 sixths of a sandwich.

Draw lines to show how much each person gets. Write the answer. Check students' lines. Possible answers are given.

1. 4 sisters share 3 pies equally.

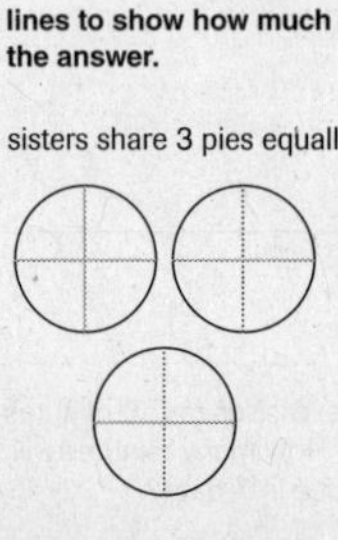

3 fourths, or 1 half and 1 fourth, of a pie

2. 6 friends share 3 fruit bars equally.

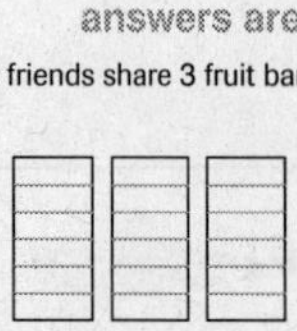

3 sixths, or 1 half, of a fruit bar

Name ______________________

Lesson 56

CC.3.NF.1

1. Three friends share 6 graham crackers equally.

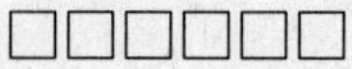

How much does each friend get?

Ⓐ 2 wholes
Ⓑ 2 wholes and 1 half
Ⓒ 3 wholes
Ⓓ 3 wholes and 1 half

2. Four brothers share 5 cookies equally.

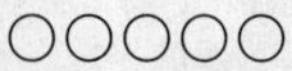

How much does each brother get?

Ⓐ 1 whole and 1 fifth
Ⓑ 1 whole and 1 fourth
Ⓒ 1 whole and 2 fourths
Ⓓ 1 whole and 4 fifths

3. Four friends share 3 fruit bars equally.

How much does each friend get?

Ⓐ 1 third
Ⓑ 2 thirds
Ⓒ 3 fourths
Ⓓ 5 eighths

4. Three teachers share 7 brownies equally.

How much does each teacher get?

Ⓐ 1 whole and 1 third
Ⓑ 1 whole and 2 thirds
Ⓒ 2 wholes and 1 third
Ⓓ 2 wholes and 2 thirds

5. Two moms share 3 sandwiches equally.

Shade the squares to show how much each mom gets. Then write the answer.

Possible answers: 1 whole and 1 half, or 3 halves, of a sandwich

Name ____________________ **Lesson 57**

COMMON CORE STANDARD CC.3.NF.1

Lesson Objective: Use a fraction to name one part of a whole that is divided into equal parts.

Unit Fractions of a Whole

A **fraction** is a number. It names part of a whole or part of a group.

The top number tells how many equal parts are being counted. The bottom number tells how many equal parts are in the whole. A **unit fraction** names 1 equal part of a whole. It always has 1 as its top number.

How much is 1 part of a fruit bar that is cut into 8 equal parts?

Step 1 Use fraction strips. Make a strip showing 8 equal parts, or eighths.

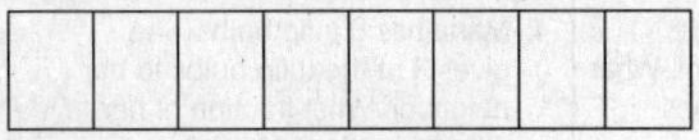

Step 2 Shade 1 of the parts and name it.

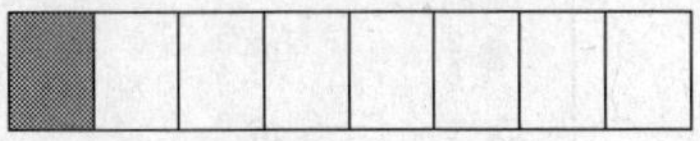

This fraction is called $\frac{1}{8}$.

So, 1 part of a fruit bar that can be divided into 8 equal parts is $\frac{1}{8}$.

Write the number of equal parts in the whole. Then write the fraction that names the shaded part.

1. 

4 equal parts

$\frac{1}{4}$

2. 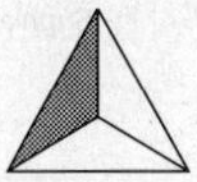

3 equal parts

$\frac{1}{3}$

3. 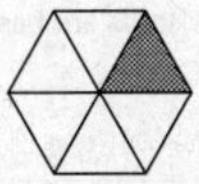

6 equal parts

$\frac{1}{6}$

Name ____________________ **Lesson 57**

CC.3.NF.1

1. The shaded part of the model shows how much cornbread was left after dinner.

What fraction of the cornbread was left?

Ⓐ $\frac{1}{3}$ Ⓑ $\frac{1}{4}$ Ⓒ $\frac{1}{6}$ Ⓓ $\frac{1}{8}$

2. Riley shaded a model to show the amount of sandwich she ate.

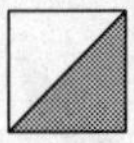

What fraction of the sandwich did Riley eat?

Ⓐ $\frac{1}{4}$ Ⓑ $\frac{1}{3}$ Ⓒ $\frac{1}{2}$ Ⓓ $\frac{1}{1}$

3. Kareena made potato salad. She shaded a model to show how much salad was left.

What fraction of the potato salad was left?

Ⓐ $\frac{1}{2}$ Ⓑ $\frac{1}{4}$ Ⓒ $\frac{1}{6}$ Ⓓ $\frac{1}{8}$

4. The shaded part of the model shows how many paintings were sold at an art show.

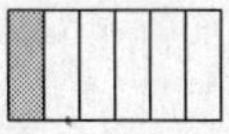

What fraction of the paintings were sold?

Ⓐ $\frac{1}{6}$ Ⓑ $\frac{1}{5}$ Ⓒ $\frac{1}{4}$ Ⓓ $\frac{1}{3}$

5. Mario drew a model to represent $\frac{1}{3}$ of the space in his bookcase. How could Mario draw a model to represent all the space in his bookcase?

Possible answer: because the rectangle represents $\frac{1}{3}$ of the space in his bookshelf, Mario could draw 2 more rectangles like the one that represented $\frac{1}{3}$.

Name ____________________ **Lesson 58**

COMMON CORE STANDARD CC.3.NF.1

Lesson Objective: Read, write, and model fractions that represent more than one part of a whole that is divided into equal parts.

Fractions of a Whole

Some shapes can be cut into equal parts. A fraction can name more than 1 equal part of a whole.

Write a fraction in words and in numbers to name the shaded part.

How many equal parts make up the whole shape? 6 equal parts

How many parts are shaded? 3 parts

So, 3 parts out of 6 equal parts are shaded. Read: three sixths. Write: $\frac{3}{6}$.

1. Shade three parts out of eight equal parts. Write a fraction in words and in numbers to name the shaded part.

Read: three eighths

Write: $\frac{3}{8}$

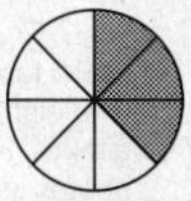

Possible shading is shown.

Write the fraction that names each part. Write a fraction in words and in numbers to name the shaded part.

2. 

Each part is $\frac{1}{6}$.

four sixths

$\frac{4}{6}$

3. 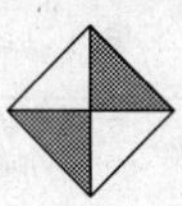

Each part is $\frac{1}{4}$.

two fourths

$\frac{2}{4}$

4. 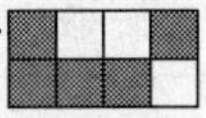

Each part is $\frac{1}{8}$.

five eighths

$\frac{5}{8}$

Name ____________________ **Lesson 58**

CC.3.NF.1

1. What fraction names the shaded part of the page?

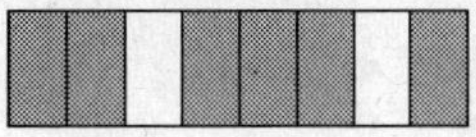

Ⓐ eight sixths
Ⓑ eight eighths
Ⓒ six eighths
Ⓓ two sixths

2. Lilly shaded this model to show what part of all the books she read are fiction.

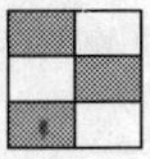

What fraction of the books Lilly read are fiction?

Ⓐ $\frac{3}{3}$ Ⓑ $\frac{5}{6}$ Ⓒ $\frac{3}{4}$ Ⓓ $\frac{3}{6}$

3. What fraction names the shaded part of the shape?

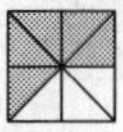

Ⓐ three eighths
Ⓑ five eighths
Ⓒ six eighths
Ⓓ eight eighths

4. Bailey shaded this model to show what part of all the baseball games his team won last season.

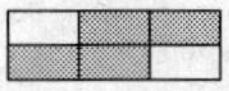

What fraction of the games did Bailey's team win?

Ⓐ $\frac{2}{6}$ Ⓑ $\frac{2}{4}$ Ⓒ $\frac{4}{6}$ Ⓓ $\frac{6}{4}$

5. Ashleigh shaded a model to show what part of the bracelets she made are blue. Explain how the model can be used to describe what part of the bracelets Ashleigh made are not blue.

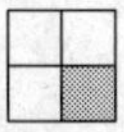

Possible answer: 3 parts are not shaded, so three fourths describes the part of the bracelets that are not blue.

Answer Key

Name ______________ **Lesson 59**

COMMON CORE STANDARD CC.3.NF.1

Lesson Objective: Model, read, and write fractional parts of a group.

Fractions of a Group

Adam has a collection of cars.
What fraction names the shaded part of the collection?

Step 1 Count how many cars are shaded. There are 3 shaded cars. This number will be the numerator, or the top number of the fraction.

Step 2 Count the total number of cars. 8 This number will be the denominator, or the bottom number of the fraction.

Step 3 Read the fraction: three eighths, or three out of eight.

So, $\frac{3}{8}$ of Adam's cars are shaded.

Write a fraction to name the shaded part of each group.

1. 

$\frac{2}{4}$

2. 

$\frac{3}{4}$

Write a whole number and a fraction greater than 1 to name the part filled.

3. 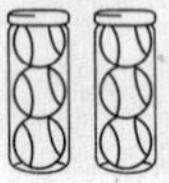

Think: 1 can = 1

2 $\frac{6}{3}$

4. 

Think: 1 pan = 1

2 $\frac{12}{6}$

Name ______________ **Lesson 59**

CC.3.NF.1

1. There are 8 rows of chairs in the auditorium. Three of the rows are empty. What fraction of the rows of chairs are empty?

Ⓐ $\frac{5}{8}$ Ⓑ $\frac{4}{8}$ **Ⓒ $\frac{3}{8}$** Ⓓ $\frac{1}{8}$

2. Greyson has 3 baseballs. He brings 2 baseballs to school. What fraction of his baseballs does Greyson bring to school?

Ⓐ $\frac{1}{3}$ Ⓑ $\frac{1}{2}$ **Ⓒ $\frac{2}{3}$** Ⓓ $\frac{3}{2}$

3. David sold 6 apple trees. He sold 5 of the apple trees to Max. What fraction of the apple trees did David sell to Max?

Ⓐ $\frac{1}{6}$ Ⓑ $\frac{3}{16}$ **Ⓒ $\frac{5}{6}$** Ⓓ $\frac{6}{5}$

4. Maria has 8 tulip bulbs. She gives 3 of the tulip bulbs to her neighbor. What fraction of her tulip bulbs does Maria give to her neighbor?

Ⓐ $\frac{3}{8}$ Ⓑ $\frac{5}{8}$ Ⓒ $\frac{3}{5}$ Ⓓ $\frac{8}{3}$

Problem Solving REAL WORLD

5. Brian has 3 basketball cards and 5 baseball cards. What fraction of Brian's cards are baseball cards?

$\frac{5}{8}$

6. Sophia has 3 pink tulips and 3 white tulips. What fraction of Sophia's tulips are pink?

$\frac{3}{6}$, or $\frac{1}{2}$

Name ______________ **Lesson 60**

COMMON CORE STANDARD CC.3.NF.1

Lesson Objective: Find fractional parts of a group using unit fractions.

Find Part of a Group Using Unit Fractions

Lauren bought 12 stamps for postcards. She gave Brianna $\frac{1}{6}$ of them. How many stamps did Lauren give to Brianna?

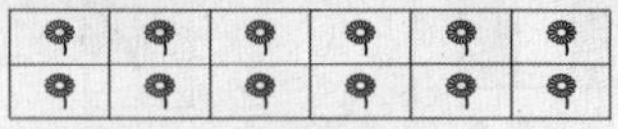

Step 1 Find the total number of stamps. 12 stamps

Step 2 Since you want to find $\frac{1}{6}$ of the group, there should be 6 equal groups. Circle one of the groups to show $\frac{1}{6}$.

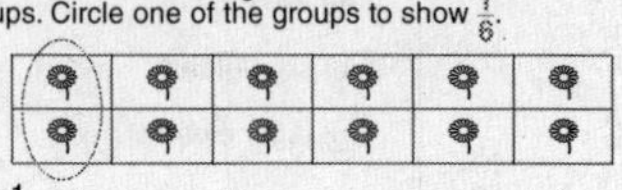

Step 3 Find $\frac{1}{6}$ of the stamps. How many stamps are in 1 group? 2 stamps

So, Lauren gave Brianna 2 stamps. $\frac{1}{6}$ of 12 = 2

Circle equal groups to solve. Count the number of shapes in 1 group. Check students' circles.

1. $\frac{1}{4}$ of 8 = 2

2. $\frac{1}{3}$ of 9 = 3

3. $\frac{1}{4}$ of 16 = 4

4. $\frac{1}{6}$ of 18 = 3

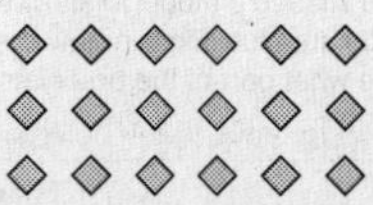

Name ______________ **Lesson 60**

CC.3.NF.1

1. Charlotte bought 16 songs. One fourth of the songs are pop songs.

How many of the songs are pop songs?

Ⓐ 16 Ⓑ 12 **Ⓒ 4** Ⓓ 1

2. Sophie uses 18 beads to make a necklace. One sixth of the beads are purple. How many of the beads are purple?

Ⓐ 1 **Ⓑ 3** Ⓒ 6 Ⓓ 18

3. Mr. Walton ordered 12 pizzas for the art class celebration. One fourth of the pizzas had only mushrooms.

How many of the pizzas had only mushrooms?

Ⓐ 1 **Ⓑ 3** Ⓒ 4 Ⓓ 9

4. Caleb took 24 photos at the zoo. One eighth of his photos are of giraffes. How many of Caleb's photos are of giraffes?

Ⓐ 1 **Ⓑ 3** Ⓒ 8 Ⓓ 24

Problem Solving REAL WORLD

5. Marco drew 24 pictures. He drew $\frac{1}{6}$ of them in art class. How many pictures did Marco draw in art class?

4 pictures

6. Caroline has 16 marbles. One eighth of them are blue. How many of Caroline's marbles are blue?

2 marbles

Answer Key

Name ____________ **Lesson 61**

COMMON CORE STANDARD CC.3.NF.1

Lesson Objective: Solve fraction problems by using the strategy *draw a diagram.*

Problem Solving • Find the Whole Group Using Unit Fractions

There are 3 apple juice boxes in the cooler. One fourth of the juice boxes in the cooler are apple juice. How many juice boxes are in the cooler?

Read the Problem	Solve the Problem
What do I need to find? I need to find how many juice boxes are in the cooler.	**Describe how to draw a diagram to solve.** The denominator in $\frac{1}{4}$ tells you that there are 4 parts in the whole group. Draw 4 circles to show 4 parts.
What information do I need to use? There are 3 apple juice boxes. One fourth of the juice boxes are apple juice.	Since 3 juice boxes are $\frac{1}{4}$ of the group, draw 3 counters in the first circle. Since there are 3 counters in the first circle, draw 3 counters in each of the remaining circles. Then count all of the counters.
How will I use the information? I will use the information in the problem to draw a diagram.	So, there are 12 juice boxes in the cooler.

1. Max has 3 beta fish in his fish tank. One half of his fish are beta fish. How many fish does Max have in his tank?

   6 fish

2. Two boys are standing in line. One sixth of the students in line are boys. How many students are standing in line?

   12 students

Name ____________ **Lesson 61**

CC.3.NF.1

1. Samuel brought 2 autographed baseballs for show and tell. They are $\frac{1}{6}$ of his whole collection. How many autographed baseballs are in Samuel's whole collection?

   Ⓐ 3 Ⓑ 4 **Ⓒ 12** Ⓓ 13

2. Together, Dillon and Leon make up $\frac{1}{4}$ of the midfielders on the soccer team. How many midfielders are on the team?

   Ⓐ 2 Ⓑ 4 Ⓒ 6 **Ⓓ 8**

3. Ben has 12 model cars in his room. These cars represent $\frac{1}{2}$ of the model cars in Ben's whole collection. How many model cars does Ben have in his whole collection?

   Ⓐ 24 Ⓑ 18 Ⓒ 15 Ⓓ 6

4. A garden has 2 yellow rose plants. These rose plants represent $\frac{1}{8}$ of the plants in the entire garden. How many plants are in the entire garden?

   Ⓐ 4 Ⓑ 6 Ⓒ 10 **Ⓓ 16**

5. Laura found 5 shells on a trip to the beach. These shells represent $\frac{1}{3}$ of the shells in her whole collection. How many shells does Laura have in her whole collection? Draw a diagram to find the answer.

   15 shells; Possible drawings are shown.

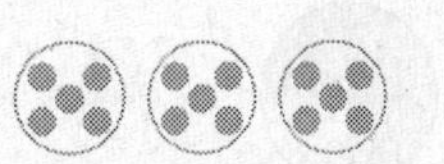

Name ____________ **Lesson 62**

COMMON CORE STANDARDS CC.3.NF.2a, CC.3.NF.2b

Lesson Objective: Represent and locate fractions on a number line.

Fractions on a Number Line

Use the fraction strips to help name the points on the number line.

Draw a point to show $\frac{1}{3}$.

Step 1 The denominator is 3, so use fraction strips for thirds. Place the fraction strips above the number line. Use the fraction strips to divide the number line into three equal lengths.

Step 2 Label each mark on the number line.
Think: The distance between each mark is $\frac{1}{3}$ of the total distance, so count the number of $\frac{1}{3}$ lengths.

Step 3 Draw a point on the number line to show $\frac{1}{3}$.

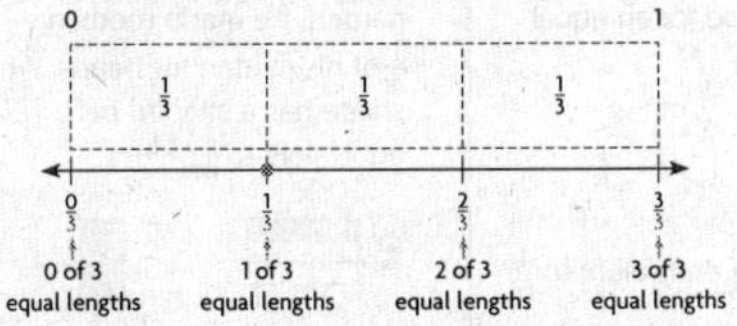

1. Complete the number line. Draw a point to show $\frac{2}{4}$.

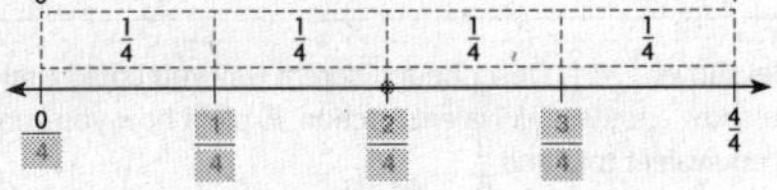

Write the fraction that names the point.

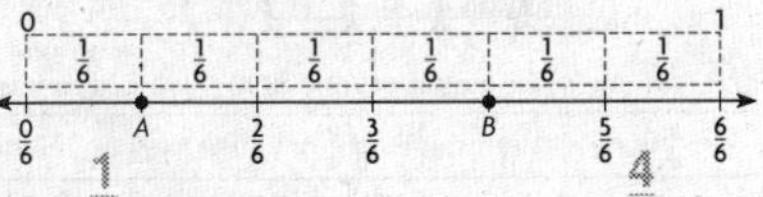

2. point A $\frac{1}{6}$ 3. point B $\frac{4}{6}$

Name ____________ **Lesson 62**

CC.3.NF.2a, CC.3.NF.2b

1. Which fraction names point A on the number line?

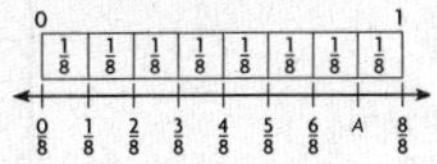

   Ⓐ $\frac{1}{8}$ Ⓑ $\frac{6}{8}$ **Ⓒ $\frac{7}{8}$** Ⓓ $\frac{8}{8}$

2. Which fraction names point A on the number line?

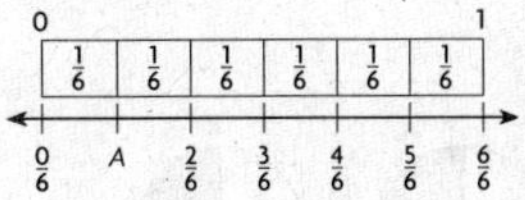

   Ⓐ $\frac{1}{6}$ Ⓑ $\frac{2}{6}$ Ⓒ $\frac{3}{6}$ Ⓓ $\frac{1}{1}$

3. Lucy can ride her bike around the block 4 times for a total of 1 mile. How many times will she ride around the block to go $\frac{3}{4}$ mile?

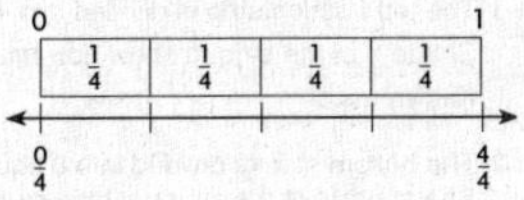

   Ⓐ 2 **Ⓑ 3** Ⓒ 6 Ⓓ 8

4. Carlos can walk around the track 8 times for a total of 1 mile. How many times will he walk around the track to go $\frac{7}{8}$ mile?

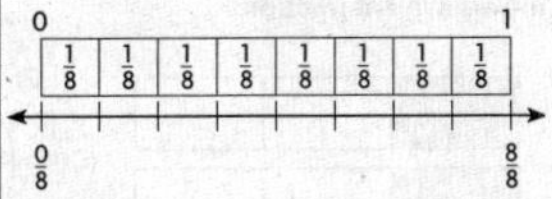

   Ⓐ 1 Ⓑ 3 Ⓒ 5 **Ⓓ 7**

Problem Solving REAL WORLD

5. Jade ran 6 times around her neighborhood to complete a total of 1 mile. How many times will she need to run to complete $\frac{5}{6}$ of a mile?

   5 times

6. A missing fraction on a number line is located exactly halfway between $\frac{3}{6}$ and $\frac{5}{6}$. What is the missing fraction?

   $\frac{4}{6}$

Answer Key

Name ______________________

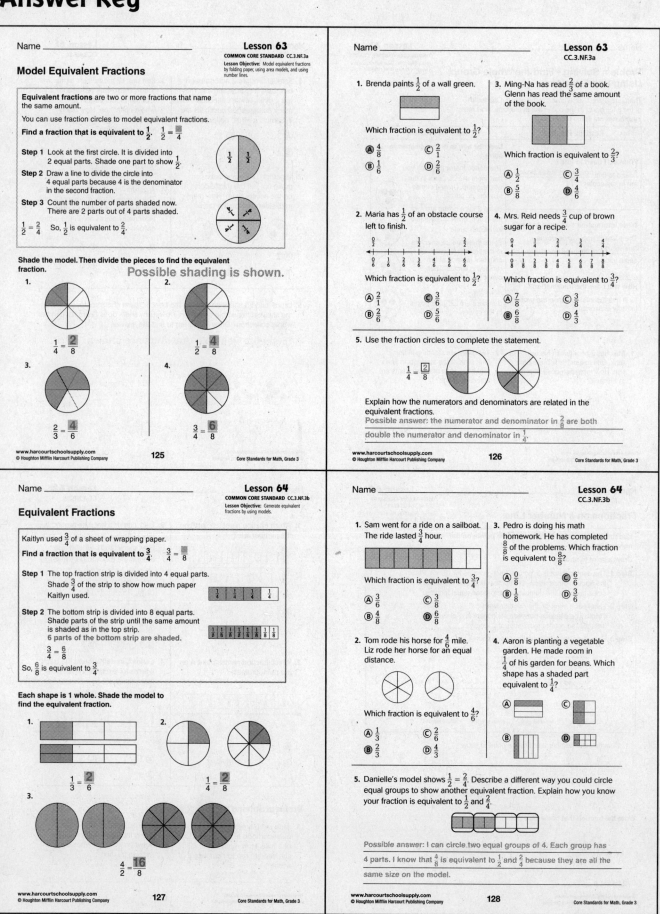

Lesson 63
COMMON CORE STANDARD CC.3.NF.3a
Lesson Objective: Model equivalent fractions by folding paper, using area models, and using number lines.

Model Equivalent Fractions

Equivalent fractions are two or more fractions that name the same amount.

You can use fraction circles to model equivalent fractions.

Find a fraction that is equivalent to $\frac{1}{2}$. $\frac{1}{2} = \frac{\blacksquare}{4}$

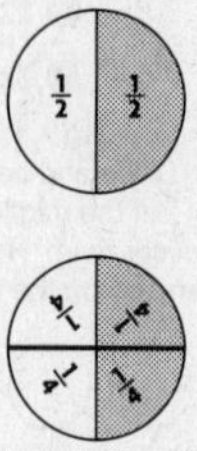

Step 1 Look at the first circle. It is divided into 2 equal parts. Shade one part to show $\frac{1}{2}$.

Step 2 Draw a line to divide the circle into 4 equal parts because 4 is the denominator in the second fraction.

Step 3 Count the number of parts shaded now. There are 2 parts out of 4 parts shaded.

$\frac{1}{2} = \frac{2}{4}$ So, $\frac{1}{2}$ is equivalent to $\frac{2}{4}$.

Shade the model. Then divide the pieces to find the equivalent fraction.

Possible shading is shown.

1. 

$\frac{1}{4} = \frac{2}{8}$

2. 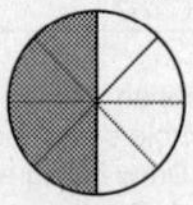

$\frac{1}{2} = \frac{4}{8}$

3. 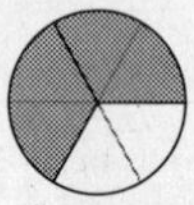

$\frac{2}{3} = \frac{4}{6}$

4. 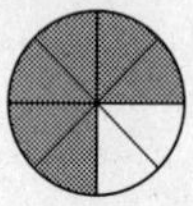

$\frac{3}{4} = \frac{6}{8}$

Name ______________________

Lesson 63
CC.3.NF.3a

1. Brenda paints $\frac{1}{2}$ of a wall green.

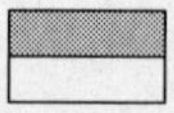

Which fraction is equivalent to $\frac{1}{2}$?

Ⓐ $\frac{4}{8}$ Ⓒ $\frac{2}{1}$
Ⓑ $\frac{1}{6}$ Ⓓ $\frac{2}{6}$

2. Maria has $\frac{1}{2}$ of an obstacle course left to finish.

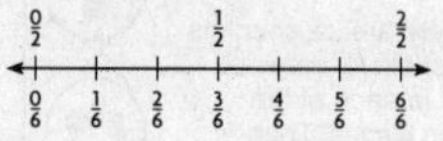

Which fraction is equivalent to $\frac{1}{2}$?

Ⓐ $\frac{2}{1}$ **Ⓒ $\frac{3}{6}$**
Ⓑ $\frac{2}{6}$ Ⓓ $\frac{5}{6}$

3. Ming-Na has read $\frac{2}{3}$ of a book. Glenn has read the same amount of the book.

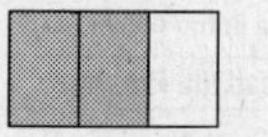

Which fraction is equivalent to $\frac{2}{3}$?

Ⓐ $\frac{1}{2}$ Ⓒ $\frac{3}{4}$
Ⓑ $\frac{5}{8}$ **Ⓓ $\frac{4}{6}$**

4. Mrs. Reid needs $\frac{3}{4}$ cup of brown sugar for a recipe.

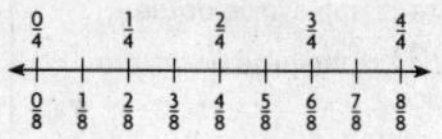

Which fraction is equivalent to $\frac{3}{4}$?

Ⓐ $\frac{7}{8}$ Ⓒ $\frac{3}{8}$
Ⓑ $\frac{6}{8}$ Ⓓ $\frac{4}{3}$

5. Use the fraction circles to complete the statement.

$\frac{1}{4} = \frac{2}{8}$

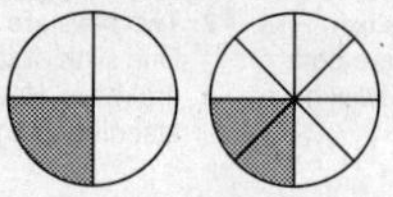

Explain how the numerators and denominators are related in the equivalent fractions.

Possible answer: the numerator and denominator in $\frac{2}{8}$ are both double the numerator and denominator in $\frac{1}{4}$.

Name ______________________

Lesson 64
COMMON CORE STANDARD CC.3.NF.3b
Lesson Objective: Generate equivalent fractions by using models.

Equivalent Fractions

Kaitlyn used $\frac{3}{4}$ of a sheet of wrapping paper.

Find a fraction that is equivalent to $\frac{3}{4}$. $\frac{3}{4} = \frac{\blacksquare}{8}$

Step 1 The top fraction strip is divided into 4 equal parts. Shade $\frac{3}{4}$ of the strip to show how much paper Kaitlyn used.

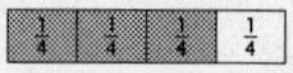

Step 2 The bottom strip is divided into 8 equal parts. Shade parts of the strip until the same amount is shaded as in the top strip.
6 parts of the bottom strip are shaded.

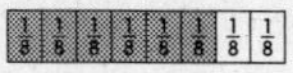

$\frac{3}{4} = \frac{6}{8}$

So, $\frac{6}{8}$ is equivalent to $\frac{3}{4}$.

Each shape is 1 whole. Shade the model to find the equivalent fraction.

1. 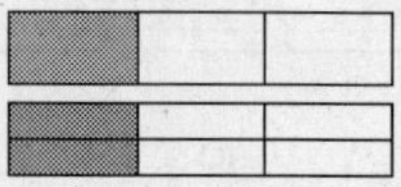

$\frac{1}{3} = \frac{2}{6}$

2. 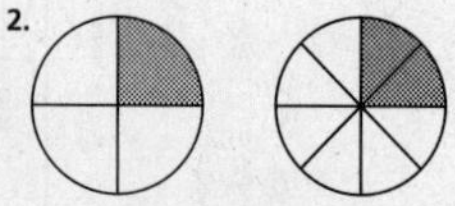

$\frac{1}{4} = \frac{2}{8}$

3. 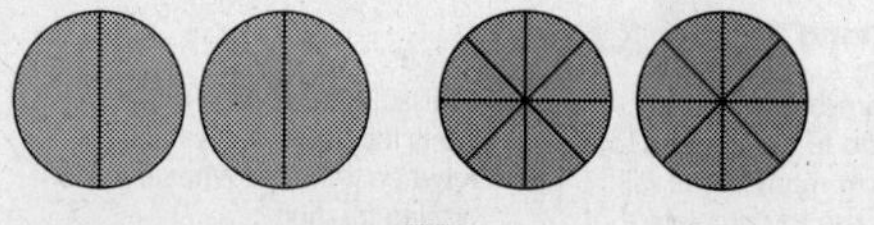

$\frac{4}{2} = \frac{16}{8}$

Name ______________________

Lesson 64
CC.3.NF.3b

1. Sam went for a ride on a sailboat. The ride lasted $\frac{3}{4}$ hour.

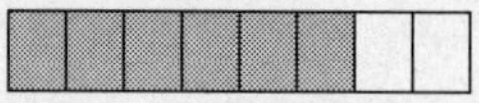

Which fraction is equivalent to $\frac{3}{4}$?

Ⓐ $\frac{3}{6}$ Ⓒ $\frac{3}{8}$
Ⓑ $\frac{4}{8}$ **Ⓓ $\frac{6}{8}$**

2. Tom rode his horse for $\frac{4}{6}$ mile. Liz rode her horse for an equal distance.

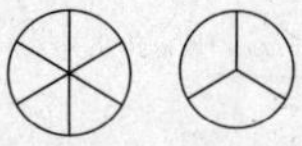

Which fraction is equivalent to $\frac{4}{6}$?

Ⓐ $\frac{1}{3}$ Ⓒ $\frac{2}{6}$
Ⓑ $\frac{2}{3}$ Ⓓ $\frac{4}{3}$

3. Pedro is doing his math homework. He has completed $\frac{8}{8}$ of the problems. Which fraction is equivalent to $\frac{8}{8}$?

Ⓐ $\frac{0}{8}$ **Ⓒ $\frac{6}{6}$**
Ⓑ $\frac{1}{8}$ Ⓓ $\frac{3}{6}$

4. Aaron is planting a vegetable garden. He made room in $\frac{1}{4}$ of his garden for beans. Which shape has a shaded part equivalent to $\frac{1}{4}$?

Ⓐ 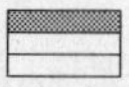 Ⓒ 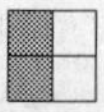

Ⓑ 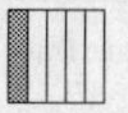 **Ⓓ** 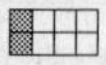

5. Danielle's model shows $\frac{1}{2} = \frac{2}{4}$. Describe a different way you could circle equal groups to show another equivalent fraction. Explain how you know your fraction is equivalent to $\frac{1}{2}$ and $\frac{2}{4}$.

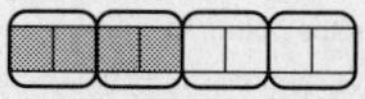

Possible answer: I can circle two equal groups of 4. Each group has 4 parts. I know that $\frac{4}{8}$ is equivalent to $\frac{1}{2}$ and $\frac{2}{4}$ because they are all the same size on the model.

Answer Key

Name ____________________ **Lesson 65**

COMMON CORE STANDARD CC.3.NF.3c

Lesson Objective: Relate fractions and whole numbers by expressing whole numbers as fractions and recognizing fractions that are equivalent to whole numbers.

Relate Fractions and Whole Numbers

A **fraction greater than 1** has a numerator greater than its denominator.

Jason ran 2 miles and Tyra ran $\frac{6}{3}$ miles. Did Jason and Tyra run the same distance?

Step 1 Use fraction strips to show the distances.
Use 2 whole strips to show Jason's distance.
Use six $\frac{1}{3}$-strips to show Tyra's distance.

Jason	1			1		
Tyra	$\frac{1}{3}$	$\frac{1}{3}$	$\frac{1}{3}$	$\frac{1}{3}$	$\frac{1}{3}$	$\frac{1}{3}$

$1 = \frac{3}{3}$ $\quad 2 = \frac{6}{3}$

Step 2 Compare the fraction strips.
Since the fraction strips for 2 and $\frac{6}{3}$ are the same length, they are equal.

So, Jason and Tyra ran the same distance.

Use the number line to find whether the two numbers are equal. Write *equal* or *not equal.*

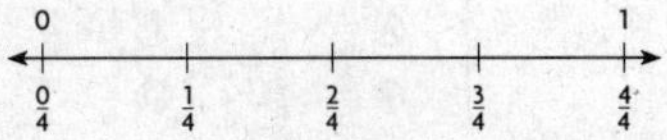

1. $\frac{4}{4}$ and 1 — equal

2. 1 and $\frac{3}{4}$ — not equal

3. $\frac{1}{4}$ and $\frac{4}{4}$ — not equal

Name ____________________ **Lesson 65**

CC.3.NF.3c

1. Which numbers from the number line are equal?

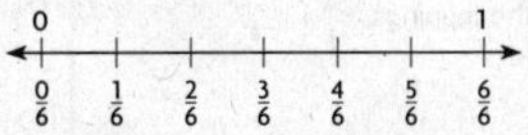

Ⓐ $\frac{6}{6}$ and 1 (answer)
Ⓑ $\frac{3}{6}$ and $\frac{6}{6}$
Ⓒ $\frac{0}{6}$ and 1
Ⓓ $\frac{0}{6}$ and $\frac{6}{6}$

2. Cora cuts the apple pies into equal parts.

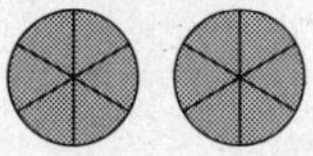

What fraction greater than 1 names both apple pies?

Ⓐ $\frac{2}{6}$
Ⓑ $\frac{6}{12}$
Ⓒ $\frac{6}{6}$
Ⓓ $\frac{12}{6}$ (answer)

3. Emma colored some shapes. What fraction greater than 1 names the parts that she shaded?

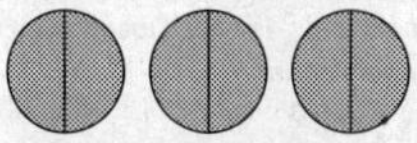

Ⓐ $\frac{6}{2}$ (answer)
Ⓑ $\frac{6}{3}$
Ⓒ $\frac{2}{3}$
Ⓓ $\frac{2}{6}$

4. Mr. Angelo sliced two pizzas into equal parts.

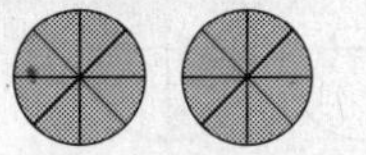

What fraction greater than 1 names both pizzas?

Ⓐ $\frac{2}{16}$
Ⓑ $\frac{8}{16}$
Ⓒ $\frac{16}{8}$ (answer)
Ⓓ $\frac{16}{4}$

Problem Solving REAL WORLD

5. Rachel jogged along a trail that was $\frac{1}{4}$ of a mile long. She jogged along the trail 8 times. How many miles did Rachel jog in all?

$\frac{8}{4}$, or 2 miles

6. Jon ran around a track that was $\frac{1}{8}$ of a mile long. He ran around the track 24 times. How many miles did Jon run in all?

$\frac{24}{8}$, or 3 miles

Name ____________________ **Lesson 66**

COMMON CORE STANDARD CC.3.NF.3d

Lesson Objective: Solve comparison problems by using the strategy *act it out.*

Problem Solving • Compare Fractions

Nick walked $\frac{2}{4}$ mile to the gym. Then he walked $\frac{3}{4}$ mile to the store. Which distance is shorter?

Read the Problem	Solve the Problem
What do I need to find? I need to find which distance is shorter.	1
What information do I need to use? Nick walked $\frac{2}{4}$ mile to the gym. Then he walked $\frac{3}{4}$ mile to the store.	$\frac{1}{4}$ $\frac{1}{4}$ $\frac{1}{4}$ $\frac{1}{4}$ (2 shaded) / $\frac{1}{4}$ $\frac{1}{4}$ $\frac{1}{4}$ $\frac{1}{4}$ (3 shaded) **Compare the lengths.** $\frac{2}{4} < \frac{3}{4}$
How will I use the information? I will use fraction strips and compare the lengths of the models to find which distance is shorter.	The length of the $\frac{2}{4}$ model is less than the length of the $\frac{3}{4}$ model. So, the distance to the gym is shorter.

1. Mariana and Shawn each had 6 pages to read. Mariana read $\frac{2}{3}$ of her pages. Shawn read $\frac{1}{3}$ of his pages. Who read more pages? **Explain.**

Mariana; Possible explanation: $\frac{2}{3} > \frac{1}{3}$

2. Carlos ran $\frac{3}{8}$ of the race course. Lori ran $\frac{3}{6}$ of the same race course. Who ran farther? **Explain.**

Lori; Possible explanation: $\frac{3}{6} > \frac{3}{8}$

Name ____________________ **Lesson 66**

CC.3.NF.3d

1. Bill used $\frac{1}{3}$ cup of raisins and $\frac{2}{3}$ cup of banana chips to make a snack. Which statement correctly compares the fractions?

Ⓐ $\frac{1}{3} > \frac{2}{3}$
Ⓑ $\frac{2}{3} < \frac{1}{3}$
Ⓒ $\frac{2}{3} > \frac{1}{3}$ (answer)
Ⓓ $\frac{2}{3} = \frac{1}{3}$

2. Mavis mixed $\frac{1}{4}$ quart of red paint with $\frac{3}{4}$ quart of yellow paint to make orange paint. Which of the following statements is **true**?

Ⓐ Mavis used less yellow paint than red paint.
Ⓑ Mavis used more red paint than yellow paint.
Ⓒ Mavis used equal amounts of red and yellow paint.
Ⓓ Mavis used more yellow paint than red paint. (answer)

3. Carlos found that $\frac{1}{2}$ of the apples in one basket are Granny Smith apples and $\frac{1}{6}$ of the apples in another basket are Granny Smith apples. The baskets are the same size. Which statement correctly compares the fractions?

Ⓐ $\frac{1}{2} = \frac{1}{6}$
Ⓑ $\frac{1}{2} < \frac{1}{6}$
Ⓒ $\frac{1}{2} > \frac{1}{6}$ (answer)
Ⓓ $\frac{1}{6} > \frac{1}{2}$

4. Of the stars on the Monroe Elementary School flag, $\frac{2}{4}$ are gold and $\frac{2}{8}$ are black. Which statement correctly compares the fractions?

Ⓐ $\frac{2}{8} > \frac{2}{4}$
Ⓑ $\frac{2}{8} < \frac{2}{4}$ (answer)
Ⓒ $\frac{2}{4} = \frac{2}{8}$
Ⓓ $\frac{2}{4} < \frac{2}{8}$

5. Tess ate $\frac{3}{8}$ of her granola bar. Gino ate $\frac{3}{4}$ of his granola bar. Both granola bars were the same size. Who ate more? Describe how you could use fraction strips to solve the problem.

Gino; Possible answer: I could model $\frac{3}{8}$ and $\frac{3}{4}$ and compare the lengths. The length of the $\frac{3}{4}$ model would be greater than the length of the $\frac{3}{8}$ model, so $\frac{3}{4}$ is greater than $\frac{3}{8}$.

Name ____________ **Lesson 67**

COMMON CORE STANDARD CC.3.NF.3d

Lesson Objective: Compare fractions with the same denominator by using models and reasoning strategies.

Compare Fractions with the Same Denominator

Pete's Prize Pizzas makes a special pizza. Of the toppings, $\frac{1}{4}$ is peppers and $\frac{3}{4}$ is ham. Does the pizza have more peppers or ham?

Compare $\frac{1}{4}$ and $\frac{3}{4}$.

Step 1 The denominators of both fractions are the same, 4. Use fraction circles divided into fourths to model the fractions.

Step 2 Shade 1 part of the first circle to show $\frac{1}{4}$.

Shade 3 parts of the second circle to show $\frac{3}{4}$.

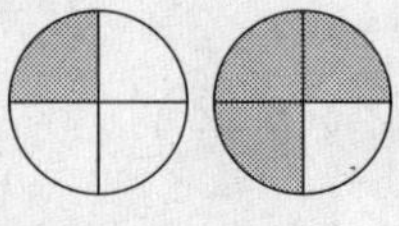

Step 3 Compare. 3 parts is more than 1 part.

$\frac{3}{4} > \frac{1}{4}$

So, the pizza has more ham.

Compare. Write <, >, or =.

1.

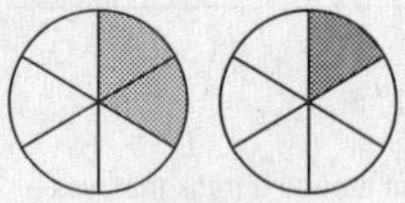

$\frac{2}{6} > \frac{1}{6}$

2.

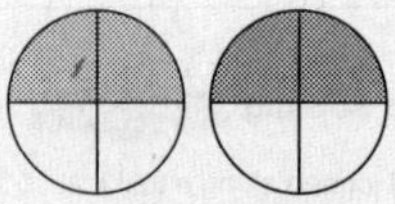

$\frac{2}{4} = \frac{2}{4}$

3. $\frac{1}{3} < \frac{2}{3}$

4. $\frac{5}{8} > \frac{3}{8}$

5. $\frac{1}{4} < \frac{3}{4}$

6. $\frac{4}{8} = \frac{4}{8}$

Name ____________ **Lesson 67**

CC.3.NF.3d

1. Dan and David are on the track team. Dan runs $\frac{1}{4}$ mile each day. David runs $\frac{3}{4}$ mile each day. Which statement is correct?

   (A) David runs farther than Dan each day.

   (B) David runs more than 1 mile each day.

   (C) David runs the same distance as Dan each day.

   (D) Dan runs farther than David each day.

2. Isabel and Raul are playing a game with fraction circles. Which statement is correct?

   (A) $\frac{1}{3} > \frac{2}{3}$ (C) $\frac{2}{3} < \frac{1}{3}$

   (B) $\frac{2}{3} = \frac{1}{3}$ **(D) $\frac{2}{3} > \frac{1}{3}$**

3. Chun lives $\frac{3}{8}$ mile from the library. Gail lives $\frac{5}{8}$ mile from the library. Which statement is correct?

   (A) Chun lives more than 1 mile from the library.

   (B) Chun lives farther from the library than Gail.

   (C) Gail lives farther from the library than Chun.

   (D) Gail and Chun live the same distance from the library.

4. Students are making quilt squares. They want $\frac{2}{6}$ of the quilt squares to be red and $\frac{4}{6}$ of the quilt squares to be white. Which statement correctly compares the fractions?

   (A) $\frac{2}{6} = \frac{4}{6}$ (C) $\frac{4}{6} < \frac{2}{6}$

   (B) $\frac{2}{6} < \frac{4}{6}$ (D) $\frac{2}{6} > \frac{4}{6}$

5. Kevin and Trevor each have a small pizza. Kevin eats $\frac{5}{6}$ of his pizza and Trevor eats $\frac{4}{6}$ of his pizza. Who eats the lesser amount? Explain how to use fraction circles to compare the fractions.

   Trevor; Possible explanation: I would use 2 fraction circles divided into sixths. 4 shaded parts is less than 5, so Trevor eats less pizza than Kevin.

Name ____________ **Lesson 68**

COMMON CORE STANDARD CC.3.NF.3d

Lesson Objective: Compare fractions with the same numerator by using models and reasoning strategies.

Compare Fractions with the Same Numerator

Ryan takes a survey of his class. $\frac{1}{8}$ of the class has dogs, and $\frac{1}{3}$ of the class has cats. Are there more dog owners or cat owners in Ryan's class?

Compare the fractions. $\frac{1}{8}$ ● $\frac{1}{3}$

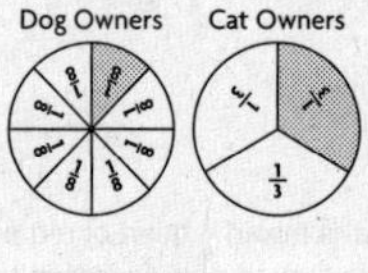

Step 1 Divide the first circle into 8 equal parts. Shade $\frac{1}{8}$ of the circle to show dog owners.

Step 2 Divide the second circle into 3 equal parts. Shade $\frac{1}{3}$ of the circle to show cat owners.

Step 3 Compare the shaded parts of the circles. Which shaded part is larger?

$\frac{1}{3}$ is larger than $\frac{1}{8}$. $\frac{1}{8} < \frac{1}{3}$

So, there are more cat owners than dog owners in Ryan's class.

Compare. Write <, >, or =.

1. $\frac{3}{4} > \frac{3}{6}$
2. $\frac{1}{8} < \frac{1}{6}$
3. $\frac{2}{4} > \frac{2}{6}$
4. $\frac{2}{3} > \frac{2}{6}$
5. $\frac{4}{6} > \frac{4}{8}$
6. $\frac{2}{8} < \frac{2}{4}$
7. $\frac{5}{6} > \frac{5}{8}$
8. $\frac{1}{3} > \frac{1}{4}$
9. $\frac{3}{6} < \frac{3}{4}$
10. $\frac{1}{3} = \frac{1}{3}$
11. $\frac{3}{3} > \frac{3}{4}$
12. $\frac{2}{4} < \frac{2}{6}$

Name ____________ **Lesson 68**

CC.3.NF.3d

1. Jenna ate $\frac{1}{8}$ of one pizza. Mark ate $\frac{1}{6}$ of another pizza. The pizzas are the same size. Which statement correctly compares the amount of pizza that was eaten?

   (A) $\frac{1}{6} < \frac{1}{8}$ (C) $\frac{1}{8} > \frac{1}{6}$

   (B) $\frac{1}{8} = \frac{1}{6}$ **(D) $\frac{1}{8} < \frac{1}{6}$**

2. Jacob and Ella are reading the same book. Jacob read $\frac{5}{8}$ of the book. Ella read $\frac{5}{6}$ of the book. Which statement is correct?

   (A) Jacob read more of the book than Ella.

   (B) Ella read less of the book than Jacob.

   (C) Jacob read less of the book than Ella.

   (D) Ella and Jacob read the same amount of the book.

3. In a survey, $\frac{1}{3}$ of the students chose soccer as their favorite sport and $\frac{1}{4}$ chose basketball. Which statement correctly compares the fractions?

   (A) $\frac{1}{3} < \frac{1}{4}$ **(C) $\frac{1}{3} > \frac{1}{4}$**

   (B) $\frac{1}{3} = \frac{1}{4}$ (D) $\frac{1}{4} > \frac{1}{3}$

4. Maria put $\frac{3}{4}$ yard of fringe around the pillow she made. Nancy put $\frac{3}{8}$ yard of fringe around her pillow. Which statement correctly compares the fractions?

   (A) $\frac{3}{4} > \frac{3}{8}$

   (B) $\frac{3}{4} < \frac{3}{8}$

   (C) $\frac{3}{4} = \frac{3}{8}$

   (D) $\frac{3}{8} > \frac{3}{4}$

Problem Solving REAL WORLD

5. Javier is buying food in the lunch line. The tray of salad plates is $\frac{3}{8}$ full. The tray of fruit plates is $\frac{3}{4}$ full. Which tray is more full?

   the fruit plate tray

6. Rachel bought some buttons. Of the buttons, $\frac{2}{4}$ are yellow and $\frac{2}{8}$ are red. Rachel bought more of which color buttons?

   yellow

Name ____________________ **Lesson 69**

COMMON CORE STANDARD CC.3.NF.3d

Lesson Objective: Compare fractions by using models and strategies involving the size of the pieces in the whole.

Compare Fractions

Mrs. Brown's recipe uses $\frac{2}{3}$ cup of flour. Mrs. Young's recipe uses $\frac{3}{4}$ cup of flour. Which recipe uses more flour?

Compare $\frac{2}{3}$ and $\frac{3}{4}$.

- You can compare fractions using fraction strips.

Step 1 Model each fraction.

Step 2 Compare the lengths of the models. The length of the $\frac{3}{4}$ model is greater than the length of the $\frac{2}{3}$ model.

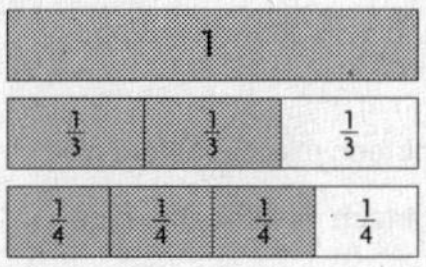

$\frac{3}{4} > \frac{2}{3}$

So, Mrs. Young's recipe uses more flour.

Compare $\frac{3}{6}$ and $\frac{4}{6}$. Which is greater?

- The denominators are the same, so compare the numerators.

$3 < 4$, so $\frac{3}{6} < \frac{4}{6}$.

So, $\frac{4}{6}$ is greater than $\frac{3}{6}$. $\frac{4}{6} > \frac{3}{6}$

Compare. Write <, >, or =. Write the strategy you used.

Possible strategies are given.

1. $\frac{2}{8} < \frac{3}{8}$ same denominator
2. $\frac{7}{8} > \frac{5}{6}$ missing pieces
3. $\frac{3}{4} > \frac{3}{6}$ same numerator
4. $\frac{3}{6} < \frac{5}{6}$ same denominator

Name ____________________ **Lesson 69**

CC.3.NF.3d

1. Floyd caught a fish that weighed $\frac{3}{4}$ pound. Kevin caught a fish that weighed $\frac{2}{3}$ pound. Which statement is correct?
   - **(A) $\frac{3}{4} > \frac{2}{3}$**
   - (B) $\frac{3}{4} < \frac{2}{3}$
   - (C) $\frac{2}{3} = \frac{3}{4}$
   - (D) $\frac{2}{3} > \frac{3}{4}$

2. There are two nature walks around the park. One trail is $\frac{7}{8}$ mile long. The other trail is $\frac{4}{8}$ mile long. Which statement is correct?
   - (A) $\frac{7}{8} < \frac{4}{8}$
   - (B) $\frac{7}{8} = \frac{4}{8}$
   - **(C) $\frac{4}{8} < \frac{7}{8}$**
   - (D) $\frac{4}{8} > \frac{7}{8}$

3. Olga is making play dough. She starts by mixing $\frac{1}{8}$ cup of salt with $\frac{1}{3}$ cup of water. Which statement is correct?
   - (A) $\frac{1}{8} = \frac{1}{3}$
   - **(B) $\frac{1}{8} < \frac{1}{3}$**
   - (C) $\frac{1}{8} > \frac{1}{3}$
   - (D) $\frac{1}{3} < \frac{1}{8}$

4. Kyle and Kelly planted seedlings. Kyle's plant is $\frac{5}{6}$ inch tall. Kelly's plant is $\frac{5}{8}$ inch tall. Which statement is correct?
   - (A) $\frac{5}{8} > \frac{5}{6}$
   - (B) $\frac{5}{8} = \frac{5}{6}$
   - (C) $\frac{5}{6} < \frac{5}{8}$
   - **(D) $\frac{5}{6} > \frac{5}{8}$**

Problem Solving REAL WORLD

5. At the third-grade party, two groups each had their own pizza. The blue group ate $\frac{7}{8}$ pizza. The green group ate $\frac{2}{8}$ pizza. Which group ate more of their pizza?

   the blue group

6. Ben and Antonio both take the same bus to school. Ben's ride is $\frac{7}{8}$ mile. Antonio's ride is $\frac{3}{4}$ mile. Who has a longer bus ride?

   Ben

Name ____________________ **Lesson 70**

COMMON CORE STANDARD CC.3.NF.3d

Lesson Objective: Compare and order fractions by using models and reasoning strategies.

Compare and Order Fractions

You can use a number line to compare and order fractions.

Order $\frac{5}{8}$, $\frac{2}{8}$, and $\frac{7}{8}$ from least to greatest.

Since you are comparing eighths, use a number line divided into eighths.

Step 1 Draw a point on the number line to show $\frac{5}{8}$.

Step 2 Repeat for $\frac{2}{8}$ and $\frac{7}{8}$.

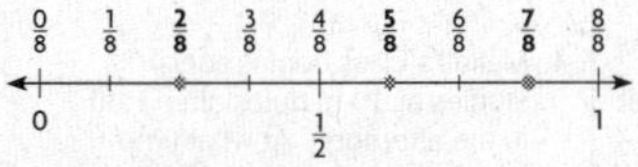

Step 3 Fractions increase in size as you move right on the number line. Write the fractions in order from left to right.

So, the order from least to greatest is $\frac{2}{8}$, $\frac{5}{8}$, $\frac{7}{8}$.

Write the fractions in order from least to greatest.

1. $\frac{4}{6}$ $\frac{6}{6}$ $\frac{3}{6}$

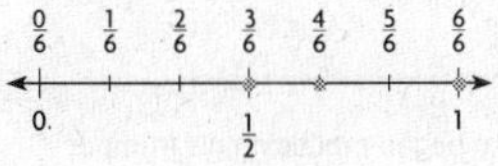

   $\frac{3}{6}$, $\frac{4}{6}$, $\frac{6}{6}$

2. $\frac{2}{3}$ $\frac{2}{6}$ $\frac{2}{4}$

   Think: When the numerators are the same, look at the denominators to compare the size of the pieces.

   $\frac{2}{6}$, $\frac{2}{4}$, $\frac{2}{3}$

3. $\frac{1}{4}$ $\frac{1}{8}$ $\frac{1}{2}$

   $\frac{1}{8}$, $\frac{1}{4}$, $\frac{1}{2}$

4. $\frac{3}{4}$ $\frac{0}{4}$ $\frac{2}{4}$

   $\frac{0}{4}$, $\frac{2}{4}$, $\frac{3}{4}$

Name ____________________ **Lesson 70**

CC.3.NF.3d

1. Pat, Elina, and Mike are meeting at the library. Pat lives $\frac{3}{4}$ mile from the library. Elina lives $\frac{1}{4}$ mile from the library. Mike lives $\frac{2}{4}$ mile from the library. Which list orders the fractions from **least** to **greatest**?
   - (A) $\frac{2}{4}, \frac{1}{4}, \frac{3}{4}$
   - (B) $\frac{1}{4}, \frac{3}{4}, \frac{2}{4}$
   - **(C) $\frac{1}{4}, \frac{2}{4}, \frac{3}{4}$**
   - (D) $\frac{3}{4}, \frac{2}{4}, \frac{1}{4}$

2. Ming is painting a picture. He has $\frac{2}{3}$ pint of red paint, $\frac{2}{8}$ pint of yellow paint, and $\frac{2}{6}$ pint of green paint. Which list orders the fractions from **greatest** to **least**?
   - (A) $\frac{2}{3}, \frac{2}{8}, \frac{2}{6}$
   - **(B) $\frac{2}{3}, \frac{2}{6}, \frac{2}{8}$**
   - (C) $\frac{2}{8}, \frac{2}{6}, \frac{2}{3}$
   - (D) $\frac{2}{6}, \frac{2}{3}, \frac{2}{8}$

3. Brian is making coconut bars. He needs $\frac{1}{3}$ cup coconut flakes, $\frac{1}{4}$ cup milk, and $\frac{1}{2}$ cup flour. Which list orders the fractions from **least** to **greatest**?
   - **(A) $\frac{1}{4}, \frac{1}{3}, \frac{1}{2}$**
   - (B) $\frac{1}{2}, \frac{1}{3}, \frac{1}{4}$
   - (C) $\frac{1}{4}, \frac{1}{2}, \frac{1}{3}$
   - (D) $\frac{1}{3}, \frac{1}{4}, \frac{1}{2}$

4. Cora measures the heights of three plants. The first plant is $\frac{4}{4}$ foot tall. The second plant is $\frac{4}{8}$ foot tall. The third plant is $\frac{4}{6}$ foot tall. Which list orders the fractions from **greatest** to **least**?
   - **(A) $\frac{4}{4}, \frac{4}{6}, \frac{4}{8}$**
   - (B) $\frac{4}{6}, \frac{4}{8}, \frac{4}{4}$
   - (C) $\frac{4}{8}, \frac{4}{6}, \frac{4}{4}$
   - (D) $\frac{4}{4}, \frac{4}{8}, \frac{4}{6}$

Problem Solving REAL WORLD

5. Mr. Jackson ran $\frac{7}{8}$ mile on Monday. He ran $\frac{3}{8}$ mile on Wednesday and $\frac{5}{8}$ mile on Friday. On which day did Mr. Jackson run the shortest distance?

   Wednesday

6. Delia has three pieces of ribbon. Her red ribbon is $\frac{2}{4}$ foot long. Her green ribbon is $\frac{2}{3}$ foot long. Her yellow ribbon is $\frac{2}{6}$ foot long. She wants to use the longest piece for a project. Which color ribbon should Delia use?

   green

Answer Key

Name ______________ **Lesson 71**

COMMON CORE STANDARD CC.3.MD.1

Lesson Objective: Read, write, and tell time on analog and digital clocks to the nearest minute.

Time to the Minute

Tommy wants to know what time the clock shows. He also wants to know one way to write the time.

Step 1 Where is the hour hand pointing? What is the hour?
It points just after the 6, so the hour is 6.

Step 2 Where is the minute hand pointing?
It points just after the 3.

Count the minutes. Count zero at the 12. Count on by fives: 5, 10, 15.

Then count on by ones: 16, 17.

So, the time is 6:17, or seventeen minutes after six.

Write the time. Write one way you can read the time. Possible answers are given.

1. 
4:16; sixteen minutes after four

2. 
8:51; nine minutes before nine

3. 
5:50; ten minutes before six

4. 
6:22; twenty-two minutes after six

Name ______________ **Lesson 71**

CC.3.MD.1

1. Brad looked at the clock on his way to football practice.

What time is shown on Brad's clock?

Ⓐ thirteen minutes before nine
Ⓑ thirteen minutes after nine
Ⓒ nine forty-five
Ⓓ thirteen minutes before ten

2. Sarah looked at her watch before she began mowing the grass. The hour hand was between the 9 and the 10. The minute hand was on the 7. At what time did Sarah begin mowing the grass?

Ⓐ 7:09 Ⓒ 9:07
Ⓑ 7:10 **Ⓓ** 9:35

3. Chris looked at his watch before he began raking the leaves. The hour hand was between the 10 and the 11. The minute hand was on the 5. At what time did Chris begin raking the leaves?

Ⓐ 10:25 Ⓒ 5:11
Ⓑ 10:05 Ⓓ 5:10

4. Jillian checked the clock before she began piano practice.

What time is shown on Jillian's clock?

Ⓐ four twenty-five
Ⓑ twenty-seven minutes after four
Ⓒ three minutes before five
Ⓓ twenty-seven minutes before five

Problem Solving REAL WORLD

5. What time is it when the hour hand is a little past the 3 and the minute hand is pointing to the 3?
3:15

6. Pete began practicing at twenty-five minutes before eight. What is another way to write this time?
7:35

Name ______________ **Lesson 72**

COMMON CORE STANDARD CC.3.MD.1

Lesson Objective: Decide when to use A.M. and P.M. when telling time to the nearest minute.

A.M. and P.M.

Lori and her father went shopping at the time shown on the clock at the right. How should Lori write the time?
Use A.M. or P.M.

Step 1 Read the time on the clock. 11:30

Step 2 Decide if the time is A.M. or P.M.

Write P.M. for times after noon and before midnight.

Write A.M. for times after midnight and before noon.

Think: Most people go shopping during the day.

So, Lori should write the time as 11:30 A.M.

REMEMBER

Noon is 12:00 in the daytime.

Midnight is 12:00 at night.

Write the time for the activity. Use A.M. or P.M.

1. leave school

2:35 P.M.

2. eat dinner

5:30 P.M.

3. arrive at school

8:20 A.M.

4. Mackenzie's violin lesson starts at the time shown on the clock. Write the time using A.M. or P.M.

4:05 P.M.

5. The diner opens for breakfast at the time shown on the clock. Write the time using A.M. or P.M.

6:30 A.M.

Name ______________ **Lesson 72**

CC.3.MD.1

1. Keisha is eating dinner at quarter after 6:00. At what time is Keisha eating dinner?

Ⓐ 5:45 A.M.
Ⓑ 6:15 A.M.
Ⓒ 5:45 P.M.
Ⓓ 6:15 P.M.

2. Terry went fishing at 6 minutes past 7:00 in the morning. At what time did Terry go fishing?

Ⓐ 6:07 A.M.
Ⓑ 7:06 A.M.
Ⓒ 6:07 P.M.
Ⓓ 7:06 P.M.

3. Ricardo wakes up at quarter to 7:00 in the morning. At what time does Ricardo wake up?

Ⓐ 6:45 A.M.
Ⓑ 7:15 A.M.
Ⓒ 6:45 P.M.
Ⓓ 7:15 P.M.

4. Makati's class begins social studies at 10 minutes after 1:00 in the afternoon. At what time does social studies begin?

Ⓐ 1:10 A.M.
Ⓑ 10:01 A.M.
Ⓒ 1:10 P.M.
Ⓓ 10:01 P.M.

Problem Solving REAL WORLD

5. Jaime is in math class. What time is it? Use A.M. or P.M.

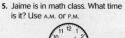

1:25 P.M.

6. Pete began practicing his trumpet at fifteen minutes past three. Write this time using A.M. or P.M.
3:15 P.M.

Name ______________________ **Lesson 73**

COMMON CORE STANDARD CC.3.MD.1

Lesson Objective: Use a number line or an analog clock to measure time intervals in minutes.

Measure Time Intervals

Julia starts her homework at 4:20 P.M. She finishes at 5:00 P.M. How much time does Julia spend doing homework?

Elapsed time is the amount of time that passes from the start of an activity to the end of the activity.

Use a number line to find elapsed time.

Step 1 Begin with the start time, 4:20.

Step 2 Skip count by tens to count the minutes from 4:20 to 5:00.

Step 3 Label the number line. Draw jumps for every 10 minutes until you get to 5:00.

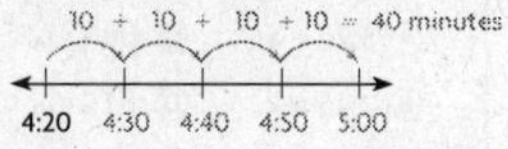

Step 4 Add the minutes that have elapsed. 40 minutes

So, Julia spends 40 minutes doing homework.

Use the number line to find the elapsed time.

Possible drawings and labels are given.

1. Start: 3:15 P.M. End: 3:45 P.M.

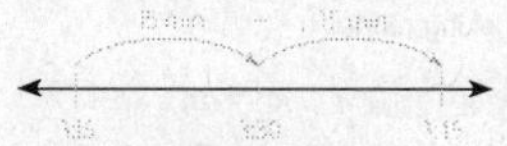

30 minutes

2. Start: 11:05 A.M. End: 11:56 A.M.

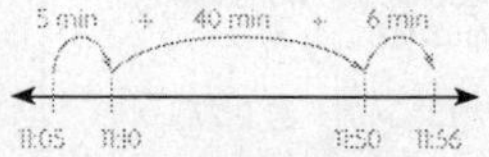

51 minutes

Find the elapsed time.

3. Start: 4:10 P.M. End: 4:46 P.M.

36 minutes

4. Start: 10:30 A.M. End: 10:59 A.M.

29 minutes

Name ______________________ **Lesson 73**

CC.3.MD.1

1. Arianna started reading her book at 11:20 A.M. and stopped reading her book at 11:43 A.M. For how long did Arianna read her book?
   - **(A) 23 minutes**
   - (B) 28 minutes
   - (C) 33 minutes
   - (D) 63 minutes

2. Hector left to take a walk at 6:25 P.M. He returned home at 6:51 P.M. How long was Hector's walk?
   - (A) 16 minutes
   - (B) 21 minutes
   - **(C) 26 minutes**
   - (D) 76 minutes

3. Victoria started her spelling homework at 4:25 P.M. and finished at 4:37 P.M. How long did it take Victoria to complete her spelling homework?
   - (A) 27 minutes
   - (B) 22 minutes
   - (C) 17 minutes
   - **(D) 12 minutes**

4. Cheung started playing basketball at 9:17 A.M. He stopped playing at 9:45 A.M. How long did Cheung play basketball?
   - **(A) 28 minutes**
   - (B) 32 minutes
   - (C) 38 minutes
   - (D) 42 minutes

Problem Solving REAL WORLD

5. A show at the museum starts at 7:40 P.M. and ends at 7:57 P.M. How long is the show?

17 minutes

6. The first train leaves the station at 6:15 A.M. The second train leaves at 6:55 A.M. How much later does the second train leave the station?

40 minutes later

Name ______________________ **Lesson 74**

COMMON CORE STANDARD CC.3.MD.1

Lesson Objective: Use a number line or an analog clock to add or subtract time intervals to find starting times or ending times.

Use Time Intervals

You can use a number line to find the starting time when you know the ending time and the elapsed time.

The ending time is 4:05 P.M. Use the number line to find the starting time if the elapsed time is 35 minutes.

Step 1	Step 2	Step 3
Find the ending time on the number line.	Jump back 5 minutes.	Jump back 30 minutes.
Think: The ending time is 4:05 P.M.	**Think:** Jump back 5 minutes to get to the hour.	**Think:** Jump back 30 minutes to get to a total of 35 minutes.
	You jump back to 4:00 P.M.	You jump back to 3:30 P.M.

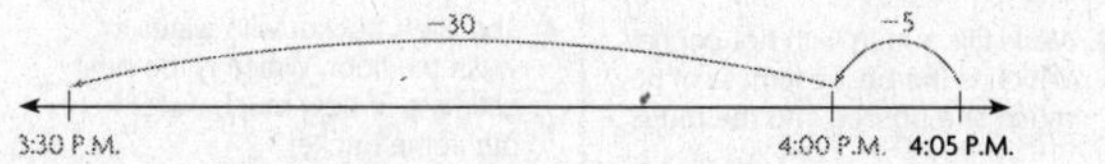

So, the starting time is 3:30 P.M.

Possible drawings and labels are given.

1. Use the number line to find the starting time if the elapsed time is 25 minutes. 1:50 A.M.

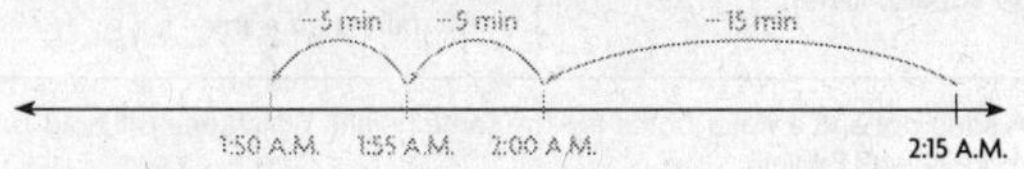

2. Use the number line to find the starting time if the elapsed time is 45 minutes. 5:15 P.M.

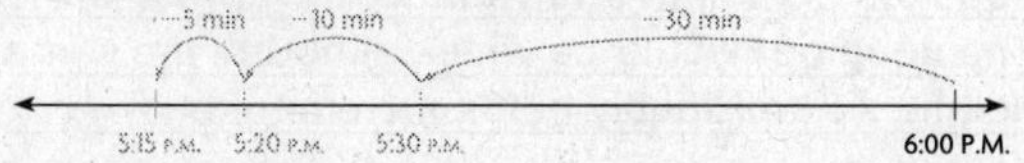

Name ______________________ **Lesson 74**

CC.3.MD.1

1. Jai's piano lesson started at 4:35 P.M. The lesson lasted 45 minutes. What time did Jai's piano lesson end?
   - (A) 3:50 P.M.
   - (B) 5:10 P.M.
   - **(C) 5:20 P.M.**
   - (D) 5:35 P.M.

2. Ky was at the skateboard park for 35 minutes. He left the park at 3:10 P.M. What time did Ky arrive at the skateboard park?
   - **(A) 2:35 P.M.**
   - (B) 2:40 P.M.
   - (C) 2:45 P.M.
   - (D) 3:45 P.M.

3. A batch of muffins needs to bake for 22 minutes. Wade puts the muffins in the oven at 10:17 A.M. At what time should Wade take the muffins out of the oven?
   - (A) 10:29 A.M.
   - **(B) 10:39 A.M.**
   - (C) 10:49 A.M.
   - (D) 10:55 A.M.

4. Yul's art class started at 11:25 A.M. The class lasted 30 minutes. At what time did Yul's art class end?
   - (A) 10:55 A.M.
   - (B) 11:35 A.M.
   - (C) 11:50 A.M.
   - **(D) 11:55 A.M.**

Problem Solving REAL WORLD

5. Jenny spent 35 minutes doing research on the Internet. She finished at 7:10 P.M. At what time did Jenny start her research?

6:35 P.M.

6. Clark left for school at 7:43 A.M. He got to school 36 minutes later. At what time did Clark get to school?

8:19 A.M.

Answer Key

Name ______________________

Lesson 75

COMMON CORE STANDARD CC.3.MD.1

Lesson Objective: Solve problems involving addition and subtraction of time intervals by using the strategy *draw a diagram.*

Problem Solving • Time Intervals

As soon as Carter got home, he worked on his book report for 45 minutes. Then he did chores for 30 minutes. He finished at 5:15 P.M. At what time did Carter get home?

Read the Problem	Solve the Problem
What do I need to find? I need to find what time Carter got home.	• Find Carter's 5:15 P.M. finishing time on the number line. • Count back 30 minutes using two 15-minute jumps to find the time Carter started his chores. 4:45 P.M.
What information do I need to use? Carter worked for 45 minutes on his report. He did chores for 30 minutes. He finished at 5:15 P.M..	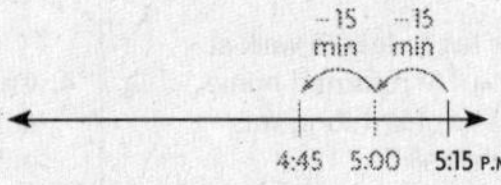
How will I use the information? I will use a number line and count back to find the time Carter got home.	• Count back 45 minutes for the time Carter worked on his report. The jumps end at 4:00 P.M.. 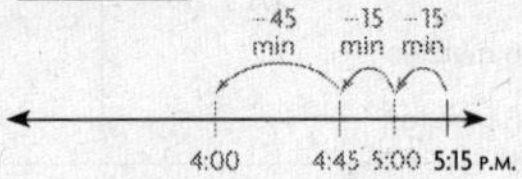 So, Carter got home at 4:00 P.M..

1. Kiera must be at school at 7:45 A.M. The ride to school takes 15 minutes. She needs 45 minutes to eat breakfast and get ready. At what time should Kiera get up?

   6:45 A.M.

2. Jack and his family go to the movies. First, they eat lunch at 1:30 P.M. It takes them 40 minutes to eat. Then they drive 25 minutes to get to the movie theater. At what time do Jack and his family get to the theater?

   2:35 P.M.

www.harcourtschoolsupply.com
© Houghton Mifflin Harcourt Publishing Company
149
Core Standards for Math, Grade 3

Name ______________________

Lesson 75

CC.3.MD.1

1. Omar rode his bike in the park for 45 minutes and rode in his neighborhood for 25 minutes. Omar stopped riding his bike at 4:40 P.M.

At what time did Omar start riding his bike?

Ⓐ 4:15 P.M.
Ⓑ 3:55 P.M.
Ⓒ 3:40 P.M.
Ⓓ 3:30 P.M. (answer)

2. Sophia folded laundry for 25 minutes. After folding laundry, she worked on a puzzle for 42 minutes. Sophia began folding laundry at 8:20 A.M. At what time did Sophia stop working on the puzzle?

Ⓐ 7:13 A.M.
Ⓑ 9:02 A.M.
Ⓒ 9:27 A.M. (answer)
Ⓓ 9:32 A.M.

3. Cheerleading practice started at 3:10 P.M. During practice, Dina practiced tumbling for 15 minutes. Then she practiced cheers for 35 minutes.

At what time did Dina's cheerleading practice end?

Ⓐ 3:25 P.M.
Ⓑ 3:45 P.M.
Ⓒ 4:00 P.M. (answer)
Ⓓ 4:15 P.M.

4. Mr. Carver spent 45 minutes making dinner. Then, he spent 18 minutes eating dinner. He finished eating at 6:15 P.M. At what time did Mr. Carver start making dinner?

Ⓐ 5:12 P.M. (answer)
Ⓑ 5:22 P.M.
Ⓒ 5:30 P.M.
Ⓓ 6:12 P.M.

5. Karl did his chores for 25 minutes. Then he read for 15 minutes. He finished reading at 5:20 P.M. Explain how you can find the time he began his chores.

   Possible explanation: I can combine 25 and 15 minutes, which is 40 minutes in all. Then I count backward on a clock 40 minutes, which is 20 minutes before 5:00 or 4:40 P.M.

www.harcourtschoolsupply.com
© Houghton Mifflin Harcourt Publishing Company
150
Core Standards for Math, Grade 3

Name ______________________

Lesson 76

COMMON CORE STANDARD CC.3.MD.2

Lesson Objective: Estimate and measure liquid volume in liters.

Estimate and Measure Liquid Volume

Liquid volume is the amount of liquid in a container. You can measure liquid volume using the metric unit **liter** (L).

A water bottle holds about 1 liter. Estimate how much liquid a plastic cup and a fish bowl will hold. Then write the containers in order from the greatest to least liquid volume.

A plastic cup holds less than 1 liter.

A water bottle holds about 1 liter.

A fish bowl holds more than 1 liter.

Think: A plastic cup is *smaller* than a water bottle.

Think: A fish bowl is *larger* than a water bottle.

So, the order of the containers from greatest to least liquid volume is fish bowl, water bottle, plastic cup.

1. A wading pool is filled with water. Is the amount *more than 1 liter, about 1 liter,* or *less than 1 liter?*

   more than 1 liter

Estimate how much liquid volume there will be when the container is filled. Write *more than 1 liter, about 1 liter,* or *less than 1 liter.*

2. vase

   about 1 liter

3. mug

   less than 1 liter

4. bathtub

   more than 1 liter

www.harcourtschoolsupply.com
© Houghton Mifflin Harcourt Publishing Company
151
Core Standards for Math, Grade 3

Name ______________________

Lesson 76

CC.3.MD.2

1. There are four bottles of punch on a shelf. The bottles are all the same size. Which bottle has the least amount of punch?

Q R S T

Ⓐ Bottle Q
Ⓑ Bottle R (answer)
Ⓒ Bottle S
Ⓓ Bottle T

2. Meiki fills a mug with hot cocoa. Which is the best estimate of how much she poured into the mug?

Ⓐ about 1 liter
Ⓑ less than 1 liter (answer)
Ⓒ more than 1 liter
Ⓓ about 5 liters

3. There are four bottles of juice on the counter. The bottles are all the same size. Which bottle has the greatest amount of juice?

A B C D

Ⓐ Bottle A (answer)
Ⓑ Bottle B
Ⓒ Bottle C
Ⓓ Bottle D

4. Jed fills a bucket with water to wash the floor. Which is the best estimate of how much water he put in the bucket?

Ⓐ a lot less than a liter
Ⓑ a little less than a liter
Ⓒ about a liter
Ⓓ more than a liter (answer)

5. A soup pot and a water bottle are the same height. Which one will hold more liquid? Explain.

   soup pot; possible explanation: liquid volume depends on height and width of the container. The soup pot would be wider, although the same height, so it probably holds more liquid.

www.harcourtschoolsupply.com
© Houghton Mifflin Harcourt Publishing Company
152
Core Standards for Math, Grade 3

© Houghton Mifflin Harcourt Publishing Company

Answer Key

Name ____________ **Lesson 77**
COMMON CORE STANDARD CC.3.MD.2
Lesson Objective: Estimate and measure mass in grams and kilograms.

Estimate and Measure Mass

Mass is the amount of matter in an object. You can measure mass using the metric units **gram** (g) and **kilogram** (kg).

Should you use gram or kilogram to measure the mass of a penny?

The mass of one grape is about 1 gram.

The mass of a book is about 1 kilogram.

Think: The mass of a penny is closer to the mass of a grape than to the mass of a book. So, use grams to measure the mass of a penny.

You can use a pan balance to compare the masses of an eraser and a stapler.

Think: The pan with the stapler is lower.

So, the mass of a stapler is more than the mass of an eraser.

Choose the unit you would use to measure the mass. Write *gram* or *kilogram*.

1. cherry

gram

2. cat

kilogram

3. pencil
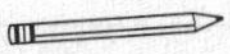
gram

4. Compare the masses of the objects. Write *is less than, is the same as,* or *is more than.*

The mass of the pencil is less than the mass of the apple.

Name ____________ **Lesson 77**
CC.3.MD.2

1. Ling uses grams to measure the mass of an object in her room. Which object would be **best** measured using grams?

Ⓐ (circled)

Ⓑ

Ⓒ

Ⓓ

2. Kylie wants to find the mass of a pair of her sneakers. Which unit should she use?

Ⓐ liter Ⓒ inch
Ⓑ kilogram (circled) Ⓓ gram

3. Jason uses a balance to compare the masses of the objects shown. What is true about the objects?

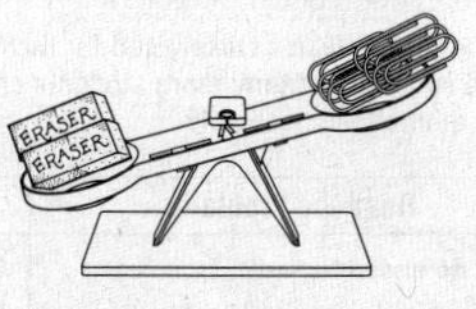

Ⓐ The mass of the erasers is the same as the mass of the paper clips.
Ⓑ The mass of the erasers is less than the mass of the paper clips.
Ⓒ The mass of the paper clips is less than the mass of the erasers. (circled)
Ⓓ The mass of the paper clips is greater than the mass of the erasers.

Problem Solving REAL WORLD

4. A red ball has a mass that is less than 1 kilogram. A blue ball has a mass of 1 kilogram. Is the mass of the blue ball more than or less than the mass of the red ball?

more than

5. Brock's dog is a collie. To find the mass of his dog, should Brock use *grams* or *kilograms*?

kilograms

Name ____________ **Lesson 78**
COMMON CORE STANDARD CC.3.MD.2
Lesson Objective: Add, subtract, multiply, or divide to solve problems involving liquid volumes or masses.

Solve Problems About Liquid Volume and Mass

You can use a model or write an equation to solve problems about liquid volume and mass.

Tina's watering can holds 4 liters of water. Todd's watering can holds 6 liters of water. What is the total liquid volume of both watering cans?

Tina's Watering Can

Todd's Watering Can

Use a bar model.

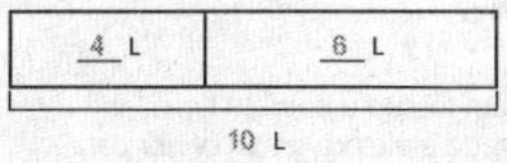

Think: Add to find the total.

4 L + 6 L = 10 L

So, the total liquid volume is 10 L.

Write an equation.

Think: I can write an addition equation to find the sum of the liquid volumes.

4 ⊕ 6 = 10

So, the total liquid volume is 10 L.

Write an equation and solve the problem.

1. Kyra has a small bucket that holds 3 liters of water and a large bucket that holds 5 liters of water. Altogether, how many liters of water do the two buckets hold?

3 ⊕ 5 = 8 8 liters

2. Rick's recipe calls for 25 grams of raisins and 40 grams of nuts. How many more grams of nuts than raisins does the recipe call for?

40 ⊖ 25 = 15 15 grams

Name ____________ **Lesson 78**
CC.3.MD.2

1. Bryce has a container completely filled with 13 liters of water. Ben has a container completely filled with 8 liters of water. What is the total liquid volume of the containers?

Ⓐ 5 liters Ⓒ 21 liters (circled)
Ⓑ 11 liters Ⓓ 24 liters

2. An online company shipped three packages. The packages had masses of 8 kilograms, 15 kilograms, and 9 kilograms. What is the total mass of the three packages?

Ⓐ 23 kilograms
Ⓑ 24 kilograms
Ⓒ 32 kilograms (circled)
Ⓓ 34 kilograms

3. Mama's Restaurant sold a total of 15 liters of orange juice in 3 hours. The same amount of orange juice was sold each hour. How many liters of orange juice were sold each hour?

Ⓐ 5 liters (circled) Ⓒ 18 liters
Ⓑ 12 liters Ⓓ 45 liters

4. Simon pours 19 liters of water into one bucket and 15 liters of water into another bucket. Each bucket is filled completely. What is the total liquid volume of the two buckets?

Ⓐ 4 liters
Ⓑ 14 liters
Ⓒ 24 liters
Ⓓ 34 liters (circled)

Problem Solving REAL WORLD

5. Zoe's fish tank holds 27 liters of water. She uses a 3-liter container to fill the tank. How many times does she have to fill the 3-liter container in order to fill her fish tank?

9 times

6. Adrian's backpack has a mass of 15 kilograms. Theresa's backpack has a mass of 8 kilograms. What is the total mass of both backpacks?

23 kilograms

Answer Key

Name ______________________ **Lesson 79**
COMMON CORE STANDARD CC.3.MD.3
Lesson Objective: Organize data in tables and solve problems using the strategy *make a table.*

Problem Solving • Organize Data

One way to show data is in a tally table. Another way to show data is in a frequency table. A **frequency table** uses numbers to record data.

The students in Jake's class voted for their favorite sport. How many more students chose soccer than chose baseball?

Favorite Sport

Sport	Tally
Soccer	卌 ||||
Baseball	卌 |
Football	||||

Read the Problem	Solve the Problem
What do I need to find? How many more students chose soccer than chose baseball?	Count the tally marks for each sport. Write the numbers in the frequency table.
What information do I need to use? the data about favorite sport from the tally table	**Think:** | = 1 vote; 卌 = 5 votes. Soccer has 1 卌 and 4 |, so write 9 in the frequency table.
How will I use the information? I will count the tally marks. Then I will write the number of tally marks for each sport in the frequency table. Next, I will subtract to compare the votes for soccer and the votes for baseball.	Subtract to find how many more students chose soccer than chose baseball. 9 − 6 = 3. So, 3 more students chose soccer than chose baseball as their favorite sport.

Favorite Sport

Sport	Number
Soccer	9
Baseball	6
Football	4

1. How many students chose football and baseball combined?
   10 students
2. How many fewer students chose football than chose soccer?
   5 fewer students

Name ______________________ **Lesson 79**
CC.3.MD.3

Use the table for 1–2.

Mike asked people what season they liked best. The tally table shows the results.

Favorite Season

Winter	卌 |||
Spring	卌 卌 |
Summer	||||
Fall	卌

1. How many people chose Winter or Summer?
   Ⓐ 4 Ⓒ 11
   Ⓑ 10 **Ⓓ 12**
2. How many **more** students chose Spring than Fall?
   Ⓐ 4 **Ⓒ 6**
   Ⓑ 5 Ⓓ 11

Use the table for 3–4.

Rory and his classmates voted for a favorite class activity. They organized the data in a tally table.

Favorite Class Activity

Science Fair	卌 卌
Bake Sale	||||
Fitness Fun Day	卌 卌 ||
Class Play	卌 ||||

3. How many students chose the Science Fair or Fitness Fun Day?
   Ⓐ 6 Ⓒ 20
   Ⓑ 12 **Ⓓ 22**
4. How many **fewer** students chose a Bake Sale than Fitness Fun Day?
   Ⓐ 4 Ⓒ 10
   Ⓑ 8 Ⓓ 12

5. Dan asked 24 members of his class how they traveled to their last vacation spot. The frequency table shows the results. Complete the table and explain how you did it.

Travel Vehicle

	Boys	Girls
Car	4	4
Airplane	6	5
Bus	2	3

I added the numbers in the table for both girls and boys. I subtracted the total, 20, from 24, and wrote 4 in the blank box.

Name ______________________ **Lesson 80**
COMMON CORE STANDARD CC.3.MD.3
Lesson Objective: Read and interpret data in a scaled picture graph.

Use Picture Graphs

A **picture graph** shows information using small pictures or symbols.

A **key** tells what the symbol stands for. A symbol can stand for more than 1.

Which state in the picture graph below has 9 national park areas?

The key for the picture graph shows that each = 6 national park areas.

Count the number of next to each state.

Oregon has one tree picture and half of a tree picture.

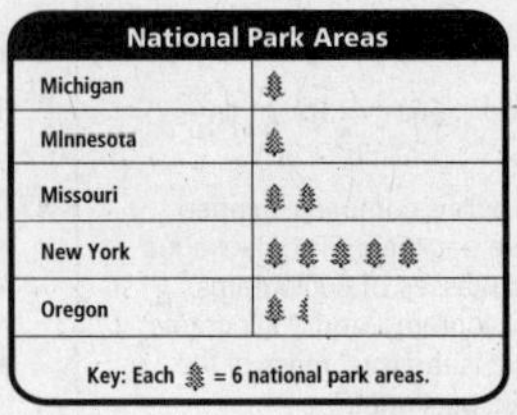

Think:
= 6 park areas
= 3 park areas

So, Oregon has 9 national park areas.

Use the Favorite Ice Pop Flavor picture graph for 1–4.

1. How many people chose orange?
   6 people
2. How many people chose lemon?
   5 people
3. How many fewer people chose lemon than chose strawberry?
   4 fewer people
4. How many people in all were surveyed?
   26 people

Name ______________________ **Lesson 80**
CC.3.MD.3

1. Ms. Sanchez's class took pictures of a lighthouse during a field trip. The picture graph shows how many pictures each student took.

How many pictures were taken in all?
Ⓐ 28 Ⓒ 52
Ⓑ 32 **Ⓓ 56**

2. The picture graph shows the number of bottles Mr. Tao's class recycled each week for an Earth Day project.

How many bottles were recycled during Week 2 and Week 3?
Ⓐ 9 **Ⓒ 85**
Ⓑ 14 Ⓓ 140

3. Mrs. Hampton's class made a picture graph to show the type of material used to make each picture at an art show.

How many **fewer** pictures were made with crayon than with paint?
Ⓐ 4 Ⓒ 9
Ⓑ 5 Ⓓ 12

4. Pam tossed a coin 20 times and made a picture graph of her data.

Coin Toss Results

Heads	○ ○ ○ ○
Tails	○ ○ ○ ○ ○ ○

Key: Each ○ = 2 coin tosses.

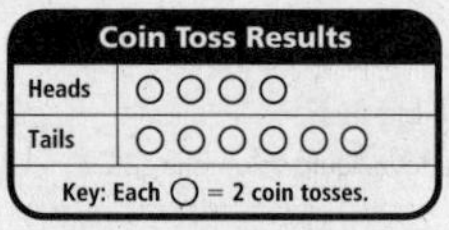

Explain how the picture graph would be different if each circle represented 4 coin tosses.

There would be 2 circles for Heads and 3 circles for Tails. The key would show that a circle represents 4 tosses instead of 2 tosses.

Name ________________________ **Lesson 81**

COMMON CORE STANDARD CC.3.MD.3

Lesson Objective: Draw a scaled picture graph to show data in a table.

Make Picture Graphs

Use the data in this table to make a picture graph.

Number of Ball Caps Sold

Basketball Game	Caps
Falcons and Mustangs	20
Sharks and Bulldogs	30
Hawks and Comets	5
Rams and Cardinals	15

Step 1 Write the title.

Step 2 Write the names of the games.

Step 3 Decide what number each picture will represent. You can count by fives to find the number of caps sold, so let each cap represent 5 caps.

Step 4 Draw one cap for every 5 caps sold during each game. There were 20 caps sold during the Falcons and Mustangs game. Count to 20 by fives. 5, 10, 15, 20. So, 4 caps should be drawn. Draw the caps for the rest of the games.

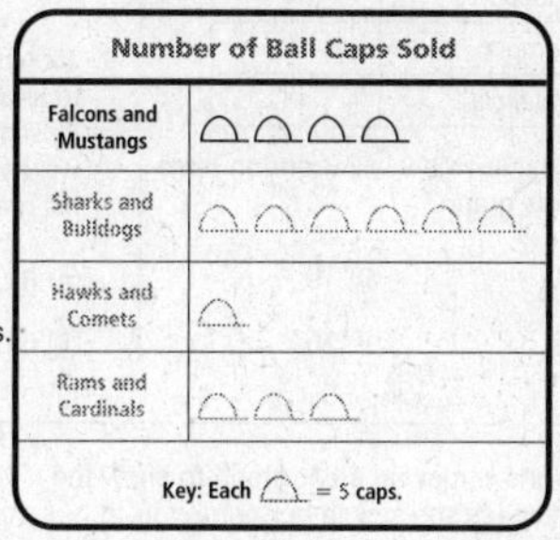

Number of Ball Caps Sold
Falcons and Mustangs
Sharks and Bulldogs
Hawks and Comets
Rams and Cardinals
Key: Each = 5 caps.

Use your picture graph above for 1–3.

1. During which game were the most ball caps sold?

   Sharks and Bulldogs

2. How many pictures would you draw if 45 ball caps were sold in a game?

   9 pictures

3. During which two games were a total of 25 caps sold?

   Falcons and Mustangs and Hawks and Comets

© Houghton Mifflin Harcourt Publishing Company

Name ________________________ **Lesson 81**

CC.3.MD.3

Use the table for 1–2.

Kim did a survey to learn which pet her classmates liked best. She wrote the results in a table and will use the data to make a picture graph with a key of ☺ = 3 students.

Favorite Pet

Kind of Pet	Number of Students
Goldfish	12
Bird	15

1. How many ☺ will Kim draw for Goldfish?

   Ⓐ 2 Ⓑ 3 **Ⓒ 4** Ⓓ 5

2. How many ☺ will Kim draw for Birds?

   Ⓐ 2 Ⓑ 3 Ⓒ 4 **Ⓓ 5**

3. Jerel made a picture graph to show the number of sunny days his city had in June and July. This is the key to Jerel's picture graph.

   Key: Each ☀ = 10 days.

   How many sunny days do ☀☀☀☀ stand for?

   Ⓐ 3 Ⓑ 4 Ⓒ 30 **Ⓓ 35**

4. Jamie saw 24 red cars and 16 blue cars. She made a picture graph to show her results. If △ = 4 cars, how many △s show the number of blue cars she saw?

   Ⓐ 4 Ⓑ 5 Ⓒ 8 Ⓓ 16

5. Jeff took a survey about the snack his 26 classmates liked best. He used the data to begin making a picture graph. Complete Jeff's picture graph. Explain your work.

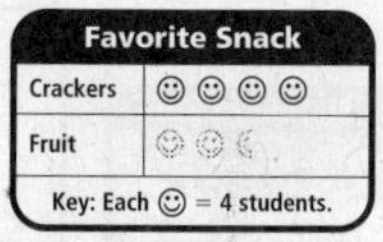

Possible answer: 16 students liked crackers. I subtracted 16 from 26 to find that 10 students liked fruit. I used the key and drew 2 ☺ and half of a ☺ in the fruit row.

© Houghton Mifflin Harcourt Publishing Company

Name ________________________ **Lesson 82**

COMMON CORE STANDARD CC.3.MD.3

Lesson Objective: Read and interpret data in a scaled bar graph.

Use Bar Graphs

How many Olympic medals did Norway win in the 2008 Summer Olympics?

- Both bar graphs show the same data about Olympic medals. The top graph is a **vertical bar graph**. The bottom graph is a **horizontal bar graph**.
- Find Norway on the vertical bar graph and follow the bar to its end. Then follow the end across to the scale to find the number of medals. 10 medals.
- Find Norway on the horizontal bar graph and follow the bar to its end. Then follow the end down to the scale to find the number of medals. 10 medals.

So, Norway won 10 medals.

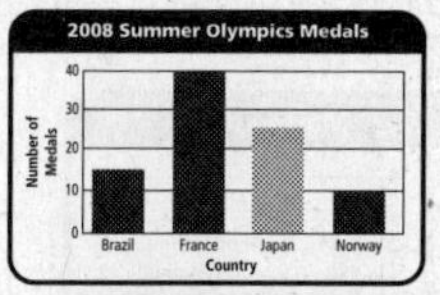

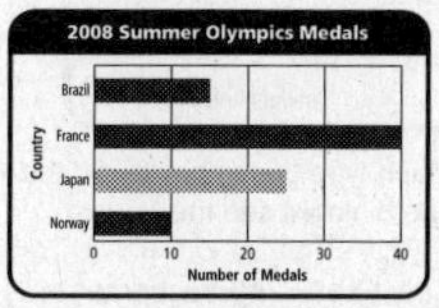

Use the Favorite Type of Book bar graph for 1–4.

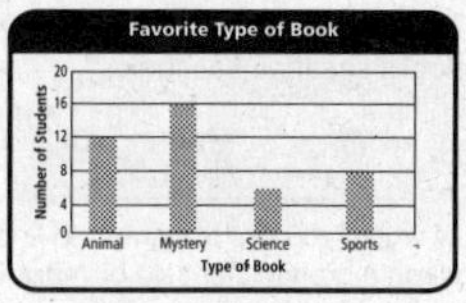

1. Which type of book did the most students choose?

   mystery

2. Which type of book received 4 fewer votes than mystery?

   animal

3. Did more students choose books about mystery or books about science and sports together?

   mystery

4. How many students in all answered the survey?

   42 students

© Houghton Mifflin Harcourt Publishing Company

Name ________________________ **Lesson 82**

CC.3.MD.3

Use the graph for 1–3.

Carrie asked people at the mall to choose a favorite type of music. The bar graph shows the results.

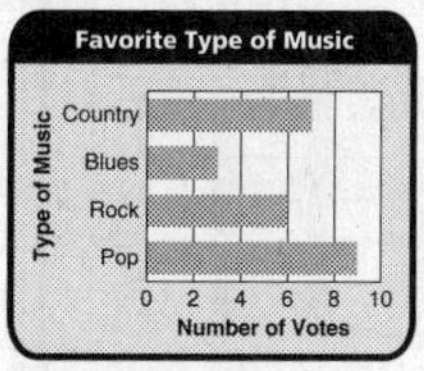

1. How many **more** people chose Rock than Blues?

   Ⓐ 2 **Ⓑ 3** Ⓒ 4 Ⓓ 9

2. How many people in all chose a type of music?

   Ⓐ 4 Ⓑ 16 Ⓒ 22 **Ⓓ 25**

3. How many **more** people would have to choose Blues to have the same number of people choose Blues and Country?

   Ⓐ 3 **Ⓑ 4** Ⓒ 6 Ⓓ 7

4. Diego made a graph to show how many butterflies he saw in his yard each day. How many **fewer** butterflies did Diego see on Tuesday than on the day that he saw the most butterflies? Explain how you used the graph to find the answer.

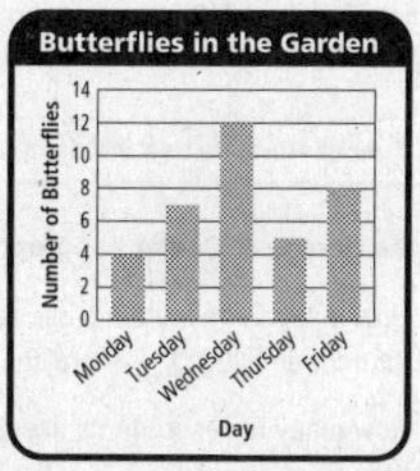

5 fewer; Sample explanation: the tallest bar, which is Wednesday, is the day he saw the most butterflies. The graph shows that he saw 7 butterflies on Tuesday and 12 butterflies on Wednesday. I subtracted 7 from 12 to find the answer.

© Houghton Mifflin Harcourt Publishing Company

© Houghton Mifflin Harcourt Publishing Company

Answer Key

Name ____________ **Lesson 83**
COMMON CORE STANDARD CC.3.MD.3
Lesson Objective: Draw a scaled bar graph to show data in a table or picture graph.

Make Bar Graphs

Use data in a table to make a bar graph.

Step 1 Write the title for the bar graph.

Step 2 Label the side and the bottom.

Step 3 Write the names of the sports.

Step 4 Choose a scale for your graph.

- The scale must be able to show the least number, 3, and the greatest number, 17.
- The numbers must be equally spaced. Start with 0 and count by twos until you reach 18.

Step 5 Draw the bar for ice skating. The bar will end halfway between 16 and 18 at 17.

Step 6 Then use the results in the table to draw the rest of the bars.

Favorite Winter Activity

Sport	Number of Votes
Ice Skating	17
Skiing	14
Sledding	12
Snowboarding	3

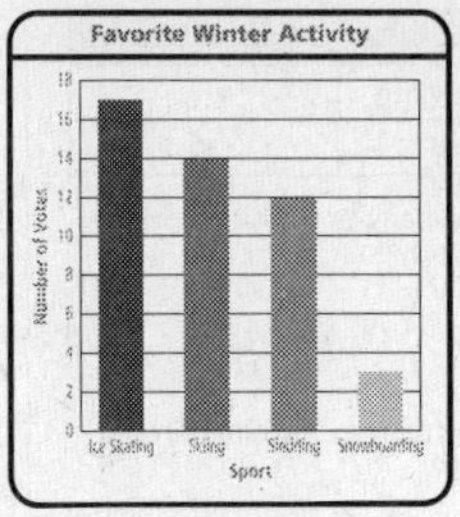

Check students' bar graphs.

Use the results in the table to make a bar graph.

Favorite Summer Sport

Sport	Number of Votes
Swimming	15
Inline Skating	10
Cycling	20

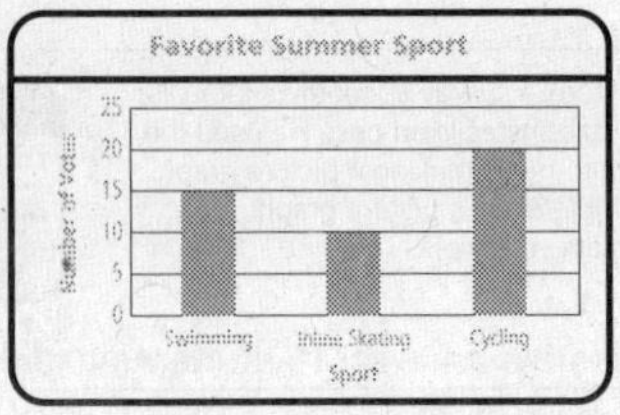

© Houghton Mifflin Harcourt Publishing Company

Name ____________ **Lesson 83**
CC.3.MD.3

Use the table for 1–2.

Brendon wants to use a table with data about the number of oranges picked to make a bar graph.

Oranges Picked

Type of Orange	Bushels
Navel	15
Pineapple	12
Temple	10
Valencia	14

1. How many bars will Brendon have on his graph?

Ⓐ 2 Ⓒ 9
Ⓑ 4 Ⓓ 16

2. Which type of orange will have the longest bar?

Ⓐ Navel
Ⓑ Pineapple
Ⓒ Temple
Ⓓ Valencia

3. Joey is making a bar graph to show how many pets his classmates have. Which pet will have the shortest bar in his graph?

Ⓐ 8 cats Ⓒ 4 dogs
Ⓑ 6 hamsters Ⓓ 3 horses

4. Martina is making a bar graph to show the 37 finches she saw in her garden from Monday through Friday. How tall should Martina make the bar to show how many finches she saw on Wednesday? Explain your answer and complete the graph.

Possible explanation: I added the finches she saw on Monday, Tuesday, Thursday, and Friday: 4 + 7 + 5 + 8 = 24. Then I subtracted 24 from 37, and drew the bar up to 13.

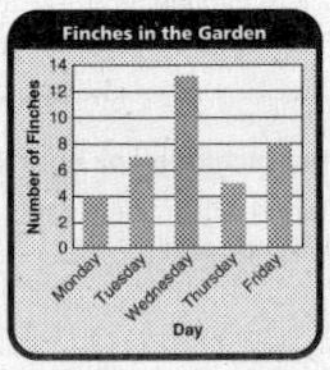

© Houghton Mifflin Harcourt Publishing Company

Name ____________ **Lesson 84**
COMMON CORE STANDARD CC.3.MD.3
Lesson Objective: Solve one- and two-step compare problems using data represented in scaled bar graphs.

Solve Problems Using Data

You can use a model or write a number sentence to help you answer questions about data.

The bar graph shows the different ways students use the computer center after school. How many more students use the computer center for projects than for games?

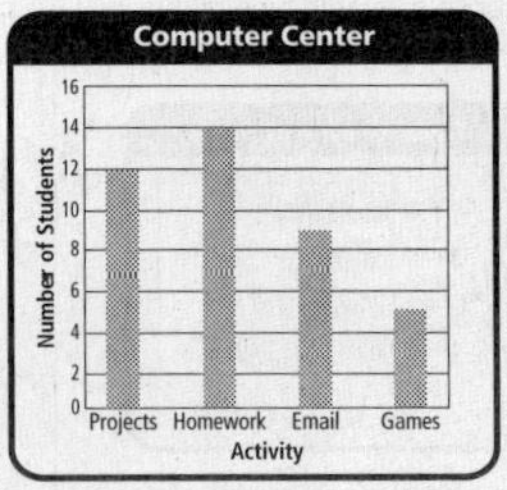

One Way Use a model.

Find the bar for projects. The bar ends at 12. So, 12 students use the computer center for projects.

Find the bar for games. The bar ends halfway between 4 and 6. So, 5 students use the computer center for games. Count back along the scale from 12 to 5 to find the difference. The difference is 7 students.

Another Way Write a number sentence.

Subtract to compare the number of students.
Think: There are 12 students who work on projects. There are 5 students who play games.

12 − 5 = 7

So, 7 more students use the computer center for projects than for games.

Use the Computer Center bar graph for 1–3.

1. How many more students use the computer center for homework than for email? 5 more students

2. How many fewer students use the computer center for games than for homework? 9 fewer students

3. Do more students use the computer center for projects or for email and games combined? **Explain.** email and games, 14 > 12

© Houghton Mifflin Harcourt Publishing Company

Name ____________ **Lesson 84**
CC.3.MD.3

Use the graph for 1–2.

A biologist made a bar graph to show how many samples of each type of marine life she saw on a dive.

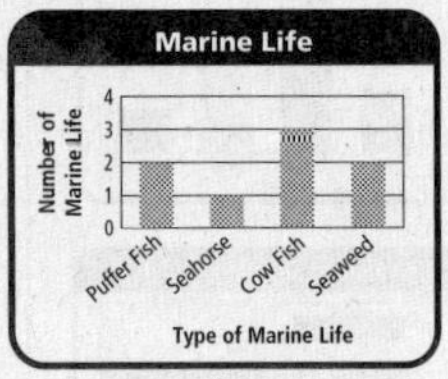

1. Of which type of marine life did the marine biologist see the **fewest**?

Ⓐ Cow Fish Ⓒ Seahorse
Ⓑ Puffer Fish Ⓓ Seaweed

2. How many more Cow Fish did the biologist see than Seahorses?

Ⓐ 1 Ⓑ 2 Ⓒ 3 Ⓓ 4

Use the graph for 3–4.

Nigel made a bar graph to show how many bushels of each type of orange are for sale at a fruit stand.

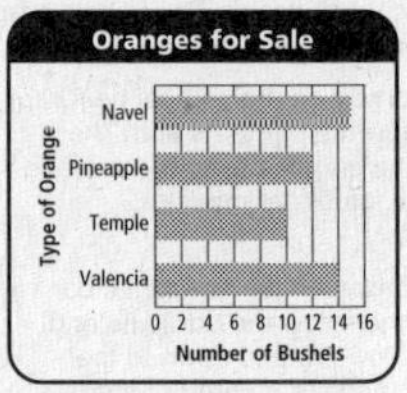

3. How many **more** bushels of Pineapple oranges and Navel oranges are there than Temple oranges and Valencia oranges?

Ⓐ 1 bushel
Ⓑ 3 bushels
Ⓒ 7 bushels
Ⓓ 24 bushels

4. How would you use the graph to find out if there were more Navel and Pineapple oranges for sale or more Temple and Valencia oranges for sale?

Possible answer: I would use the data in the graph and add the total number of bushels of Navel and Pineapple oranges for sale and then the number of Temple and Valencia oranges for sale. By comparing the sums, I could tell which groups of oranges there were more of.

© Houghton Mifflin Harcourt Publishing Company

© Houghton Mifflin Harcourt Publishing Company

Name ______________________

Lesson 85

COMMON CORE STANDARD CC.3.MD.4

Lesson Objective: Read and interpret data in a line plot and use data to make a line plot.

Use and Make Line Plots

A **line plot** uses marks to record each piece of data above a number line.

Louise measured the heights of tomato plants in her garden. She recorded the height of each plant.

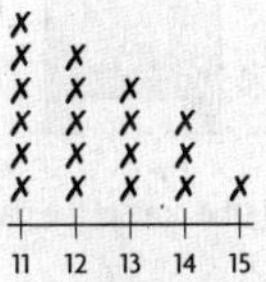

Heights of Tomato Plants (inches)

How many tomato plants are there?

Each ✗ stands for 1 plant.

Count all the ✗s. There are 19 in all.

This tells the total number of plants.

How many plants are taller than 13 inches?

Add the number of ✗s for 14 and 15.

3 plants are 14 inches tall. 1 plant is 15 inches tall.

3 + 1 = 4 So, 4 plants are taller than 13 inches.

Use the Spelling Test Scores line plot for 1–3.

Spelling Test Scores

1. Which test score did the most students receive?

85

2. How many more students scored 90 than 100?

4 more students

3. How many students in all took the spelling test?

28 students

© Houghton Mifflin Harcourt Publishing Company

Name ______________________

Lesson 85

CC.3.MD.4

Use the line plot for 1–2.

Mr. Robinson's students made a line plot to show the number of hats they each have.

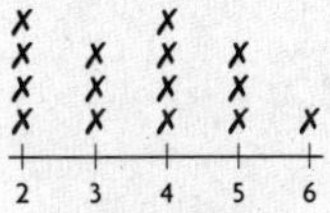

Number of Hats

1. How many students have 4 or fewer hats?

Ⓐ 3 Ⓒ 7
Ⓑ 4 **Ⓓ 11**

2. How many students were included in the line plot?

Ⓐ 13 **Ⓒ 15**
Ⓑ 14 Ⓓ 16

Use the line plot for 3–4.

Anna made a line plot to show the number of books each student in her class read for a reading contest.

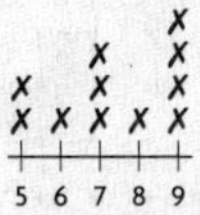

Number of Books Read

3. How many students read 9 books?

Ⓐ 4 Ⓒ 2
Ⓑ 3 Ⓓ 1

4. How many students read **fewer** than 8 books?

Ⓐ 4 **Ⓒ 6**
Ⓑ 5 Ⓓ 7

5. Lewis made a line plot to show the number of hours students in his class spend at practice each week. Find the total number of students and the total number of hours. Explain how you found your answers.

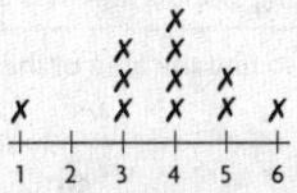

Number of Hours

Possible explanation: I found the total number of students, 11, by adding the number of Xs on the line plot. I found the total number of hours, 42, by multiplying each hour number by the number of Xs above it and then adding all the products together.

© Houghton Mifflin Harcourt Publishing Company

Name ______________________

Lesson 86

COMMON CORE STANDARD CC.3.MD.4

Lesson Objective: Measure length to the nearest half or fourth inch and use measurement data to make a line plot.

Measure Length

You can measure length to the nearest half or fourth inch.

Use a ruler to measure lines A–C to the nearest half inch.

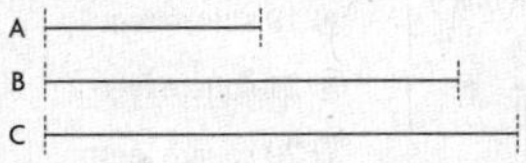

Step 1 Line up the left end of Line A with the zero mark on the ruler.

Step 2 The right end of Line A is between the half-inch marks for $\underline{1}$ and $\underline{1\frac{1}{2}}$.

The mark that is closest to the right end is for $\underline{1\frac{1}{2}}$ inches.

So, the length of Line A to the nearest half inch is $\underline{1\frac{1}{2}}$ inches.

Repeat Steps 1 and 2 for lines B and C.

The length of Line B to the nearest half inch is $\underline{2\frac{1}{2}}$ inches.

The length of Line C to the nearest half inch is $\underline{3}$ inches.

Measure the length to the nearest half inch. Is the crayon closest to $1\frac{1}{2}$ inches, 2 inches, or $2\frac{1}{2}$ inches?

1.

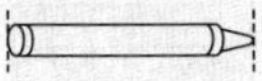

$\underline{1\frac{1}{2}}$ inches

2.

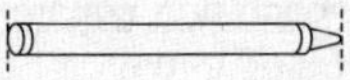

$\underline{2}$ inches

© Houghton Mifflin Harcourt Publishing Company

Name ______________________

Lesson 86

CC.3.MD.4

1. Mrs. Williams uses an inch ruler to measure a flower in a picture. How tall is the flower to the nearest fourth inch?

Ⓐ 2 inches Ⓒ $2\frac{3}{4}$ inches
Ⓑ $2\frac{1}{4}$ inches Ⓓ 3 inches

2. Hector uses an inch ruler to measure a screw. What is the length of the screw to the nearest half inch?

Ⓐ $1\frac{1}{2}$ inches Ⓒ $2\frac{1}{2}$ inches
Ⓑ 2 inches Ⓓ 3 inches

3. Julio uses an inch ruler to measure a pencil sharpener. What is the length of the pencil sharpener to the nearest fourth inch?

Ⓐ $\frac{1}{4}$ inch Ⓒ 1 inch
Ⓑ $\frac{3}{4}$ inch Ⓓ $1\frac{3}{4}$ inches

Problem Solving REAL WORLD

Use a separate sheet of paper for 4.

4. Draw 8 lines that are between 1 inch and 3 inches long. Measure each line to the nearest fourth inch, and make a line plot.

Check students' drawings, measurements, and line plots.

5. The tail on Alex's dog is $5\frac{1}{4}$ inches long. This length is between which two inch-marks on a ruler?

between 5 and 6 inches

© Houghton Mifflin Harcourt Publishing Company

© Houghton Mifflin Harcourt Publishing Company

Answer Key

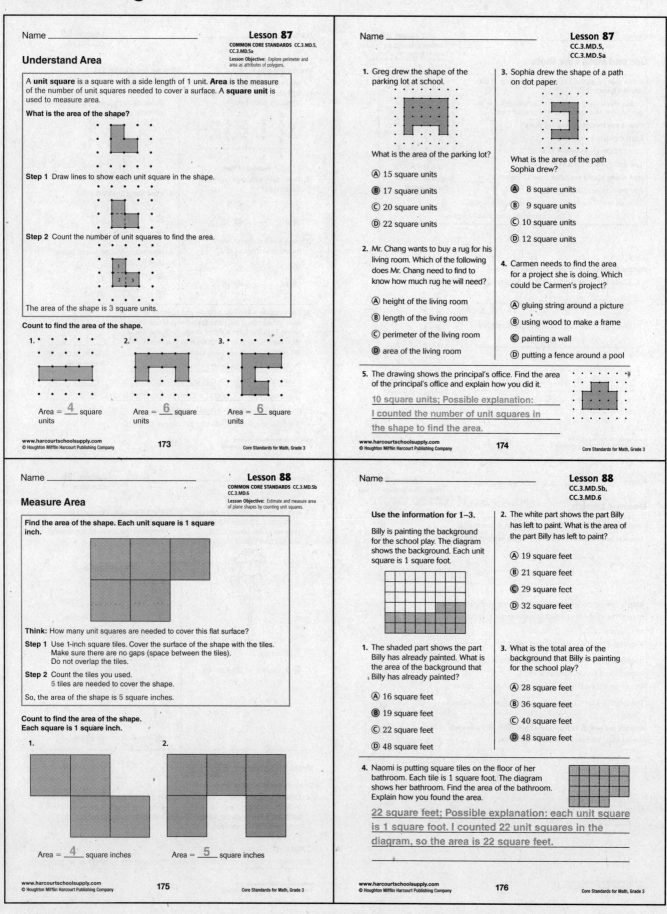

Name ______________________ **Lesson 87**

COMMON CORE STANDARDS CC.3.MD.5, CC.3.MD.5a

Lesson Objective: Explore perimeter and area as attributes of polygons.

Understand Area

A **unit square** is a square with a side length of 1 unit. **Area** is the measure of the number of unit squares needed to cover a surface. A **square unit** is used to measure area.

What is the area of the shape?

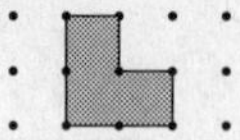

Step 1 Draw lines to show each unit square in the shape.

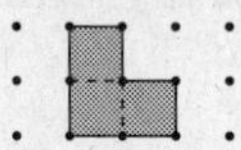

Step 2 Count the number of unit squares to find the area.

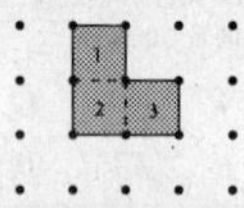

The area of the shape is 3 square units.

Count to find the area of the shape.

1. 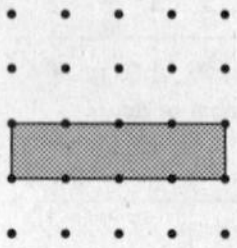

Area = 4 square units

2. 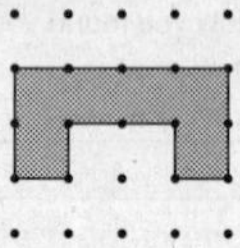

Area = 6 square units

3. 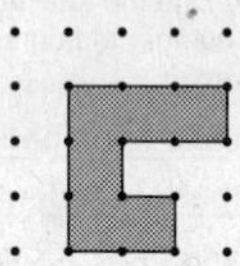

Area = 6 square units

Name ______________________ **Lesson 87**

CC.3.MD.5, CC.3.MD.5a

1. Greg drew the shape of the parking lot at school.

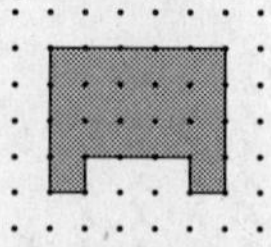

What is the area of the parking lot?

Ⓐ 15 square units
Ⓑ 17 square units
Ⓒ 20 square units
Ⓓ 22 square units

2. Mr. Chang wants to buy a rug for his living room. Which of the following does Mr. Chang need to find to know how much rug he will need?

Ⓐ height of the living room
Ⓑ length of the living room
Ⓒ perimeter of the living room
Ⓓ area of the living room

3. Sophia drew the shape of a path on dot paper.

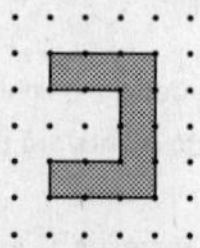

What is the area of the path Sophia drew?

Ⓐ 8 square units
Ⓑ 9 square units
Ⓒ 10 square units
Ⓓ 12 square units

4. Carmen needs to find the area for a project she is doing. Which could be Carmen's project?

Ⓐ gluing string around a picture
Ⓑ using wood to make a frame
Ⓒ painting a wall
Ⓓ putting a fence around a pool

5. The drawing shows the principal's office. Find the area of the principal's office and explain how you did it.

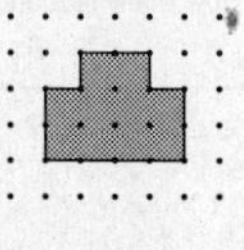

10 square units; Possible explanation: I counted the number of unit squares in the shape to find the area.

Name ______________________ **Lesson 88**

COMMON CORE STANDARDS CC.3.MD.5b CC.3.MD.6

Lesson Objective: Estimate and measure area of plane shapes by counting unit squares.

Measure Area

Find the area of the shape. Each unit square is 1 square inch.

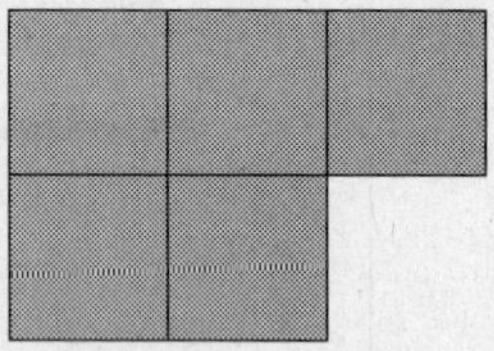

Think: How many unit squares are needed to cover this flat surface?

Step 1 Use 1-inch square tiles. Cover the surface of the shape with the tiles. Make sure there are no gaps (space between the tiles). Do not overlap the tiles.

Step 2 Count the tiles you used. 5 tiles are needed to cover the shape.

So, the area of the shape is 5 square inches.

Count to find the area of the shape. Each square is 1 square inch.

1. 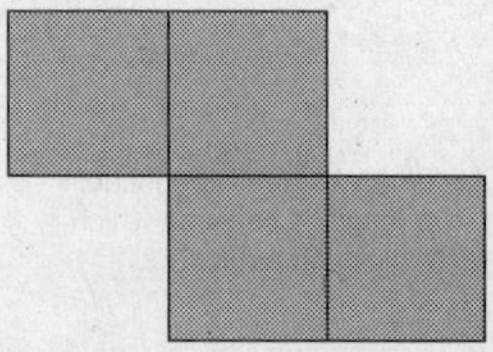

Area = 4 square inches

2. 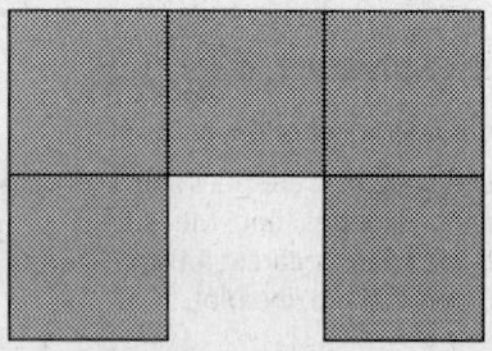

Area = 5 square inches

Name ______________________ **Lesson 88**

CC.3.MD.5b, CC.3.MD.6

Use the information for 1–3.

Billy is painting the background for the school play. The diagram shows the background. Each unit square is 1 square foot.

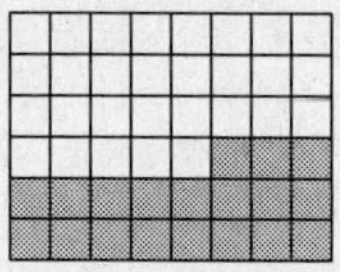

1. The shaded part shows the part Billy has already painted. What is the area of the background that Billy has already painted?

Ⓐ 16 square feet
Ⓑ 19 square feet
Ⓒ 22 square feet
Ⓓ 48 square feet

2. The white part shows the part Billy has left to paint. What is the area of the part Billy has left to paint?

Ⓐ 19 square feet
Ⓑ 21 square feet
Ⓒ 29 square feet
Ⓓ 32 square feet

3. What is the total area of the background that Billy is painting for the school play?

Ⓐ 28 square feet
Ⓑ 36 square feet
Ⓒ 40 square feet
Ⓓ 48 square feet

4. Naomi is putting square tiles on the floor of her bathroom. Each tile is 1 square foot. The diagram shows her bathroom. Find the area of the bathroom. Explain how you found the area.

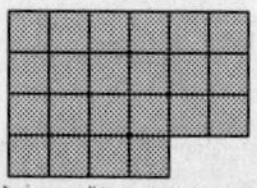

22 square feet; Possible explanation: each unit square is 1 square foot. I counted 22 unit squares in the diagram, so the area is 22 square feet.

Name ____________________

Lesson 89

COMMON CORE STANDARD CC.3.MD.7a

Lesson Objective: Relate area to addition and multiplication by using area models.

Use Area Models

Use multiplication to find the area of the shape. Each unit square is 1 square meter.

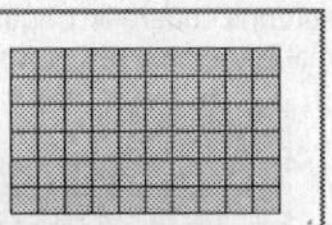

Step 1 Count the number of rows. There are 6 rows.

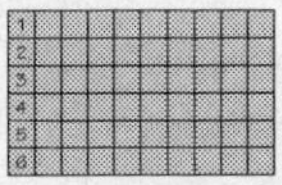

Step 2 Count the number of unit squares in each row. There are 10 unit squares.

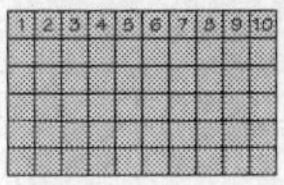

Step 3 Multiply the number of rows by the number in each row to find the area.

number of rows × number in each row = area

6 × 10 = 60

So, the area of the shape is 60 square meters.

Find the area of the shape. Each unit square is 1 square meter.

1. 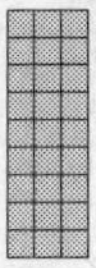

27 square meters

2. 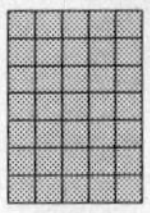

35 square meters

Name ____________________

Lesson 89

CC.3.MD.7a

1. The drawing shows Seth's plan for a footpath through his garden. Each unit square is 1 square foot. What is the area of Seth's footpath?

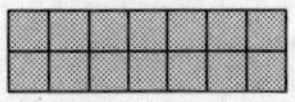

Ⓐ 14 square feet
Ⓑ 16 square feet
Ⓒ 18 square feet
Ⓓ 21 square feet

2. Keisha draws a sketch of a tile mosaic she wants to make on grid paper. Each unit square is 1 square inch. What is the area of Keisha's mosaic?

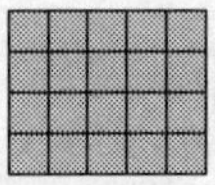

Ⓐ 9 square inches
Ⓑ 18 square inches
Ⓒ 20 square inches
Ⓓ 25 square inches

3. The drawing represents a vegetable garden in the Wilsons' backyard. Each unit square is 1 square meter. What is the area of the Wilsons' vegetable garden?

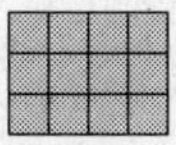

Ⓐ 7 square meters
Ⓑ 12 square meters
Ⓒ 14 square meters
Ⓓ 24 square meters

4. Roberto put square tiles down in the entryway. Each tile is 1 square foot. Write the area of the entryway floor. Explain how you found the area.

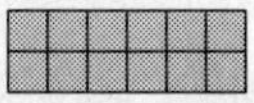

12 square feet; Possible explanation: I counted the number of rows (2) and the number of square tiles in each row (6). I then multiplied to find the area: 2 × 6 = 12, so the area is 12 square feet.

Name ____________________

Lesson 90

COMMON CORE STANDARD CC.3.MD.7b

Lesson Objective: Solve area problems by using the strategy *find a pattern*.

Problem Solving • Area of Rectangles

Mrs. Wilson wants to plant a garden, so she drew plans for some sample gardens. She wants to know how the areas of the gardens are related. How will the areas of Gardens A and B change? How will the areas of Gardens C and D change?

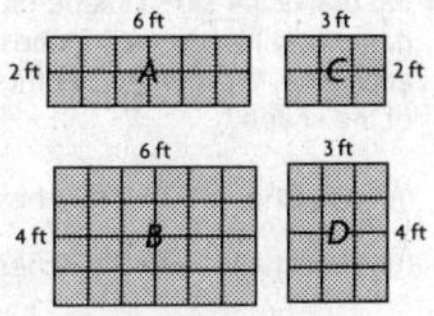

Use the graphic organizer to help you solve the problem.

Read the Problem

What do I need to find?	What information do I need to use?	How will I use the information?
I need to know how the areas will change from *A* to *B* and from *C* to *D*.	I need to use the length and width of each garden to find its area.	I will record the areas in a table. Then I will look for a pattern to see how the areas will change.

Solve the Problem

	Length	Width	Area		Length	Width	Area
Garden A	2 ft	6 ft	12 sq ft	Garden C	2 ft	3 ft	6 sq ft
Garden B	4 ft	6 ft	24 sq ft	Garden D	4 ft	3 ft	12 sq ft

From the table, I see that the lengths will be doubled and the widths will be the same.

The areas in square feet will change from 12 to 24 and from 6 to 12.

So, the area will be doubled.

Solve.

1. Mrs. Rios made a flower garden that is 8 feet long and 2 feet wide. She made a vegetable garden that is 4 feet long and 2 feet wide. How do the areas change?

The area of the flower garden is double the area of the vegetable garden.

Name ____________________

Lesson 90

CC.3.MD.7b

1. Brian drew these shapes. If the pattern continues, the next shape will have an area of 24 square units. What will be its length?

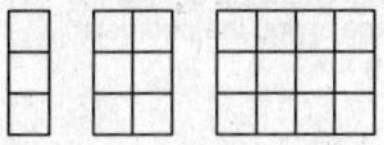

Ⓐ 4 units
Ⓑ 6 units
Ⓒ 8 units
Ⓓ 16 units

2. Brent uses carpet squares to make the pattern. Each unit square is 1 square foot. If the pattern continues, what will be the area of the fourth shape?

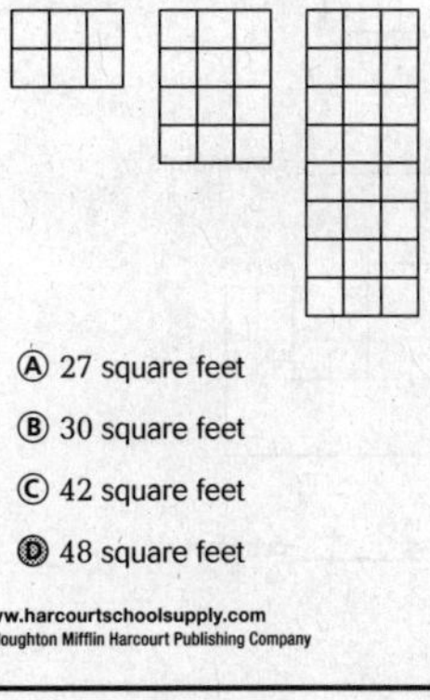

Ⓐ 27 square feet
Ⓑ 30 square feet
Ⓒ 42 square feet
Ⓓ 48 square feet

3. Julia uses tiles to make the pattern below. Each unit square is 1 square inch. If the pattern continues, what will be the area of the fourth shape?

Ⓐ 6 square inches
Ⓑ 8 square inches
Ⓒ 10 square inches
Ⓓ 12 square inches

4. Amy measured two rooms at her school. The first room is 8 feet wide and 10 feet long. The second room is 16 feet wide and 10 feet long. Describe how the lengths and widths of the rooms are related. Then use this information to explain how the areas of the two rooms are related.

Possible answer: the width of the second room is twice the width of the first room. The lengths of both rooms are the same. Because of this relationship between length and width, the area of the second room is twice the area of the first room.

© Houghton Mifflin Harcourt Publishing Company

Answer Key

Name ____________________

Lesson 91

COMMON CORE STANDARDS CC.3.MD.7c, CC.3.MD.7d

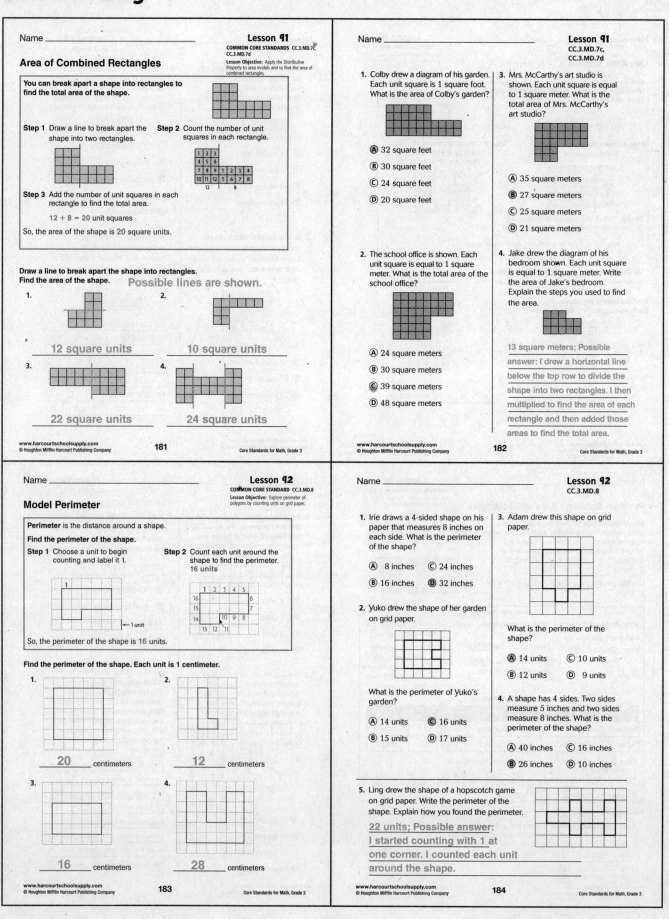

Lesson Objective: Apply the Distributive Property to area models and to find the area of combined rectangles.

Area of Combined Rectangles

You can break apart a shape into rectangles to find the total area of the shape.

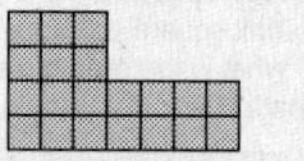

Step 1 Draw a line to break apart the shape into two rectangles.

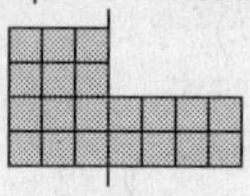

Step 2 Count the number of unit squares in each rectangle.

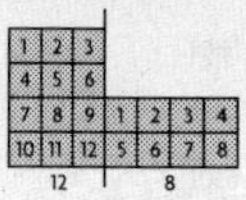

Step 3 Add the number of unit squares in each rectangle to find the total area.

12 + 8 = 20 unit squares

So, the area of the shape is 20 square units.

Draw a line to break apart the shape into rectangles. Find the area of the shape. Possible lines are shown.

1. 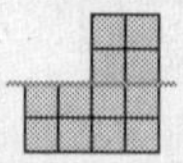

12 square units

2. 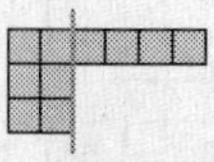

10 square units

3. 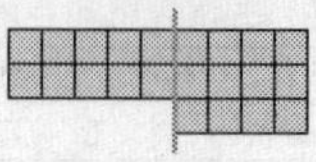

22 square units

4. 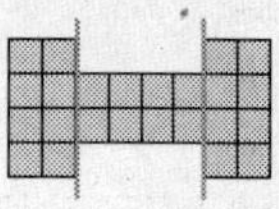

24 square units

www.harcourtschoolsupply.com
© Houghton Mifflin Harcourt Publishing Company

Name ____________________

Lesson 91

CC.3.MD.7c, CC.3.MD.7d

1. Colby drew a diagram of his garden. Each unit square is 1 square foot. What is the area of Colby's garden?

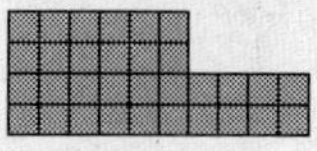

(A) 32 square feet
(B) 30 square feet
(C) 24 square feet
(D) 20 square feet

2. The school office is shown. Each unit square is equal to 1 square meter. What is the total area of the school office?

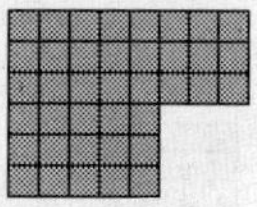

(A) 24 square meters
(B) 30 square meters
(C) 39 square meters
(D) 48 square meters

3. Mrs. McCarthy's art studio is shown. Each unit square is equal to 1 square meter. What is the total area of Mrs. McCarthy's art studio?

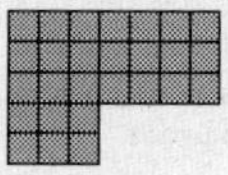

(A) 35 square meters
(B) 27 square meters
(C) 25 square meters
(D) 21 square meters

4. Jake drew the diagram of his bedroom shown. Each unit square is equal to 1 square meter. Write the area of Jake's bedroom. Explain the steps you used to find the area.

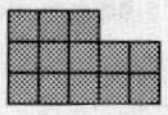

13 square meters; Possible answer: I drew a horizontal line below the top row to divide the shape into two rectangles. I then multiplied to find the area of each rectangle and then added those areas to find the total area.

www.harcourtschoolsupply.com
© Houghton Mifflin Harcourt Publishing Company

Name ____________________

Lesson 92

COMMON CORE STANDARD CC.3.MD.8

Lesson Objective: Explore perimeter of polygons by counting units on grid paper.

Model Perimeter

Perimeter is the distance around a shape.

Find the perimeter of the shape.

Step 1 Choose a unit to begin counting and label it 1.

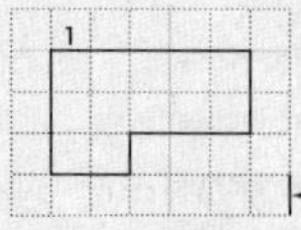

Step 2 Count each unit around the shape to find the perimeter.
16 units

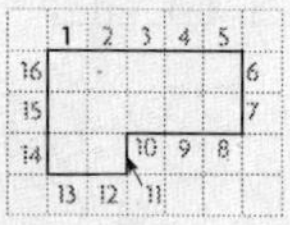

So, the perimeter of the shape is 16 units.

Find the perimeter of the shape. Each unit is 1 centimeter.

1. 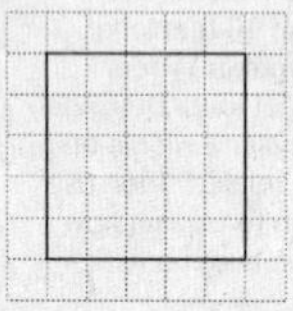

20 centimeters

2. 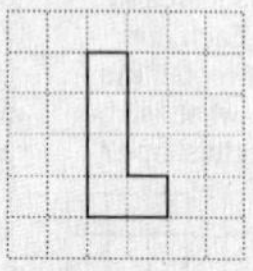

12 centimeters

3. 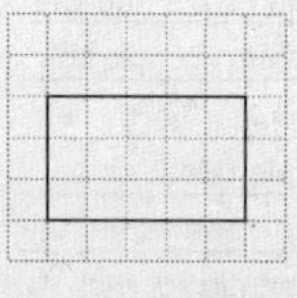

16 centimeters

4. 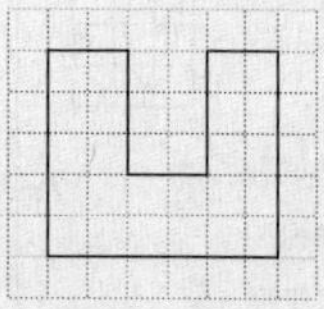

28 centimeters

www.harcourtschoolsupply.com
© Houghton Mifflin Harcourt Publishing Company

Name ____________________

Lesson 92

CC.3.MD.8

1. Irie draws a 4-sided shape on his paper that measures 8 inches on each side. What is the perimeter of the shape?

(A) 8 inches
(B) 16 inches
(C) 24 inches
(D) 32 inches

2. Yuko drew the shape of her garden on grid paper.

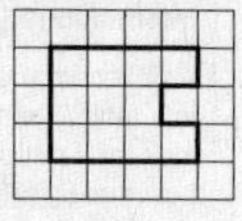

What is the perimeter of Yuko's garden?

(A) 14 units
(B) 15 units
(C) 16 units
(D) 17 units

3. Adam drew this shape on grid paper.

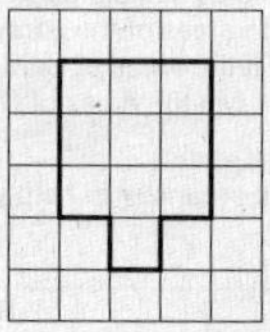

What is the perimeter of the shape?

(A) 14 units
(B) 12 units
(C) 10 units
(D) 9 units

4. A shape has 4 sides. Two sides measure 5 inches and two sides measure 8 inches. What is the perimeter of the shape?

(A) 40 inches
(B) 26 inches
(C) 16 inches
(D) 10 inches

5. Ling drew the shape of a hopscotch game on grid paper. Write the perimeter of the shape. Explain how you found the perimeter.

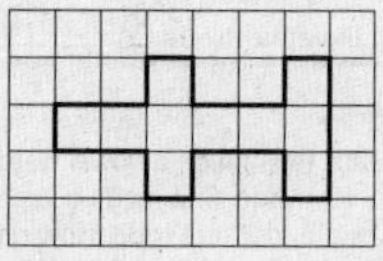

22 units; Possible answer: I started counting with 1 at one corner. I counted each unit around the shape.

www.harcourtschoolsupply.com
© Houghton Mifflin Harcourt Publishing Company

www.harcourtschoolsupply.com
© Houghton Mifflin Harcourt Publishing Company

Name ____________ **Lesson 93**

COMMON CORE STANDARD CC.3.MD.8

Lesson Objective: Estimate and measure perimeter of polygons using inch and centimeter rulers.

Find Perimeter

Kelsey wants to know the perimeter of the shape below. She can use an inch ruler to find the perimeter.

Step 1 Choose one side of the shape to measure. Place the zero mark of the ruler on the end of the side. Measure to the nearest inch. Write the length.

Step 2 Use the ruler to measure the other three sides. Write the lengths.

Step 3 Add the lengths of all the sides.
1 + 1 + 2 + 1 = 5

So, the perimeter of the shape is 5 inches.

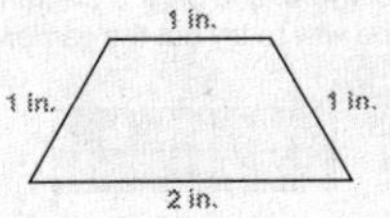

Use an inch ruler to find the perimeter.

1.

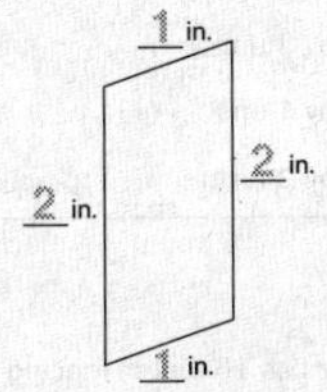

6 inches

2.

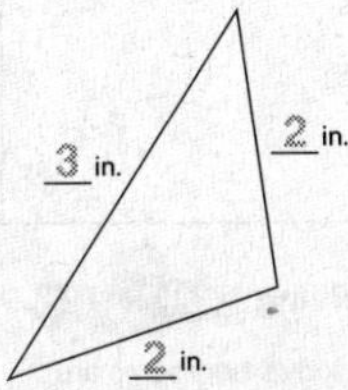

7 inches

Name ____________ **Lesson 93**
CC.3.MD.8

1. Fiona bought a picture with a perimeter of 24 inches. Which picture did she buy?

Ⓐ
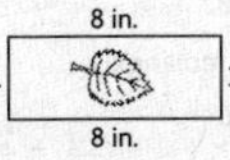

Ⓑ
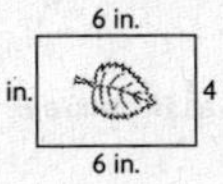

Ⓒ
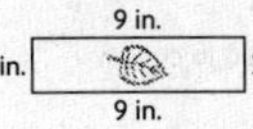

Ⓓ (marked)
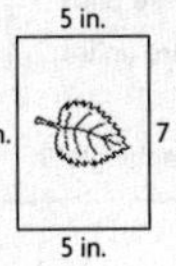

2. Kim wants to put trim around a picture she drew. How many centimeters of trim does Kim need for the perimeter of the picture?

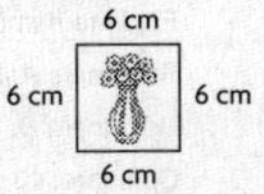

Ⓐ 6 cm Ⓒ 24 cm (marked)
Ⓑ 12 cm Ⓓ 36 cm

3. Mr. Gasper is putting wood trim around this window. How many feet of wood trim does Mr. Gasper need for the perimeter of the window?

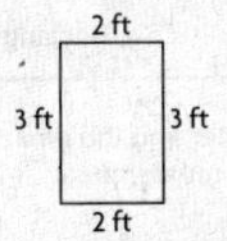

Ⓐ 6 feet Ⓒ 12 feet
Ⓑ 10 feet (marked) Ⓓ 13 feet

4. Dylan used a centimeter ruler to draw this square. Find the perimeter of Dylan's square and explain how you did it.

8 centimeters; Possible explanation: I used the ruler to measure the length of each side of the square. Each side was 2 centimeters long. I then added the lengths of the sides to find the perimeter: 2 + 2 + 2 + 2 = 8.

Name ____________ **Lesson 94**

COMMON CORE STANDARD CC.3.MD.8

Lesson Objective: Find the unknown length of a side of a polygon when you know its perimeter.

Algebra • Find Unknown Side Lengths

An unknown side length is a side that does not have its length labeled with a number. Instead the side is labeled with a symbol or letter, such as *a*.

The perimeter of the shape is 20 meters. Find the length of side *a*.

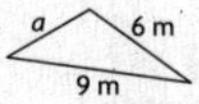

Think: There is only one unknown side length.

Step 1 Add the *known* side lengths.
6 + 9 = 15

Step 2 Subtract the sum of the known side lengths from the perimeter.
20 − 15 = 5

Step 3 Add to check your work.
6 + 9 + 5 = 20 ✓

So, the unknown side length, *a*, is 5 meters.

The perimeter of the square is 12 feet. What is the length of each side of the square?

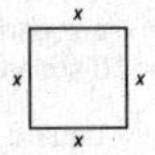

Think: A square has four sides of equal length.

Step 1 Divide the perimeter by the number of sides.
12 ÷ 4 = 3

Step 2 Multiply to check your work.
4 × 3 = 12 ✓

So, the length of each side, *x*, is 3 feet.

Find the unknown side lengths.

1. Perimeter = 18 centimeters

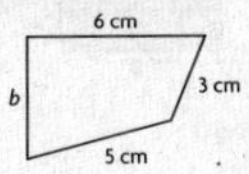

b = 4 centimeters

2. Perimeter = 20 yards

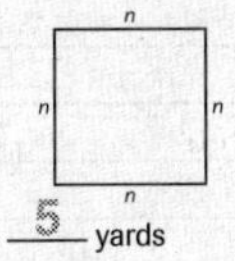

n = 5 yards

Name ____________ **Lesson 94**
CC.3.MD.8

1. Natasha cut out a rectangle that has a perimeter of 34 centimeters. The width of the rectangle is 7 centimeters. What is the length of the rectangle?

Ⓐ 5 centimeters
Ⓑ 10 centimeters (marked)
Ⓒ 20 centimeters
Ⓓ 27 centimeters

2. Vanessa uses a ruler to draw a square. The perimeter of the square is 12 centimeters. What is the length of each side of the square?

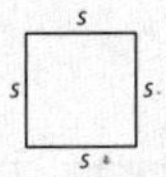

Ⓐ 3 cm (marked) Ⓒ 6 cm
Ⓑ 4 cm Ⓓ 48 cm

3. Mrs. Rios wants to put a wallpaper border around the room shown. She will use 36 feet of wallpaper border. What is the unknown side length?

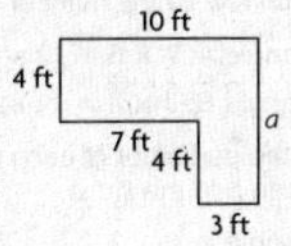

Ⓐ 6 feet Ⓒ 14 feet
Ⓑ 8 feet (marked) Ⓓ 28 feet

4. Frank uses 16 feet of fencing around the perimeter of a rectangular garden. The garden is 5 feet long. What is the width of the garden?

Ⓐ 11 feet Ⓒ 3 feet (marked)
Ⓑ 6 feet Ⓓ 2 feet

5. Mr. Rios has a rectangular rug. The perimeter of the rug is 28 feet. The width of the rug is 6 feet. Find the length of the rug. Explain the steps you used to find the missing length.

8 feet; Possible explanation: I drew a diagram, labeled each width 6, and each length *l*. I knew the sum was 28, so 6 + 6 + *l* + *l* = 28. I found the unknown number or length must be 8 feet.

© Houghton Mifflin Harcourt Publishing Company

Answer Key

Name ______________________ **Lesson 95**

COMMON CORE STANDARD CC.3.MD.8

Lesson Objective: Compare areas of rectangles that have the same perimeter.

Same Perimeter, Different Areas

You can use perimeter and area to compare rectangles.

Compare the perimeters of Rectangle *A* and Rectangle *B*.

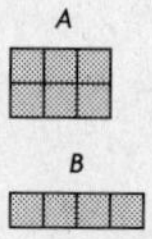

Find the number of units around each rectangle.

Rectangle *A*: 3 + 2 + 3 + 2 = 10 units

Rectangle *B*: 4 + 1 + 4 + 1 = 10 units

Compare: 10 units = 10 units

So, Rectangle *A* has the same perimeter as Rectangle *B*.

Compare the areas of Rectangle *A* and Rectangle *B*.

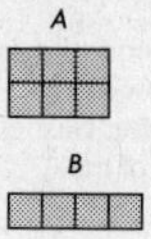

Find the number of unit squares needed to cover each rectangle.

Rectangle *A*: 2 rows of 3 = 2 × 3, or 6 square units

Rectangle *B*: 1 row of 4 = 1 × 4, or 4 square units

Compare: 6 square units > 4 square units

So, Rectangle *A* has a greater area than Rectangle *B*.

Find the perimeter and the area. Tell which rectangle has a greater area.

1. 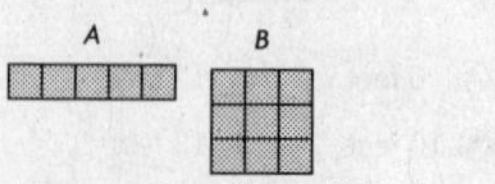

A: Perimeter = 12 units;
Area = 5 square units
B: Perimeter = 12 units;
Area = 9 square units
Rectangle B has a greater area.

2. 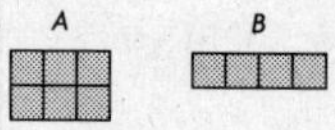

A: Perimeter = 10 units;
Area = 6 square units
B: Perimeter = 10 units;
Area = 4 square units
Rectangle A has a greater area.

Name ______________________ **Lesson 95**

CC.3.MD.8

Use the information for 1–3.

Sarah is building a garden in the backyard. She drew a diagram of one way to lay out the garden.

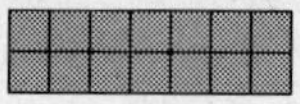

1. What is the perimeter of the garden?

Ⓐ 9 units
Ⓑ 12 units
Ⓒ 14 units
Ⓓ 18 units

2. What is the area of the garden?

Ⓐ 6 square units
Ⓑ 12 square units
Ⓒ 14 square units
Ⓓ 18 square units

3. Sarah wants her rectangular garden to have the greatest possible area, but she wants the same perimeter as shown in her diagram. Which could be the length and width of Sarah's garden?

Ⓐ 5 units by 4 units
Ⓑ 6 units by 3 units
Ⓒ 8 units by 1 unit
Ⓓ 5 units by 2 units

Problem Solving REAL WORLD

4. Tara's and Jody's bedrooms are shaped like rectangles. Tara's bedroom is 9 feet long and 8 feet wide. Jody's bedroom is 7 feet long and 10 feet wide. Whose bedroom has the greater area? **Explain.**

Tara's; 9 × 8 = 72 and 7 × 10 = 70; 72 > 70

5. Mr. Sanchez has 16 feet of fencing to put around a rectangular garden. He wants the garden to have the greatest possible area. How long should the sides of the garden be?

All four sides should be 4 feet long.

Name ______________________ **Lesson 96**

COMMON CORE STANDARD CC.3.MD.8

Lesson Objective: Compare perimeters of rectangles that have the same area.

Same Area, Different Perimeters

Find the perimeter and area of Rectangles *A* and *B*. Tell which rectangle has a greater perimeter.

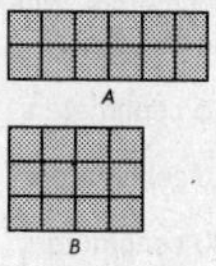

Step 1 Find the area of each rectangle. You can multiply the number of unit squares in each row by the number of rows.

Rectangle *A*: 2 × 6 = 12 square units

Rectangle *B*: 3 × 4 = 12 square units

Step 2 Find the perimeter of each rectangle. You can add the sides.

Rectangle *A*: 6 + 2 + 6 + 2 = 16 units

Rectangle *B*: 4 + 3 + 4 + 3 = 14 units

Step 3 Compare the perimeters. 16 units > 14 units.

So, Rectangle *A* has a greater perimeter.

Find the perimeter and the area. Tell which rectangle has a greater perimeter.

1. 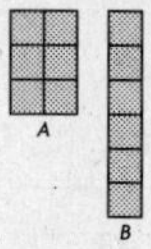

A: Area = 6 square units;
Perimeter = 10 units
B: Area = 6 square units;
Perimeter = 14 units
Rectangle B has a greater perimeter.

2. 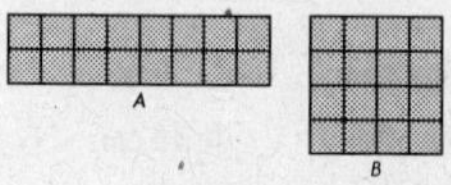

A: Area = 16 square units;
Perimeter = 20 units
B: Area = 16 square units;
Perimeter = 16 units
Rectangle A has a greater perimeter.

Name ______________________ **Lesson 96**

CC.3.MD.8

Use the information for 1–3.

Cheung drew two rectangles on grid paper.

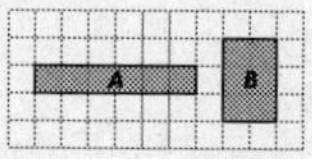

1. What is the area of each rectangle?

Ⓐ *A*: Area = 6 square units; *B*: Area = 6 square units
Ⓑ *A*: Area = 6 square units; *B*: Area = 3 square units
Ⓒ *A*: Area = 14 square units; *B*: Area = 10 square units
Ⓓ *A*: Area = 7 square units; *B*: Area = 5 square units

2. What is the perimeter of rectangle *B*?

Ⓐ 5 units
Ⓑ 6 units
Ⓒ 8 units
Ⓓ 10 units

3. Which statement about the perimeters and areas of Cheung's rectangles is true?

Ⓐ The areas are the same and the perimeters are the same.
Ⓑ The areas are the same and the perimeters are different.
Ⓒ The areas are different and the perimeters are different.
Ⓓ The areas are different and the perimeters are the same.

4. Shawana used square tiles to make the rectangles shown. Compare and contrast the areas and perimeters of her two rectangles.

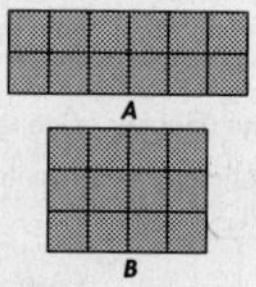

Possible answer: the perimeter of rectangle A is 16 units and the area is 12 square units. The perimeter of rectangle B is 14 units and the area is 12 square units. The perimeters of the two rectangles are different, but the areas are the same.

Name ______________________

Lesson 97
COMMON CORE STANDARD CC.3.G.1
Lesson Objective: Identify and describe attributes of plane shapes.

Describe Plane Shapes

You can use math words to describe plane shapes.

- **point** — an exact position or location
- **line** — a straight path that goes in two directions without end
- **endpoints** — points that are used to show segments of lines
- **line segment** — part of a straight line and has 2 endpoints
- **ray** — part of a straight line that has 1 endpoint and continues in one direction

A **plane shape** is a shape on a flat surface. It is formed by points that make curved paths, line segments, or both. Plane shapes can be open or closed.

A **closed shape** starts and ends at the same point. An **open shape** does not start and end at the same point.

Look at this plane shape called a triangle.
It is a closed shape.
It has 3 line segments.
The line segments meet at the endpoints.

Circle all the words that describe the shape.

1. line / (line segment)
2. (point) / ray
3. closed shape / (open shape)
4. (closed shape) / open shape

Write whether the shape is *open* or *closed*.

5. open
6. closed
7. closed
8. open

Name ______________________

Lesson 97
CC.3.G.1

1. Abby drew a point. Which shows a point?
   - (A) •
   - (B) line segment
   - (C) ray
   - (D) line

2. Cyrus uses line segments to draw a shape.

How many line segments does Cyrus's shape have?
   - (A) 6
   - (B) 7
   - (C) 8
   - (D) 9

3. Four friends draw shapes. Rachel, Zoe, and Jorge draw closed shapes. Andy draws an open shape. Which is Andy's shape?
   - (A) (B) (C) (D) — answer: (B)

4. Jamey drew this shape.
   What shape did Jamey draw?
   - (A) line
   - (B) line segment
   - (C) point
   - (D) ray

Problem Solving REAL WORLD

5. Carl wants to show a closed shape in his drawing. Show and explain how to make the drawing a closed shape.

Add a fourth line segment, so the shape starts and ends at the same point.

6. The shape of a fish pond at a park is shown below. Is the shape open or closed?

closed

Name ______________________

Lesson 98
COMMON CORE STANDARD CC.3.G.1
Lesson Objective: Describe angles in plane shapes.

Describe Angles in Plane Shapes

There are different types of angles.

A **right angle** forms a square corner. Some angles are less than a right angle. Some angles are greater than a right angle.

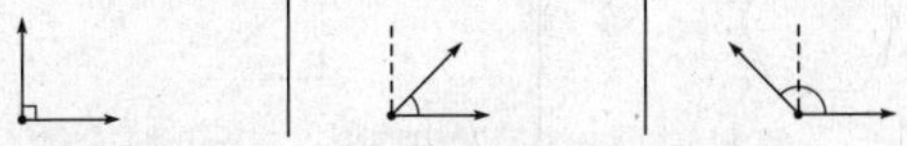

Look at this shape. Describe the angles.

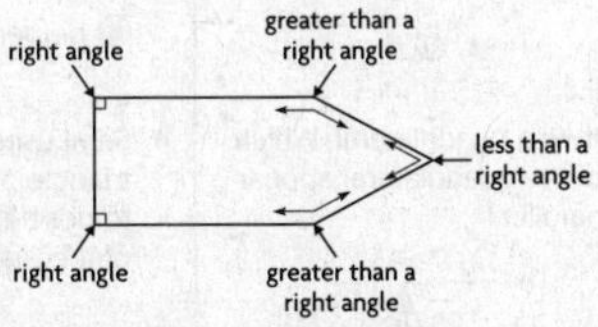

There are 2 right angles.
There are 2 angles greater than a right angle.
There is 1 angle less than a right angle.

Use the corner of a sheet of paper to tell whether the angle is a *right angle*, *less than a right angle*, or *greater than a right angle*.

1. less than a right angle
2. greater than a right angle
3. right angle

Write how many of each type of angle the shape has.

4. 4 right; 0 less than a right; 0 greater than a right
5. 1 right; 0 less than a right; 5 greater than a right
6. 0 right; 2 less than a right; 2 greater than a right

Name ______________________

Lesson 98
CC.3.G.1

1. How many right angles does this shape appear to have?

   - (A) 0
   - (B) 1
   - (C) 2
   - (D) 5

2. Look at the shape.

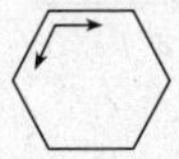

Which **best** describes the marked angle?
   - (A) less than a right angle
   - (B) greater than a right angle
   - (C) a right angle
   - (D) a straight angle

3. Which describes the angles of this triangle?

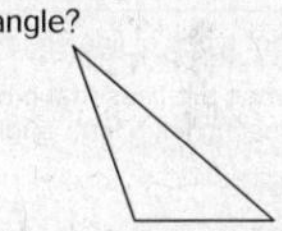

   - (A) 1 greater than a right angle; 2 less than a right angle
   - (B) 1 greater than a right angle; 2 right angles
   - (C) 2 greater than a right angle; 1 less than a right angle
   - (D) 1 greater than a right angle; 1 right angle; 1 less than a right angle

4. Which capital letter appears to have an angle that is less than a right angle?
   - (A) H
   - (B) L
   - (C) T
   - (D) Z

5. Mrs. Simpson drew this shape. Explain how to classify the marked angle.

Possible explanation: I compared the marked angle to the corner of a sheet of paper. The marked angle is greater than the corner, so it is greater than a right angle.

Answer Key

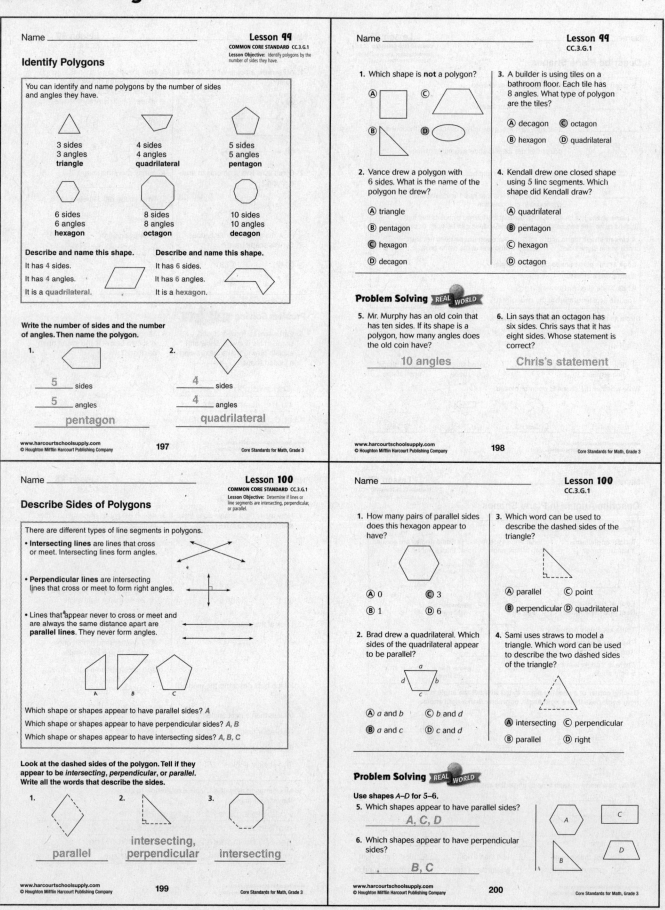

Name

Lesson 99

COMMON CORE STANDARD CC.3.G.1

Lesson Objective: Identify polygons by the number of sides they have.

Identify Polygons

You can identify and name polygons by the number of sides and angles they have.

  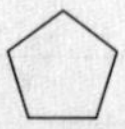

3 sides 3 angles **triangle**	4 sides 4 angles **quadrilateral**	5 sides 5 angles **pentagon**

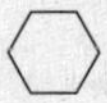 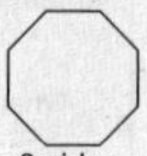 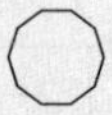

6 sides 6 angles **hexagon**	8 sides 8 angles **octagon**	10 sides 10 angles **decagon**

Describe and name this shape.

It has 4 sides.

It has 4 angles.

It is a quadrilateral.

Describe and name this shape.

It has 6 sides.

It has 6 angles.

It is a hexagon.

Write the number of sides and the number of angles. Then name the polygon.

1. 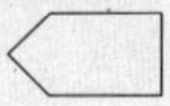

5 sides

5 angles

pentagon

2. 

4 sides

4 angles

quadrilateral

© Houghton Mifflin Harcourt Publishing Company

Name

Lesson 99

CC.3.G.1

1. Which shape is **not** a polygon?

Ⓐ  Ⓒ 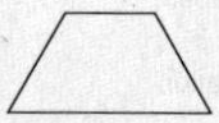

Ⓑ  Ⓓ (filled) 

2. Vance drew a polygon with 6 sides. What is the name of the polygon he drew?

Ⓐ triangle

Ⓑ pentagon

Ⓒ (filled) hexagon

Ⓓ decagon

3. A builder is using tiles on a bathroom floor. Each tile has 8 angles. What type of polygon are the tiles?

Ⓐ decagon Ⓒ (filled) octagon

Ⓑ hexagon Ⓓ quadrilateral

4. Kendall drew one closed shape using 5 line segments. Which shape did Kendall draw?

Ⓐ quadrilateral

Ⓑ (filled) pentagon

Ⓒ hexagon

Ⓓ octagon

Problem Solving REAL WORLD

5. Mr. Murphy has an old coin that has ten sides. If its shape is a polygon, how many angles does the old coin have?

10 angles

6. Lin says that an octagon has six sides. Chris says that it has eight sides. Whose statement is correct?

Chris's statement

© Houghton Mifflin Harcourt Publishing Company

Name

Lesson 100

COMMON CORE STANDARD CC.3.G.1

Lesson Objective: Determine if lines or line segments are intersecting, perpendicular, or parallel.

Describe Sides of Polygons

There are different types of line segments in polygons.

- **Intersecting lines** are lines that cross or meet. Intersecting lines form angles.

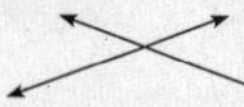

- **Perpendicular lines** are intersecting lines that cross or meet to form right angles.

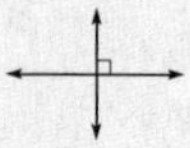

- Lines that appear never to cross or meet and are always the same distance apart are **parallel lines**. They never form angles.

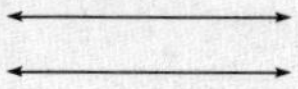

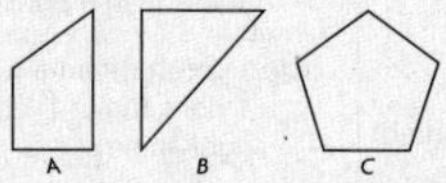

Which shape or shapes appear to have parallel sides? *A*

Which shape or shapes appear to have perpendicular sides? *A, B*

Which shape or shapes appear to have intersecting sides? *A, B, C*

Look at the dashed sides of the polygon. Tell if they appear to be *intersecting*, *perpendicular*, or *parallel*. Write all the words that describe the sides.

1. 

parallel

2. 

intersecting, perpendicular

3. 

intersecting

© Houghton Mifflin Harcourt Publishing Company

Name

Lesson 100

CC.3.G.1

1. How many pairs of parallel sides does this hexagon appear to have?

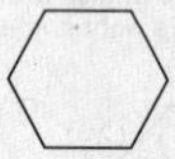

Ⓐ 0 Ⓒ (filled) 3

Ⓑ 1 Ⓓ 6

2. Brad drew a quadrilateral. Which sides of the quadrilateral appear to be parallel?

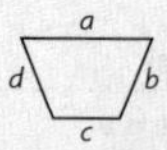

Ⓐ *a* and *b* Ⓒ *b* and *d*

Ⓑ (filled) *a* and *c* Ⓓ *c* and *d*

3. Which word can be used to describe the dashed sides of the triangle?

Ⓐ parallel Ⓒ point

Ⓑ (filled) perpendicular Ⓓ quadrilateral

4. Sami uses straws to model a triangle. Which word can be used to describe the two dashed sides of the triangle?

Ⓐ (filled) intersecting Ⓒ perpendicular

Ⓑ parallel Ⓓ right

Problem Solving REAL WORLD

Use shapes *A–D* for 5–6.

5. Which shapes appear to have parallel sides?

A, C, D

6. Which shapes appear to have perpendicular sides?

B, C

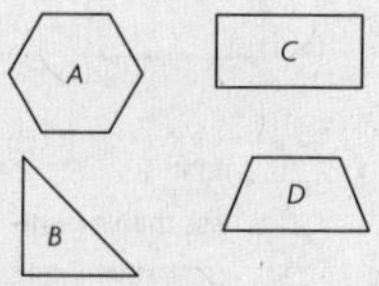

© Houghton Mifflin Harcourt Publishing Company

© Houghton Mifflin Harcourt Publishing Company

Name ____________ **Lesson 101**
COMMON CORE STANDARD CC.3.G.1
Lesson Objective: Describe, classify, and compare quadrilaterals based on their sides and angles.

Classify Quadrilaterals

You can classify quadrilaterals by their sides and by their angles.

2 pairs of opposite sides that are parallel
4 sides that are of equal length
4 right angles

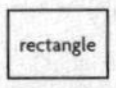

2 pairs of opposite sides that are parallel
2 pairs of sides that are of equal length
4 right angles

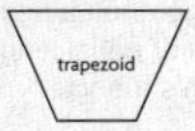

1 pair of opposite sides that are parallel
lengths of sides could be the same

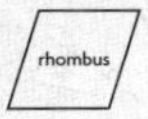

2 pairs of opposite sides that are parallel
4 sides that are of equal length

How can you classify the quadrilateral?

It has only 1 pair of opposite sides that are parallel.
The lengths of all 4 sides are not equal.
So, the quadrilateral is a trapezoid.

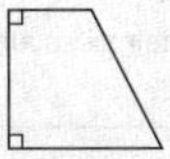

Circle all the words that describe the quadrilateral.

1. 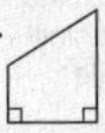
square
rhombus
trapezoid

2. 
square
rectangle
quadrilateral

3. 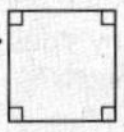
square
rectangle
rhombus

Name ____________ **Lesson 101**
CC.3.G.1

1. Hillary drew this shape.

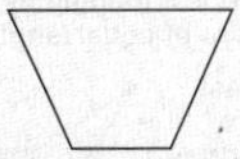

Which word **best** describes the shape Hillary drew?

Ⓐ square Ⓒ rhombus
Ⓑ rectangle **Ⓓ trapezoid**

2. Cooper used toothpicks to make a shape.

Which **best** describes the shape Cooper made?

Ⓐ decagon **Ⓒ square**
Ⓑ open shape Ⓓ trapezoid

3. Edward says he drew a quadrilateral. Which of these could **not** be Edward's shape?

Ⓐ 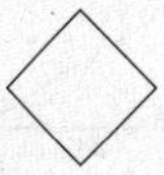 Ⓒ 
Ⓑ  **Ⓓ** 

4. Helen drew this shape.

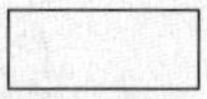

Which word **best** describes the shape Helen drew?

Ⓐ rectangle Ⓒ square
Ⓑ rhombus Ⓓ trapezoid

Problem Solving REAL WORLD

5. A picture on the wall in Jeremy's classroom has 4 right angles, 4 sides of equal length, and 2 pairs of opposite sides that are parallel. What quadrilateral best describes the picture?

square

6. Sofia has a plate that has 4 sides of equal length, 2 pairs of opposite sides that are parallel, and no right angles. What quadrilateral best describes the plate?

rhombus

Name ____________ **Lesson 102**
COMMON CORE STANDARD CC.3.G.1
Lesson Objective: Draw quadrilaterals.

Draw Quadrilaterals

Use grid paper to draw a quadrilateral.

Step 1 Use a ruler to draw line segments. Connect *A* to *B*.

Step 2 Connect *B* to *C*.

Step 3 Connect *C* to *D*.

Step 4 Connect *D* to *A*.

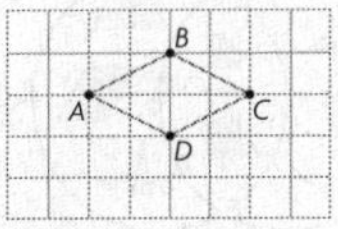

Write the name of your quadrilateral.
rhombus

For 1–4, possible drawings are shown.

1. Choose four endpoints that connect to make a square.

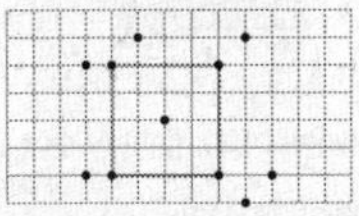

2. Choose four endpoints that connect to make a trapezoid.

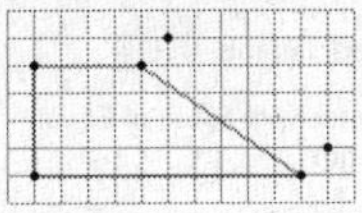

Use grid paper to draw a quadrilateral that is described. Name the quadrilateral you drew.

3. 4 right angles

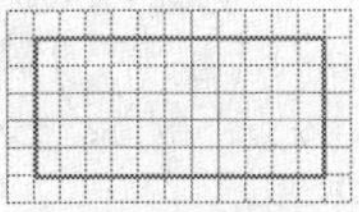

rectangle

4. 2 pairs of opposite sides that are parallel

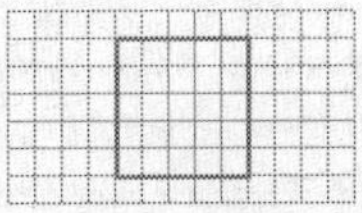

square

Name ____________ **Lesson 102**
CC.3.G.1

1. Melody draws a quadrilateral with 2 pairs of opposite sides that are parallel. Which could be the quadrilateral Melody draws?

Ⓐ  **Ⓒ** 
Ⓑ  Ⓓ 

2. Gina drew a quadrilateral that has 4 sides of equal length and 4 right angles. Which shape did she draw?

Ⓐ pentagon Ⓒ trapezoid
Ⓑ square Ⓓ triangle

3. Hannah drew a quadrilateral with exactly 1 pair of opposite sides that are parallel. Which shows a shape Hannah could have drawn?

Ⓐ  **Ⓒ** 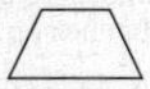
Ⓑ 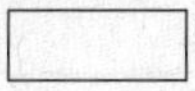 Ⓓ 

4. Henry drew a quadrilateral that has 2 pairs of sides of equal length and 4 right angles. Which shape did he draw?

Ⓐ hexagon Ⓒ trapezoid
Ⓑ pentagon **Ⓓ rectangle**

Problem Solving REAL WORLD

5. Layla drew a quadrilateral with 4 right angles and 2 pairs of opposite sides that are parallel. Name the quadrilateral she could have drawn.

square or rectangle

6. Victor drew a quadrilateral with no right angles and 4 sides of equal length. What quadrilateral could Victor have drawn?

rhombus

Answer Key

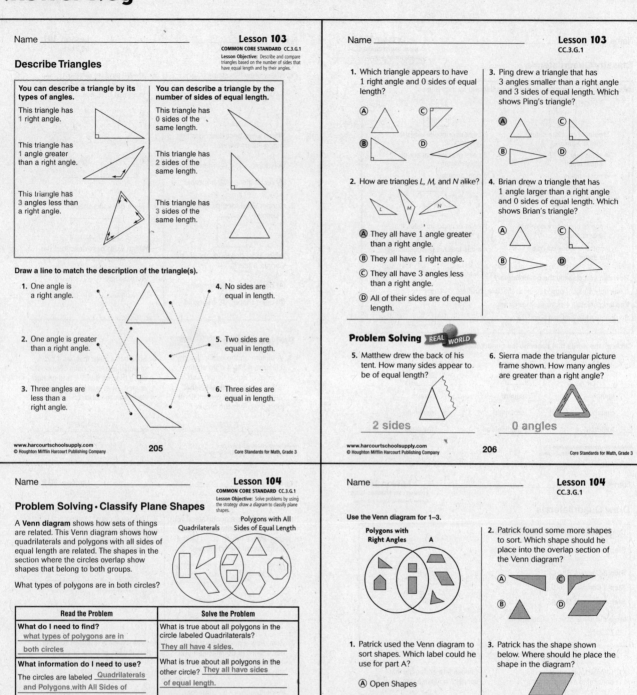

Name ______________ **Lesson 103**
COMMON CORE STANDARD CC.3.G.1
Lesson Objective: Describe and compare triangles based on the number of sides that have equal length and by their angles.

Describe Triangles

You can describe a triangle by its types of angles.		**You can describe a triangle by the number of sides of equal length.**	
This triangle has 1 right angle.	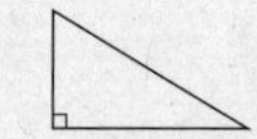	This triangle has 0 sides of the same length.	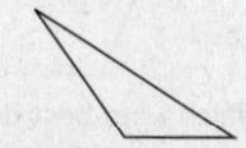
This triangle has 1 angle greater than a right angle.	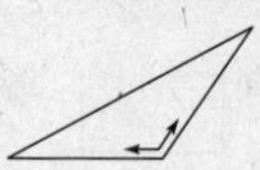	This triangle has 2 sides of the same length.	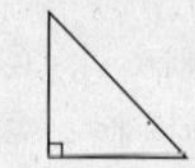
This triangle has 3 angles less than a right angle.	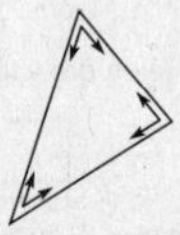	This triangle has 3 sides of the same length.	

Draw a line to match the description of the triangle(s).

1. One angle is a right angle.
2. One angle is greater than a right angle.
3. Three angles are less than a right angle.

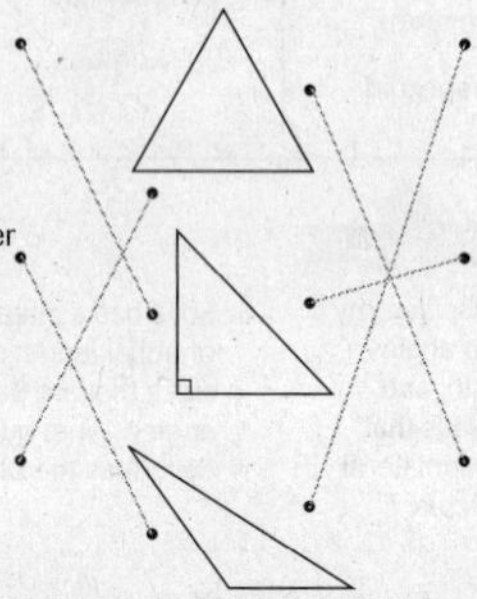

4. No sides are equal in length.
5. Two sides are equal in length.
6. Three sides are equal in length.

Name ______________ **Lesson 103**
CC.3.G.1

1. Which triangle appears to have 1 right angle and 0 sides of equal length?

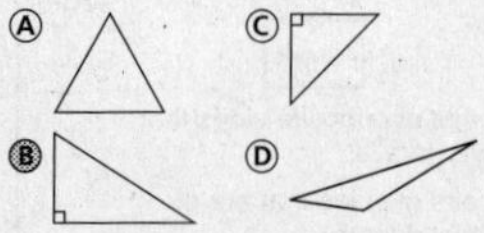

(A) (**B**) (C) (D)

2. How are triangles *L*, *M*, and *N* alike?

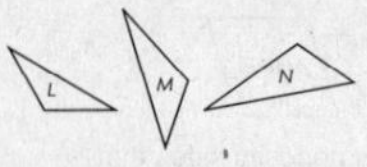

(**A**) They all have 1 angle greater than a right angle.
(B) They all have 1 right angle.
(C) They all have 3 angles less than a right angle.
(D) All of their sides are of equal length.

3. Ping drew a triangle that has 3 angles smaller than a right angle and 3 sides of equal length. Which shows Ping's triangle?

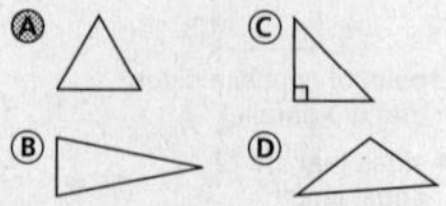

(**A**) (B) (C) (D)

4. Brian drew a triangle that has 1 angle larger than a right angle and 0 sides of equal length. Which shows Brian's triangle?

(A) (B) (C) (**D**)

Problem Solving REAL WORLD

5. Matthew drew the back of his tent. How many sides appear to be of equal length?

2 sides

6. Sierra made the triangular picture frame shown. How many angles are greater than a right angle?

0 angles

Name ______________ **Lesson 104**
COMMON CORE STANDARD CC.3.G.1
Lesson Objective: Solve problems by using the strategy *draw a diagram* to classify plane shapes.

Problem Solving • Classify Plane Shapes

A **Venn diagram** shows how sets of things are related. This Venn diagram shows how quadrilaterals and polygons with all sides of equal length are related. The shapes in the section where the circles overlap show shapes that belong to both groups.

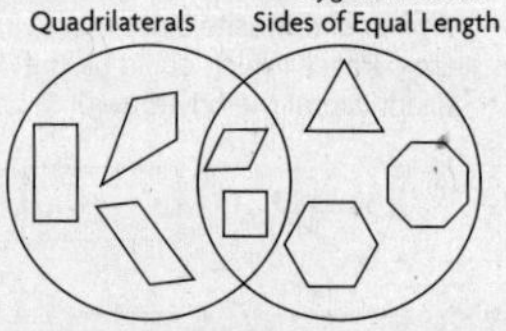

What types of polygons are in both circles?

Read the Problem	Solve the Problem
What do I need to find? what types of polygons are in both circles	What is true about all polygons in the circle labeled Quadrilaterals? They all have 4 sides.
What information do I need to use? The circles are labeled Quadrilaterals and Polygons with All Sides of Equal Length	What is true about all polygons in the other circle? They all have sides of equal length.
How will I use the information? I will describe the shapes in the section where the circles overlap	Which polygons are in the section where the circles overlap? shapes that are quadrilaterals and that have 4 sides that are of equal length
	So, a square and a rhombus are in the section where the circles overlap.

1. Brad drew the Venn diagram at the right. What type of shapes are in the section where the circles overlap?

triangles that have 1 right angle

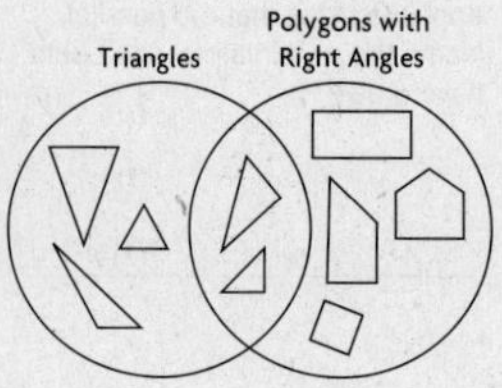

Name ______________ **Lesson 104**
CC.3.G.1

Use the Venn diagram for 1–3.

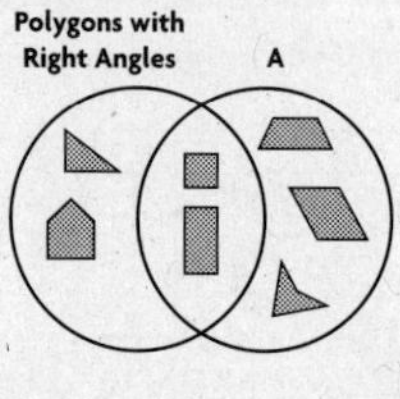

1. Patrick used the Venn diagram to sort shapes. Which label could he use for part A?

(A) Open Shapes
(**B**) Quadrilaterals
(C) Shapes with Sides of Equal Length
(D) Shapes with 1 Right Angle

2. Patrick found some more shapes to sort. Which shape should he place into the overlap section of the Venn diagram?

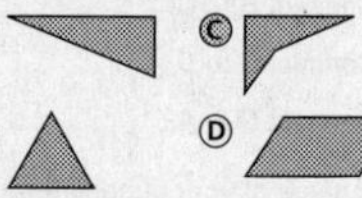

(A) (B) (**C**) (D)

3. Patrick has the shape shown below. Where should he place the shape in the diagram?

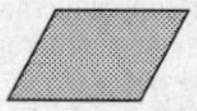

(**A**) part A
(B) Polygons with Right Angles
(C) overlap section
(D) outside the Venn diagram

4. Kendra used a Venn diagram to sort shapes. Write a label she could use for circle A. Explain your reasoning.

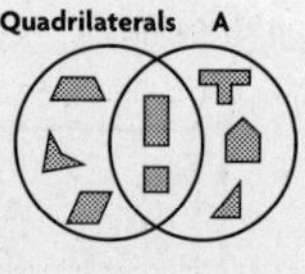

Possible answer: Polygons with Perpendicular Sides; I looked at the five shapes in circle A, including the shapes in the overlap section. All of the shapes had at least 1 pair of perpendicular sides, while the other three shapes did not.

Name ______________________

Lesson 105

COMMON CORE STANDARD CC.3.G.2

Lesson Objective: Partition shapes into parts with equal areas and express the area as a unit fraction of the whole.

Relate Shapes, Fractions, and Area

You can separate a plane shape into equal parts to explore the relationship between fractions and area.

Divide the rectangle into 6 parts with equal area. Write the fraction that names the area of each part of the whole.

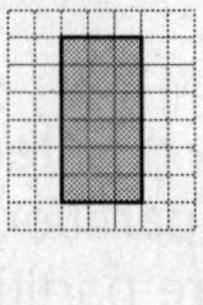

Step 1 Draw lines to divide the rectangle into 6 parts with equal area. Use the grid to help you.

Step 2 Write the fraction that names each part of the divided whole.

Think: Each part is 1 part out of 6 equal parts.

Each part is $\frac{1}{6}$ of the whole shape's area.

Step 3 Write the fraction that names the whole area.

Think: There are 6 equal parts.

The fraction that names the whole area is $\frac{6}{6}$.

Draw lines to divide the shape into parts with equal area. Write the area of each part as a unit fraction.

1. 4 equal parts

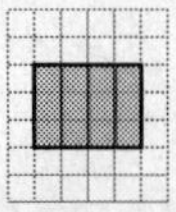

Each part is $\frac{1}{4}$ of the whole shape's area.

2. 8 equal parts

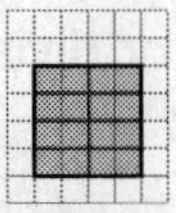

Each part is $\frac{1}{8}$ of the whole shape's area.

Possible drawings are shown.

Name ______________________

Lesson 105

CC.3.G.2

1. Talon divides a square into equal parts that each show $\frac{1}{6}$. Which could be Talon's square?

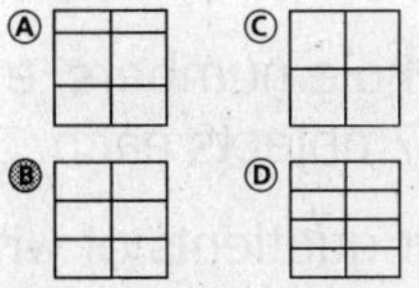

2. Colleen drew lines to divide a trapezoid into equal parts that each represent $\frac{1}{3}$ of the whole area. Which could be Colleen's trapezoid?

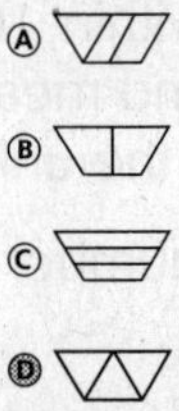

3. Tad divides a rhombus into equal parts that each show $\frac{1}{2}$. Which could be Tad's rhombus?

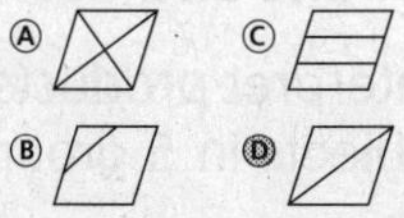

4. Dennie drew lines to divide a shape into 3 parts each with equal area. Which could be Dennie's shape?

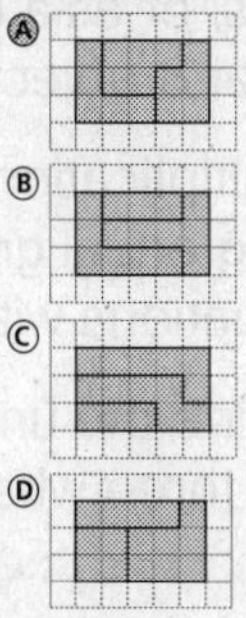

5. Reese divided the shaded shape into equal parts. Write the unit fraction that names each part of the divided whole. Explain your reasoning.

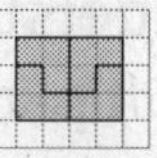

$\frac{1}{4}$; Possible explanation: the shape is divided into 4 equal parts, so each part is $\frac{1}{4}$ of the whole.

© Houghton Mifflin Harcourt Publishing Company

Common Core State Standards

Operations and Algebraic Thinking CC.3.OA

Represent and solve problems involving multiplication and division.

1. Interpret products of whole numbers, e.g., interpret 5×7 as the total number of objects in 5 groups of 7 objects each.
2. Interpret whole-number quotients of whole numbers, e.g., interpret $56 \div 8$ as the number of objects in each share when 56 objects are partitioned equally into 8 shares, or as a number of shares when 56 objects are partitioned into equal shares of 8 objects each.
3. Use multiplication and division within 100 to solve word problems in situations involving equal groups, arrays, and measurement quantities, e.g., by using drawings and equations with a symbol for the unknown number to represent the problem.
4. Determine the unknown whole number in a multiplication or division equation relating three whole numbers.

Understand properties of multiplication and the relationship between multiplication and division.

5. Apply properties of operations as strategies to multiply and divide.
6. Understand division as an unknown-factor problem.

Multiply and divide within 100.

7. Fluently multiply and divide within 100, using strategies such as the relationship between multiplication and division (e.g., knowing that $8 \times 5 = 40$, one knows $40 \div 5 = 8$) or properties of operations. By the end of Grade 3, know from memory all products of two one-digit numbers.

Solve problems involving the four operations, and identify and explain patterns in arithmetic.

8. Solve two-step word problems using the four operations. Represent these problems using equations with a letter standing for the unknown quantity. Assess the reasonableness of answers using mental computation and estimation strategies including rounding.
9. Identify arithmetic patterns (including patterns in the addition table or multiplication table), and explain them using properties of operations.

© Houghton Mifflin Harcourt Publishing Company

Number and Operations in Base Ten CC.3.NBT

Use place value understanding and properties of operations to perform multi-digit arithmetic.

1. Use place value understanding to round whole numbers to the nearest 10 or 100.
2. Fluently add and subtract within 1000 using strategies and algorithms based on place value, properties of operations, and/or the relationship between addition and subtraction.
3. Multiply one-digit whole numbers by multiples of 10 in the range 10–90 (e.g., 9 × 80, 5 × 60) using strategies based on place value and properties of operations.

© Houghton Mifflin Harcourt Publishing Company

Common Core State Standards

Number and Operations – Fractions CC.3.NF

Develop understanding of fractions as numbers.

1. Understand a fraction $1/b$ as the quantity formed by 1 part when a whole is partitioned into b equal parts; understand a fraction a/b as the quantity formed by a parts of size $1/b$.
2. Understand a fraction as a number on the number line; represent fractions on a number line diagram.
   a. Represent a fraction $1/b$ on a number line diagram by defining the interval from 0 to 1 as the whole and partitioning it into b equal parts. Recognize that each part has size $1/b$ and that the endpoint of the part based at 0 locates the number $1/b$ on the number line.
   b. Represent a fraction a/b on a number line diagram by marking off a lengths $1/b$ from 0. Recognize that the resulting interval has size a/b and that its endpoint locates the number a/b on the number line.
3. Explain equivalence of fractions in special cases, and compare fractions by reasoning about their size.
   a. Understand two fractions as equivalent (equal) if they are the same size, or the same point on a number line.
   b. Recognize and generate simple equivalent fractions, e.g., $1/2 = 2/4$, $4/6 = 2/3$. Explain why the fractions are equivalent, e.g., by using a visual fraction model.
   c. Express whole numbers as fractions, and recognize fractions that are equivalent to whole numbers.
   d. Compare two fractions with the same numerator or the same denominator by reasoning about their size. Recognize that comparisons are valid only when the two fractions refer to the same whole. Record the results of comparisons with the symbols $>$, $=$, or $<$, and justify the conclusions, e.g., by using a visual fraction model.

© Houghton Mifflin Harcourt Publishing Company

Measurement and Data CC.3.MD

Solve problems involving measurement and estimation of intervals of time, liquid volumes, and masses of objects.

1. Tell and write time to the nearest minute and measure time intervals in minutes. Solve word problems involving addition and subtraction of time intervals in minutes, e.g., by representing the problem on a number line diagram.
2. Measure and estimate liquid volumes and masses of objects using standard units of grams (g), kilograms (kg), and liters (l). Add, subtract, multiply, or divide to solve one-step word problems involving masses or volumes that are given in the same units, e.g., by using drawings (such as a beaker with a measurement scale) to represent the problem.

Represent and interpret data.

3. Draw a scaled picture graph and a scaled bar graph to represent a data set with several categories. Solve one- and two-step "how many more" and "how many less" problems using information presented in scaled bar graphs.
4. Generate measurement data by measuring lengths using rulers marked with halves and fourths of an inch. Show the data by making a line plot, where the horizontal scale is marked off in appropriate units— whole numbers, halves, or quarters.

Geometric measurement: understand concepts of area and relate area to multiplication and to addition.

5. Recognize area as an attribute of plane figures and understand concepts of area measurement.
   a. A square with side length 1 unit, called "a unit square," is said to have "one square unit" of area, and can be used to measure area.
   b. A plane figure which can be covered without gaps or overlaps by n unit squares is said to have an area of n square units.
6. Measure areas by counting unit squares (square cm, square m, square in, square ft, and improvised units).
7. Relate area to the operations of multiplication and addition.
   a. Find the area of a rectangle with whole-number side lengths by tiling it, and show that the area is the same as would be found by multiplying the side lengths.
   b. Multiply side lengths to find areas of rectangles with whole-number side lengths in the context of solving real world and mathematical problems, and represent whole-number products as rectangular areas in mathematical reasoning.
   c. Use tiling to show in a concrete case that the area of a rectangle with whole-number side lengths a and $b + c$ is the sum of $a \times b$ and $a \times c$. Use area models to represent the distributive property in mathematical reasoning.
   d. Recognize area as additive. Find areas of rectilinear figures by decomposing them into non-overlapping rectangles and adding the areas of the non-overlapping parts, applying this technique to solve real world problems.

© Houghton Mifflin Harcourt Publishing Company

Common Core State Standards

Measurement and Data *(continued)* CC.3.MD

Geometric measurement: recognize perimeter as an attribute of plane figures and distinguish between linear and area measures.

8. Solve real world and mathematical problems involving perimeters of polygons, including finding the perimeter given the side lengths, finding an unknown side length, and exhibiting rectangles with the same perimeter and different areas or with the same area and different perimeters.

Geometry CC.3.G

Reason with shapes and their attributes.

1. Understand that shapes in different categories (e.g., rhombuses, rectangles, and others) may share attributes (e.g., having four sides), and that the shared attributes can define a larger category (e.g., quadrilaterals). Recognize rhombuses, rectangles, and squares as examples of quadrilaterals, and draw examples of quadrilaterals that do not belong to any of these subcategories.
2. Partition shapes into parts with equal areas. Express the area of each part as a unit fraction of the whole.

© Houghton Mifflin Harcourt Publishing Company